# Praise for PassPorter®

"A nifty travel guide that works overtime as a planner, organizer, and journal..."
— Jacky Runice
Daily Herald—Chicago

"[PassPorter] is a brilliant travel aid... the most practical, sanity-saving guide you could take along to Disney World."
— Stephanie Gold, Amazon.com

"[PassPorter] has become the Bible for those of us who want to experience Walt Disney World to the max."
— Kim Cool, Venice Gondolier Sun

"Vacationers who want to enjoy all that Disney World has to offer should make sure they take along this PassPorter guide."
— ForeWord Reviews

PassPorter is a life saver! I never had so much information at my fingertips! No question went unanswered.
— Michelle Marshall in Georgia

I love everything about PassPorter! It is so full of information that it makes the trip much more enjoyable and hassle-free.
— Maura Scott in Massachusetts

PassPorter keeps everything organized in one place. This helps me to plan my trip and make the most of my visit to prioritize exactly what we want to do each day. Great resource!
— Trese in Ohio

PassPorter is THE ultimate resource for Walt Disney World!
— Janine Robison in California

# What's Unique in PassPorter

- **Coverage of the most recent changes** throughout Walt Disney World—thanks to our later production schedule, this is the most up-to-date 2008 guidebook available! We have the recent pass price changes, Disney-MGM Studios' name change, resort season changes and price increases, and the Disney Dining Plan changes.
- **Comprehensive yet concise information** is packed into our pages—PassPorter is information-rich and padding-free!
- **Full color** brings life and clarity to our maps and photos.
- **Blending of personal experience** from your authors and the collective wisdom of tens of thousands of readers means a guidebook that's full of heart and soul.
- **Well-organized chapters and pages** make it easy to find what you need. We edit our information carefully so that sections always begin at the top of a page.
- **Worksheets** to jot notes and make travel arrangements.
- **Our famous organizer PassPockets** to plan your trip, store your maps and papers, and record your vacation memories.
- **Floorplans of Disney resort hotel rooms** to give you a better sense of the layout.
- **Fold-out maps** of the four major Disney theme parks, printed in full color on heavy paper to stand up to rugged use.
- **Custom-designed attraction charts** provide all the information you need at a glance.
- **ToddlerTips, KidTips, TweenTips, and TeenTips** offer advice for kids by kids.
- **Color, self-stick tabs** to mark your chapters in whatever way you prefer for quick and easy reference.
- **Original color photos** to see the *real* Walt Disney World!
- **Personalization labels and fun stickers** to custom-design your PassPockets to your own vacation.
- **Magical memories** from fellow travelers convey the spirit and wonder of Walt Disney World.
- **Disney changes highlighted** with a light green background to mark significant changes since our last edition.
- **Expert peer reviewers** to ensure accuracy and thoroughness.

*...and much more! Visit us at http://www.passporter.com for a complete list of what's new and unique in PassPorter Walt Disney World 2008!*

# PassPorter® Walt Disney World® Resort

## 2008 Edition

### The unique travel guide, planner, organizer, journal, and keepsake

Jennifer Marx,
Dave Marx,
and
Allison Cerel Marx

**PassPorter Travel Press**

An imprint of MediaMarx, Inc.
P.O. Box 3880, Ann Arbor, Michigan 48106
877-WAYFARER
http://www.passporter.com

**PassPorter's® Walt Disney World®–2008 Edition**
by Jennifer Marx, Dave Marx, and Allison Cerel Marx



P.O. Box 3880, Ann Arbor, Michigan 48106
877-WAYFARER or 877-929-3273 (toll-free)
Visit us online at http://www.passporter.com



Special Sales: PassPorter Travel Press publications are available at special discounts for bulk purchases for sales premiums or promotions. Special editions, including personalized covers and excerpts of existing guides, can be created in large quantities. For information, write to Special Sales, P.O. Box 3880, Ann Arbor, Michigan, 48106.

Distributed by Publishers Group West

ISBN-13: 978-1-58771-049-0
ISBN-10: 1-58771-049-8

10 9 8 7 6 5 4 3 2 1

Printed in Hong Kong

# About the Authors

Name: Jennifer Marx
Date of birth: 10/09/68
Residence: Ann Arbor, MI
Signature: Jennifer Marx

**Jennifer Marx** fell in love with Walt Disney World on her first visit as a teenager in 1983. She has since returned more times than she can count on her fingers and toes many times over, visiting every park, attraction, resort, and restaurant at least once. As author of more than a dozen popular books, she yearned to write one about Walt Disney World but felt no interest in churning out yet another travel guide when there were so many excellent books already available. When she hit upon the idea of the PassPorter, she knew she could offer her fellow vacationers something unique and valuable. With the help of the PassPorter, Jennifer has organized gatherings at Walt Disney World for individuals, groups, and families of all ages and stages. Jennifer lives in Ann Arbor, Michigan, where she makes her home with husband Dave and young son Alexander.

**Dave Marx** may be considered a Renaissance Man, a jack-of-all-trades, or a dilettante, depending on how you look at things. He took a 20-year hiatus between his early journalism training and the commencement of his full-time writing career. Beyond co-authoring numerous books with Jennifer, he's been a radio writer/producer; recording engineer; motion picture music editor; broadcast engineering supervisor; tax preparer; cab driver; whitewater safety and rescue instructor; developer and instructor of online publishing courses; and chairman of MouseFest (see page 282). He has also co-authored and contributed to numerous books about America Online and the Internet. He discovered the "World" (Walt Disney World, that is) in 1997 and spent more than six months there over the following five years. Dave is from New Jersey and now makes his home in Ann Arbor, Michigan.

Name: Dave Marx
Date of birth: 04/07/55
Residence: Ann Arbor, MI
Signature: Dave Marx

**Allison Cerel Marx** ("Allie") is a veteran visitor to Walt Disney World (and Dave's 15-year-old daughter). She has a maniacal grin, especially when spinning one of Mad Hatter's teacups at top speed. She's camped at Fort Wilderness, celebrated New Year's Eve in the Magic Kingdom, and photographed animals at Animal Kingdom Lodge Resort. She shares her "A-OK!" ratings and her popular tips for kids, "tweens" (pre-teens), and teens on the attractions in the Touring the 'World' chapter. Allie also offers her thoughts on the childcare clubs on property. (Allie is pictured here with her little brother, Alexander, who "contributes" his ToddlerTips in this edition.)

# PassPorter Team

**Our 25 Expert Peer Reviewers** painstakingly checked our text and maps and helped us ensure PassPorter's accuracy, readability, and thoroughness. Special thank yous to Brad K. Maureen Austin, Lesley Duncan, Linda Holland, Sue Kulick, Kris Lindsey, and Sheana Perry.

**Amy Bedore** took her first trip to Walt Disney World when she was five, and has since returned more than 20 times. Amy is an alumnus of the Disney College Program. She is also a Guide on the PassPorter Message Boards.

**Sandy Bostwick** is an occupational therapist, college professor, speaker, and writer. Her educational consulting and coaching practice helps people with challenges excel. She visits Walt Disney World yearly for pixie dust refills.

**Dyan K. Chaplin** enjoys traveling to Walt Disney World with her husband, Jeffrey, and teenage son, Kyle, who share her enthusiasm for all things Disney. Dyan serves as a PassPorter Message Board Guide, has a love for baseball and the Boston Red Sox.

**Dianne Cook** and her husband Tom had a Disney honeymoon and now "do Disney" twice a year with their sons Andrew and Matthew. A Disney Vacation Club member since 1996, Dianne is also a PassPorter Guide.

**Rob Gatto** is a Disney Vacation Club member and visits Walt Disney World regularly with his wife Margaret and children Joseph and Nicholas. He enjoys sharing tips and providing advice as a Guide on the PassPorter Message Boards.

**Marisa Garber-Brown** is a Destination Specialist with MouseEarsVacations.com. Her parents started taking her to Disney in 1979 and she has visited multiple times every year since. She enjoys being a PassPorter Guide and spending time with her husband Tim.

**LauraBelle Hime** visits Disney World and Disneyland as often as she can, especially enjoying vacations with her grandchildren Alexis, Olivia, Caleb, Jacob, and Samantha. She offers help and guidance as a PassPorter Guide and to family and friends almost daily.

**Deb Koma**, co-author of *PassPorter's Open Mouse for Walt Disney World and the Disney Cruise Line*, is also senior editor of the weekly e-newsletter ALL EARS® and the web site AllEars.net. She indulges her passion for travel with at least four visits to the World each year.

**Denise Lang** and her family love the magic of Disney. She is a PassPorter Message Board Guide. and has made seven trips to the World. Denise enjoys assisting others plan their magical memories as a Travel Consultant with Ears To You Travel.

**Bruce Metcalf** has loved and studied Disney parks since 1958. He works at a major Central Florida resort and co-writes the delightful "Iago & Zazu's Attraction of the Week" at http://aotw.figzu.com.

**Sarah Mudd** is a military wife, PassPorter Message Board Guide, and frequent visitor to Disney's U.S. parks. She, her husband Mike, and 7-year-old daughter Emilie live in Virginia, and can't wait to get back to "The World!"

**Rebecca Oberg** is always ready for her next Disney Vacation adventure. With countless Disneyland trips, five Walt Disney World jaunts, and two Disney Cruises under her belt, she eagerly awaits the next voyage in March 2008.

**Cheryl Pendry** and her husband Mark usually visit Walt Disney World every year, despite the fact they live in England. They became Disney Vacation Club members in 2002 and Cheryl is also a PassPorter Message Board Guide.

**Jennifer Savickas** and her husband Jim have made the trek from New Hampshire to Walt Disney World more than 18 times since 1996 (four times in one year alone)! Now with their son, Jameson, they visit twice a year.

**Ann Smith**, a PassPorter Message Board Guide, has visited Disney World more than 15 times with her family. She is especially looking forward to watching her son Jamie's high school band march in the Magic Kingdom Parade in March 2008.

**Jeff Spencer**, a veteran of more than 35 Disney World trips, enjoys helping family, friends, and fellow Disney fans plan their vacations. For Disney trip reports, tips, links, and other Disney information, visit http://home.hiwaay.net/~jlspence.

**Marnie Urmaza**, her husband Matt, and children Alexa and Colin have made six trips to Walt Disney World since 2003, including a Disney cruise. Marnie also enjoys being a PassPorter Message Board Guide.

**Deb Wills** is recognized as a Disney expert by the national press and others in the Disney travel planning field. She's the founder of AllEars.net and the ALL EARS® newsletter, and is the co-author of *PassPorter's Open Mouse for Walt Disney World and the Disney Cruise Line*.

# Acknowledgments

A "world" of thanks to our readers, who've contributed loads of tips and stories since PassPorter's debut. A special thanks to those who generously allowed us to include their **contributions** in this edition:

Michelle Marshall, Maura Scott, Trese, and Janine Robison (page i); Angela J., Kristine Asselin, Christa White, and Jodi Leeper (page 12); Brandy Dorsch, Julie Pagano, Helen Friedlander, and Teresa Weddelman (page 24); Barbara Hargrove, Matt Riker, Tom Anderson, and Bonnie M. (page 112); Anthony Steeples, Celine Johnson, Bob Kennedy, and Diane Barrette (page 198); Laura B., Chris Oakleaf, and Sandra Johnson (page 242); Tracy Eastridge, Marnie Walsh, and Bob Kennedy (page 262). May each of you receive a new magical memory for every reader your words touch.

A very special thank you to our in-house research wizards and office managers, **Nicole Larner and Chad Larner**—this phenomenal brother-and-sister team unearthed tidbits of new and updated information, checked the accuracy of addresses and phone numbers, updated the index, and assisted in the peer review process. Their contributions really shine in chapter 5—Nikki did the primary page layout work for this chapter, and Chad did extensive research on menu items and prices. Their essential position on the team enables PassPorter to grow and thrive! Nikki and Chad are both fans of Disney World, having made numerous trips there in recent years.

PassPorter would not be where it is today without the help and support of the many members of the **Internet Disney fan community**. Our thanks to the friendly folks below and to all whom we didn't have room to include!

- AllEarsNet.com (http://www.allears.net). Thanks, Deb and Deb!
- DIS—Unofficial Disney Information Station (http://www.wdwinfo.com). Thanks, Pete!
- Hidden Mickeys of Disney (http://www.hiddenmickeys.org). Thanks, Tom!
- Intercot (http://www.intercot.com). Thank you, John!
- LaughingPlace.com (http://www.laughingplace.com). Thanks, Doobie and Rebekah!
- MouseEarVacations.com (http//www.mouseearvacations.com). Thanks, Jami!
- Mouse Fan Travel (http://www.mousefantravel.com). Thanks, Beci!
- MousePlanet.com (http://www.mouseplanet.com). Thanks, Mike, Mark, Adrienne, & Tony!
- MouseSavers.com (http://www.mousesavers.com). Thanks, Mary!
- Our Laughing Place (http://www.ourlaughingplace.com). Thanks, Ahnalira!
- Planning Strategy Calculator (http://pscalculator.net). Thanks, Scott!

Big thanks to the **Guides (moderators) of our own message boards**: Maureen Austin, Amy Bedore, Tiffany Bendes, Dyan Chaplin, Michelle Clark, Dianne Cook, Lesley Duncan, Dawn Erickson, Joanne and Tim Ernest, Marisa Garber-Brown, Rob Gatto, Kristin Grey, Debbie Hendrickson, LauraBelle Hime, Linda Holland, Christina Holland-Radvon, Claudine Jamba, Robin Krening-Capra, Susan Kulick, Marcie LaCava, Denise Lang, Kris Lindsey, Yvonne Mitchell, Sarah Mudd, Bill Myers, Michelle Nash, Rebecca Oberg, Allison Palmer-Gleicher, Cheryl Pendry, Sheana Perry, Tina Peterson, Susan Rannestad, Sabine Rautenberg, Carol Ray, Crystal Remaly, Jennifer Sanborn, Jennifer Savickas, Ann Smith, Donna Sonmor, Kelly Spratt, Marie St. Martin, Suzanne Torrey, Marnie Urmaza, Sara Varney, Dave Walsh, Suzi Waters, Brant Wigginton, Don Willis, Debbie Wright, and the 20,000+ readers in our amazing community at http://www.passporterboards.com.

A heartfelt thank you to our **family and friends** for their patience while we were away on trips or cloistered at our computers, and for their support of our dream: Alexander Marx; Carolyn Tody; Tom Anderson; Fred and Adele Marx; Kim, Chad, Megan, and Natalie Larner; Dan, Jeannie, Kayleigh, Melanie, and Nina Marx; Gale Cerel; Jeanne and David Beroza; Robert and Sharon Larner; Gordon Watson and Marianne Couch; Ben Foxworth; and Marta Metcalf.

A special thanks to these very important folks "behind the scenes" at PassPorter:

**Office Managers and Research Wizards**: Nicole Larner and Chad Larner
**Proofreader Extraordinaire**: Sandy Livingston
**Printer**: Magnum Printing, Ltd., Hong Kong (thank you, Anita Lam!)
**Online Coordinator and Newsletter Editor**: Sara Varney
**Visibility Specialists**: Kate and Doug Bandos, KSB Promotions
**Assorted Pixies**: Tom Anderson, Dave Hunter, Kim Larner, Bob Sehlinger, and Dirk Uhlenbrock

Last but not least, we thank Walter Elias Disney for his dream.

# Contents



*List of Maps, Worksheets, and Charts*

## Touring the "World" .......................113

## Contents
*(continued)*



**Bonus Features...**

# Congratulations!

First, congratulations are in order—you're going to Walt Disney World! You are about to embark on an experience that will amaze and, hopefully, delight you. This isn't an ordinary, run-of-the-mill trip—after all, you're going to spend your vacation in the heart of Mickey Mouse land!

The Walt Disney World Resort is a world unto itself, full of heralded amusements and hidden gems. Yet the very fact that it is so vast can make a visit to Walt Disney World seem more like a race in a maze than a relaxed vacation. And worse yet, pleasant memories of a great vacation may disappear beneath the stress and worries that accompanied it.

Happily, after fifty-plus trips to Walt Disney World, we've learned to dispel our stress with one simple and enjoyable task: **planning ahead**. In fact, it is no task at all—planning is as much fun as the vacation itself. Planning gave birth to the PassPorter concept. Originally, Jennifer made itineraries on her computer and placed them in a binder. During the trip she kept the binder handy, using it to store passes, brochures, and receipts. After the vacation, these organizers had turned into scrapbooks, full of pixie-dusted memories and goofy smiles. When Jennifer's writing career took off, she didn't have the time to create binders for every trip. She wished for a simpler version that she could use each trip without a lot of fuss. It was on a Disney bus that the idea came to her. She could make an easy-to-use, book-based version and offer it as a resource to fellow vacationers!

Now, after much work, you hold PassPorter in your hands. The first edition of PassPorter debuted in 1999, creating a sensation in the Disney fan community, winning 12 national awards, and helping hundreds of thousands plan great vacations. This edition, our tenth, is our best yet!

It is our greatest hope that PassPorter helps you "discover the magic" through your own eyes, as it did for us. To get you in the spirit, read "Disney Dreaming" on the next page and prepare for your adventure!

Smiles and laughter,

Jennifer, Dave, and Allison

We'd love to hear from you! Visit us on the Internet (http://www.passporter.com) or drop us a postcard from Walt Disney World!

P.S. We finished this edition's updates in August 2007. For the latest changes, updates, and news, be sure to consult our page of free book updates at http://www.passporter.com/customs/bookupdates.htm.

# Disney Dreaming

A good part of the fun of going to the Walt Disney World Resort is the anticipation before your trip! To really get you into "Disney Dreaming," we present some of our favorite tips to feed your excitement and prepare you for the adventure that lies ahead. This is magical stuff—don't blame us if you get the urge to hop on the next plane to Orlando.

**Watch a Movie**

Disney movies—animations and live action alike—capture the Disney spirit wonderfully. Rent your favorite from the local video store and settle in for a cozy evening. You can also request a free vacation planning video of the Walt Disney World Resort— call Disney at 407-934-7639 to order your free video. (To get a free Disney Cruise Line video, call 888-325-2500.)

**Go Shopping**

You may enjoy a visit to The Disney Store—while many of these closed over the last few years and the chain was recently sold, plenty are still found in major shopping malls. The stores continue to offer delightful theming and foot-tapping music. You can buy park admission at a discount, and special offers may be had with the Disney Rewards Visa (see page 10).

**Reminisce**

If you've visited the "World" before, think back to your vacation and the things you enjoyed most about it. Dig out your souvenirs, photos, and home movies and view them with fresh eyes. If you used a PassPorter last time, go through your PassPockets carefully to refresh your memory and find the notes you made "for next time." If you haven't gone to Walt Disney World before, talk to all the friends and family members who have gone and get their impressions, tips, and stories.

**Network With Others**

Disney fans tend to gravitate toward online services and the Internet. If you've got an Internet connection, you'll find many Disney sites—even one for PassPorter planners! (See page 7 for more information.) No access to the Internet? Look to your communities for other vacationers who'd like to swap ideas and plans—try your workplace and school.

**Plan, Plan, Plan**

Few things are better than planning your own trip to the Walt Disney World Resort. Cuddle up with your PassPorter, read it through, and use it to the fullest—it makes planning fun and easy. PassPorter really is the ultimate in Disney Dreaming!

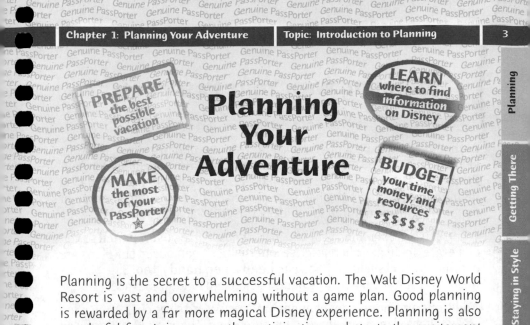

# Planning Your Adventure

Planning is the secret to a successful vacation. The Walt Disney World Resort is vast and overwhelming without a game plan. Good planning is rewarded by a far more magical Disney experience. Planning is also wonderful fun. It increases the anticipation and starts the excitement months before the vacation begins.

Planning begins with learning about the Walt Disney World Resort. Your PassPorter has all the information you need for a great vacation, and then some! Written to be complete yet compact, PassPorter can be your only guidebook or act as a companion to another. You can use it in a variety of ways: as a travel guide, a vacation planner, an organizer, a trip journal, and a keepsake. We designed it for heavy use–you can take it with you and revisit it after your trip is just a fond memory. You can personalize it with your plans, notes, souvenirs, and memories. We even crafted it with extra room in the binding to hold the things you'll squeeze and jam into the pockets along the way. PassPorter is the ultimate Walt Disney World Resort guide–before, during, and after your vacation.

This first chapter helps you with the initial planning stage: gathering information and budgeting. Your PassPorter then continues through the planning stages in order of priority. Sprinkled throughout are ways to personalize your trip, little-known tips, and magical Disney memories.

Above all else, have fun with your plans, both now and when you reach the Walt Disney World Resort. Leave room for flexibility, and include time to relax and refresh. You might be tempted to see and do it all, but an overly ambitious plan will be more exhausting (and frustrating) than fun. Don't get so bogged down with planning and recording that you miss the spontaneous magic of a Disney vacation. To paraphrase Robert Burns, "The best laid plans of mice and of men go oft astray." Use your PassPorter to plan ahead and be aware of your options so you can relax and enjoy your vacation, no matter what it brings.

# Planning With Your PassPorter

Each important aspect of your vacation—budgeting, traveling, packing, lodging, touring, and eating—has a **special, dedicated worksheet** in your PassPorter. Don't be shy; we designed these worksheets to be scribbled upon at will. Not only do they take the place of easy-to-lose scraps of paper, they are structured specifically for your vacation.

When you start planning your trip in your PassPorter, **use a pencil** so you can erase and make changes. Use a permanent pen once your plans are definite to avoid smudging. You can **keep a pen handy, too**! Slip it inside the book's spiral binding. The pen's pocket clip holds it in place.

**Additions and significant changes** at Disney World since our 2007 edition are highlighted in green, just like this paragraph. This is not to be confused with general changes to PassPorter—almost every page has changed!

Your PassPorter is most useful when you keep it handy before and during your vacation. It fits compactly into backpacks and shoulder bags. Or tuck your PassPorter into a **waist pack** (at least 6.5" x 9" or 17 x 23 cm).

Your PassPorter loves to go on rides with you, but try to **keep it dry** on Splash Mountain and Kali River Rapids. The heavy cover offers good protection, but a simple resealable plastic bag (gallon size) is a big help.

Personalize your PassPorter! **Write your name** under the front cover flap, along with other information you feel comfortable listing (we recommend that you do not list your room number for safety reasons). Your hotel name, trip dates, and phone number help if you misplace your PassPorter. Under the back cover flap are places for your important **phone numbers**, **reminders**, and **addresses**. Use the checkboxes to mark items when done. The **label page** at the end of the text is a fun feature—use the labels to personalize your PassPockets and attach the tabs to mark your chapters!

Two tools you may find helpful for planning are a **highlighter** (to mark "must-sees") and those sticky **page flags** (to mark favorite pages).

It's normal for the **handy spiral binding** in your PassPorter to rotate as you flip pages. If this causes your binding to creep up, you can easily rotate it back—just twist the binding while holding the pages securely.

Your PassPorter's **sturdy cover** wraps around your book for protection, and you can fold it back and leave the book open. The binding is a bit bigger than necessary to fit your stuff. We crafted a pocket for each day of your trip (up to 10 days), plus special ones for your journey, lodging, and memories. Read more about these "PassPockets" on the next page.

*Note: Most of the tips on these two pages apply to the regular edition (spiral-bound); if you have a deluxe edition (ring-bound), visit http://www.passporter.com/wdw/deluxe.htm.*

# Using Your PassPockets

In the back of your PassPorter are 14 unique "PassPockets" to help you plan before you go, keep items handy while you're there, and save memories for your return. Just pencil in your trip information and itinerary on the front; store brochures, maps, receipts, and such inside; and jot down impressions, memories, expenses, and notes on the back. Use the PassPockets in any way that suits you, filling in as much or as little as you like. You can even personalize your PassPockets with the included labels!

*Read the advice or tip.*

*Use the pockets as printed, or personalize with a label.*

*Write your itinerary here, including times, names, and confirmation numbers. Or just record what you did.*

*Jot down things you want to remember, do, or visit.*

*Make notes before you go or add notes during your trip.*

*Store items you want to have on hand during your trip, or things you collect along the way, in this roomy pocket. Guidemaps, brochures, and envelopes all fit inside.*

*Slip small items in this smaller slot, such as receipts, claim tags, and ticket stubs.*

*Write the day of the week and the date for quick reference.*

*Record memories of your vacation to share with others or to keep to yourself. You can jot these down as you go or reminisce at the end of the day.*

*Keep track of photos taken so you can find them later!*

*Watch your expenses to stay within a budget or to track your resort charge account balance.*

*Remember all those great (or not-so-great) meals and snacks by noting them here. You can even include the price of the meal or snack, too!*

*What did you forget? What do you want to do again? What would you like to try next time? What wouldn't you touch again with a ten-foot pole? Make a note of it here!*

Use the Vacation-at-a-Glance page just in front of your PassPockets to record park hours, showtimes, meals, or anything that helps you plan your trip. If you prefer to travel light, don't be shy about removing a PassPocket and carrying it around for the day instead of toting your entire PassPorter. Just tuck it back in here at the end of the day! (If you have the spiral version and feel uncomfortable about tearing out a PassPocket, you may prefer our ring-bound Deluxe Edition with looseleaf pockets—see page 284.) You can also purchase extra PassPockets—visit http://www.passporterstore.com/store.

# Finding Disney Information

PassPorter can act as your **first source** of information for the Walt Disney World Resort. It can also be a companion to other Disney books you may already own or purchase later. Either way, we like to think it packs a lot of information into a small package. Everything you need to know to plan a wonderful Disney vacation can be found within its pages.

Do keep in mind that the Walt Disney World Resort is constantly changing. We've taken every step to ensure that your PassPorter is as up-to-date as possible, but we cannot foresee the future. So to help your PassPorter remain current, we **make free updates available** to you at our web site (http://www.passporter.com/customs/bookupdates.htm). If you have ideas, questions, or corrections, please contact us—see page 280.

Oodles of **travel guidebooks** are available if you have a hankering for second opinions. We highly recommend *The Unofficial Guide to Walt Disney World* by Bob Sehlinger for its irreverence, detail, and touring plans. *Birnbaum's Walt Disney World* offers the official line and colorful graphics. *PassPorter's Open Mouse for Walt Disney World and the Disney Cruise Line* guidebook (formerly *PassPorter's Walt Disney World for Your Special Needs*) by Deb Wills and Debra Martin Koma has more than 400 pages filled with super detail for issues like ADHD, autism, allergies, diet, fears, pregnancy, infants, seniors, mobility issues, vision, and more—see details on page 284.

Call the **Walt Disney World Resort** at 407-WDW-MAGIC (407-939-6244) or e-mail them through their web site (http://www.disneyworld.com) when you need answers to specific questions. In our experience, their representatives are very friendly, but they rarely volunteer information and won't offer opinions. Prepare questions in advance. If the person you reach doesn't have an answer, call back—several times if necessary. Don't hesitate to ask for a manager if you can't get the information you need.

**Travel agents** you know and trust can be a great source of information—many have web sites, too. Also check with **membership organizations** that arrange travel, such as AAA (see page 11).

**Magazines and newsletters** about Disney are also available. Our own free weekly PassPorter newsletter has Disney and other travel features, book updates, news, reviews, reports, contests, tips, and deals—subscribe at http://www.passporter.com/news.htm (subscribers are also entitled to a discount on PassPorter guidebooks). ALL EARS® Newsletter is a free unofficial weekly e-mail with Disney news, reviews, and reports—subscribe at http://www.allearsnet.com. Annual Passholders in the United States (see page 10) receive a quarterly newsletter from Disney.

➢

# Exploring a Whole New World Wide Web

The ultimate source of information, in our opinion, is the **Internet**. Of course, this requires access to a computer with access to the Internet, but with this you can connect to millions of vacationers happy to share their Disney knowledge.

The web offers hundreds of Disney-related sites. In fact, **PassPorter** has its own web site with updates, tips, ideas, articles, forums, and links. Visit us at http://www.passporter.com. More details are on page 281.

As you might expect, Disney has a web site for all things Walt Disney World at http://www.disneyworld.com. While **Disney's official web site** doesn't offer opinions, it is an excellent source for basic information, including operating hours, rates, maps, and resort room layouts. Late changes to operating hours are best verified at 407-824-4321, however.

We also highly recommend several **unofficial web sites**, which we frequent ourselves when planning a trip. We introduce these web sites as appropriate throughout the book (check pages 274–275 in the index for a full list). One special site deserves mention now: **AllEars.net®**. This is a comprehensive and up-to-date guide to the Walt Disney World Resort. AllEars.net is located at http://www.allears.net. When you stop by, tell Deb we said "Hi!"

Another source of information (and camaraderie) is **discussion groups**. PassPorter has its own set of message boards with an active, supportive community of vacationers at http://www.passporterboards.com—come chat with us, ask your questions, and share the fun! Fans also gather at **Tagrel.com** at http://www.tagrel.com, at Pete Werner's **Unofficial Disney Information Station** at http://www.wdwinfo.com, as well as at **Intercot** at http://www.intercot.com and **DisneyEcho** at http://disneyecho.emuck.com. We also recommend the **rec.arts.disney.parks (RADP)** newsgroup at news://rec.arts.disney.parks. Last but not least, those of you on **America Online** can visit the Disney message boards at keyword: TRAVEL BOARDS.

**E-mail lists** are yet another valuable Internet resource, allowing you to observe and participate in discussions from the safety of your e-mailbox. We host both a discussion list and a newsletter list with regular feature articles—subscribe for free at our web site. Many other mailing lists are available, including **The Mouse For Less** for Disney fans on a budget—visit at http://www.themouseforless.com.

Planning | Getting There | Staying in Style | Touring | Feasting | Making Magic | Index | Notes & More

# Budgeting for Your Vacation

There's nothing magical about depleting your nest egg to finance a vacation. Too many Disney vacationers can tell you that money concerns overshadowed all the fun. Yet you can avoid both the realities and worries of overspending by planning within a budget. Budgeting ahead of time not only keeps you from spending too much, it encourages you to seek out ways to save money. With just a little bit of research, you can often get **more for less**, resulting in a richer, more relaxed vacation.

If you purchase a **vacation package**, you have the advantage of covering most of your major expenses up front. And while Disney's package prices haven't offered a real savings in the past, they've recently been offering excellent deals. Consider adding Disney's Dining Plan (if offered) to your package (see pages 202–203). Can't find a package with a great deal? Planning each aspect of your vacation yourself often saves you even more money, as we show throughout this book. You can learn about vacation packages on page 30 and inquire into prices with the Walt Disney Travel Co. at 800-828-0228 or on the Internet at http://www.disneytravel.com.

Your **vacation expenses** usually fall into six categories: planning, transportation, lodging, admission, food, and extras. How you budget for each depends upon the total amount you have available to spend and your priorities. Planning, transportation, lodging, and admission are the easiest to factor ahead of time, as costs are more or less fixed. The final two—food and extras—are harder to control, but can usually be estimated.

Begin your vacation budgeting with the **worksheet** on the following page. Enter the minimum you prefer to spend and the maximum you can afford in the topmost row. Establish as many of these ranges as possible before you delve into the other chapters. Your excitement may grow as you read more about Walt Disney World, but it is doubtful your bank account will.

As you uncover costs and ways to save money later, return to this worksheet and **update it**. Think of your budget as a work in progress. Flexibility within your minimum and maximum figures is important. As plans begin to crystallize, write the amount you expect to pay (and can afford) in the Estimated Costs column. Finally, when you are satisfied with your budget, **transfer the amounts** from the Estimated Costs column to the back of each PassPocket. Note that each PassPocket also provides space to record actual expenses, which helps you stay within your budget. Tip: This worksheet and many others are available in electronic, interactive versions, and some even do the calculations for you—see page 287 for details.

Electronic, interactive worksheet available–see page 287

# Budget Worksheet

Use this worksheet to identify your resources, record estimated costs, and create a budget for your vacation. When complete, transfer the figures from the Estimated Costs column to the back of each PassPocket.

| | **Minimum** | | **Maximum** | | **Est. Costs** | |
|---|---|---|---|---|---|---|
| **Total Projected Expenses** | $ | | $ | | $ | |
| **Planning**: | | | | | | |
| Phone Calls/Faxes: | | | | | | |
| Guides/Magazines: | | | | | | |
| **Transportation**: | *(transfer to your Journey PassPocket)* | | | | | |
| Rental Car: | | | | | | |
| Fuel/Maintenance/Tolls: | | | | | | |
| Airfare/Travel Tickets: | | | | | | |
| Shuttle/Town Car/Taxi: | | | | | | |
| Stroller/Wheelchair: | | | | | | |
| ECV/Golf Cart: | | | | | | |
| Parking: | | | | | | |
| **Lodging**: | *(transfer to your Rooms PassPocket)* | | | | | |
| En Route Motel/Other: | | | | | | |
| Resort/Hotel: | | | | | | |
| **Admission**: | *(transfer to appropriate PassPocket)* | | | | | |
| Theme Park Passes: | | | | | | |
| Water Park Passes: | | | | | | |
| DisneyQuest Passes: | | | | | | |
| Pleasure Island Passes: | | | | | | |
| Guided Tours/Other: | | | | | | |
| **Food***: | Daily | Total | Daily | Total | Daily | Total |
| Breakfast: | | | | | | |
| Lunch: | | | | | | |
| Dinner: | | | | | | |
| Snacks: | | | | | | |
| Groceries/Other: | | | | | | |
| | *(transfer to each daily PassPocket)* | | | | | |
| **Extras**: | | | | | | |
| Souvenirs/Clothing: | | | | | | |
| Gratuities: | | | | | | |
| Vacation Wardrobe: | | | | | | |
| Photos: | | | | | | |
| Other: | | | | | | |
| **Total Budgeted Expenses** | $ | | $ | | $ | |

* If you're on the Disney Dining Plan package (see pages 202-203), you may want to check off your included meals in the worksheet so you don't budget money for them.

# Money-Saving Programs

You can save real money on a Walt Disney World Resort vacation by taking advantage of the following money-saving programs. Some require a membership fee, but they often pay for themselves quite quickly.

**Disney Rewards Visa Card**—This credit card from Chase gives cardholders special discounts on Disney resorts, packages, and tours, plus onboard credits on the Disney cruise. The card itself has no annual fee and earns "Disney Dream Reward Dollars" equal to 1% or more of your purchases. You can redeem your dollars relatively quickly for Disney travel, entertainment, and merchandise. Exclusive cardholder benefits are also typically offered, such as special character meet and greets. Another perk is the "pay no interest for 6 months" offer on Disney packages and cruises, but keep in mind initial deposits and all payments must be made with the card or you can lose the deal. Be sure to read the fine print carefully, too—if you carry a separate balance while floating a 0% vacation deal, your payments may apply to the higher interest balance first and you could end up paying some steep interest. Also, double check exactly when you need to pay off the balance and be careful about confusing terminology. We have a Disney Visa ourselves and we think the "rewards" are just average, interest rates are high, and the available discounts are sparse (but attractive when offered). Disney Rewards Visa is available to U.S. residents only. If you have a Disney Rewards Visa, be sure to mention this when making reservations so they can offer any available incentives or deals. For details, visit http://chase.com/disney or call 877-252-6576. Also see our in-depth article at http://www.passporter.com/credit.asp.

**Annual Pass (AP)**—An Annual Pass (regular or premium) saves big money on admission if you plan to visit for more than 10–14 days in a one-year period (depending on the pass)—this is the point at which it becomes less expensive than regular admission. It may also deliver discounts at selected resorts, meals, tours, and ticketed events, plus invitations to special events. And let's not forget Disney Dining Experience eligibility (see below). See pages 116–117 for details and call 407-WDW-MAGIC for prices.

**Florida Residents**—Those of you with proof of Florida residency (such as a valid Florida driver's license) can enjoy great savings on Disney tickets, resorts, cruises, and more. The deals are so good we're almost tempted to move to Florida. For more information, visit http://www.disneyworld.com/flresidents.

**Disney Dining Experience (DDE)**—This program offers 20% discounts on food and alcohol (for up to 10 persons, paying with one credit card) at most Disney eateries, plus free theme park parking after 5:00 pm, free resort valet parking when dining at the resort, and half-price Pleasure Island admission. Available to Annual and Seasonal Passholders and Florida residents ages 21 and up with a valid Florida driver's license or ID card. Membership is $65 for Annual/Seasonal Passholders; $85/year for Florida residents without an Annual or Seasonal Pass (renewals are $70/year). A second membership for your spouse or partner is $25/year. Call 407-566-5858 to order (allow 4–6 weeks, or request a confirmation letter if traveling within 6 weeks). Note that DDE cannot be combined with any other discount or package, and there are some blackout dates (e.g., major holidays like Mother's Day, Easter, Independence Day, Thanksgiving, Christmas Eve/Day, and New Year's Eve/Day).

## Money-Saving Programs

*(continued)*

**Disney Vacation Club (DVC)**—This timeshare program may save money for families who plan ahead. DVC members also get discounts on select meals, admission, and backstage tours. See pages 102–103 for details.

**Disney "Postcard" Specials and Advertisements**—Disney sometimes offers lodging discounts in direct mail and mass media advertisements. These offers may be sent to previous Disney guests and vacationers who've requested planning materials, or they may appear in newspaper or TV ads. These offers usually have eligibility requirements, such as residence in a particular state, or can only be used by the person who received the mailing. If you receive an offer, be sure to save it for your records. You'll need the "coupon code" and perhaps an ID number to make your reservation. Be sure you are eligible for the offer—if you show up at Disney and can't prove eligibility, you'll lose your "deal." Visit http://www.mousesavers.com for a listing of current offers.

**Orlando Magicard**—This free card offers discounts on many non-Disney shows and park tickets, as well as rental cars and hotels. Call 888-416-4026 or visit http://www.orlandoinfo.com/magicard.

**Entertainment Book**—This annual discount book offers coupons for rental cars, off-property hotels and restaurants, and non-Disney theme parks like Universal Orlando, SeaWorld, and Busch Gardens. Cost is about $30 for a new edition (older editions may be less). Call 888-231-SAVE (888-231-7283) or visit http://www.entertainment.com.

**American Automobile Association (AAA)**—Members enjoy discounts ranging from 10% to 20%, including tickets (when purchased from AAA). Contact your local office, call 800-222-6424, or visit http://www.aaa.com.

### Money-Saving Tips

- ✔ *MouseSavers.com is a web site dedicated to cataloging available Disney discounts and deals. Webmaster Mary Waring has built a huge following, both at http://www.mousesavers.com and through her free monthly newsletter.*
- ✔ *If you are flying, check newspapers and the Internet for fare sales—they occur more frequently than you might think and offer savings. Expedia.com (http://www.expedia.com) has great combo deals on fares and hotel rooms!*
- ✔ *If you are driving or arriving late in the evening, consider staying a night at a less expensive motel your first night.*
- ✔ *You can save money on meals by sharing entrees or by eating only two meals a day, as Disney portions tend to be quite large. Bring quick breakfast foods and snacks from home to quell the munchies and keep up your energy.*
- ✔ *Always ask about discounts when you make reservations, dine, or shop. You may discover little-known specials for AAA, Disney Visa Card, Florida residents, Annual Passholders, or simply vacationers in the right place at the right time.*
- ✔ *Join The Mouse For Less community for more money-saving tips—you can subscribe for free at http://www.themouseforless.com.*

# Plan It Up!

Use these tips to make planning your vacation fun and rewarding:

"To **save money for our upcoming Disney trip**, we went to the local 'big box' store and bought a seven-gallon water jug from the camping department. We found some great Disney scrapbooking stickers and decorated the jug. We're now using the jug to save all of our change!" – *Contributed by Angela J., a winner in our 2007 Reader Tip Contest*

If you have access to the **Internet**, make it a point to get online once a week for the latest news on the "World." We have many trip reports from fellow vacationers posted on our message boards at http://www.passporterboards.com. MousePlanet also offers trip reports at http://www.mouseplanet.com/dtp/trip.rpt.

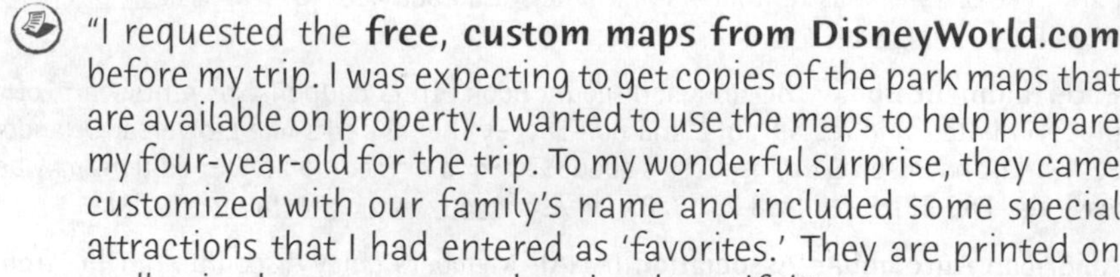

"I requested the **free, custom maps from DisneyWorld.com** before my trip. I was expecting to get copies of the park maps that are available on property. I wanted to use the maps to help prepare my four-year-old for the trip. To my wonderful surprise, they came customized with our family's name and included some special attractions that I had entered as 'favorites.' They are printed on really nice heavy paper and are just beautiful!"

– *Contributed by Kristine Asselin, a winner in our 2007 Reader Tip Contest*

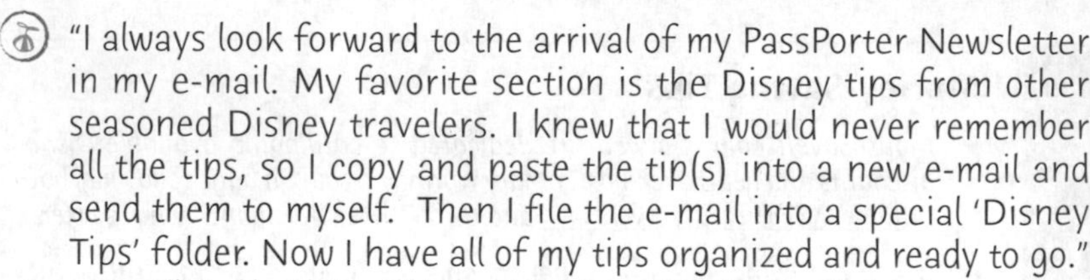

"I always look forward to the arrival of my PassPorter Newsletter in my e-mail. My favorite section is the Disney tips from other seasoned Disney travelers. I knew that I would never remember all the tips, so I copy and paste the tip(s) into a new e-mail and send them to myself. Then I file the e-mail into a special 'Disney Tips' folder. Now I have all of my tips organized and ready to go."

– *Contributed by Christa White, a winner in our 2007 Reader Tip Contest*

## Magical Memory

*"We planned to take our 8-year-old daughter Brianna on her very first Walt Disney World trip in August 2006. We told Brianna about the trip well in advance and, to Brianna, it felt like forever until August. Being a scrapbook mom, I had lots of leftover Disney papers and stickers. I used all those leftovers and scraps for fun notes in her school lunch each day. I decided to start at 101 days and use the '101 Dalmatians' story as a theme to kick off the day-by-day countdown until our trip. For each day, the notes included some fun Disney facts or trivia and the number of days remaining until we left for our trip. Not only was Brianna excited to read her notes, but her classmates couldn't wait to see the notes, too! It was a hit and the highlight of lunchtime. What a joy for Brianna to get those notes and share the fun and excitement of her first Walt Disney World trip with her friends and classmates!"*

*...as told by Disney vacationer Jodi Leeper*

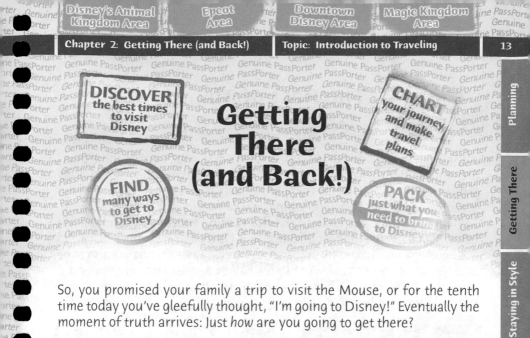

# Getting There (and Back!)

FIND many ways to get to Disney

PACK just what you need to bring to Disney

So, you promised your family a trip to visit the Mouse, or for the tenth time today you've gleefully thought, "I'm going to Disney!" Eventually the moment of truth arrives: Just *how* are you going to get there?

Traveling in this age of tightened security requires more planning and patience, but you'll discover it is quite easy to get to the Walt Disney World Resort. The path to Orlando is well traveled by cars, planes, trains, buses, and tours. On the other hand, "easy" isn't always convenient or inexpensive. Choosing the best and most affordable way to get to Disney can take some doing. We can help!

In this chapter, we walk you through the process of making your travel arrangements. We brief you on weather, attendance levels, park hours, and seasonal rates so you can pick the best time to go or make the most of the dates you've already chosen. You'll find descriptions of each major path to the Walt Disney World Resort and a worksheet to help you pick a route and make your reservations. Then it's time to get packing, with the help of our special packing lists. Finally, we help you smile and enjoy your journey with tips for having fun along the way.

What we won't do is take up space with the phone numbers of airlines and car rental companies or travel directions from every city. You can find that information in your phone book or on the World Wide Web. Just jot down numbers and notes on the worksheet, and transfer the winners to the appropriate PassPocket in the back.

It's important to note that due to reservation change penalties, air and rail travel is generally less flexible than lodging. Thus, we find it works much better to make traveling decisions before finalizing hotel arrangements. However, you may prefer to skip to the next chapter and shop for your lodging first. Just return here to tailor your travel plans to your lodging choice.

Your journey begins...

# The Best of Times

Most Disney veterans can tell you, in no uncertain terms, that some times are much better than others to visit the "World." We wholeheartedly agree, but there's more to it. While there are certainly times of the year that are less crowded or more temperate, only you can decide the best time to visit. To help you decide, we charted the **fluctuating factors** for each month below. If you ask us, the best time to visit is November–February, but avoid the holidays, when parks fill to capacity. Three-day weekends are also to be avoided whenever possible. The latter half of August and September are uncrowded, though you'll battle the heat. For links to more temperature and rainfall data, visit http://www.passporter.com/wdw/bestoftimes.htm.

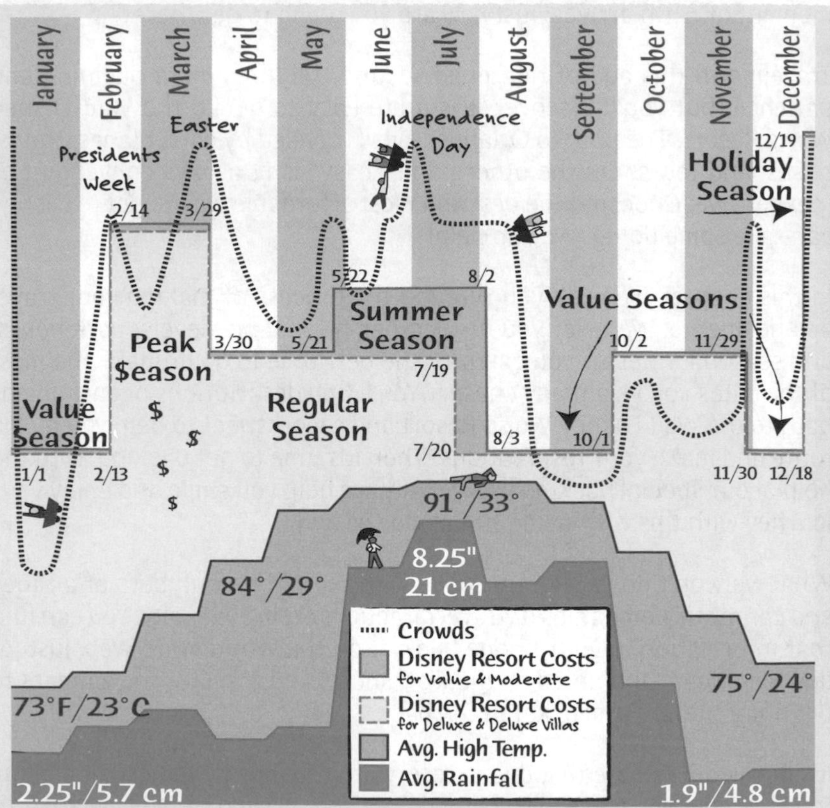


## 2008 Disney resort cost seasons are as follows:

***Value Season*** *is Jan. 1–Feb. 13 (all), Jul. 20–Oct. 1 (deluxe, deluxe villas, and Ft. Wilderness cabins), Aug. 3–Nov. 20 (Ft. Wilderness campsites), Aug. 3–Oct. 1 (value and moderate), Nov. 30–Dec. 18 (all but campsites);* ***Regular Season*** *is Mar. 30–Jul. 19 (deluxe, cabins, and deluxe villas), Mar. 30–Aug. 2 (campsites), Mar. 30–May 21 (value and moderate), Oct. 2–Nov. 29 (all but campsites);* ***Summer Season*** *is May 22–Aug. 2 (value and moderates);* ***Peak Season*** *is Feb. 14–Mar. 29 (all);* ***Pre-Holiday Season*** *is Nov. 21–Dec. 18 (campsites only); and* ***Holiday Season*** *is Dec. 19–31 (all).*

# Getting There

One of the major hurdles to a Walt Disney World Resort vacation is figuring out how to get there in the first place. Many of us think along the traditional (and expensive) lines first and become discouraged. It doesn't have to be like that. There are **more ways** to get to Disney than you probably realize. Below we describe each, beginning with the most popular. At the end of the list, on page 21, a worksheet gives you space to make notes, jot down prices, and note reservation numbers. When your travel plans are finalized, record them on the first PassPocket.

## By Car, Van, Truck, or Motorcycle

Many vacationers arrive at Disney in their own vehicle. It's hard to beat the **slowly rising sense of excitement** as you draw closer or the freedom of having your own wheels once you arrive. Driving may also eliminate the concerns you or family members may have with air travel. Additionally, driving can be less expensive than air travel, especially for large families. Be sure to compare the costs of driving versus flying before you decide. On the down side, you may spend long hours or even days on the road, which cuts deeply into your time with Mickey.

If you opt to drive, carefully **map your course** ahead of time. You can do this with a AAA TripTik—a strip map that guides you to and from your destination. You must be a AAA member (see page 11) to get a TripTik, but that is easily done for $60–$75/year (visit http://www.aaa.com for more information). If you're driving, we heartily recommend *Along Interstate-75* (http://www.i75online.com) and/or *Drive I-95* (http://www.drivei95.com). I-95 drivers should also visit http://www.usastar.com/i95/homepage.htm. Or try a trip routing service, such as http://www.mapquest.com or http://www.freetrip.com. **Tip**: Have exact change ready for the unmanned toll booths along the Florida toll roads on your route. Check toll prices at http://www.floridasturnpike.com/TRI/index.htm and http://epass.oocea.com.

If you live more than 500 miles away, **spread out your drive** over more than one day, allotting one day for every 500 miles. Arriving at Walt Disney World overly road-weary is no way to begin a vacation. If your journey spans more than one day, decide in advance where to stop each night and make reservations accordingly. Check that your air-conditioning is in good working order and your cell phone is charged before heading out (bring a cell phone charger and headset, too). Secure rest areas are available once you hit the Florida border, making it a bit easier to drive at night. Also see our in-depth articles on driving at http://www.passporter.com/driving.asp.

# By Airplane

Air travel is the fastest way for most vacationers to get to Orlando. In fact, air travel may be less expensive than you think if you know the tricks to getting an **affordable flight**. First, be flexible on the day and time of departure and return—fares can differ greatly depending on when you fly and how long you stay. Second, take advantage of the many "fare sales." To learn about sales, visit airlines' web sites or travel sites such as Expedia (http://www.expedia.com), Orbitz (http://www.orbitz.com), Travelocity (http://www.travelocity.com), or Kayak (http://www.kayak.com)—note that not all airlines are represented on these travel sites, however. Subscribe to e-mail fare alerts from travel sites and from the airlines that serve your home airport(s)—if Southwest Airlines is an option, be sure to check out DING! (see http://www.southwest.com). Third, try alternate airports, such as Sanford or Tampa, when researching fares (see the in-depth PassPorter article at http://www.passporter.com/sanford.asp). Fourth, be persistent. Ask for their lowest fare if you call the airline directly. When you find a good deal, put it on hold immediately (if possible), note your reservation number on page 21, and cancel later if necessary. Fifth, consider Priceline.com (http://www.priceline.com), where you name your own price for a round-trip ticket (but once your price is met, you can't cancel). Finally, don't stop shopping. If your airline offers a cheaper fare later, you may be able to rebook at the lower rate (watch out for penalties).

Once you reserve a flight, **make a note** of the reservation numbers, flight numbers, seat assignments, and layovers on your first PassPocket. To arrange **ground transportation** from the airport, see pages 19–20.

## Our Top 10 Flying Tips, Reminders, and Warnings

1. Visit http://www.tsa.gov for travel security news and updates.
2. Check the status of your flight before departing for the airport. Use online check-in if it is offered by your airline (most now offer it).
3. Pick up a meal and drinks for the flight after you pass through security, as most domestic flights have discontinued meal service for security reasons.
4. Pack sharp or potentially dangerous items in checked luggage (or just leave them at home). This includes pocket knives and sport sticks. Cigarette lighters, scissors with blades under 4" and nail clippers are allowed. For details, visit http://www.tsa.gov.
5. Remember the **3-1-1 rule** for liquids/gels in carry-ons: They must be in **3 oz. or less** bottle(s), all in **1 quart-sized, clear, zip-top bag**, and **1 bag per person**, placed in screening bin. Limit your carry-ons to one bag and one personal item (e.g., purse).
6. Keep your luggage unlocked for inspections, or it may be damaged.
7. Plan to arrive at the airport at least two hours prior to departure.
8. Curbside check-in may be available (fee may apply), but you may need to obtain a boarding pass from your airline's customer service desk anyway.
9. E-ticket holders should bring a confirmation and/or boarding pass. If you don't have one, print it from your airline's web site (your hotel's front desk may also be able to print boarding passes within 24 hours of departure).
10. Keep your ID handy. We carry ours in PassHolder Pouches (see page 283).

## Getting Around the Orlando Airport

Orlando International Airport is a large, sprawling hub and one of the better (and cleaner) airports we've flown into. When you arrive, your plane docks at one of the **satellite terminals** (see map below). From there, follow the signs to the automated **shuttle** that takes you to the main terminal—there you'll find **baggage claim** and ground transportation. Once you reach the main terminal (Level 3), follow the signs down to baggage claim (Level 2). Shuttles, taxis, town cars, rental cars, and buses are found down on Level 1 (take the elevators opposite the baggage carousels). Disney's Magical Express (see page 19) check-in is located on Level 1, Side B. Each shuttle and bus company has its own ticket booth. If you get lost, look about for signs or an information desk that can get you back on track.

As your authors used to live in different cities, we became quite good at **meeting up at the airport**. It's best to meet your party at their baggage claim area as you won't be allowed past security without a valid boarding pass. The trick is knowing which airline and baggage claim area. Use the map and airline list below, or call the airport directly at 407-825-2001. Be careful when differentiating between Side A's and Side B's baggage claims. Gates 1–29 and 100–129 use Side A, while gates 30–99 use Side B. Check the arrival/departure boards in the terminal for flight status, too! Other terminal meeting spots are the Disney Stores (see stars on map below), the Borders bookstore (noted on map below—they carry PassPorter books!), or an eatery. Be sure to exchange cell phone numbers, too.

For **more details** on the Orlando International Airport, call 407-825-2001 or visit http://www.orlandoairports.net. Page travelers at 407-825-2000.

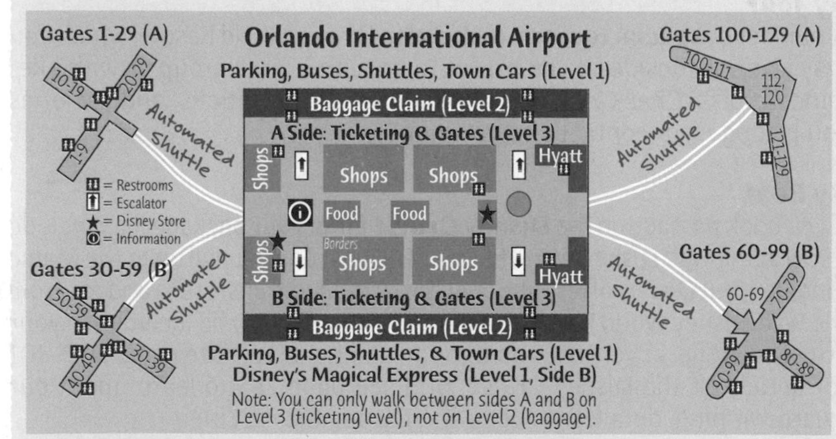


Air Canada, Alaska Airlines, American Airlines, CanJet, Continental, Midwest, and Sun Country use Gates 1–29; America West, ANA, KLM, Northwest, Spirit, Ted, United, and US Airways use Gates 30–59; Air France, AirTran, British Airways, Delta, Frontier Airlines, and Virgin Atlantic use Gates 60–99; and ATA, JetBlue, and Southwest use Gates 100–129.

# By Train, Bus, Tour, and Boat

**By Train**

The train is a uniquely relaxing way to travel to the Walt Disney World Resort. **Amtrak** serves the Orlando area daily with both **passenger trains** and an Auto Train, which carries your family and your car. The **Auto Train** runs between suburban Washington, DC (Lorton, VA) and suburban Orlando (Sanford, FL). Other trains may go through to Kissimmee, which is a closer, less-crowded station. Prices vary depending upon the season, the direction, and how far in advance you make your reservation. The Auto Train is also available one-way, and in many seasons, one direction is less expensive than the other direction. You may need to take a taxi or town car (see page 20) from the train station to the Disney property. Hertz rental cars are available from the Sanford and Orlando stations, but not the Kissimmee station. For Amtrak reservations, call 800-USA-RAIL or visit them at http://www.amtrak.com. Also see the in-depth PassPorter article at http://www.passporter.com/autotrain.asp.

**By Bus**

Buses make good economic and environmental sense. **Greyhound** serves Orlando and Kissimmee. You can take the local LYNX buses from there, but it's not easy (for more information on LYNX, see page 20 under "Riding a Bus"). Buses often take longer to reach a destination than do cars or trains driving the same route. Fares are lowest if you live within 10 hours of Walt Disney World. For fares, schedules, and tickets, call Greyhound at 800-231-2222 or visit them at http://www.greyhound.com.

**By Tour**

A number of **special tours** go to the Walt Disney World Resort, which you may want to consider if you prefer to go with a large group or with like-minded folks. Check with the associations, organizations, and societies you belong to, or contact a travel agent.

**By Boat**

If you book passage on the **Disney Cruise Line**, your package may include a stay at the Walt Disney World Resort. The boat doesn't pull up to the Magic Kingdom, but Disney offers optional, prearranged transfers to and/or from the Walt Disney World Resort—this transportation may be included in your cruise package, or you may add it for an additional fee. See pages 100–101 for details on the Disney Cruise, and see page 285 to learn about our award-winning, detailed guide to the Disney Cruise Line.

**By Everything Else!**

The list of ways to get to Disney is really endless. You could even combine business with pleasure, as many others do!

# Are We There Yet?

Once you reach Orlando Airport, you need to continue about 20 miles before you actually reach Disney property. Your options are to take advantage of Disney's Magical Express shuttle service, use a shuttle or town car, rent a car, ride a bus, or call a taxi. Here are the details of each:

**Disney's Magical Express**

Disney's Magical Express is a free perk for Disney's resort hotel guests, providing **free ground transportation** to and from Orlando International Airport and luggage "intercept" on arrival in Orlando—properly tagged luggage is pulled off the conveyor and is delivered directly to your Disney resort hotel room. Just walk off the plane and head directly to Disney's Welcome Center (Level 1, Side B). For the return trip to the airport, you may be able to check in for your flight (and check your bags) before you leave your Disney resort. Disney's Magical Express is efficient, with guests being whisked to their resort with little wait and few (if any) stops at other hotels (though long waits and delays can still occur during peak arrival times). Nonetheless, Disney's Magical Express does take extra time. If you want another hour or two of park time on your first or last day, we suggest you pay for a town car service (see next page).

Tip: Travel with a **carry-on containing all your necessities**, including a swimsuit and a change of clothes. It may be many hours before your checked luggage arrives at your resort or before you're aware of any lost luggage. If you arrive late at night, your luggage may not arrive at your hotel until the next morning, so get your luggage yourself or pack your necessities.

You must **make reservations** for Disney's Magical Express at least one day prior to your arrival in Orlando (but do it at least ten days prior to allow time to receive your materials in the mail). To add this service, call Disney's regular reservations phone line or your travel agent, or visit http://www.disneyworld.com. Disney will need your airline flight numbers. Once reserved, Disney will send you special luggage tags (two per person age 3 and above; more available on request) and an instruction booklet. If your flight is changed or delayed, notify Disney's Magical Express Guest Services at 866-599-0951.

Only **guests at Disney-owned resorts** can use Disney's Magical Express. Swan, Dolphin, Shades of Green, and all hotels on Hotel Plaza Boulevard (Grosvenor, DoubleTree Suites, Hilton, etc.) are not included, and neither are travelers using Sanford International Airport. Disney Vacation Club members wishing to use this service should contact DVC Member Services.

Disney's Magical Express service is **available at least through 2011**.

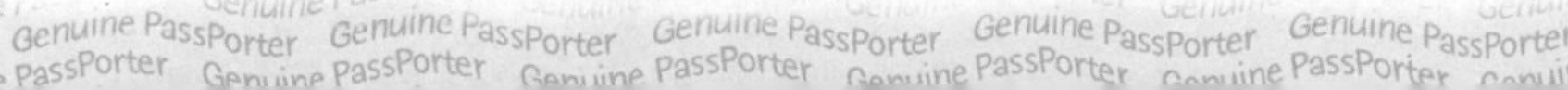

# Are We There Yet?

*(continued)*

**Taking a Shuttle or Town Car**

A number of companies stay in business largely by transporting guests to and from Disney. Shuttle stands are located at the Orlando International Airport (Level 1), but all other pickup locations require advance notice. The major shuttle operator is Mears (800-759-5219). We prefer and recommend a **town car**, however. The town car driver greets us at baggage claim, carries our luggage, drives us to our hotel, and charges less than it costs a family of four to use a shuttle, taxi, or rental car. If you'd like to stop at a grocery store or if you need a car/booster seat, request this at reservation. Town car companies we've used include:
Happy Limo—888-394-4277, http://www.happylimo.com
Quicksilver—888-468-6939, http://www.quicksilver-tours.com

**Driving a Car**

If you're driving to Walt Disney World, you'll need specific directions. You can find detailed directions through a trip routing service (see page 15) or Disney (call 407-939-4636). Fliers planning to drive a car while in Orlando should rent at the airport. We don't feel a rental car is needed if you stay only on Disney property, as their internal transportation system works well (see pages 118–119) and even an occasional taxi fare can be cheaper than a rental car. If you plan to go off-property often, you may find a rental car helpful. Alamo (Disney's official rental car agency), Avis, Budget, Dollar, and National are located right at the airport on Level 1 (in-airport rentals incur a 10% fee). Enterprise, Hertz, and many others are off-site, and you'll need to take a shuttle on Level 1 to reach them (off-site rentals carry an 8.67% fee). The Dolphin Resort and several off-property hotels offer rental car desks, too. Inquire about all taxes and surcharges. See our rental car tips at http://www.passporter.com/rentalcars.asp. Tip: Vacationers using I-75/Florida Turnpike can arrive via the recently-added Western Beltway (FL 429 Toll) and Disney's Western Way—see maps on cover flaps.

**Riding a Bus**

The regional bus system, LYNX, has limited service to the Walt Disney World property. Call 407-841-LYNX (5969) or visit http://www.golynx.com. Please note that it takes about three hours to get from the Orlando Airport to Walt Disney World via LYNX. If you need to get from your hotel to any other theme park in the Orlando area, Mears offers transportation ($16 round-trip)—call a day in advance.

**Using a Taxi**

While taxis are available, we don't recommend them for airport travel due to cost. Large parties may be able to ride in a taxi mini-van economically, however, especially for occasional travel within Walt Disney World.

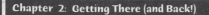

Electronic, interactive worksheet available— see page 287

# Travel Worksheet

Use this worksheet to jot down preferences, scribble information during phone calls, and keep all your discoveries together. Don't worry about being neat—just be thorough! When everything is confirmed, transfer it to your first PassPocket in the back of the book. Circle the names and numbers once you decide to go with them to avoid confusion.

Arrival date: ______________ Alternate: ______________
Return date: ______________ Alternate: ______________

We plan to travel by: ❑ Car/Van ❑ Airplane ❑ Train ❑ Bus ❑ Tour
❑ Other: ______________

**For Drivers:**
Miles to get to Orlando: ________ ÷ 500 = ______ days on the road
We need to stay at a motel on: ______________
Tune-up scheduled for: ______________
Rental car info: ______________

**For Fliers:**
Airline phone numbers: ______________
Flight preferences: ______________
Flight availabilities: ______________
Reserved flight times and numbers: ______________

**For Ground Transportation:**
Magical Express/town car/shuttle/rental car reservations: ________

______________

Package ground transportation details: ______________

______________

**Additional Notes:**

*Reminder: Don't forget to confirm holds or cancel reservations within the allotted time frame.*

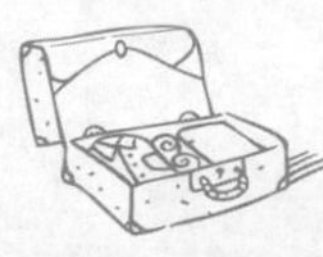

# Packing List

Electronic, interactive worksheet available—see page 287

Packing for a vacation is fun when you feel confident you're packing the right things. Over the years, we've compiled this packing list for a great vacation. Just note the quantity you plan to bring and check off items as you pack. Consider carrying items in **magenta** on a daily basis as you tour.

## The Essentials

- ❑ Casual clothing you can layer—the dress code nearly everywhere at Disney is casual, even at dinner. One "nice" outfit is usually enough.
  - ___ *Shorts/skirts* ___ *Pants/jeans* ___ *Shirts* ___ *Sweaters*
  - ___ *Underwear* ___ *Socks* ___ *Pajamas* ___ ________
- ❑ Jacket and/or sweatshirt (light ones for the warmer months)
  - ___ ***Jackets*** ___ *Sweatshirts* ___ *Sweaters* ___ *Vests*
- ❑ Comfortable, well-broken-in shoes ... plus a second pair, just in case!
  - ___ *Walking shoes* ___ *Sandals/Crocs* ___ *Sneakers* ___ ________
- ❑ Swim gear (bring one-piece suits for water slides)
  - ___ *Suits/swim diapers* ___ *Cover-ups/towels* ___ *Water shoes* ___ *Goggles*
- ❑ Sun protection (the Florida sun can be brutal)
  - ___ ***Sunblock*** ___ ***Lip balm*** ___ ***Sunburn relief*** ___ ***Sunglasses***
  - ___ ***Hats w/brims*** ___ ***Caps*** ___ ***Visors*** ___ ________
- ❑ Rain gear (compact and light so you don't mind carrying it)
  - ___ *Raincoat* ___ ***Poncho*** ___ ***Umbrella*** ___ ***Extra socks***
- ❑ Comfortable bags with padded straps to carry items during the day
  - ___ ***Backpacks*** ___ ***Waist packs*** ___ *Shoulder bags* ___ ***Camera bag***
- ❑ Toiletries (in a bag or bathroom kit to keep them organized)
  - ___ ***Brush/comb*** ___ *Toothbrush* ___ *Toothpaste* ___ *Dental floss*
  - ___ *Favorite soap, shampoo, and conditioner* ___ *Deodorant* ___ ***Baby wipes***
  - ___ ***Aspirin/acetaminophen/ibuprofen*** ___ ***Bandages*** ___ ***First aid kit***
  - ___ ***Prescriptions*** *(in original containers)* ___ *Vitamins* ___ *Fem. hygiene*
  - ___ *Hair dryer/iron* ___ ***Anti-blister tape*** ___ *Makeup* ___ *Hair spray*
  - ___ *Razors* ___ *Shaving cream* ___ *Cotton buds* ___ *Lotion*
  - ___ *Nail clippers* ___ *Spare eyeglasses* ___ *Lens solution* ___ ***Bug repellent***
  - ___ *Mending kit* ___ *Small scissors* ___ ***Safety pins*** ___ ***Insect sting kit***
- ❑ Camera/camcorder and more film/tape than you think you need
  - ___ ***Camera*** ___ ***Camcorder*** ___ ***Film/tapes*** ___ ***Memory cards***
  - ___ ***Batteries*** ___ *Chargers* ___ ***Case/tripod*** ___ ________
- ❑ Money in various forms and various places
  - ___ ***Charge cards*** ___ ***Traveler's checks*** ___ ***Bank cards*** ___ ***Cash***
- ❑ Personal identification, passes, and membership cards
  - ___ ***Driver's licenses*** ___ ***Other photo ID*** ___ ***Passports*** ___ *Birth certificate*
  - ___ ***AAA card*** ___ ***Discount cards*** ___ *Air miles card* ___ ________
  - ___ ***Tickets/passes*** ___ ***Insurance cards*** ___ ***Calling cards*** ___ ________

**Tip:** Label everything with your name, phone, and hotel to help reunite you with your stuff if lost. Every bag should have this info on a luggage tag as well as on a slip of paper inside it. Use our Luggage Tag Maker at http://www.passporter.com/wdw/luggagelog.htm.

## For Your Carry-On

- ❑ Your **PassPorter**, **tickets**, **maps**, **guides**, and a **pen** or **pencil**! Remember to pack any sharp or potentially dangerous items in your checked luggage, not your carry-on.
- ❑ **Camera** and/or **camcorder**, along with **film**, **memory cards**, **tapes**, and **batteries**.
- ❑ Any **prescriptions**, important toiletries, **sunblock**, **sunglasses**, **hats**, **bug repellent**–liquids/gels in your carry-on must each be 3 oz. or less and all fit in a quart-size bag.
- ❑ **Snacks**, **gum**, favorite books, **toys**, **games**, blankets, change of clothes.

## For Families

- ❑ Snacks and juice boxes
- ❑ Books, toys, and games
- ❑ Stroller, carrier, and accessories
- ❑ **Autograph books and fat pens**
- ❑ EarPlanes (http://www.earplanes.com)

## For Couples

- ❑ Corkscrew and wine glasses
- ❑ Candles and matches
- ❑ Evening wear for nights out
- ❑ Jacket (if going to Victoria & Albert's)
- ❑ Portable CD player and CDs

## For Connected Travelers

- ❑ Laptop and power supply
- ❑ Extension cord/surge suppressor
- ❑ Phone/network cables, coupler, splitter
- ❑ Security cable with lock
- ❑ **Cell phones** and chargers
- ❑ **Two-way radios**
- ❑ Local access numbers
- ❑ **Handheld/Palm organizer**

## For Heat-Sensitive Travelers

- ❑ **Personal fans/water misters**
- ❑ **Water bottles** (frozen, if possible)
- ❑ **Washcloth** to cool off face and neck
- ❑ Loose, breezy clothing
- ❑ **Hats** with wide brims
- ❑ **Sunshades** (for baby strollers)
- ❑ **Elastics** to keep long hair off neck
- ❑ **Sweatbands**

## Everyone Should Consider

- ❑ Big beach towels (for pools and water parks)
- ❑ **Penlight** or flashlight (for reading/writing in dark places and to alleviate kids' fears)
- ❑ **Water bottles** and personal **fan/water misters**
- ❑ **Snacks** for any time of the day (plus gum, if you chew it)
- ❑ Plastic resealable bags (many uses) and plastic cutlery for snacks or leftovers
- ❑ **Quarters and pennies** (and a way to hold them) for the coin presses and/or laundry
- ❑ Plastic storage bags that seal (large and small), plus trash bags
- ❑ Address book, stamps, and envelopes
- ❑ Laundry detergent/tablets, bleach, dryer sheets, stain stick, and a laundry tote
- ❑ **Binoculars**
- ❑ Collapsible bag or suitcase inside another suitcase to hold souvenirs on your return
- ❑ **Spare pair of prescription eyeglasses and a copy of your eyeglass prescription**

## Your Personal Packing List

| ❑ ____________ | ❑ ____________ |
|---|---|
| ❑ ____________ | ❑ ____________ |
| ❑ ____________ | ❑ ____________ |
| ❑ ____________ | ❑ ____________ |
| ❑ ____________ | ❑ ____________ |
| ❑ ____________ | ❑ ____________ |
| ❑ ____________ | ❑ ____________ |
| ❑ ____________ | ❑ ____________ |
| ❑ ____________ | ❑ ____________ |

# Adventuring!

Your journey is more pleasant when you consider it an adventure rather than a tiring trek. Here are our tried-and-true adventuring tips:

 Bring your own **snacks and beverages** (purchased after you pass through security) aboard the plane. We also suggest you bring chewing gum (to offset air pressure), 3 oz. lotion (to offset dry air), and a DVD/CD player (to offset boredom).

 "Line the bottom of your suitcase with a **garbage bag** when packing. I place everything inside then wrap another around the top. This keeps everything dry and the bags double as laundry bags on the way home." – *Contributed by Brandy Dorsch in our 2007 Traveling Tip Contest*

 "I always bring an **extension cord or power strip** on vacation to charge all of our electronics: cell phone, camera, laptop, DVD player, iPods, etc. The rooms don't always have enough convenient outlets." – *Contributed by Julie Pagano, a winner in our 2007 Traveling Tip Contest*

## Magical Memories

 *"We live near Atlantic City, NJ and usually fly out of Philadelphia, about an hour away. We use more gas, pay for parking, and have an hour ride each way when we fly out of Philadelphia. With gas prices being so high, I have been checking airfares, especially at Atlantic City airport just 15 minutes away. One day I saw a round-trip fare on Spirit for $209, but never got the time to book it and only saw fares increase over the next few days. Soon thereafter, I opened my e-mail and saw my Travelzoo newsletter, which advertised Spirit Airlines' $0.01 sale. Knowing it would not be on our dates, I opened it anyway and went through the booking process. Lo and behold, if we left in the morning of our trip instead of the evening, I could get a one-way fare for $9.99 (yes, just $9.99) and a return fare of $95. Needless to say, we booked it. Sign up for all travel web site e-mails because it is definitely worth it."*

*...as told by Disney vacationer Helen Friedlander*

 *"Before our first trip, we purchased Disney character pillowcases. When our children were toddlers, we slit the seams at the open end a bit and inserted drawstrings to make bags. We used the 'bags' to hold their toys and travel items in our van. As they have grown into teenagers, we use the pillowcases on pillows for use in the van during the trip. When we get to Disney, we use them as our laundry bags. As we wear our clothes, we sort them into the appropriate pillowcase—white for whites, colored for colored clothes. When the pillowcase is full, we take it to the laundry, throw the clothes in the washer, along with the pillowcase. Voila! Clean clothes and a clean tote to get them back to the room. Over the years, the pillowcases have became a bit worn and even have a few patches. They are a part of our children's trips, and have grown and adapted with our children and their ever-changing needs. You can also get pillowcases autographed. If you are already carrying the pillowcases into the parks for autographs, you can get double duty by using them to sit on during parades and shows. Hot seats, wet seats; not a problem. Need a tote bag for the free robots at Epcot's Innoventions? Put the pillowcase to use."*

*...as told by Disney vacationer Teresa Weddelman*

UNLOCK
the door to
resort basics,
information,
and tips


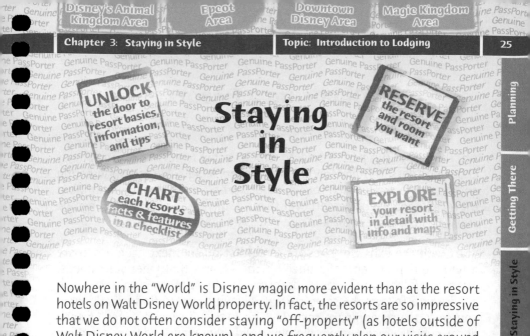

# Staying in Style

CHART each resort's facts & features in a checklist

EXPLORE your resort in detail with info and maps

Nowhere in the "World" is Disney magic more evident than at the resort hotels on Walt Disney World property. In fact, the resorts are so impressive that we do not often consider staying "off-property" (as hotels outside of Walt Disney World are known), and we frequently plan our visits around our favorite resorts rather than our favorite parks. Staying in a Disney resort is unlike any other hotel experience we've had, and we've visited both the exotic and the expensive. It isn't just that staying at a Disney resort provides total immersion in the Walt Disney World experience. The resorts are miniature theme parks in their own right, with hidden surprises and a remarkable attention to detail.

With more than 31,000 guest rooms and campsites throughout the Walt Disney World Resort, it would take more than 80 years to stay once in each room. (Sign us up!) There's something for every taste and budget. Whether you want a romantic setting, space for a family reunion, disabled access, or bunk beds, you can find it somewhere in the "World." There are enough choices to preclude staying at a non-Disney hotel, but bargains off-property are also a factor. If you visit with friends or family, prefer to stay in another hotel, or even take a cruise, your PassPorter still serves you well—you can record your arrangements here with the same ease. We include basic information on the Disney Cruise Line, Disney Vacation Club, and off-site hotels at the end of this chapter, too.

If you've already decided to stay at a Disney resort, your PassPorter puts you a step ahead! Our Walt Disney World resort descriptions are the most comprehensive of any guidebook, and our resort maps, photos, floor plans, tips, notes, and recommendations can help the veteran vacationer, as well as the novice, get the most out of their resort.

To help you find your way through the staggering array of choices, we've prepared a detailed guide to choosing your resort. We heartily recommend you turn the page and take advantage of it.

.................................................................➢

# Choosing a Resort

Ah, this is the fun part! Deciding which resort to stay at reminds us of choosing a dessert from a tray laden with every imaginable, mouth-watering goodie. Some are too rich for us, others aren't quite sweet enough, but there are enough choices left over to make us feel spoiled. Sometimes we stay at two or more resorts in one visit. Are you surprised?

Start with the exhaustive **resort checklist** on the next page. Compare it with your preferences to uncover the resorts that meet your needs. Then carefully read the resort descriptions, beginning on page 35. Each description follows the same format, allowing you to find exactly what you seek as you **compare resorts**. The first and second pages of each description list resort essentials, along with floor plans and transportation times. The third page lists the best tips, notes, and ratings for each resort—this is the "good stuff" to help you make the most out of your experience. In the Ratings section, we and our readers grade each resort for value, magic, and satisfaction. An explanation of the ratings is at the bottom of this page. The fourth page features a detailed resort map and our ideas for the best rooms in the resort. Rates, addresses, and phone/fax numbers are listed at the end of each description. **Tip:** When researching resorts, use the darkest "stamp" (tab) at the top of the page to locate parks and eateries in the vicinity, which will have the same "stamp" at the top of their pages.

When you're ready, use the Lodging Worksheet on pages 110–111 to record your dates, preferences, and reservation options.

## Resort Ratings Explained

We offer a variety of resort ratings in PassPorter to help you make the best decisions. Even so, we recommend you use these ratings as a guide, not gospel.

**Value Ratings** range from 1 (poor) to 10 (excellent) and are based on **quality** (cleanliness, maintenance, and freshness); **accessibility** (how fast and easy it is to get to attractions); and **affordability** (rates for the standard rooms)—**overall value** represents an average of the above three values. **Magic Ratings** are based on **theme** (execution and sense of immersion); **amenities** (guest perks and luxuries); and **fun factor** (number and quality of resort activities)—**overall magic** represents an average of the above three values. We use a point accumulation method to determine value and magic ratings.

**Readers' Ratings** are calculated from surveys submitted by experienced vacationers at our web site (http://www.passporter.com/wdw/rate.htm).

**Guest satisfaction** is based on our and our readers' experiences with how different types of guests enjoy the resort: ❤❤❤❤❤=love it ❤❤❤❤=enjoy it ❤❤❤=like it ❤❤=tolerate it ❤=don't like it

➤

# Resort Comparisons

| * Kitchen facilities are present only in the villas or family suites of indicated resorts | All-Star Resorts | Animal King. Lodge/Villas | Beach Club/Villas | BoardWalk Inn/Villas | Caribbean Beach | Contemporary | Coronado Springs | Dolphin | Fort Wilderness | Grand Floridian | Old Key West | Polynesian | Pop Century | Port Orleans | Saratoga Springs | Shades of Green | Swan | Wild. Lodge/Villas | Yacht Club |
|---|---|---|---|---|---|---|---|---|---|---|---|---|---|---|---|---|---|---|---|
| Deluxe | | ✓ | ✓ | ✓ | | ✓ | | ✓ | | ✓ | | ✓ | | | | ✓ | ✓ | ✓ | ✓ |
| Disney's Deluxe Villas | | ✓ | ✓ | ✓ | | | | | | | ✓ | | | | ✓ | | | ✓ | |
| Moderate | | | | | ✓ | | ✓ | | | | | | | ✓ | | | | | |
| Value | ✓ | | | | | | | | | | | | ✓ | | | | | | |
| **Rooms and Amenities** | | | | | | | | | | | | | | | | | | | |
| Total Rooms | 5568 | 1293 | 785 | 910 | 2112 | 1041 | 1967 | 1509 | 1195 | 900 | 761 | 853 | 2880 | 3056 | 1260 | 586 | 758 | 864 | 634 |
| Occupancy | 4-6 | 4-12 | 4-8 | 4-12 | 4 | 5 | 4 | 5 | 4-10 | 5 | 4-12 | 5 | 4 | 4-5 | 4-12 | 5-8 | 5 | 4-8 | 5 |
| Mini-Bars | | | | | | | | ✓ | | ✓ | | | | | | | ✓ | | |
| Coffeemakers | | ✓ | ✓ | ✓ | ✓ | ✓ | ✓ | ✓ | ✓ | ✓ | ✓ | ✓ | | ✓ | ✓ | ✓ | ✓ | ✓ | |
| Hair Dryers | ✓ | ✓ | ✓ | ✓ | ✓ | ✓ | ✓ | ✓ | ✓ | ✓ | ✓ | ✓ | ✓ | ✓ | ✓ | ✓ | ✓ | ✓ | ✓ |
| In-Room Safes | ✓ | ✓ | ✓ | ✓ | ✓ | ✓ | ✓ | ✓ | ✓ | ✓ | ✓ | ✓ | ✓ | ✓ | ✓ | ✓ | ✓ | ✓ | ✓ |
| Kitchen Facilities* | ✓ | ✓ | ✓ | ✓ | | | | | ✓ | | ✓ | | | | ✓ | | | ✓ | |
| Turndown (on req.) | | ✓ | ✓ | ✓ | | ✓ | | ✓ | | ✓ | | ✓ | | | | | ✓ | ✓ | ✓ |
| Wireless Internet | | | ✓ | ✓ | | ✓ | ✓ | ✓ | | ✓ | | | | | | | ✓ | | ✓ |
| **Eating and Drinking** | | | | | | | | | | | | | | | | | | | |
| Restaurants/Cafes | – | 2 | 3 | 7 | 1 | 3 | 1 | 2 | 2 | 4 | 2 | 3 | – | 1 | 2 | 4 | 3 | 3 | 3 |
| Character Meals | | | ✓ | | | ✓ | | | ✓ | ✓ | | ✓ | | | | | ✓ | | |
| Lounges | 3 | 3 | 3 | 4 | 1 | 3 | 2 | 1 | 1 | 3 | 1 | 2 | 1 | 4 | 2 | 1 | 2 | 2 | 2 |
| Food Courts | 3 | 1 | – | – | 1 | 1 | 1 | 1 | – | 1 | – | 1 | 1 | 2 | 1 | – | – | – | – |
| Room Service | | ✓ | ✓ | ✓ | ✓ | ✓ | ✓ | ✓ | | ✓ | | ✓ | | | | ✓ | ✓ | ✓ | ✓ |
| Pizza Delivery | ✓ | | | | ✓ | | | | | | ✓ | | ✓ | ✓ | | ✓ | | | ✓ |
| **Recreational Activities** | | | | | | | | | | | | | | | | | | | |
| Beach (no swim) | | | ✓ | | ✓ | ✓ | ✓ | ✓ | ✓ | ✓ | | ✓ | | | | | ✓ | ✓ | ✓ |
| Pools | 6 | 1 | 2 | 3 | 7 | 2 | 4 | 2 | 2 | 2 | 4 | 2 | 6 | 7 | 4 | 2 | 2 | 2 | 2 |
| Kid Pool | 3 | 1 | 1 | 1 | 1 | 1 | 1 | 1 | 1 | 1 | 1 | 1 | 2 | 2 | 1 | 1 | 1 | 1 | 1 |
| Spa (Hot Tub) | – | 2 | 5 | 3 | 1 | 2 | 1 | 1 | – | 1 | 2 | – | – | 2 | 5 | 1 | 1 | 3 | 5 |
| Spa (Services) | | | ✓ | ✓ | | | ✓ | ✓ | | ✓ | ✓ | | | | ✓ | | ✓ | | ✓ |
| Health Club | | ✓ | ✓ | ✓ | | ✓ | ✓ | ✓ | | ✓ | ✓ | | | | ✓ | ✓ | ✓ | ✓ | ✓ |
| Marina | | | ✓ | ✓ | ✓ | ✓ | ✓ | ✓ | ✓ | ✓ | ✓ | ✓ | | ✓ | | | ✓ | ✓ | ✓ |
| Tennis | | | ✓ | ✓ | | | | ✓ | ✓ | ✓ | ✓ | | | | ✓ | ✓ | ✓ | | ✓ |
| Jogging Path | ✓ | | ✓ | ✓ | ✓ | ✓ | ✓ | ✓ | ✓ | ✓ | ✓ | ✓ | ✓ | ✓ | ✓ | | ✓ | ✓ | ✓ |
| Playground | ✓ | ✓ | ✓ | ✓ | ✓ | | ✓ | ✓ | ✓ | ✓ | ✓ | ✓ | ✓ | ✓ | ✓ | ✓ | ✓ | ✓ | ✓ |
| Kids' Program | | ✓ | ✓ | | | | | ✓ | | ✓ | | ✓ | | | | | ✓ | ✓ | ✓ |
| **Access and Facilities** | | | | | | | | | | | | | | | | | | | |
| Monorail | | | | | | ✓ | | | | ✓ | | ✓ | | | | | | | |
| Disabled Rooms | 288 | 66 | 10 | 51 | 22 | 6 | 99 | 43 | 13 | 5 | 67 | 17 | 126 | 34 | 16 | 22 | 8 | 46 | 10 |
| Conf. Center | | | ✓ | ✓ | | ✓ | ✓ | ✓ | | ✓ | | | | | | | ✓ | | ✓ |
| **Your Favorites** | | | | | | | | | | | | | | | | | | | |

# Reserving a Room

Once you have an idea of where you want to stay at the Walt Disney World Resort, it's time to **make reservations**. A travel agent is not needed, but if you have a great travel agent, by all means consult him or her (they do not generally charge any fees for their services). Here's the lowdown on reservations:

Before you make your reservations, **use the worksheet** on pages 110–111 to jot down the dates you prefer to visit along with any alternates. Even a one-day change in your travel dates can open the door to availabilities. Be familiar with all resorts in your price range. We also suggest you finalize resort reservations after you make your flight reservations. Hotel room reservations may be changed or canceled, but flight changes often incur a fee.

You can make reservations for all Walt Disney World resort hotels at **407-WDW-MAGIC** (407-939-6244) or 800-828-0228 (Walt Disney Travel Company). Note that Walt Disney Travel Company agents answer both numbers. Disney representatives can offer assistance in English, Spanish, Japanese, French, Portuguese, and German. If you have Internet access, you can research room rates and make reservations online at http://www.disneyworld.com (click on "Resorts")–discounts are sometimes available on the web site, but you must follow the specific links for the specials or you'll be charged regular rates. You may also want to try Travelocity or Expedia, both of which are popular Internet reservation systems–you can visit them at http://www.travelocity.com and http://www.expedia.com. Be sure to look for promotional rates while you're there, too! If you prefer, you can also make reservations through the mail by writing to Walt Disney World at Box 10100, Lake Buena Vista, Florida 32830.

Reservations can be made for just **lodging ("room only")** or for **vacation packages**, which include lodging, admission, and more (see page 30 for more details on the types of packages available). Prices and policies differ for each type of booking, which we describe on the next page.

Research **special deals or packages** by visiting MouseSavers.com (see page 11) or by calling Disney Reservations. If you have a Disney Visa card or Annual Pass, or if you are a Florida resident or military family, ask about those discounts, too. (The Swan and Dolphin offer discounts to nurses, teachers, government employees, and AllEars.net readers.) If your dates aren't available, ask about alternates. Sometimes you can get a discount for part of your stay. Lock in whatever discount you can get, and book at full price for the remainder. Keep calling back, as canceled reservations are released every morning. If a lower rate comes out later, you may be able to call back and get it applied.

Make any **special requests** at the time of reservation and again when you check in. If you need a barrier-free room, a refrigerator, or a crib, request this now. If you have a particular location or room in mind (we make many suggestions later), make sure to tell the reservations agent. It's best to make your request as general as possible. You'll have better luck requesting a "high floor with views of fireworks" than simply "room 5409." If Disney doesn't know why you want room 5409, they can't choose a suitable substitute. Disney will not guarantee a particular room or view, but if your request is "in the system," they will try their best to make your wish come true. Call your resort about three days before your arrival to confirm any requests you made.

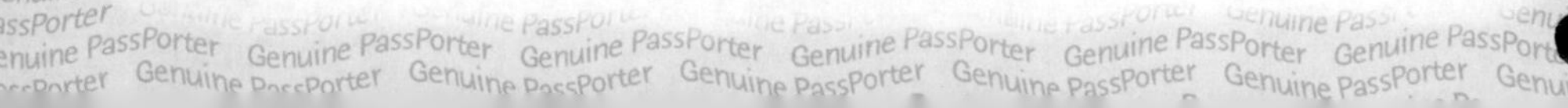

Do you need **ground transportation** between Orlando International Airport and your Disney-owned resort? Disney's Magical Express provides free shuttle bus service from and to the airport, as well as luggage handling. If your reservation agent doesn't mention it, be sure to ask. If you forget, the service can be added to your reservation at least one day before your scheduled arrival. See page 19 for the full details on Disney's Magical Express.

© MediaMarx, Inc.
*Onboard a Magical Express motorcoach*

You may be able to hold more than one reservation for the same date, but eventually you have to put down a deposit or lose the reservation. Typically, Disney resort reservations are held 10–14 days without confirmation as a courtesy, but only if you have at least 45 days until your stay. **Deposit and cancellation policies do differ** between packages and room-only reservations. Room-only reservations have a more liberal deposit policy—the cost of one night's lodging is all that's required (due in 14 days), with a no-penalty cancellation possible up to six days prior. With less than six days' notice, you forfeit the full one-night deposit. Packages require a deposit of $200, also due in 14 days, and full payment for your vacation is due 45 days in advance. Packages and room-only reservations made online also incur a $100 charge for cancellations made between 6 and 45 days prior, and $200 for cancellations made less than 6 days prior. There's a $50 charge for modifying package reservations within 21 days of your arrival.

Be sure to **pay your deposit** by midnight on your due date, or your reservation will be canceled. Your deposit can be made over the phone with American Express, MasterCard, Visa, Discover, JCB, Diner's Club, or through mail or fax with the same credit cards or a personal check. The Lodging Worksheet at the end of the chapter (pages 110–111) has spaces to check off confirmations and deposits made, too! **Tip**: You may be able to request an extension on your deposit if needed—inquire with Disney.

Once you've made your reservations, **record the details** on your Room(s) PassPocket, including the name of the resort, dates, type of room, price, reservation number, and any special information you want to note. This is also an ideal place to note any special requests you want to check on at check-in. Use a pencil if plans aren't final.

### Reservation Changes Beginning in 2008

Beginning on January 1, 2008, Disney may charge you a different rate for each night of your stay. The days of being able to get the same rate for every night of your stay based on your first night's rate are gone. So a stay that straddles both value season and peak season (see seasons on page 14) will be charged both value and peak season rates for the appropriate nights of your stay. Additionally, Disney is bumping up rates by $5-$30 per night at the value, moderate, and deluxe resorts on weekends and special holiday periods like Martin Luther King Weekend (January 18–20, 2008), Presidents Day Weekend (February 15–17, 2008), Easter Week (March 16–27, 2008), Independence Day Weekend (July 4–5, 2008), and Thanksgiving Weekend (November 26–29, 2008). You can learn the nightly rate for a given time period by calling Disney at 800-828-0228 or going online at http://www.disneyworld.com.

# Choosing a Package

Disney's vacation packages offer the promise of peace of mind and luxury. Package rates may be lower than the list price for each component, but may include more components than you can possibly use. A good number of veteran vacationers tell us they love these packages! Note that everyone in your room must be on the same package and plan. For more information and reservations, ask your travel agent, call 800-828-0228, or visit http://www.disneyworld.com. Below are the 2008 packages:

**Magic Your Way Basic Package**—Get three or more nights at a Disney resort hotel, a Magic Your Way Base Ticket (see page 116), one luggage tag/person, and other goodies. You may choose to add Park Hopping, Water Parks and More Option, and/or No Expiration features to your Base Ticket. From $357/adult.

**Magic Your Way Dining Package**—Everything in the basic package described above plus dining at more than 100 participating Disney restaurants.* For each night of your package, you get one table-service meal, one counter-service meal, and one snack**—you can exchange two table-service meals for a signature meal or a dinner show. From $471/adult.

**Magic Your Way Deluxe Dining Package (new for 2008)**—Everything in the above package, except you get three dining credits (good at table-service or counter-service) and two snack credits per person per night, plus one refillable mug per person. From $566/adult.

**Magic Your Way Premium Package**—Everything in the basic package, plus breakfast, lunch, and dinner per person per night at more than 100 participating Disney restaurants,* unlimited recreation, unlimited admission to Disney childcare clubs, Cirque du Soleil tickets, Grand Gathering experiences (if there are at least 8 in your party), and unlimited admission to selected theme park tours***. From $804/adult.

**Magic Your Way Platinum Package**—Everything in the premium package listed above, but you can eat at any Disney eatery, including Victoria & Albert's, character meals, and dinner shows (not all Downtown Disney eateries, however). You also receive two "magical evenings"—reserved seating at one showing of Fantasmic! and one fireworks cruise. Additional benefits include one selected spa treatment, a specially created keepsake, and itinerary planning services. From $1,378/adult.

**Magic Your Way Wine and Dine Package (new for 2008)**—An add-on to another package that includes dining, this gives you one bottle of wine per night per room. Adds $40/room.

* Participating Disney restaurants include all restaurants described in chapter 5 (see pages 199–242) **except the following eateries, which are excluded**: Victoria & Albert's (Grand Floridian); Bistro de Paris and Tokyo Dining (Epcot); Rainforest Cafe (Animal Kingdom); Ghirardelli, Rainforest Cafe, Ronald's Fun House, Wolfgang Puck's Grand Cafe, Fulton's Crab House, Portobello Yacht Club, Bongos, House of Blues, Wetzel's Pretzels, and Wonderland Cafe (Downtown Disney); and Big River Grille (BoardWalk Resort). Note that this list is subject to change at any time—be sure to check with Disney before making plans. Kids ages 3–9 must order off the children's menu when available at an eatery. Dining Plan credits may also be used for in-room private dining.

** Table-service meals on the 2008 Magic Your Way Basic Dining Package include entree, dessert, nonalcoholic beverage, and tax (but not appetizer or gratuity). Table-service meals on the 2008 Magic Your Way Deluxe Dining Package also include an appetizer. Counter-service meals include entree/combo meal, dessert, nonalcoholic beverage, and tax. Snacks include most items under $4, such as a nonalcoholic beverage, ice cream, cookie, popcorn, fruit, chips, or juice—even Dole Whips and French fries may be considered snacks. More details on Disney's Dining Plan are provided on pages 202–203.

*** Selected theme park tours include all tours described on pages 244–245 except the Around the World at Epcot tour, Backstage Magic, VIP Tours, and Yuletide Fantasy.

# Resort Key

**Resort Locations**—The Disney resorts described in your PassPorter are all located within minutes of the theme parks. We organize them into four areas: Magic Kingdom, Downtown Disney, Epcot, and Disney's Animal Kingdom (use the map on the inside back cover for reference). Each resort's area is identified in its description. You can also use the blue "stamps" at the top of each page to locate all resorts in a neighborhood.

**Room Locations**—Room locations, such as a building or room number, can be requested, but are not guaranteed. However, if you note your preferences when you make your reservation, via phone about three days before arrival, and again when you check in, there is a chance you will get the room you want. Resort maps and suggestions are given for each resort in this chapter. If you don't like the particular room you've been assigned, do as you would with any hotel and politely ask for another.

**Room Occupancy**—All resorts have rooms that hold at least four guests, plus one child under 3 in a crib. Port Orleans Riverside (Alligator Bayou) rooms allow up to five guests with an optional trundle bed, as do many of the deluxe resorts. Ft. Wilderness Cabins and All-Star Music family suites allow up to six. The two-bedroom villas in Disney's Deluxe Villa Resorts allow up to eight, and Grand Villas allow up to 12. There is an extra charge of $2–$25 per adult for more than two adults in a single room, except at Disney's Deluxe Villa Resorts.

---

**Amenities**—All rooms have the basics: television with remote control, phone, drawers, clothing rod with hangers, small table, and chairs, as well as simple toiletries. Additional amenities differ at each resort and are detailed later. **Tip**: If your room doesn't have a coffeemaker or iron/ironing board, request it from housekeeping.

**Check-In Time**—Check-in time is 3:00 pm or 4:00 pm (varies by resort), although rooms may be available earlier if you inquire upon your arrival. If your room is not available, you can register, leave your luggage, and go play in the parks while your room is being prepared.

**Check-Out Time**—Check-out time is 11:00 am. If you need to check out an hour or two later (up to 1:00 pm), ask the Front Desk the morning of check-out. If the resort isn't busy, they may grant your request at no extra cost. Extended check-out may also be available for an extra fee. You can also leave your bags with Bell Services and go play in the parks.

**Childcare**—Children's childcare "clubs" for ages 4–12 are available in many of the deluxe resorts (refer to the chart on page 27). In-room sitting is also available. See pages 254–255 for details and opinions on childcare.

**Concierge**—All of the deluxe resorts offer concierge services, which give you extra perks like a continental breakfast, afternoon snacks, and planning services. Concierge services are associated with certain rooms (often on the higher floors) that come at a higher rate.

**Convention Centers**—Several resort hotels at the Walt Disney World Resort are popular among convention-goers due to their excellent facilities, including the BoardWalk, Contemporary, Coronado Springs, Grand Floridian, Swan, Dolphin, and Yacht Club. For more details on convention facilities, call 407-828-3200. Business Centers are available at each of the above resorts.

**Data Services (Internet)**—All Disney resorts now have high-speed Internet access for $9.95 for a continuous 24-hour period, and some even have wireless (wi-fi) in select areas of the resorts (see page 27) available at the same rate. If you need technical support, call 407-938-4357. All phones have data ports for dial-up access. Local calls are now free. The front desk will also receive your faxes for a fee.

........................................➢

## Resort Key: Disabled Access to Information

**Disabled Access**—All resorts offer accommodations and access for differently abled guests. For details and reservations, call Disney's Special Requests Department at 407-939-7807 (voice) or 407-939-7670 (TTY). Be sure to ask that "Special Needs" be noted on your reservation. See page 27 for the number of barrier-free rooms at each resort and page 284 for *PassPorter's Open Mouse for Walt Disney World and the Disney Cruise Line* guidebook.

**Extra Magic Hours**—Guests at Disney resorts and the Swan, Dolphin, Shades of Green, and Hilton can enter the parks up to one hour earlier or stay three hours later than everyone else. Disney resort ID is required for entry, along with a valid admission. Only certain parks and attractions are open for Extra Magic Hours on any given day, however. The schedule changes from week to week (check http://www.disneyworld.com for the schedule during your visit), but here's a sample Extra Magic Hour schedule:

| | Sunday | Monday | Tuesday | Wednesday | Thursday | Friday | Saturday |
|---|---|---|---|---|---|---|---|
| am | none | Animal Kingdom | Epcot | none | Magic Kingdom | none | Disney's Hollywood Studios |
| pm | Magic Kingdom | Disney's Hollywood Studios | none | Animal Kingdom | none | Epcot | none |

SAMPLE

**Extra Magic Hour Attractions** (underlined attractions are open only during evening Extra Magic Hours)—In the Magic Kingdom, this usually includes Space Mountain, Buzz Lightyear's Space Ranger Spin, Big Thunder Mountain, Stitch's Great Escape, Tomorrowland Indy Speedway, Haunted Mansion, Pirates of the Caribbean, Splash Mountain, Magic Carpets of Aladdin, and most of Fantasyland. Epcot opens Soarin', Mission: SPACE, Spaceship Earth, Test Track, Journey Into Imagination, "Honey, I Shrunk the Audience," Living with the Land, Gran Fiesta Tour Starring The Three Caballeros, American Adventure, and Maelstrom. Disney's Hollywood Studios (formerly called Disney-MGM Studios) opens Rock 'n' Roller Coaster, Tower of Terror, Star Tours, Muppet*Vision 3-D, The Great Movie Ride, and Voyage of the Little Mermaid. Disney's Animal Kingdom opens Expedition Everest, It's Tough to be a Bug!, Kali River Rapids, Festival of the Lion King, Dinosaur, TriceraTop Spin, Primeval Whirl, The Boneyard, Pangani Forest Exploration Trail, and Kilimanjaro Safaris. Attractions are subject to change.

**Food**—Every resort has places to eat, such as food courts, cafes, fine dining, and room service. All resort eateries are noted in each resort's dining section later in this chapter. Details on the table-service restaurants start on page 226. If you are looking for snacks or groceries, each resort has a store with a small selection of food and drinks. No gum is sold on property. Special dietary requests can be made (see page 204).

**Housekeeping Services**—Every Disney resort has daily "mousekeeping" services and happily provides you with extra towels, pillows, and blankets upon request, as well as a hair dryer, iron, and ironing board. If you require extra toiletries, just ask for them. For tipping suggestions, see page 34. Note: Disney's Deluxe Villa Resorts provide reduced services to DVC members using their points.

**Ice and Soda**—All resorts have ice machines within easy walking distance. Most, but not all, also have soda machines. The rule seems to be the more plush the resort, the harder it is to find a soda machine. If soda is important, pick up some before you arrive (it's cheaper anyway). Another option is to purchase a refillable souvenir mug (offered at most resorts) for free (or low-cost) refills of soda, coffee, tea, and cocoa at your resort—see page 34.

**Information**—Check the Walt Disney World information channels on your in-room TV. These channels are available at every resort and offer a nice introduction for newcomers, plus a peek at what's new. You can touch "0" on any resort phone for more information.

## Resort Key: Laundry to Recreation

**Laundry**—Every resort has either coin-operated machines in a laundry room near the pool (expect to pay at least 8 quarters/load) or a washer and dryer in your room. **Tip**: Old Key West, The Villas at Wilderness Lodge, and Beach Club Villas offer complimentary self-service laundry facilities (no coins needed). Laundry bags and forms are available in your resort room for same-day service (it's very expensive). **Tip**: Store your dirty laundry in the laundry bags.

**Lobby Concierge (formerly Guest Services)**—Each resort has a Lobby Concierge desk where you can purchase park passes, make dining reservations, and find answers to just about any question. You can also connect to Lobby Concierge (and other Disney services) through a button on your in-room phone.

**Mail and Packages**—Purchase stamps at Lobby Concierge and in many shops; mail can be dropped off at Lobby Concierge or placed in mailboxes. Federal Express also picks up and drops off packages. A full-service Post Office is at the Shoppes at Lake Buena Vista at 12133 Apopka-Vineland Rd., about one mile north of the Crossroads Shopping Center.

**Merchandise Delivery**—Resort guests can have park and Downtown Disney purchases delivered free to their resort, usually by the next afternoon or the day after. Inquire before your purchase is rung up. Your package is delivered to your resort's gift shop or front desk for pick-up, not your room. (Includes Swan/Dolphin guests.)

**Money**—Cash, Disney Dollars and Gift Cards, traveler's checks, MasterCard, Visa, American Express, Discover, Diner's Club, and JCB are accepted. Personal checks are not accepted on property. ATMs are located near the front desk. Make your room deposit over the phone or fax with the above credit cards or by mail with a credit card or check.

**Parking**—Secured, free, gated parking lots are available at all Disney resorts. The deluxe resorts also offer valet ($10/day, free to those with handicap parking permit/tags); Swan & Dolphin valet is $16/day. Show your resort ID or confirmation at the security gate—parking is reserved for resort guests and those using a resort's restaurants or recreation.

**Pets**—Pets are not allowed in the parks or resorts (except for a few campsites at Fort Wilderness—see page 61) unless you travel with a companion (service) animal. Kennel fees are $6/day or $9/night per animal for Disney resort hotel guests ($11 per night for non-Disney resort hotel guests). Although the kennels are designed primarily for dogs and cats, they can also accommodate birds, ferrets, small rodents, rabbits, and nonvenomous snakes. Pets in kennels must be walked two to three times per day by their owners.

**Pools**—Every Disney resort has at least one swimming pool. Hours vary, but usually the "themed" pools close in the evenings while the "leisure" pools may stay open all night. Only guests staying at a resort can use its pool, though some resorts share pools and Disney Vacation Club members using their points have access to all but Stormalong Bay (Yacht & Beach Club) and the pool at Animal Kingdom Lodge (unless they are staying there).

**Preferred Rooms**—Disney's value and moderate resorts offer preferred rooms with better locations and higher rates.

**Recreation**—Every resort has something to do, with many offering a wide variety of outdoor activities. You can visit another resort to use its recreational facilities (with the exception of swimming pools). Be sure to note the operating hours upon arrival or by phoning ahead.

*The themed pool at the Polynesian Resort*

## Resort Key: Refillable Mugs to Voice Mail

Refillable mugs with the 2007 design

**Refillable Mugs**—All resorts sell thermal mugs that can be refilled free for the length of your stay in which you purchased the mug. If you drink a lot of soda, tea, coffee, or hot chocolate, these are a blessing—and they make fun souvenirs. Mugs are about $12 and can generally be refilled at a resort's food court or snack shop. In 2007, the resort-specific mugs changed to a general design available at all resorts. Neither milk nor juice is a refill option unless it appears on the soda fountain.

**Refrigerators**—In-room refrigerators are provided at no charge in Disney's deluxe and moderate resorts. You may request a refrigerator for a $10/night fee at the value resorts (except the All Star Music family suites, which have refrigerators already in the suites).

**Room Service**—The deluxe resorts and some of the moderate resorts offer room service. Most resorts offer a pizza delivery service in the afternoon and evenings.

**Security**—A gatehouse guards entry into every resort. If you arrive by car, plan to show your resort ID and photo ID and explain that you are checking in, dining, or using the resort's recreational facilities. All resort rooms have electronic locks that open with your resort ID for added security. In addition, you can store small valuables in your in-room safe (most, though not all, rooms have them) or with the front desk.

**Smoking**—All Disney resort guest rooms (including patios/balconies) are now nonsmoking. Designated outdoor smoking areas are indicated on resort maps.

**Spa**—Disney-speak for a hot tub. There's at least one spa at every Disney resort, with the exception of the All-Stars, Fort Wilderness, Polynesian, and Pop Century. Traditional spa facilities (massages and manicures) are available in some resorts.

**Tax**—Sales tax is 6.5% in Orange County (most of Walt Disney World) and 7% in Osceola County (Pop Century and some parts of All-Star Resorts); sales tax is charged on all purchases and lodging. An additional lodging tax is assessed on guest rooms: 6% in Orange County and 6% in Osceola County.

**Telephones**—All rooms have a phone and information on how to use it. Local and toll-free calls are free; long-distance calls are the cost of the call plus a 50% surcharge. Use calling cards or cell phones instead. Incoming calls are free.

**Tipping**—It's customary to tip valet parking attendants $1–$2 upon arrival and departure, bell services $1–$2/bag upon delivery and pick-up, and housekeeping $1/person/day. **Tip**: Leave your housekeeping tip with the housekeeper's name card so it's recognized.

**Transportation**—Every resort provides free transit to and from the parks via bus, boat, monorail, and/or pathway. We list each resort's options and in-transit times in this chapter.

**Wheelchairs**—You can borrow a wheelchair from any resort (inquire at Bell Services). A deposit may be required; availability is limited. Motorized wheelchairs (ECVs) may be rented at the parks for in-park-only use. You can rent ECVs at the BoardWalk Resort for use anywhere from Buena Vista Scooters (866-484-4797, http://www.buenavistascooters.com)—they also deliver to resorts. Other sources are Care Medical (800-741-2282—http://caremedicalequipment.com) and Walker Mobility (888-726-6837—http://walkermobility.com).

**Voice Mail**—Every resort offers free voice mail that can be retrieved from your room or any other phone in or outside of the Walt Disney World Resort. You can even personalize the message callers hear when they are connected to your room. If you are on the phone when a call comes in, the voice mail system still takes your caller's message.

# Disney's All-Star Resorts

Both economical and magical, the All-Star Resorts bring movies, music, and sports to life in three independent yet connected resort hotels. The All-Star Movies, All-Star Music, and All-Star Sports Resorts are located near Disney's Animal Kingdom theme park and the Blizzard Beach water park (use the blue tab at the top of the page for parks and eateries in the vicinity).

AMBIENCE

A star-studded production awaits you at the All-Star Resorts. From the painted stars everywhere you look to the autographed photos of famous celebrities lining the lobby walls, each resort greets you as a star in its **main hall**—Cinema Hall in All-Star Movies, Melody Hall in All-Star Music, and Stadium Hall in All-Star Sports. The halls house the registration desks, food courts, general stores, and arcades. Outside, the stars give way to larger-than-life movie, music, and sports icons, such as a towering Buzz Lightyear, a four-story-high conga drum, and a Coke cup that could hold 240 million ounces. Music plays in the background, providing you with an ever-changing soundtrack as you stroll through the grounds.

RESORT LAYOUT & ROOMS

The 5,568 guest rooms (1,728–1,920 in each resort) are situated in 15 differently themed areas encompassing a total of 30 buildings. **All-Star Movies Resort** showcases 101 Dalmatians, Fantasia and Fantasia 2000, The Love Bug, Toy Story, and Mighty Ducks; **All-Star Music Resort** features Calypso, Jazz Inn, Rock Inn, Country Fair, and Broadway; and **All-Star Sports Resort** sports Surf's Up!, Hoops Hotel, Center Court, Touchdown!, and Home Run Hotel. Each of the 15 areas features a themed courtyard created by two of the T-shaped buildings. The energetic and colorful themes are echoed in the guest rooms, with themed bedspreads, drapes, wallpaper, and a vanity area with one sink. Standard rooms have either two double beds or one king bed, a TV, a small table with two chairs, and drawers. Rooms with king-size beds are also the barrier-free rooms; thus, some of these rooms have only showers (no tubs). Rooms are small—260 sq. feet—but we find them adequate with the simple furnishings. 192 Family Suites are also available in All-Star Music—see page 37. No private balconies or patios, but each room has individual climate controls.

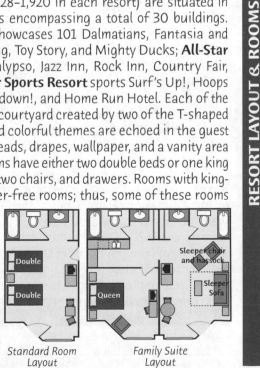

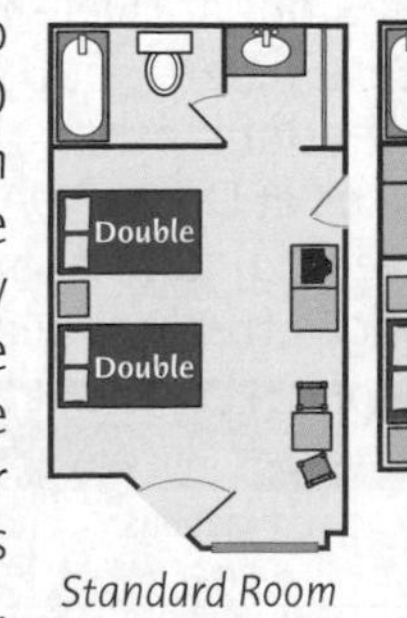

*Standard Room Layout*

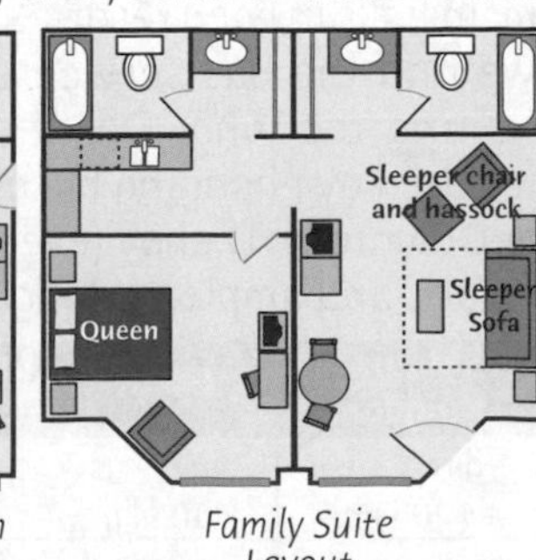

*Family Suite Layout*

# Using the Amenities at Disney's All-Star Resorts

## EATING & DRINKING

**Food courts**: World Premiere (Movies), Intermission (Music), and End Zone (Sports), each with four food stations plus a snack shop. Breakfast (6:00 am to 11:00 am) menu items typically include a Breakfast Platter for $5.59, a Western omelet for $6.49, and child meals for $3.59. Lunch and dinner (11:00 am to midnight) items include a 16" pizza for $15.49, chicken strips for $6.69, a Caesar salad for $6.99, a double cheeseburger for $6.89, and child meals for $3.99. Souvenir mugs ($12) offer unlimited soft drink refills. A **pizza delivery service** is available from 4:00 pm to midnight. **Walk-up bars** are at each food court and main pool.

*Family Suite at All-Star Music*
*200+ more photos at http://www.passporter.com/photos*

## PLAYING & RELAXING

**For Athletes**: Well-marked paths are ideal for walks and jogs.
**For Children**: Quiet playgrounds are located within each resort (locations vary—see map on page 38 for playground locations).
**For Gamers**: Each resort's main hall has an arcade—some games reward players with tickets that can be redeemed for small prizes.
**For Shoppers**: Donald's Double Feature (Movies), Maestro Mickey's (Music), and Sport Goofy (Sports) offer gifts and sundries.
**For Swimmers**: Each resort offers a main pool and a smaller pool. Movies' main pool conjures up the fun of Fantasia, Music's main pool is in the shape of a guitar, and Sports' main pool is styled after a surfing lagoon. All main pools have children's wading pools nearby.

## GETTING ABOUT

**Buses** (see chart below for in-transit times) are found outside the main halls in each resort. Stops are well-marked and offer benches. We find the bus service efficient, but some guests complain of waiting too long. Destinations other than those below can be reached by changing buses at Disney's Animal Kingdom (daytime) or Downtown Disney (evening). Guests may find a car useful at this resort, and ample parking is freely available around the resort.

| Magic Kingdom | Epcot | Disney's Hollywood Studios | Disney's Animal Kingdom | Downtown Disney |
|---|---|---|---|---|
| direct bus ~20 min. | direct bus ~10 min. | direct bus ~10 min. | direct bus ~10 min. | direct bus ~15 min. |

*Approximate time you will spend in transit from resort to destination during normal operation.*

# Making the Most of Disney's All-Star Resorts

TIPS

All-Star Music boasts **192 "Family Suites"** (see photo on previous page). These 520 sq. ft. rooms sport two full bathrooms, a kitchenette, a queen bed, a sofa bed, and two convertible twin beds. Each suite sleeps up to 6 people, plus one child under 3 in a crib. We love them!

**Walk around** the resorts to catch all the neat props and details that make these resorts so fun. Even the walkways have fun designs.

If you need an escape from the activity of the All-Stars, look for the **quiet spots** around the resorts. Relax in a hammock behind a stand of palm trees in Fantasia at All-Star Movies, or try the picnic tables in Country Fair's courtyard in All-Star Music for a leisurely lunch.

All-Star Music's rooms were renovated in 2007.

You can rent a **small refrigerator** for $10/night—request one when you reserve your room. (Family Suites already have refrigerators.)

NOTES

Plan to either carry your own luggage or wait a while (often 45–60 minutes) for their **luggage assistance service** to drop it off at your building. Unlike other Disney resorts, luggage is delivered at their convenience, not yours. Arrangements to pick up luggage on your departure day should be made the night before. You can borrow a luggage cart from the luggage assistance desk in the main hall, and you may need to leave your ID while you use the cart.

**Toiletries** are limited to a bar of facial soap at the sink and bath soap and shampoo in the shower/tub. You may want to bring your own.

Towels are not provided near the pools, so bring your own or use your room **towels**. Contact housekeeping for extra towels.

**Check-in time** is 4:00 pm. Check-out time is 11:00 am.

RATINGS

*Ratings are explained on page 26.*

| Our Value Ratings: | | Our Magic Ratings: | | Readers' Ratings: |
|---|---|---|---|---|
| Quality: | 6/10 | Theme: | 6/10 | 42% fell in love with it |
| Accessibility: | 5/10 | Amenities: | 4/10 | 35% liked it well enough |
| Affordability: | 9/10 | Fun Factor: | 2/10 | 12% had mixed feelings |
| **Overall Value:** | **7/10** | **Overall Magic:** | **4/10** | 11% were disappointed |

| The All-Stars are enjoyed by... | (rated by both authors and readers) | |
|---|---|---|
| Younger Kids: ♥♥♥♥♥ | Young Adults: ♥♥♥♥ | Families: ♥♥♥♥ |
| Older Kids: ♥♥♥♥♥ | Mid Adults: ♥♥♥ | Couples: ♥♥ |
| Teenagers: ♥♥♥ | Mature Adults: ♥♥ | Singles: ♥♥♥ |

# Finding Your Place at Disney's All-Star Resorts

ALL-STAR RESORT MAP

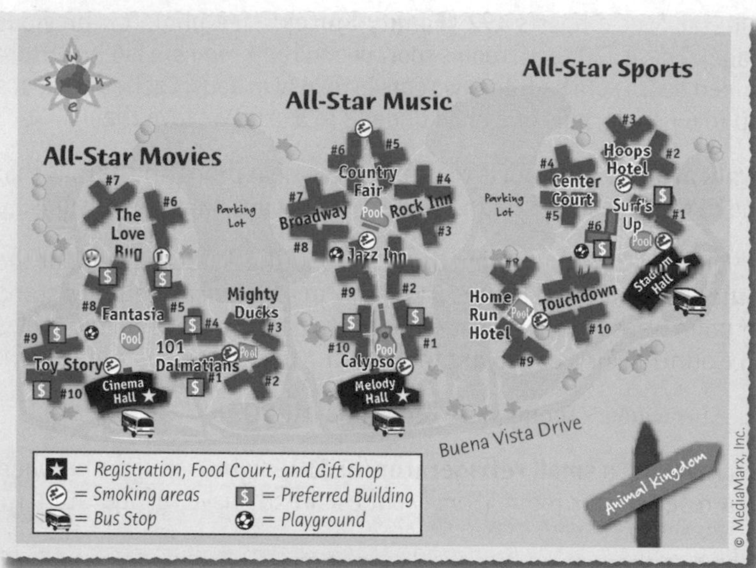


BEST LOCATIONS

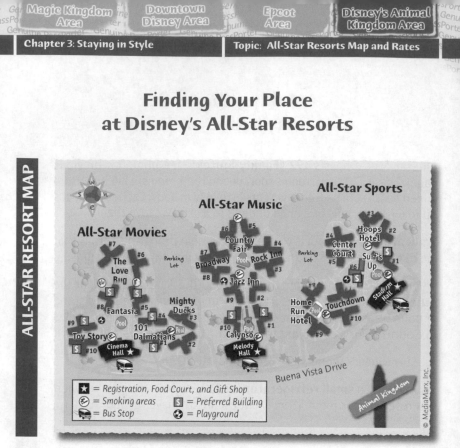

Rooms at the All-Star Resorts vary mostly by location within the resorts and floor. For convenience, we recommend **101 Dalmatians**, **Fantasia**, or **Toy Story** (at All-Star Movies), **Calypso** (at All-Star Music), and **Surf's Up!** (at All-Star Sports)—they are closest to the main pools, food, and transportation. Our personal preferences are **Fantasia** (at All-Star Movies), **Country Fair** (at All-Star Music), and **Home Run Hotel** (at All-Star Sports) as they are relatively quiet and have good views from most windows—the latter two are a good distance from the main hall, however. Quieter rooms are those that face away from the pools and are on the **top floor**.

RATES

## 2008 Sample Room Rates

*Seasons are noted on page 14.*

| Room Type | Value | Regular | Summer | Peak | Holiday |
|---|---|---|---|---|---|
| Standard Room | $82 | $99–$109 | $109–$124 | $119–$134 | $129–$139 |
| Preferred Room | $94 | $111–$121 | $121–$136 | $131–$146 | $141–$151 |
| Family Suites | $184 | $220–$240 | $250–$280 | $275–$305 | $295–$315 |

*13% tax not included in above rates. Preferred rooms are Fantasia, Toy Story, 101 Dalmatians, Calypso, and Surf's Up. Higher rate ranges are for weekend and holiday periods.*

INFO

## Disney's All-Star Movies/Music/Sports Resorts

1901/1801/1701 W. Buena Vista Dr., Lake Buena Vista, FL 32830
Phone: 407-939-7000/407-939-6000/407-939-5000
Fax: 407-939-7111/407-939-7222/407-939-7333
For reservations, call Central Reservations: 407-939-6244

# Disney's Animal Kingdom Lodge & Villas Resort

Disney's Animal Kingdom Lodge and Villas shares the ambience of its neighboring park, Disney's Animal Kingdom (use the blue tab at the top of the page for nearby parks/eateries). Guests at this deluxe resort can watch grazing wildlife on 33 acres of African savanna from their balconies.

AMBIENCE

Your trek to the Lodge is rewarded as soon as you step into the atrium lobby, which offers a dramatic view to the animal reserve and "kopje" (rock outcrop) beyond. Sunlight pours in through high windows, painting the lobby's thatched ceiling and carved wooden decorations in a warm, intimate glow. African artwork, much of it museum quality, greets you at every turn. Designed by the architect behind Disney's Wilderness Lodge, the six-story hotel shares its sister resort's **rustic appeal**, but adds a welcome warmth and intimacy, even in the largest public spaces. Then, of course, there are the animals, which add a sense of delight unique to this resort.

LAYOUT & ROOMS

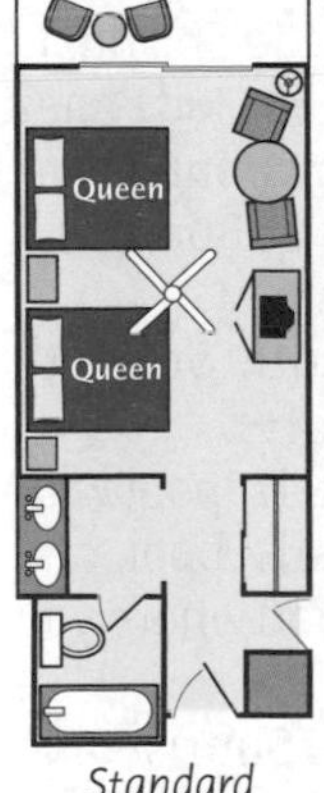

*Standard Room Layout*

This **horseshoe-shaped lodge**, inspired by African Kraal (corral) villages, gives most rooms a view of the private wildlife reserve. Rooms feature hand-carved furniture, gauze hangings at the head of the beds, and Kente-inspired fabrics. Standard rooms (344 sq. ft.) have two queen beds; one king bed and a daybed; or one queen bed and bunk beds. Disney's Deluxe Villas are also now available here in studio and one-bedroom villa configurations—see page 41 for more details. All rooms have a balcony, ceiling fan, table and chairs, refrigerator, coffeemaker, armoire with TV and drawers, double sinks, in-room safe, iron and ironing board, hair dryer, voice mail, and newspaper delivery.

DINING

A casual yet upscale restaurant, **Jiko**, is open for guests who want an elegantly inventive dinner. **Boma**, which means "place of refuge," offers an exciting, African-flavored dining adventure with all-you-care-to-eat buffets at breakfast and dinner. These two table-service restaurants are reviewed on page 226. **The Mara** is a quick-service cafe open all day. Typical breakfast menu items include an omelet sandwich ($5.59), a breakfast platter ($5.59), and a kid's breakfast ($3.99). Typical lunch/dinner items include African stew ($7.49), Mara house salad ($4.99), and flatbread pizza ($7.39). Refillable mugs ($12) can be purchased at The Mara. Room service is also available.

# Using the Amenities at Disney's Animal Kingdom Lodge & Villas Resort

## LOUNGING

**Victoria Falls Lounge**, which overlooks Boma, serves coffees, African wines, and international beer in the evenings. The **Cape Town Lounge and Wine Bar**, inside Jiko, serves remarkable wines from South Africa. **Uzima Springs** is a poolside bar offering beer and mixed drinks. Snacks, beer, and wine are at the **Zawadi Marketplace** and **The Mara**.

*Alexander enjoys the flamingos at Animal Kingdom Lodge*

## PLAYING & RELAXING

**For Animal Watchers**: Bring plenty of film/memory cards for your camera—you may also want a tripod. Binoculars are handy, too.
**For Athletes**: Keep in shape in the Zahanati Fitness Center near the pool. Massage treatments are also offered. There are no jogging paths—drive or bus to another resort (such as Coronado Springs).
**For Children**: Simba's Cubhouse is a supervised club for kids ages 4–12 (see page 255). There's also the Hakuna Matata playground near the pool, storytelling at the fire pit, and daily activities at Boma.
**For Gamers**: Pumbaa's Fun and Games has video games.
**For Shoppers**: The festive Zawadi Marketplace can outfit you with sundries, foodstuffs, books, clothing, and African crafts.
**For Swimmers**: Soak in the Uzima Pool, an 11,000 sq. ft. pool with an African theme, water slide (closes at 10:00 pm), kids' pool, and two spas (hot tubs). The pool features a zero-entry section where you can wade into the water. A pool wheelchair is available.
**For Concierge Guests**: Inquire in advance about the Sunrise and Sunset Safari experiences that include a special tour of the Lodge savannas plus a breakfast at Tusker House or dinner at Jiko.

## GETTING ABOUT

**Buses** to theme parks and Downtown Disney (see chart below for in-transit times) are a short walk out front (see the map on page 42). Travel to other resorts via Disney's Animal Kingdom theme park (daytime) or Downtown Disney (evening). Ample parking is available, as is valet parking ($10/day). This is the only deluxe resort to lack boat or monorail access to a nearby park.

| Magic Kingdom | Epcot | Disney's Hollywood Studios | Disney's Animal Kingdom | Downtown Disney |
|---|---|---|---|---|
| direct bus ~20 min. | direct bus ~15 min. | direct bus ~10 min. | direct bus ~5 min. | direct bus ~15 min. |

*Approximate time you will spend in transit from resort to destination during normal operation.*

➢

# Making the Most of Disney's Animal Kingdom Lodge & Villas Resort

TIPS

**Disney Vacation Club** is adding villas to this popular resort. 134 villas (studios and one-bedroom villas) opened in 2007, located on the fifth and sixth floors of the existing building (the "Jambo House"). In spring 2008, a new building (the "Kidani Village") opens with 324 villas, a new full-service restaurant, savanna, pool, water play area, and lobby area.

The Lodge's own **33-acre savanna**, which is distinct from the theme park, is home to 36 species of mammals and 26 species of birds—more than 330 animals in all. Guests can see zebras, antelopes, giraffes, gazelle, wildebeests, ostriches, cranes, vultures, and storks. Animals may come within 15–30 feet from you, day or night. Each savanna has a few animal species that are unique to it. Each savanna closes daily for cleaning and animal care, but at least two savannas are always open. Best viewing times are typically early to mid-morning, and at dusk (ask about night-vision goggles).

**African storytelling** is held nightly around the firepit. In inclement weather, storytelling moves to one of the overlooks inside. "Safari guides" are also on hand to educate guests.

NOTES

Tour the resort's **African art collection** on a free self-guided tour or a daily guided tour in the afternoons. Inquire at the front desk.

**Three separate savannas** (each about 11 acres) can be viewed 24 hours a day. If your room doesn't have a view of the savanna, **watch the animals** from the kopje (the large observation area that extends into the savanna), the Sunset Overlook (a delightful room on the west side of the lobby), the overlook near the pool, and the alcoves along Zebra Trail and Kudu Trail (visit the second floor for outdoor viewing platforms that feature rocking chairs and binoculars).

**Check-in time** is 3:00 pm. Check-out is 11:00 am. No late check-outs.

RATINGS

*Ratings are explained on page 26.*

| Our Value Ratings: | | Our Magic Ratings: | | Readers' Ratings: |
|---|---|---|---|---|
| Quality: | 9/10 | Theme: | 10/10 | 70% fell in love with it |
| Accessibility: | 5/10 | Amenities: | 5/10 | 23% liked it well enough |
| Affordability: | 6/10 | Fun Factor: | 8/10 | 7% had mixed feelings |
| **Overall Value:** | **6/10** | **Overall Magic:** | **8/10** | 0% were disappointed |

| Disney's Animal Kingdom Lodge is enjoyed by... (rated by both authors and readers) | | |
|---|---|---|
| Younger Kids: ♥♥♥♥♥ | Young Adults: ♥♥♥♥ | Families: ♥♥♥♥♥ |
| Older Kids: ♥♥♥♥♥ | Mid Adults: ♥♥♥♥♥ | Couples: ♥♥♥ |
| Teenagers: ♥♥♥ | Mature Adults: ♥♥ | Singles: ♥♥♥♥ |

# Finding Your Place at Disney's Animal Kingdom Lodge & Villas Resort

## ANIMAL KINGDOM LODGE MAP

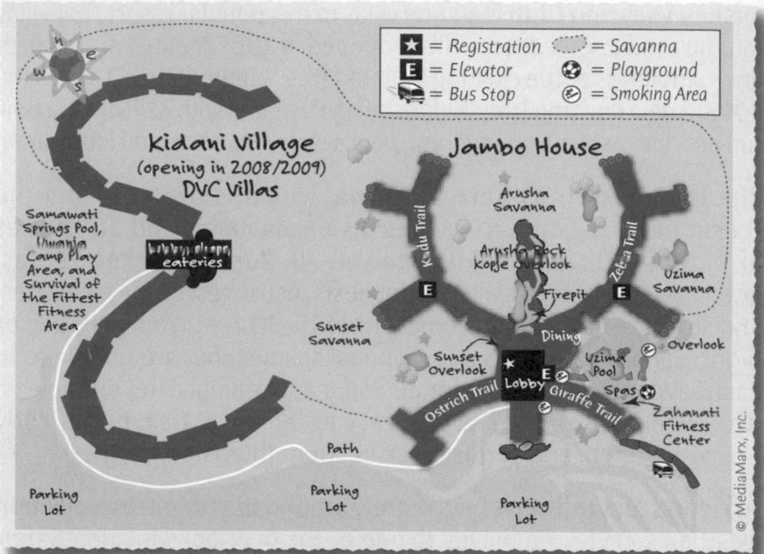

## BEST LOCATIONS

**Standard rooms** for up to four guests are located on floors 1–4. Rooms come in three views: standard (Giraffe and Ostrich Trails), pool (Giraffe and Zebra Trails), and savanna (Zebra, Kudu, and Ostrich Trails). If animal-watching is your main draw, reserve a savanna-view room. Rooms on the far ends of the Zebra and Kudu Trails require a long walk. **Concierge rooms** (floors 5 and 6) are also available in pool and savanna views, as are several suites. **Villas** are currently located on floors 5 and 6, also. Note that only the 6th floor is key-protected.

## RATES

### 2008 Sample Room Rates

*Seasons are noted on page 14.*

| Room Type | Value | Regular | Peak | Holiday |
|---|---|---|---|---|
| Standard View | \$225–\$245 | \$275–\$295 | \$340–\$370 | \$370–\$390 |
| Water/Pool View | \$235–\$255 | \$285–\$305 | \$350–\$380 | \$385–\$405 |
| Savanna View | \$290–\$310 | \$345–\$365 | \$410–\$430 | \$445–\$465 |
| Concierge (Club) | \$335–\$355 | \$390–\$410 | \$470–\$500 | \$520–\$540 |
| Studio Villa Savanna View | \$395 | \$440 | \$510 | \$565 |
| One-Bedroom Villa Savanna | \$606 | \$565 | \$645 | \$705 |

*12.5% tax not included in above prices. Suites start in the low \$700's. Higher rates in price ranges are for weekends and holiday periods (see page 29).*

## INFO

**Disney's Animal Kingdom Lodge & Villas Resort**
2901 Osceola Parkway, Lake Buena Vista, FL 32830
Phone: 407-938-3000 Fax: 407-938-7102
For reservations, call Central Reservations: 407-939-6244

*Looking for the Beach Club and Villas? See pages 93–97.*

# Disney's BoardWalk Inn & Villas Resort

BoardWalk Inn & Villas Resort enjoys a favored location in the middle of the action, fronting Crescent Lake between Epcot and Disney's Hollywood Studios (use the blue tab at the top of the page for parks and eateries in the area). The Villas are affiliated with the Disney Vacation Club (see pages 102–103).

## AMBIENCE

This **"seaside" resort** takes you back to the heyday of the Atlantic City Boardwalk in the 1920s and 1930s, where carefree days floated by on the summer breeze. Reminiscent of an elegant bed-and-breakfast inn, the BoardWalk continues this impression inside with its old-fashioned furnishings and soft, muted colors. Outside, a stroll along the vibrant promenade offers great views, family fun, and more eateries, clubs, and shops than you can visit.

## LAYOUT & ROOMS

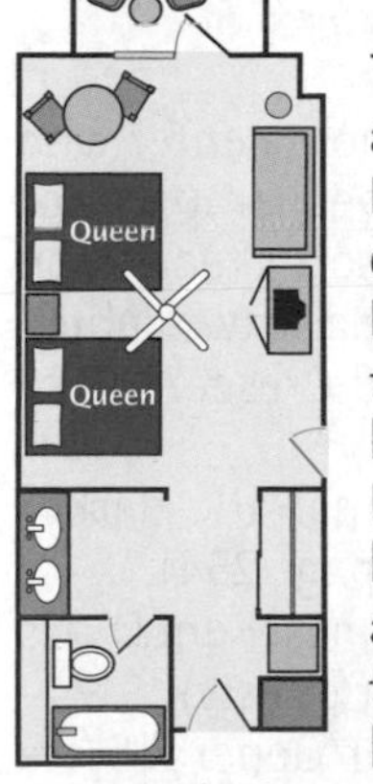

*Standard Room Layout (Inn)*

The two different sides of this resort offer varying accommodations, ranging from 359 to 2,142 sq. ft. **BoardWalk Inn** has 378 rooms with one king or two queens plus a daybed or queen sofa bed, and suites. **BoardWalk Villas** feature 532 studios and one-, two-, and three-bedroom villas (suites)—studios have a kitchenette, suites have a full kitchen, big-screen TV, DVD player, and washer/dryer. All rooms in the resort have a balcony or patio, double sinks, a marble vanity, a table and chairs, a sofa, an armoire, TV, ceiling fan, toiletries, and a hair dryer. Also available are housekeeping, turndown service (on request), voice mail, and, in most rooms, an in-room safe.

## DINING

Unique to this resort is a lively entertainment complex along the waterfront promenade. This innovative mini-park offers a variety of dining options. BoardWalk table-service restaurants, detailed on pages 226–227, include **Big River Grille & Brewing Works**, a modern brewpub; **ESPN Club**, an All-American sports cafe; **Flying Fish Cafe**, fine dining with an ever-changing menu; and **Spoodles**, delicious Mediterranean food. Spoodles also has an outside counter for take-out—pick up a slice of pepperoni pizza ($3.49/$3.99) or sangria ($6.95). The **Belle Vue Room** offers a quick bite in the mornings. Two quick-service cafes round out the menu. **BoardWalk Bakery** tempts you with baked goods and coffee—try the chocolate croissant ($2.79), breakfast burrito ($3.99), or a Lunch Bag (sandwich plus salad or chips for $8.09). **Seashore Sweets** offers ice cream, cookies, fudge, saltwater taffy, and coffees.

Planning | Getting There | Staying in Style | Touring | Feasting | Making Magic | Index | Notes & More

# Using the Amenities at Disney's BoardWalk Inn & Villas Resort

## LOUNGING

The BoardWalk is rich with lounges and clubs. **Atlantic Dance Hall** and **Jellyrolls** (see page 192) serve up drinks and fun. In the resort itself is the **Belle Vue Room**, perfect for a quiet drink and a game of chess. **Leaping Horse Libations** is the pool bar near Luna Park. 24-hour room service is also available.

*Alexander frolics on the lawn at the BoardWalk*

## PLAYING & RELAXING

**For Athletes**: Muscles and Bustles Fitness is a fitness center with exercise equipment, steam room, sauna, and massage therapies (for an extra fee). Rent bikes at Community Hall (the resort's recreation center) and surrey bikes on the BoardWalk. There are also two lighted tennis courts and a walking/jogging circuit around Crescent Lake and along the path to Disney's Hollywood Studios.
**For Children**: A playground and wading pool is at Luna Park. Harbor Club kids' care club is closed, but may reopen (see page 254).
**For Gamers**: Side Show Games Arcade has video games. Rent DVDs at Community Hall (free to DVC members, $3.16 for guests).
**For Shoppers**: Dundy's Sundries and Screen Door General Store offer the basics, while Thimbles & Threads and Disney's Character Carnival stock apparel and gifts. Wyland Galleries has collectibles.
**For Swimmers**: Of the three pools, the largest is Luna Park with a 200-ft. "wooden coaster" slide. All pools have spas (hot tubs).

## GETTING ABOUT

**Buses** are boarded in the front of the resort, while **boats** depart from the marina (see the chart below for in-transit times). Travel elsewhere via a park (daytime) or Downtown Disney (evening). You can **walk** to Disney's Hollywood Studios, Epcot, Yacht & Beach Club, and Swan & Dolphin. If you miss the Disney's Hollywood Studios boat, just walk to the Swan & Dolphin boat dock before your missed boat reaches it and hop on. Valet parking is a $10/day option.

| Magic Kingdom | Epcot | Disney's Hollywood Studios | Disney's Animal Kingdom | Downtown Disney |
|---|---|---|---|---|
| direct bus ~20 min. | walk/boat ~10/~5 min. | walk/boat ~15/~20 min. | direct bus ~10 min. | direct bus ~15 min. |

*Approximate time you will spend in transit from resort to destination during normal operation.*

# Making the Most of Disney's BoardWalk Inn & Villas Resort

TIPS

The BoardWalk Inn is being **extensively refurbished** in late 2007, and guest rooms are expected to receive flat-screen televisions.

The **Belle Vue Room** is a marvel of nostalgia. It's tucked away in a corner down the hall from the lobby on the Inn side of the resort. You'll find backgammon, chess, and checkers tables (ask a cast member for game pieces), as well as a single-malt scotch menu.

Take a stroll through the grounds, away from the busy Promenade. The **landscaping** is a delight. If you prefer the bustle of the BoardWalk, rent a **surrey bike** and tour around the promenade and lake.

The BoardWalk Inn's **Garden Suites** have to be the most romantic in the "World." Each of the 14 suites looks like a two-story cottage. All suites have private entrances and most have a unique garden surrounded by a white picket fence with a trellised arbor gate. Suites have a separate living room, sleeper sofa, and a wet bar on the first floor, while the open second floor has a king-size bed, a separate shower, and a large whirlpool tub.

Look for several quaint **sitting areas** scattered about the resort.

NOTES

Guests with rooms in the **small courtyard building** on the Inn side must use their room key to enter the building itself.

**Noise** and **light** levels are important considerations here due to the proximity of the BoardWalk Promenade. If these are concerns, request a room away from both the promenade and the pools.

**Conference facilities** are available at the BoardWalk.

**Check-in time** is 3:00 pm (BoardWalk Inn) or 4:00 pm (BoardWalk Villas). Check-out time is 11:00 am for both.

RATINGS

*Ratings are explained on page 26.*

| Our Value Ratings: | | Our Magic Ratings: | | Readers' Ratings: |
|---|---|---|---|---|
| Quality: | 9/10 | Theme: | 8/10 | 72% fell in love with it |
| Accessibility: | 7/10 | Amenities: | 8/10 | 17% liked it well enough |
| Affordability: | 3/10 | Fun Factor: | 6/10 | 8% had mixed feelings |
| **Overall Value:** | **6/10** | **Overall Magic:** | **7/10** | 3% were disappointed |

| The BoardWalk is enjoyed by... | (rated by both authors and readers) | |
|---|---|---|
| Younger Kids: ♥♥♥♥ | Young Adults: ♥♥♥♥ | Families: ♥♥♥♥♥ |
| Older Kids: ♥♥♥♥ | Mid Adults: ♥♥♥♥♥ | Couples: ♥♥♥♥♥ |
| Teenagers: ♥♥♥ | Mature Adults: ♥♥♥♥♥ | Singles: ♥♥♥ |

# Finding Your Place at Disney's BoardWalk Inn & Villas Resort

## BOARDWALK RESORT MAP

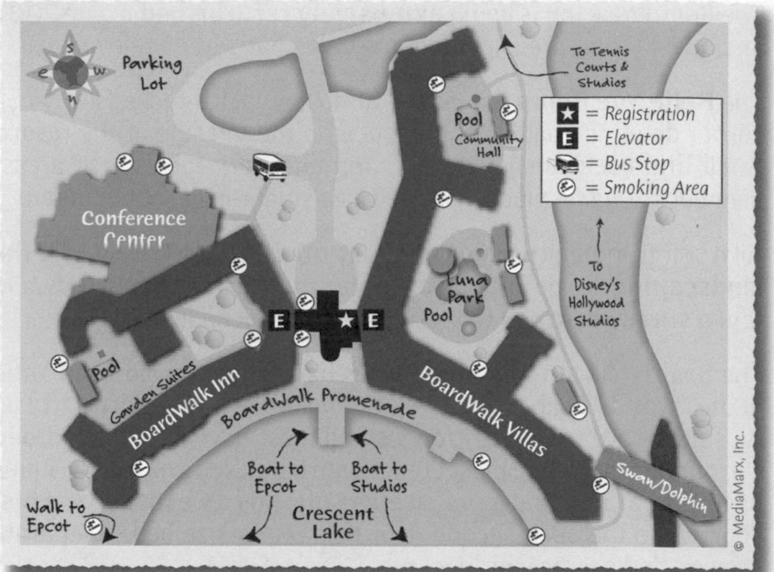

## BEST LOCATIONS

It's hard to get a bad room at either the BoardWalk Inn or Villas. Request a **water view** at the Inn if you want to watch the bustling BoardWalk Promenade, but keep in mind it can be noisy. Water views in the Villas may overlook the canal leading to the Studios, but may also overlook the Promenade (you may request this). **Standard views** overlook attractive courtyards or the entrance driveway (which isn't so bad as trees shield the parking areas). **Preferred views** in the Villas can overlook anything but a parking area. Rooms around the leisure pools are more peaceful than those around Luna Park.

## RATES

### 2008 Sample Room Rates

*Seasons are noted on page 14.*

| Room Type | Value | Regular | Peak | Holiday |
|---|---|---|---|---|
| Standard (Inn) or Studio (Villas) | $325-$345 | $370-$390 | $440-$470 | $490-$510 |
| Water View (Inn) | $400-$420 | $465-$485 | $525-$555 | $600-$620 |
| One-Bedroom (Villas) | $435 | $495 | $575 | $645 |
| Two-Bedroom (Villas) | $610 | $795 | $1,005 | $1,140 |

*12.5% tax not included in above prices. Concierge-level rooms begin in the mid-$400s and suites begin in the mid-$600s. Two-bedroom concierge suites begin in the $1,200s. Higher rates in price ranges are for weekends and holiday periods at the Inn (see page 29).*

## INFO

**Disney's BoardWalk Inn & Villas Resort**

2101 N. Epcot Resort Blvd., Lake Buena Vista, FL 32830

Phone: 407-939-5100 Fax: 407-939-5150

For reservations, call Central Reservations: 407-939-6244

# Disney's Caribbean Beach Resort

The free spirit of the tropics greets you at the Caribbean Beach Resort, Disney's original moderately priced resort. Within easy distance of both Epcot and Disney's Hollywood Studios (use the blue tab at the top of the page for parks and eateries in the area), this large and sprawling resort is popular with families.

AMBIENCE

The bright, sunny colors of the buildings and rooftops are your first sign of the **laid-back lifestyle** you'll find at the Caribbean. After you check in at the Customs House, you make your way to one of the six "islands" that encircle 45-acre Barefoot Bay. Lush tropical foliage, hidden courtyards, and white sand beaches are the setting for your lively Caribbean adventure.

RESORT LAYOUT & ROOMS

The 2,112 rooms are well spread out among the six exotic "**islands**" of the Caribe—Aruba, Barbados, Martinique, Jamaica, Trinidad North, and Trinidad South. Each island has a cluster of stucco, pitched-roof buildings without elevators that make up the "village centers," all painted in their own distinctive colors. The rooms in the two-storied buildings have bright colors and oak furnishings. The beds (one king or two doubles) have posts carved into pineapples, the symbol of hospitality. Guest rooms have double sinks in the separate vanity area with under-sink shelves and a privacy curtain, a table and chairs, an armoire with TV, a set of drawers, and a ceiling fan. There are no balconies or patios. Guest rooms here are the largest of all the moderate resorts at 340 sq. ft. Amenities include a coffeemaker, refrigerator, toiletries, housekeeping, limited room service, and voice mail.

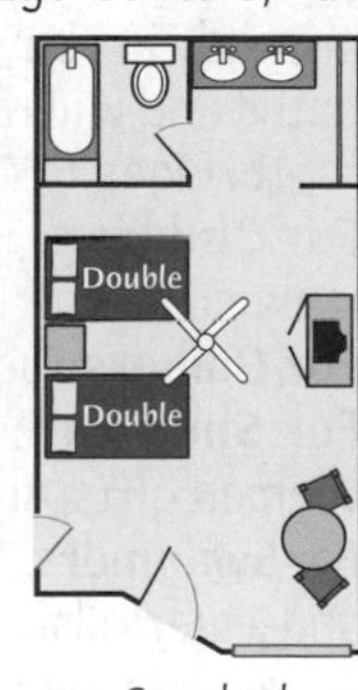


*Standard Room Layout*

DINING

The Caribbean Beach offers a table-service restaurant, as well as a breezy food court and the ubiquitous pool bar. All are available in **Old Port Royale**, also called "Center Towne," housing the eateries, shops, main pool, and marina. The food court's hours are 6:00 am–11:30 pm. **Banana Cabana**, a pool bar located at Old Port Royale, offers a variety of specialty drinks ($6.50+) and beer ($4.00–$5.00) during pool hours. **Bluerunner** is a limited room delivery service—typical menu items include domestic beer ($5.00), wine ($8.95+ for 1/2 bottles), 16" pizza ($16.99), and cheesecake ($3.59). **Shutters**, the table-service restaurant, serves Caribbean-flavored fare for dinner only—see the restaurant's description on page 227.

# Using the Amenities at Disney's Caribbean Beach Resort

## MORE DINING

A bustling village atmosphere sets the stage for **Market Street**, the resort's updated food court. The various food stations offer chicken, pasta, sandwiches, burgers, pizza, and baked goods. Menu items include French toast with bacon ($4.99), Cobb salad ($6.99), bacon double cheeseburger with fries ($7.39), turkey club ($6.29), kids' grilled cheese ($3.99), and carrot cake ($2.99). Get refills at the beverage island with a mug ($12).

© MediaMarx, Inc.

*Relaxing in our Caribbean Beach room*
*150+ more photos at http://www.passporter.com/photos*

## PLAYING & RELAXING

**For Athletes**: The Barefoot Bay Boat Yard rents boats and "toobies" (motorized inner tubes). Rent a bicycle or surrey bike for a ride around the bay. Walkers and joggers enjoy the many beautiful paths and will really enjoy the circuit around Barefoot Bay and the footbridges to Caribbean Cay island.
**For Children**: There are playgrounds on the beaches in Barbados, Jamaica, and Trinidad South.
**For Gamers**: Goombay Games in Old Port Royale has video games.
**For Shoppers**: The Calypso Trading Post & Straw Market offers themed gifts, sundries, clothing, and Caribbean items.
**For Swimmers**: The themed pool near Old Port Royale features cannons and waterfalls, as well as a wading pool for kids, a spa (hot tub), and a water slide. Note: The themed pool is slated for renovation January–June, 2008. Six leisure pools are in each of the resort's "islands."
**For Sunbathers**: Each "island" has a beautiful, white sand beach.

## GETTING ABOUT

Transportation to the theme parks and water parks (see chart below for in-transit times) is via frequent **buses**. Other resorts are accessible by changing buses at a nearby theme park (daytime) or Downtown Disney (evening). You can also take an internal resort bus if you need to reach other areas within the resort. To go to the Customs House (lobby concierge/luggage services), get off at Barbados.

| Magic Kingdom | Epcot | Disney's Hollywood Studios | Disney's Animal Kingdom | Downtown Disney |
|---|---|---|---|---|
| direct bus ~20 min. | direct bus ~15 min. | direct bus ~12 min. | direct bus ~20 min. | direct bus ~25 min. |

*Approximate time you will spend in transit from resort to destination during normal operation.*

# Making the Most of Disney's Caribbean Beach Resort

TIPS

We stayed at this **beautiful resort** in June 2007 and are delighted to report that it is looking wonderful!

While you can't swim in the bay, the **white sand beaches** are great spots to relax. We found several hammocks set up along the beach—take some time to just kick back and watch the palm trees flutter.

You can catch a glimpse of the **Epcot globe** between Old Port Royale and Martinique—look in the evenings for a glimpse of IllumiNations.

There are "hidden" **courtyards** sporting tables with umbrellas in every "island" of the resort—these are now the designated smoking areas, but can still be very rewarding places to relax. Be sure to take a trip across the bridge to **Caribbean Cay** (formerly Parrot Cay) in the middle of Barefoot Bay. Beyond the lush foliage and dense bamboo stands, you'll find gazebos, picnic areas, and hammocks.

*Caribbean Cay*

In-room **refrigerators** are complimentary.

There are **no elevators** at this resort.

NOTES

One of the biggest drawbacks of this resort is how spread out it is, making it difficult to get to Old Port Royale to eat or shop. You may find it easier to **stock up** on snacks and quick breakfast foods. Board the bus marked "Internal" to move around the resort a little easier.

All rooms in Martinique and Trinidad North are **preferred rooms** and are priced the same as a water-view or king-bed room.

**Check-in time** is 3:00 pm. Check-out time is 11:00 am.

RATINGS

*Ratings are explained on page 26.*

| Our Value Ratings: | | Our Magic Ratings: | | Readers' Ratings: |
|---|---|---|---|---|
| Quality: | 6/10 | Theme: | 6/10 | 47% fell in love with it |
| Accessibility: | 5/10 | Amenities: | 6/10 | 43% liked it well enough |
| Affordability: | 8/10 | Fun Factor: | 6/10 | 8% had mixed feelings |
| **Overall Value:** | **6/10** | **Overall Magic:** | **6/10** | 2% were disappointed |

| Caribbean Beach is enjoyed by... | (rated by both authors and readers) | |
|---|---|---|
| Younger Kids: ♥♥♥♥♥ | Young Adults: ♥♥♥♥ | Families: ♥♥♥♥ |
| Older Kids: ♥♥♥♥♥ | Mid Adults: ♥♥♥♥ | Couples: ♥♥♥♥♥ |
| Teenagers: ♥♥♥♥ | Mature Adults: ♥♥♥♥ | Singles: ♥♥♥ |

# Finding Your Place at Disney's Caribbean Beach Resort

**CARIBBEAN BEACH RESORT MAP**

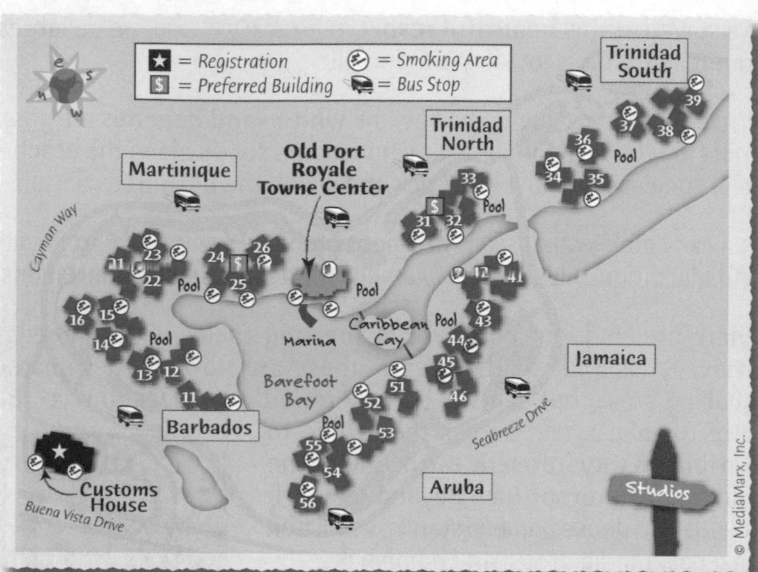


**BEST LOCATIONS**

Your "island" can make or break your experience. Though more expensive, we suggest you request **Martinique** or **Trinidad North**, both of which are close to Old Port Royale (dining and shopping). **Aruba** and **Jamaica**, across the Barefoot Bay bridge, are good choices if you wish to be a bit secluded. You don't need a **water view** to enjoy your room here, but if you prefer one, we found the following rooms to have outstanding water views: 2524, 2525, 2556, and 2557 in Martinique; and 3117, 3149, 3225–3228, and 3257–3261 in Trinidad North. Corner rooms (available with either double- or king-size beds) seem larger as they often have an extra window.

**RATES**

## 2008 Sample Room Rates

*Seasons are noted on page 14.*

| Room Type | Value | Regular | Summer | Peak | Holiday |
|---|---|---|---|---|---|
| Standard Room | $149–$159 | $165–$175 | $179–$194 | $189–$204 | $205–$215 |
| Preferred, Water, or King | $165–$175 | $185–$195 | $199–$214 | $215–$230 | $230–$240 |

*12.5% tax not included in above rates. King-bed rooms come in both standard or water view, and both are the same rate as a water-view room. Preferred rooms (any view, any bed size) are located in Martinique and Trinidad North. Higher rates in price ranges are for weekends and holiday periods (see page 29).*

**INFO**

## Disney's Caribbean Beach Resort

900 Cayman Way, Lake Buena Vista, FL 32830
Phone: 407-934-3400 Fax: 407-934-3288
For reservations, call Central Reservations: 407-939-6244

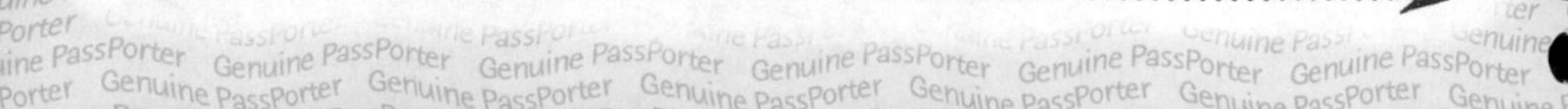

# Disney's Contemporary Resort

The Contemporary Resort is one of the original and quintessential Walt Disney World hotels, built at the same time as nearby Magic Kingdom (use the blue tab at the top of the page for parks and eateries in the area). Bay Lake and the Seven Seas Lagoon surround the resort on three sides.

## AMBIENCE

Every time we enter the Contemporary Resort, we get the sense we've entered the **center of the "World."** It isn't just the soaring architecture, the massive steel and glass tower, or the monorail running right through it, though those are all a part of it. Rather, it is akin to the feeling city dwellers boast about: Everything you need, everyone you like, and every place that matters is right there. And that seems to be exactly the way Disney intended it, with the Grand Concourse housing several of the resort's services, restaurants, and shops. There's even a restaurant at the top of the tower, overlooking the "World" below.

## RESORT LAYOUT & ROOMS

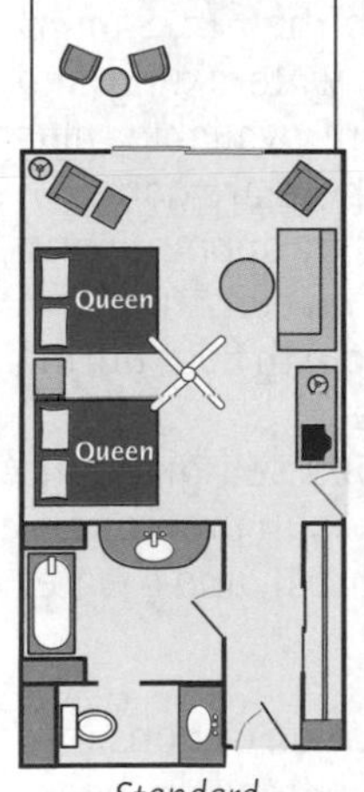

*Standard Room Layout*

The 1,041 guest rooms are housed along the outside of the 15-story, A-frame **Tower** or within the flanking, three-story **Garden Wing**. The rooms are spacious (about 436 sq. ft.). The recently renovated rooms are now modern and Feng Shui-like with flat-screen TVs, double closets, and dark cherry wood details with two queens or one king bed, and a daybed. All rooms have spacious bathrooms with two sinks. Some rooms have large patios or balconies. Amenities include housekeeping, toiletries, safe, newspaper delivery, coffeemaker, refrigerator, hair dryer, turndown service (on request), voice mail, and valet parking.

## DINING

The Contemporary's dining options are getting some contemporary updates! The two most popular table-service restaurants—**Chef Mickey's** (a character dining experience) and the trendy **California Grill** (the Contemporary's centerpiece)—remain as they are (see details on pages 227–228). The **Food and Fun Center** is now closed, and in its place a new table-service restaurant called **The Wave** (rumored to serve Asian food) will open in 2008/2009. Until then, a temporary quick-service eatery, **Tempo Grab and Go**, is open near the Outer Rim lounge. Once The Wave is open, **Concourse Steakhouse** will close and reopen in summer 2008 as a new quick-service eatery. Refillable mugs are available at the resort for $12. The **Sand Bar** by the pool also offers drinks, sandwiches, and ice cream.

# Using the Amenities at Disney's Contemporary Resort

## LOUNGING

**California Grill Lounge** offers California wines and appetizers along with a magnificent view of the Magic Kingdom. The **Outer Rim Cocktail Lounge**, overlooking Bay Lake, offers a full bar and snacks. **Contemporary Grounds** is a coffee bar near the front desk. **Room service** is also available 24 hours a day.

*The Contemporary Resort at dusk*

## PLAYING & RELAXING

**For Athletes**: The Olympiad fitness center has exercise equipment, sauna, and massage therapies. Boat rentals add to the fun. Sammy Duvall's Watersports Centre at the resort offers waterskiing and parasailing. Volleyball and shuffleboard courts are available, plus jogging paths. The tennis courts formerly located here are gone.
**For Charmers**: A full-service salon offers services by appointment.
**For Children**: Note: The playground is closed during construction.
**For Gamers**: The resort arcade has moved to the fourth floor during construction, with pinball, video, and action games.
**For Shoppers**: The fourth-floor Concourse shops sell gifts and clothing. The marina pavilion offers swimwear and sun protection.
**For Swimmers**: Two heated pools, two spas (hot tubs), and a water slide, as well as a sand beach for sunbathers.

## GETTING ABOUT

The Contemporary Resort offers myriad transportation options (see the chart below for in-transit times). For the Magic Kingdom, board the **monorail** on the fourth floor or walk the **path** on the north side (see map on page 54). For Epcot, monorail to the Transportation and Ticket Center (TTC) and transfer to the Epcot monorail. For other parks, take the **direct bus** just outside the lobby. For the Polynesian or Grand Floridian, take the monorail. For Fort Wilderness or the Wilderness Lodge, take the **boat**. For other destinations, go to the Magic Kingdom (daytime) or Downtown Disney (evening) and transfer to the appropriate resort bus. Valet parking is a $10/day option.

| Magic Kingdom | Epcot | Disney's Hollywood Studios | Disney's Animal Kingdom | Downtown Disney |
|---|---|---|---|---|
| monorail/walk ~20/~10 min. | monorail x 2 ~5+10 min. | direct bus ~20 min. | direct bus ~20 min. | direct bus ~35 min. |

*Approximate time you will spend in transit from resort to destination during normal operation.*

# Making the Most of Disney's Contemporary Resort

TIPS

The **Electrical Water Pageant**, a whimsical parade of lighted barges and music, can be seen from the shore of Bay Lake at 10:00 pm.

The resort also offers one- and two-bedroom suites and two concierge levels, all with special amenities. Among the many amenities in the **suites** (bathrobes, triple sheeting, turndown service, etc.), the two-line speakerphones are great for those who use dataports often.

The obvious method of transportation to Magic Kingdom is via the monorail, but consider **walking** instead on busy mornings or when the park lets out—it's much faster! The monorail goes around the lagoon clockwise, so it can take a while to reach the Magic Kingdom.

Guest rooms in the **Garden Wing** can be a hike from the Tower's restaurants and services. If this is a concern, reserve a Tower room.

The resort has been recently **renovated** with entirely redecorated guest rooms and public areas. Very classy!

NOTES

Construction on the north side of the resort (where the North Garden Wing was located) is rumored to be new **Deluxe Villas** or perhaps even family suite accommodations, but this has yet to be officially confirmed by Disney.

For some, the Contemporary lacks the whimsy seen in most other Disney resorts. It feels much more like a traditional hotel. Even so, it is a very deluxe, modern, sparkling-clean hotel with a powerful presence. You'll be delighted by **subtler details** and **little luxuries**. Wireless Internet access is available in some public areas, too.

**Check-in time** is 3:00 pm. Check-out time is 11:00 am.

RATINGS

*Ratings are explained on page 26.*

| Our Value Ratings: | | Our Magic Ratings: | | Readers' Ratings: |
|---|---|---|---|---|
| Quality: | 8/10 | Theme: | 4/10 | 50% fell in love with it |
| Accessibility: | 9/10 | Amenities: | 9/10 | 24% liked it well enough |
| Affordability: | 5/10 | Fun Factor: | 5/10 | 10% had mixed feelings |
| **Overall Value:** | **7/10** | **Overall Magic:** | **6/10** | 16% were disappointed |

| Contemporary is enjoyed by... | (rated by both authors and readers) | |
|---|---|---|
| Younger Kids: ❤❤❤ | Young Adults: ❤❤❤❤❤ | Families: ❤❤❤❤❤ |
| Older Kids: ❤❤❤❤❤ | Mid Adults: ❤❤❤❤ | Couples: ❤❤❤❤ |
| Teenagers: ❤❤❤❤❤ | Mature Adults: ❤❤❤ | Singles: ❤❤❤❤ |

# Finding Your Place at Disney's Contemporary Resort

CONTEMPORARY RESORT MAP

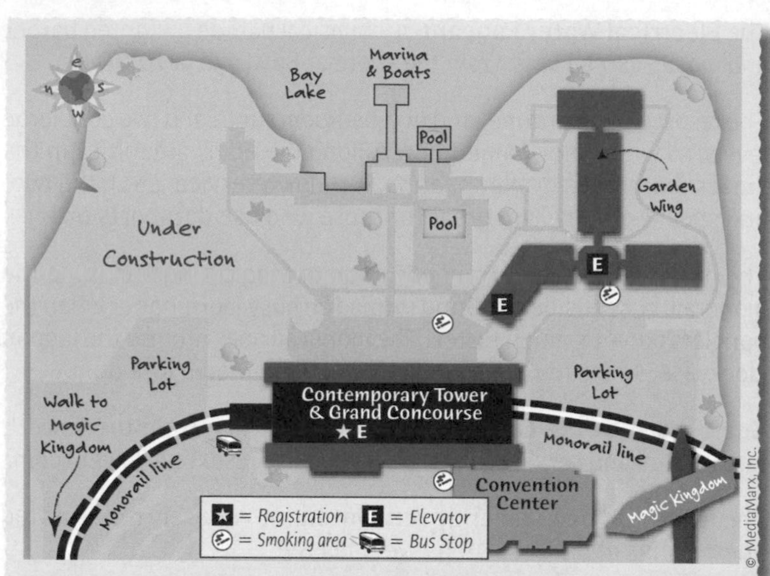


BEST LOCATIONS

If you are drawn to the Contemporary by its proximity to the Magic Kingdom and you want to **see the castle** from your room, be sure to request this specifically when reserving—only certain **Tower** rooms get this breathtaking view. The **Garden Wing** may lack the Tower's excitement, but we found the rooms delightful and relaxing, especially those facing the water. Garden Wing rooms fronting Bay Lake feel far removed from the bustle of the Tower and are quite relaxing. Very few of the Garden Wing rooms have **balconies**, but first-floor rooms have **patios**.

RATES

## 2008 Sample Room Rates

*Seasons are noted on page 14.*

| Room Type | Value | Regular | Peak | Holiday |
|---|---|---|---|---|
| Standard View (Wing) | $270-$290 | $315-$335 | $350-$380 | $410-$430 |
| Garden/Water View (Wing) | $320-$340 | $365-$385 | $405-$435 | $470-$500 |
| Tower Room (Bay View) | $380-$400 | $430-$450 | $485-$515 | $540-$560 |
| Tower (Magic Kingdom view) | $410-$430 | $465-$485 | $540-$570 | $600-$620 |

*12.5% tax not included in above rates. Concierge-level rooms (floors 12 and 14) start in the low $500s. Suites come in a variety of views and start in the high $800s. Higher rates in price ranges are for weekends and holiday periods (see page 29).*

INFO

**Disney's Contemporary Resort**

4600 North World Drive, Lake Buena Vista, FL 32830
Phone: 407-824-1000 Fax: 407-824-3539
For reservations, call Central Reservations: 407-939-6244

# Disney's Coronado Springs Resort

Coronado Springs is located near Disney's Animal Kingdom and Disney's Hollywood Studios (use the blue tab at the top of the page for parks and eateries in the area). The resort offers moderately priced rooms and convention facilities. The resort surrounds a 15-acre lake known as Lago (Lake) Dorado.

**AMBIENCE**

The architecture and decor trace the travels of explorer Francisco de Coronado in colonial Mexico and the **American Southwest**. Adventure awaits around every corner, from the colorful, bustling market to the Mayan pyramid overlooking the main swimming pool. Your visit begins in a sunny plaza, which leads to the large, open lobby graced by beamed ceilings, elegant columns, and intricately inlaid floors. Around the corner, a festive market offers native foods, just the thing to eat on the lakeside terrace. The resort's buildings are clustered around sparkling Lago Dorado, including the stately main building, El Centro.

**RESORT LAYOUT & ROOMS**

The guest rooms in this 1,967-room resort are divided into three districts. Closest to El Centro are the **Casitas**, a bustling village of three- and four-story stucco buildings painted in soft pastels. Next around the lagoon are the rustic adobe-and-wood **Ranchos**. You could imagine Zorro dashing under the porch roofs and amid the cactus, while bubbling springs cascade into rock-strewn stream beds, ultimately to disappear into the parched desert earth. Finally, you reach the tropical **Cabanas**, vibrantly colored two-story buildings with the corrugated tin roofs of a rustic beach resort. Rooms are about 314 sq. ft. and offer two extra-long double beds or one king bed, a separate vanity area with just one sink, table and chairs, armoire, and a TV. Amenities include toiletries, housekeeping, limited room service, hair dryer, iron and ironing board, coffeemaker, refrigerator, in-room safe, and voice mail. Newspaper delivery is available for $1.50/day. A number of junior, one-bedroom, and executive suites are also available.

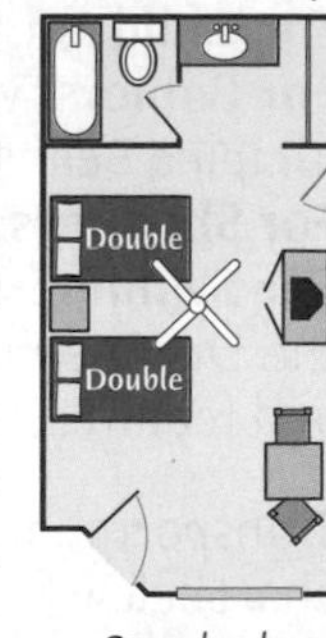

*Standard Room Layout*

The large 95,000 sq. ft. **Conference Center** is quite modern and generally lacks the regional character of the resort. It boasts the largest ballroom in the Southeast (60,214 sq. ft.). Several smaller-sized meeting rooms, another 20,000 sq. ft. ballroom, and patios round out the facilities. The center has recently undergone a major expansion. A full-service business center is available.

# Using the Amenities at Disney's Coronado Springs Resort

DINING

Coronado Springs' dining options are the real enchilada. **Maya Grill** (see page 228) is an upscale table-service restaurant open for breakfast and dinner. **Pepper Market** is an upscale food court dressed up like a festive, outdoor market for breakfast, lunch, and dinner. Typical menu items include breakfast burrito ($7.95), cheese omelet ($6.99), catch of the day tacos ($11.95), chicken fajitas ($12.95), ham sandwich ($7.50), and kids' chicken strips ($4.75), plus an automatic 10% gratuity. **Siesta's** is the poolside bar serving sandwiches, nachos, fries, and various drinks. **Francisco's** is a large lounge where you can also get light snacks and appetizers. **Limited room service** is offered in the mornings and evenings. Refillable mugs ($12) are available at the Pepper Market.

© MediaMarx, Inc.

*Home on the Ranchos*

PLAYING & RELAXING

**For Athletes**: La Vida Health Club has exercise equipment, whirlpool, and massage treatments. Boats, bikes, surreys, and fishing poles can be rented at La Marina, and there is a volleyball court. Enjoy a nature trail and a walk/jog around the lagoon.
**For Charmers**: Casa de Belleza offers beauty and hair treatments.
**For Children**: The Explorer's Playground is near the main pool.
**For Gamers**: Video games of all sorts are found at the two arcades: Jumping Beans (in El Centro) and Iguana (near the main pool).
**For Shoppers**: Panchito's has sundries, character items, and gifts.
**For Swimmers**: A leisure pool in each of the three districts, plus the Dig Site main pool, which is built around an ancient pyramid and features a water slide, spa (hot tub), and kids' pool.

GETTING ABOUT

Transportation to the theme parks is by frequent, direct **buses** (see chart below for in-transit times). There are four bus stops (see map on page 58). For other destinations, transfer at a nearby theme park (daytime) or at Downtown Disney (evening). A sidewalk connects the resort to Blizzard Beach, and it's a quick drive to both Disney's Hollywood Studios and Disney's Animal Kingdom.

| Magic Kingdom | Epcot | Disney's Hollywood Studios | Disney's Animal Kingdom | Downtown Disney |
|---|---|---|---|---|
| direct bus ~15 min. | direct bus ~15 min. | direct bus ~15 min. | direct bus ~10 min. | direct bus ~25 min. |

*Approximate time you will spend in transit from resort to destination during normal operation.*

# Making the Most of Disney's Coronado Springs Resort

The **Dig Site** is really a miniature water park with delightful scenery and fun water attractions. The pool itself is huge (10,800 sq. ft.), and there's a large sandbox that masquerades as the "dig site" of the Mayan pyramid. The 123-foot-long water slide has a jaguar atop it that spits water. Oh, and they have the largest outdoor spa (hot tub) of any Disney resort—it fits 22 people!

Small **refrigerators** are available at no extra charge. Roll-away beds are available for $15/day (but rooms are still limited to four guests). Request these with your reservations and again at check-in.

The **Pepper Market** food court works differently than other food courts. Upon arrival, you are seated by a cast member and given a ticket. You then visit the various food stations, and when you find an item you want, your ticket is stamped. You pay after your meal. A 10% gratuity is added (unless you get your food to go).

This resort goes for the sun-drenched effect and, in the process, seems to **lack enough shade** to protect you from the scorching Florida sun. Use caution if you are fair-skinned (as Jennifer is) or if you are going during the summer months.

Coronado Springs strikes us as a bit more **buttoned-down** than the other moderate resorts, no doubt due to the conference center and business facilities. While we have no major complaints, it also didn't delight us in the same way that other moderate Disney resorts have. On the other hand, some of our fellow vacationers are very impressed with the resort, especially its quality service. We definitely feel this is a great resort for business travelers.

**Check-in time** is 3:00 pm. Check-out time is 11:00 am.

*Ratings are explained on page 26.*

| Our Value Ratings: | | Our Magic Ratings: | | Readers' Ratings: |
|---|---|---|---|---|
| Quality: | 7/10 | Theme: | 8/10 | 35% fell in love with it |
| Accessibility: | 6/10 | Amenities: | 5/10 | 47% liked it well enough |
| Affordability: | 8/10 | Fun Factor: | 4/10 | 15% had mixed feelings |
| **Overall Value:** | **7/10** | **Overall Magic:** | **6/10** | 3% were disappointed |

| Coronado Springs is enjoyed by... | (rated by both authors and readers) | |
|---|---|---|
| Younger Kids: ♥♥♥♥ | Young Adults: ♥♥♥♥♥ | Families: ♥♥♥♥ |
| Older Kids: ♥♥♥♥ | Mid Adults: ♥♥♥♥ | Couples: ♥♥♥♥♥ |
| Teenagers: ♥♥♥♥ | Mature Adults: ♥♥♥ | Singles: ♥♥♥♥ |

# Finding Your Place at Disney's Coronado Springs Resort

CORONADO SPRINGS RESORT MAP

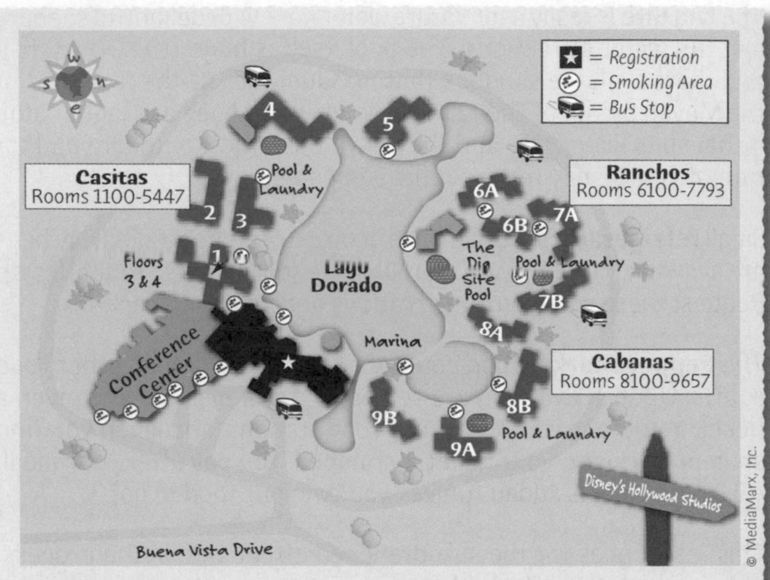


BEST LOCATIONS

The **Casitas** are the least interesting visually, but they are convenient to the Convention Center—in fact, they house the only rooms that you can reach from El Centro without leaving the protection of a roof or overhang. Building 1 is the closest to the Conference Center. The charming **Ranchos** are closest to the main pool and farthest from El Centro. We recommend building 6B for its view and proximity to the leisure pool. The **Cabanas** are convenient to El Centro. We loved our room in building 8B (close to pools and the bus); building 8A has good views, and 9B is next door to El Centro.

RATES

## 2008 Sample Room Rates

*Seasons are noted on page 14.*

| Room Type | Value | Regular | Summer | Peak | Holiday |
|---|---|---|---|---|---|
| Standard Room | $149-$159 | $165-$175 | $179-$194 | $189-$204 | $205-$215 |
| Water or King Room | $165-$175 | $185-$195 | $199-$214 | $215-$230 | $230-$240 |
| Junior Suite (double beds) | $340-$350 | $390-$400 | $430-$445 | $465-$480 | $530-$540 |
| One-Bedroom Suite | $635-$645 | $695-$705 | $735-$750 | $775-$790 | $845-$855 |

*12.5% tax not included in above rates. Higher rates in price ranges are for weekends and holiday periods (see page 29).*

INFO

**Disney's Coronado Springs Resort**

1000 W. Buena Vista Drive, Lake Buena Vista, FL 32830

Phone: 407-939-1000 Fax: 407-939-1001

For reservations, call Central Reservations: 407-939-6244

*Looking for the Dolphin Resort? See page 99.*

# Disney's Fort Wilderness Resort & Campground

Much more than tents and hookups, Fort Wilderness is a resort in every sense of the word. It is pleasantly situated in a shady forest on Bay Lake, connected by a scenic waterway to the nearby Magic Kingdom theme park (use the blue tab at the top of the page for parks and eateries in the vicinity).

## AMBIENCE

Enveloped by pine, cypress, and oak, this 700-acre campground is a **relaxing haven** after the noise and excitement of a long day at the parks. Rough-hewn log common buildings are nestled among towering pine trees and flowering meadows. Wilderness this is not, however. There are enough daily conveniences and services that the tents may be the only reminder that you are camping.

## RESORT LAYOUT & ROOMS

All types of camping are available—tent, pop-up, trailer, and motor home (RV)—throughout the 788 **campsites**. Located on small loop roads connecting to larger thoroughfares, each site is relatively secluded by trees and shrubs and offers its own paved driveway, Coquina rock bed, charcoal grill, picnic table, and 110V/220V electrical service. Of the three types of campsites, partial hookups supply water, full hookups offer sewer and water, and preferred sites have cable TV, sewer, and water—preferred sites are also closest to the marina and eateries. Each site accommodates up to ten people and one car; pets are welcome at certain sites. All sites are close to very clean, air-conditioned "Comfort Stations" with restrooms, private showers, telephones, ice machines (extra fee), and laundry facilities. For guests without a tent or trailer, the 407 **Wilderness Cabins** are roomy, air-conditioned "log cabins" (504 sq. ft.) that accommodate up to six guests plus a child under 3 in a crib. Each cabin has a living room, bedroom, a full kitchen, and modern bathroom. Charmingly rustic yet comfortable, each cabin comes stocked with pots and utensils, plus a coffeemaker, stove, microwave, refrigerator, dishwasher, cable TV, DVD player, high-speed Internet (fee), phone, hair dryer, and safe. The living room has a pull-down double bed. The bedroom has a separate vanity, TV, a double bed, and bunk beds. Outside is a charcoal grill, picnic table, and deck. Amenities include voice mail and housekeeping—they even do dishes! All guests staying in the cabins must be accommodated within them; no tents are permitted outside the cabin.

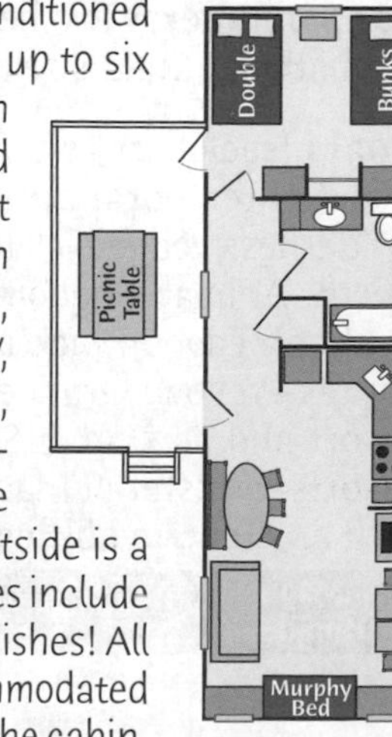

*Cabin Layout*

# Using the Amenities at Disney's Fort Wilderness Resort

## DINING

Many guests cook at their sites or cabins. If cooking isn't your thing, try **The Chuck Wagon**—it's open during the nightly campfire and serves snacks. Typical menu items: a hot dog ($2.35), popcorn ($2.36), and s'mores ($4.93). **Hoop-Dee-Doo Musical Revue** and **Mickey's Backyard BBQ** are dinner shows (see page 236). **Trail's End Restaurant** is a buffeteria (page 228). **Crockett's Tavern** serves drinks and snacks.

© MediaMarx, Inc.

*A Fort Wilderness Cabin*

## PLAYING & RELAXING

**For Athletes**: You'll find two lighted tennis courts, plus volleyball, tetherball, basketball, and horseshoes. Rent a boat at the marina or a canoe or bike at the Bike Barn. Horseback rides ($42) at the livery (must be 9+ years, 48"+). Nature walks, too!
**For Children**: A free petting zoo with pony rides ($3) and a nearby playground delight kids. Free nightly campfires with Chip and Dale and Disney movies, or go on a "hay ride" ($8/adult and $4/kids).
**For Fishers**: Try a bass fishing excursion in Bay Lake for $200–$230.
**For Gamers**: Two video arcades are within the resort.
**For Romantics**: Enjoy a relaxing, private carriage ride for $35.
**For Shoppers**: Gifts, sundries, and groceries at two trading posts.
**For Show-Goers**: Two dinner shows! See page 236 for details.
**For Swimmers**: Two heated pools, a wading pool, and a beach for sunbathers. Child-size life vests are at the pools (no charge).

## GETTING ABOUT

**Boats** (see chart below) go to Magic Kingdom, Wilderness Lodge, and Contemporary. **Buses** to Disney's Hollywood Studios and Wilderness Lodge pick up/drop off at Settlement Depot. Buses for Epcot, Animal Kingdom/Blizzard Beach, and Downtown Disney/Typhoon Lagoon pick up/drop off at Outpost Depot. Three bus routes—Yellow, Orange, and Purple—serve locations within the resort and all stop at Settlement Depot and Outpost Depot. For resorts, transfer at Magic Kingdom or Downtown Disney. You can rent an **electric golf cart** to move about the resort easier.

| Magic Kingdom | Epcot | Disney's Hollywood Studios | Disney's Animal Kingdom | Downtown Disney |
|---|---|---|---|---|
| boat ~15 min. | direct bus ~25 min. | direct bus ~30 min. | direct bus ~30 min. | direct bus ~35 min. |

*Approximate time you will spend in transit from resort to destination during normal operation.*

# Making the Most of Disney's Fort Wilderness Resort

TIPS

**Electric golf carts** are very popular for moving about the resort but are hard to get. To reserve one up to a year in advance, call the Bike Barn at 407-824-2742. Rates are $47+tax per 24-hour period.

The **Electrical Water Pageant**, a light and music barge parade on Bay Lake, can be seen from the beach at around 9:45 pm.

Fort Wilderness offers **many special features** not found at other resorts, including the nightly campfire and movie (see previous page), trail rides, petting zoo, and more. See page 193 for details.

Seasonal, weekly, and monthly **discounts** may exist for campsites.

NOTES

A **car** may come in handy at this resort, and there is 15-minute parking available at the Meadows Trading Post. Disney transportation to and from Fort Wilderness requires a transfer from internal to external transport, making it more time-consuming than most resorts. To reduce transit time, request a site in loops 100–800, as these are within walking distance of Settlement Depot and the marina.

Bring your **groceries**, or buy them at Gooding's at Crossroads near Downtown Disney. You can pick up some items from the trading posts.

**Pets** are allowed for $5/day, but only in loops 300, 700, 800, and 1600–1900 (request at booking). No pets in pop-ups or tents.

Creekside Meadow offers rustic **group camping** with a Comfort Station, grills, and fire pits. Tents and cots can be rented.

**Campfires** are not allowed at individual campsites.

**Check-in time** is 1:00 pm (campsites) or 3:00 pm (cabins). Check-out time for all is 11:00 am.

RATINGS

*Note: The two Affordability Ratings below correspond to lodging and camping.*

*Ratings are explained on page 26.*

| Our Value Ratings: | | Our Magic Ratings: | | Readers' Ratings: |
|---|---|---|---|---|
| Quality: | 7/10 | Theme: | 6/10 | 80% fell in love with it |
| Accessibility: | 4/10 | Amenities: | 5/10 | 7% liked it well enough |
| Affordability: | 6 & 10/10 | Fun Factor: | 8/10 | 10% had mixed feelings |
| **Overall Value:** | **6 & 7/10** | **Overall Magic:** | **6/10** | 3% were disappointed |

| Fort Wilderness is enjoyed by... | (rated by both authors and readers) | |
|---|---|---|
| Younger Kids: ♥♥♥♥♥ | Young Adults: ♥♥♥♥ | Families: ♥♥♥♥♥ |
| Older Kids: ♥♥♥♥ | Mid Adults: ♥♥♥♥ | Couples: ♥♥♥ |
| Teenagers: ♥♥♥♥ | Mature Adults: ♥♥♥♥ | Singles: ♥♥ |

# Finding Your Place at Disney's Fort Wilderness Resort

FORT WILDERNESS RESORT MAP

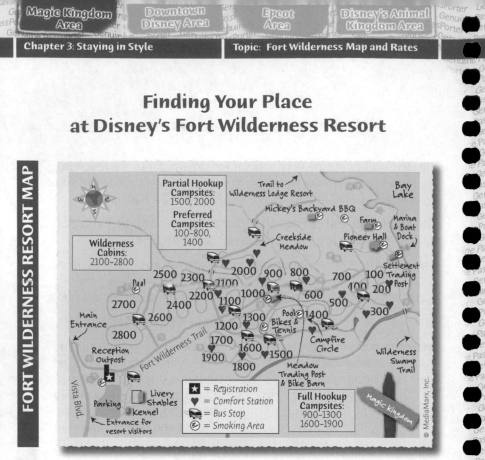

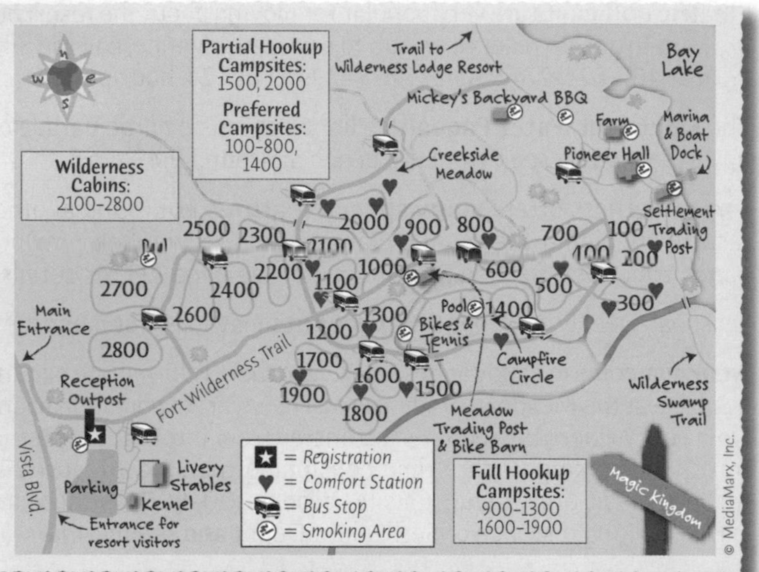


BEST SPOTS

Campsites and cabins are located on loops, which are circular drives with about 40 sites or cabins each. The most popular **cabin** locations are on loops 2500-2700 near the west pool, though we loved our cabin on loop 2100 near a bus stop. The most popular **campsites** are on loops 100 and 200. Preferred sites are **closest to Pioneer Hall** in the 100-800 and 1400 loops. **Full hookup campsites** are in loops 900-1300 and 1600-1900—we highly recommend loop 1300. **Partial hookups** are located in the 1500 and 2000 loops.

RATES

## 2008 Sample Campsite/Cabin Rates

*Seasons are noted on page 14.*

| Room Type | Value | Regular | Peak | Pre-Holiday | Holiday |
|---|---|---|---|---|---|
| Partial Hookup Campsite | $42-$44 | $60-$63 | $70-$72 | $46-$48 | $81-$83 |
| Full Hookup Campsite | $47-$49 | $71-$74 | $82-$85 | $52-$54 | $94-$96 |
| Preferred Campsite | $56-$58 | $77-$80 | $88-$91 | $60-$62 | $99-$101 |
| Wilderness Cabin | $255-$270 | $299-$319 | $340-$360 | – | $380-$395 |

*12.5% tax not included in above rates. There is an additional charge of $5/night for more than two adults in a cabin, or $2/night for more than two adults at a campsite. Higher rates in price ranges are for weekends and holiday periods (see page 29).*

INFO

**Disney's Fort Wilderness Resort & Campground**

4510 N. Fort Wilderness Trail, Lake Buena Vista, FL 32830
Phone: 407-824-2900 Fax: 407-824-3508
For reservations, call Central Reservations: 407-939-6244
For details: http://home.hiwaay.net/~jlspence/faq_fw.htm

# Disney's Grand Floridian Resort & Spa

The most luxurious of Disney's resorts, the Grand Floridian Resort & Spa is a breathtaking Victorian hotel with turrets and gabled roofs. It extends into the Seven Seas Lagoon between the Polynesian and the Magic Kingdom (use the blue tab at the top of the page for parks and eateries in the area).

## AMBIENCE

From the moment you step into the **Grand Lobby**, you will feel as though you've been transported back to the 1890s and the days when the well-to-do wintered in style at grand seaside resorts. As in that unhurried time, the warm whites and soft pastels draw you in, just as the towering lobby and stained glass skylights draw your eyes upward. It is the picture of charm, romance, and luxury.

## RESORT LAYOUT & ROOMS

900 guest rooms are generously spread out among five **lodge** buildings and the Grand Lobby. The luxurious rooms are decorated in four different whimsical-yet-subtle themes: floral, cameo (fairies), swans (Wind in the Willows), and Alice in Wonderland. Rooms are about 400 sq. ft. and are resplendent with marble-topped double sinks and balconies or patios. Most guest rooms offer two queen-size beds and a daybed, accommodating five people. The lodge buildings also house the slightly smaller "dormer" rooms, plus suites. Amenities include signature toiletries, turndown service, mini-bar, large in-room safe, hair dryer, newspaper delivery, valet parking, 24-hour room service, high-speed Internet (fee)—and best of all—comfy robes to relax in after a long day.

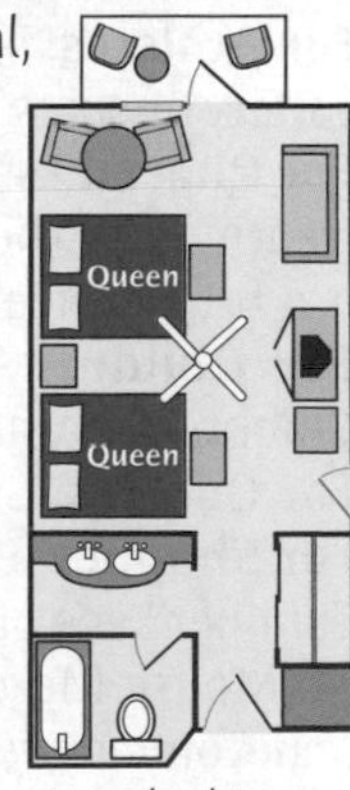

*Standard Room Layout*

## DINING

Culinary delights await you in any of the restaurants and lounges, largely located on the first two floors of the Grand Lobby. Table-service restaurants, which are described on pages 229–230, include: **1900 Park Fare**, a festive character dining experience; **Cítricos**, sophisticated Floridian and Mediterranean cuisine; **Grand Floridian Cafe**, a sun-splashed cafe with traditional fare; **Garden View Lounge**, high tea in the afternoon; **Narcoossee's**, seafood with a view of Seven Seas Lagoon; and **Victoria & Albert's**, Disney's finest restaurant. Quick-service options include the **Grand Floridian Pool Bar** for snacks and **Gasparilla's Grill and Games** for light fare 24 hours a day. Typical menu items at Gasparilla's Grill include an egg croissant ($5.59), a double cheeseburger ($6.89), a whole cheese pizza ($13.99, toppings are $1.50), and chili ($3.50).

# Using the Amenities at Disney's Grand Floridian Resort & Spa

## LOUNGING

Lounges at the Grand Floridian include the **Garden View Lounge**, which offers drinks in the evening. **Mizner's** serves cocktails and light snacks within earshot of the musicians who often perform in the Grand Lobby. The **Grand Floridian Pool Bar** also serves drinks and snacks, such as a cheeseburger with fries ($11.95) or a Cobb salad ($12.95). Visit **Gasparilla's Grill and Games** to buy refillable mugs (about $12) and get refills.

*Jennifer and Dave enjoy a Turret Suite*

## PLAYING & RELAXING

**For Athletes**: Two clay tennis courts are available for a fee. Rent a variety of boats at the marina. You'll also find walking/jogging paths.
**For Charmers**: The Ivy Trellis Salon pampers you with hair and nail treatments. The Grand Floridian Spa & Health Club (see page 193) is a full-service spa facility. Call 407-824-2332 for information.
**For Children**: A playground is adjacent to the Mouseketeer Clubhouse, a supervised program for kids 4–12 (see page 255).
**For Gamers**: Gasparilla's Grill and Games has a video arcade.
**For Shoppers**: On the first floor, Sandy Cove stocks sundries and Summer Lace offers upscale women's clothing. On the second floor, M. Mouse Mercantile has gifts; Bally offers luxury leather goods; and Commander Porter's has men's and women's apparel.
**For Swimmers**: A moderately-sized leisure pool and hot tub are available, as is a themed, zero-entry pool near the beach with a slide and play fountain. Sunbathers enjoy the beach (no swimming).

## GETTING ABOUT

A **monorail** goes to Magic Kingdom as well as the Contemporary, the Polynesian, and the Transportation and Ticket Center (TTC), where you can transfer to the Epcot monorail. **Boats** also take you to the Magic Kingdom and the Polynesian. For other parks (see chart below for in-transit times), use the **direct buses** in front of the resort. For other resorts, monorail to the Magic Kingdom (daytime) or bus to Downtown Disney (evening) and transfer to a resort bus.

| Magic Kingdom | Epcot | Disney's Hollywood Studios | Disney's Animal Kingdom | Downtown Disney |
|---|---|---|---|---|
| monorail/boat ~3/~10 min. | monorail x 2 ~12+10 min. | direct bus ~10 min. | direct bus ~15 min. | direct bus ~20 min. |

*Approximate time you will spend in transit from resort to destination during normal operation.*

# Making the Most of Disney's Grand Floridian Resort & Spa

TIPS

The Grand Lobby is often filled with the sound of **live music**, ranging from solo pianists to full dance bands.

Many **children's activities** are offered, including scavenger hunts, arts and crafts, and story time (complimentary). Additional-fee activities like fishing trips, the Wonderland Tea Party, the Pirate Cruise, and a cooking class (see page 246) are also available.

**Private dining** is available for a quiet or romantic evening. You can have a meal on your balcony, on the beach, or even on a boat in the lagoon. Make arrangements in advance with room service.

For a touch of magic, end your day with a romantic, nighttime **stroll along the beach**. You may even catch the Electrical Water Pageant on the Seven Seas Lagoon around 9:15 pm.

NOTES

Four extra-special types of rooms are available. The **lodge tower** rooms have a separate sitting area, an extra TV and phone, and five windows. **Concierge** rooms offer personalized services, continental breakfast, evening refreshments, and a private elevator. Of the concierge rooms, special **turret rooms** (see our honeymoon photo on previous page) have wet bars and windows all around, while **honeymoon suites** pamper with whirlpool tubs!

The Grand Floridian Resort & Spa is also a **conference center**.

Even though this is a luxury resort, don't feel you need to dress up. **Casual wear** is the norm here. The only exception is Victoria & Albert's restaurant, which requires evening attire.

**Check-in time** is 3:00 pm. Check-out time is 11:00 am.

RATINGS

*Ratings are explained on page 26.*

| Our Value Ratings: | | Our Magic Ratings: | | Readers' Ratings: |
|---|---|---|---|---|
| Quality: | 10/10 | Theme: | 8/10 | 80% fell in love with it |
| Accessibility: | 8/10 | Amenities: | 9/10 | 4% liked it well enough |
| Affordability: | 2/10 | Fun Factor: | 6/10 | 11% had mixed feelings |
| **Overall Value:** | **7/10** | **Overall Magic:** | **8/10** | 5% were disappointed |

| Grand Floridian is enjoyed by... | (rated by both authors and readers) | |
|---|---|---|
| Younger Kids: ♥♥♥♥ | Young Adults: ♥♥♥♥ | Families: ♥♥♥ |
| Older Kids: ♥♥♥♥ | Mid Adults: ♥♥♥♥♥ | Couples: ♥♥♥♥♥ |
| Teenagers: ♥♥♥ | Mature Adults: ♥♥♥♥♥ | Singles: ♥♥♥ |

# Finding Your Place at Disney's Grand Floridian Resort & Spa

GRAND FLORIDIAN RESORT MAP

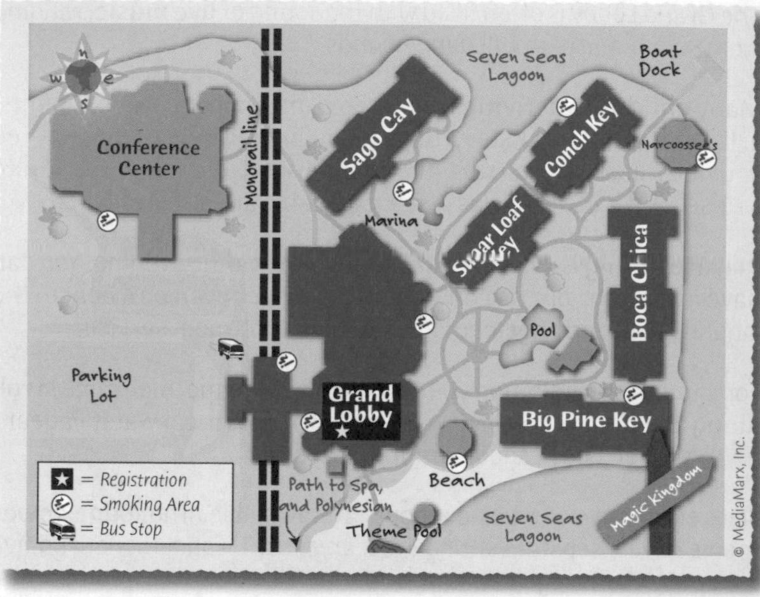

Conference Center
Monorail line
Sago Cay
Seven Seas Lagoon
Boat Dock
Conch Key
Narcoossee's
Marina
Sugar Loaf Key
Boca Chica
Pool
Parking Lot
Grand Lobby
Big Pine Key
★ = Registration
= Smoking Area
= Bus Stop
Path to Spa and Polynesian
Beach
Theme Pool
Seven Seas Lagoon
Magic Kingdom
© MediaMarx, Inc.

BEST SPOTS

The **dormer rooms** on the top floors of the lodge buildings may be a bit smaller (they only fit 4 rather than 5), but they feature vaulted ceilings, a secluded balcony, and a charming window above the French doors. The **best views of Cinderella Castle** come in the theme park-view rooms in Sago Cay and Conch Key lodges. Sugar Loaf Key is the closest lodge house to the Grand Lobby, but also sees the most traffic and hears the most noise. Big Pine Key is near the beach, and its lagoon-view rooms offer picturesque views.

RATES

## 2008 Sample Room Rates

*Seasons are noted on page 14.*

| Room Type | Value | Regular | Peak | Holiday |
|---|---|---|---|---|
| Garden View | $385-$405 | $435-$455 | $510-$540 | $605-$625 |
| Lagoon View | $445-$465 | $515-$535 | $605-$635 | $705-$725 |
| Lodge Tower | $470-$490 | $535-$555 | $635-$655 | $710-$730 |
| Lodge Concierge (Sugar Loaf Key) | $505-$525 | $580-$600 | $685-$715 | $775-$795 |
| Main Building Concierge | $665-$685 | $745-$765 | $860-$890 | $950-$970 |

*12.5% tax is not included in above room rates. Honeymoon concierge rooms start in the high $600s. Suites, which are available in one- and two-bedrooms, are upwards of $1,000. Higher rates in price ranges are for weekends and holiday periods (see page 29).*

INFO

## Disney's Grand Floridian Resort & Spa

4401 Floridian Way, Lake Buena Vista, FL 32830
Phone: 407-824-3000 Fax: 407-824-3186
For reservations, call Central Reservations: 407-939-6244

# Disney's Old Key West Resort

Old Key West Resort caters primarily (but not exclusively) to Disney Vacation Club members. Old Key West is located roughly between Downtown Disney and Epcot (use the blue tab at the top of the page for parks and eateries in the area).

AMBIENCE

If Disney's Grand Floridian and BoardWalk set the pace for elegant turn-of-the-century seaside resorts, this is the dressed-down, laid-back antidote. Lush vegetation and low, white **clapboard buildings** with sky-blue eaves evoke authentic Key West style, and the public areas of the resort exude small-town intimacy. Quaint waterside shops and restaurants are connected by wooden walkways, and the Conch Flats Community Hall offers homey choices like table tennis and board games. The atmosphere is lively, friendly, and not at all hectic. Accommodations are spacious, comfy, and attractive.

RESORT LAYOUT & ROOMS

Intimate is not necessarily small. Old Key West is big enough to get lost in. (We speak from experience!) The resort's 761 guest "homes" range from **studios** (390 sq. ft.) with kitchenettes that sleep four adults, to spacious **one-bedrooms** (942 sq. ft.) with full kitchens that sleep four adults, **two-bedrooms** (1,395 sq. ft.) also with full kitchens that sleep eight adults, and the incredible three-bedroom/four-bath **Grand Villas** (2,375 sq. ft.) that sleep up to 12. All have a private patio or balcony perfect for breakfast, and all but the studios include a master suite with a large two-person whirlpool tub; a sprawling great room with full kitchen, dining area, and queen-size sleeper sofa; and washer and dryer. Villas sport views of the golf course, waterways, or woods. Amenities in all rooms include a TV, refrigerator, microwave, coffeemaker, high-speed Internet (fee), and voice mail. One-bedroom and larger villas boast a fully equipped kitchen, big-screen TV, DVD player, and in-room safe. These "homes" are excellent for groups and families who wish to stay together.

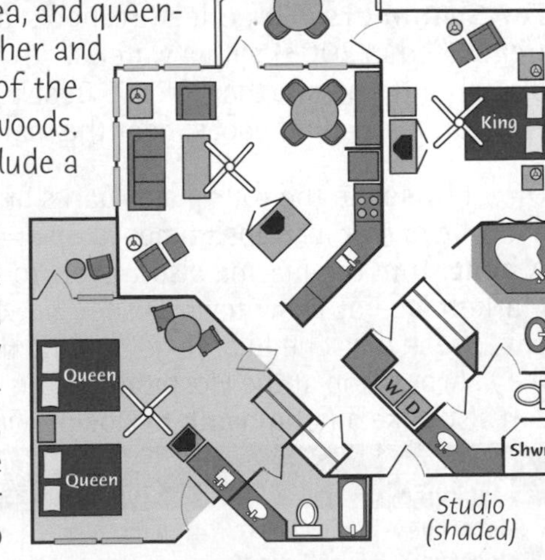

Entire layout represents a Two-Bedroom Home

# Using the Amenities at Disney's Old Key West Resort

## DINING & LOUNGING

**Olivia's Cafe** (see page 230) is a kind of casual, small-town place loved by locals. **Good's Food to Go** over by the main pool serves up breakfasts, burgers, and snacks—typical menu items include a tuna sandwich ($6.69) and a child's sandpail meal ($5.49). Refillable mugs are available for $12. Also by the main pool, the **Gurgling Suitcase** has drinks and appetizers like shrimp fritters ($5.99) and crab cake ($7.59). **Turtle Shack** by the Turtle Pond Road pool offers snacks seasonally. **Pizza delivery** is also available.

© MediaMarx, Inc.

*Father, son, and grandma enjoy a one-bedroom villa at Old Key West*

## PLAYING & RELAXING

**For Athletes**: Tennis, basketball, shuffleboard, and volleyball courts are available. Rent boats and bikes at Hank's Rent 'N Return. Golf at the nearby course, or try the walking/jogging path. A health club has Nautilus equipment, plus a sauna and massages.
**For Children**: The Conch Flats Community Hall offers games and organized events for kids. Playgrounds are near some of the pools.
**For Gamers**: The two arcades—Electric Eel Arcade and The Flying Fisherman—have plenty of video games to keep the kids happy.
**For Shoppers**: The Conch Flats General Store offers general and Disney merchandise, plus groceries and sundries.
**For Swimmers**: Three leisure pools and a large themed pool (renovated in 2005) with a water slide, hot tub, sauna, and sandy play area round out the "R.E.S.T. Beach Recreation Department." A children's wading pool is near the main pool.

## GETTING ABOUT

Direct **buses** to the four major parks and Downtown Disney (see chart below for in-transit times) stop at the resort's five bus stops. A **boat** from the marina also travels to Saratoga Springs and the Marketplace at Downtown Disney between 11:00 am and 11:00 pm—check the schedule. To get around the resort, hop on a bus, as they always stop at the Hospitality House before heading out. You can also take a (long) **walk** to Downtown Disney via a footpath.

| Magic Kingdom | Epcot | Disney's Hollywood Studios | Disney's Animal Kingdom | Downtown Disney |
|---|---|---|---|---|
| direct bus ~25 min. | direct bus ~10 min. | direct bus ~10 min. | direct bus ~15 min. | bus/boat ~5/~15 min. |

*Approximate time you will spend in transit from resort to destination during normal operation.*

# Making the Most of Disney's Old Key West Resort

TIPS

Some one-bedroom homes have a slight variation that can make a big difference if your party is large: There is a **second door to the bathroom** through the laundry room (see layout on page 67) that avoids the master bedroom. If this is important, request buildings 30 or higher at reservation and again at check-in.

**Buildings 62–64** are the newest—they opened in early 2000. These are also the only buildings that have elevators.

The **three-bedroom Grand Villas** are luxurious (and expensive). They are two-storied with private baths for each bedroom plus an extra one for guests sleeping on the sleeper sofa. They have all the amenities of the other vacation homes, plus a 32" television and a stereo. They are phenomenally popular with families, though, so reserve as early as possible.

**Hank's Rent 'N Return** offers more than just bikes and boats. You can rent videos, board games, balls, and more. There are often daily activities and games—inquire when checking in.

NOTES

If you stay in a studio, you won't have a washer and dryer in your room, but there are air-conditioned **laundry rooms** available near the pools at no extra charge. You can buy soap and bleach, too.

Studios have **no in-room safes**, but there are safe deposit boxes at the front desk. Note that ice is available from ice machines at the bus stops.

**Check-in time** is 4:00 pm. Check-out time is 11:00 am.

RATINGS

*Ratings are explained on page 26.*

| Our Value Ratings: | | Our Magic Ratings: | | Readers' Ratings: |
|---|---|---|---|---|
| Quality: | 7/10 | Theme: | 7/10 | 85% fell in love with it |
| Accessibility: | 5/10 | Amenities: | 6/10 | 15% liked it well enough |
| Affordability: | 4/10 | Fun Factor: | 5/10 | 0% had mixed feelings |
| **Overall Value:** | **5/10** | **Overall Magic:** | **6/10** | 0% were disappointed |

| Old Key West is enjoyed by... | | (rated by both authors and readers) |
|---|---|---|
| Younger Kids: ♥♥♥ | Young Adults: ♥♥♥♥ | Families: ♥♥♥♥♥ |
| Older Kids: ♥♥♥♥ | Mid Adults: ♥♥♥♥♥ | Couples: ♥♥♥♥♥ |
| Teenagers: ♥♥♥♥ | Mature Adults: ♥♥♥♥♥ | Singles: ♥♥♥ |

# Finding Your Place at Disney's Old Key West Resort

## OLD KEY WEST RESORT MAP

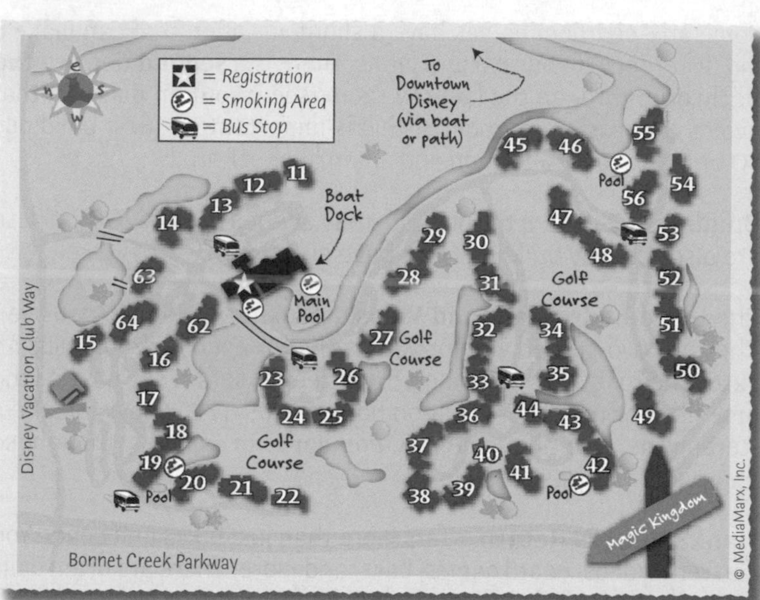


## BEST LOCATIONS

Location is important in this sprawling resort. Though there are bus stops throughout the resort, we found staying near the **Hospitality House** to be a huge benefit. Buildings 11–14 and 62–64 are the closest (we loved our one-bedroom home in building 11), with buildings 15–16 and 23–26 also within reasonable walking distance. Most locations enjoy relative **peace and quiet**, but if you really want seclusion, 47–48 and 52–54 are nice as they are away from pools and roads, yet are near a bus stop. We suggest you avoid 30–44 as they feel remote, have traffic noise, and bus stops are often inconvenient.

## RATES

### 2008 Sample Villa Rates

*Seasons are noted on page 14.*

| Room Type | Value | Regular | Peak | Holiday |
|---|---|---|---|---|
| Studio Villa | $285 | $315 | $370 | $410 |
| One-Bedroom Villa | $380 | $430 | $500 | $575 |
| Two-Bedroom Villa | $530 | $630 | $765 | $875 |
| Grand Villa | $1,170 | $1,305 | $1,475 | $1,645 |

*12.5% tax is not included in the above rates. Three views are available—water, golf course, and woods—but with no difference in price.*

## INFO

**Disney's Old Key West Resort**

1510 North Cove Road, Lake Buena Vista, FL 32830

Phone: 407-827-7700 Fax: 407-827-7710

For reservations, call Central Reservations: 407-939-6244

# Disney's Polynesian Resort

The Polynesian Resort is a lush, tropical paradise that brings the romance of the South Pacific to life. It rests tranquilly on the Seven Seas Lagoon between the Transportation and Ticket Center and the Grand Floridian Resort (use the blue tab at the top of the page for parks and eateries in the area).

AMBIENCE

The blooming gardens are your first hint of the beauty and color of the **tropics**, which are captured so splendidly here. You may not even notice that you've entered the main building, the Great Ceremonial House, with its atrium filled with falling waters and flowering tropical plants. "Aloha!" is more than a word here—it is a way of life—and you will be reminded of this again and again during your visit.

RESORT LAYOUT & ROOMS

853 guest rooms are arranged throughout **longhouses** on 11 "islands" of Polynesia. The longhouses are two or three stories; the first-floor rooms have patios, and many of the upper-floor rooms have balconies. The lush, laid-back feeling of the resort is carried into the recently renovated rooms with tropical blues and greens, dark, hand-carved wood furniture, and flat-screen TVs. Spacious rooms (409–448 sq. ft.) offer two queen beds and a daybed, accommodating five people. The roomy bathroom has a large mirror and toilet behind a partition. Suites and concierge-level rooms housed in the Tonga and Hawaii longhouses offer personal service and great views. Amenities for all rooms include toiletries, 24-hour room service, coffeemakers, refrigerators, housekeeping, turndown service (on request), and voice mail.

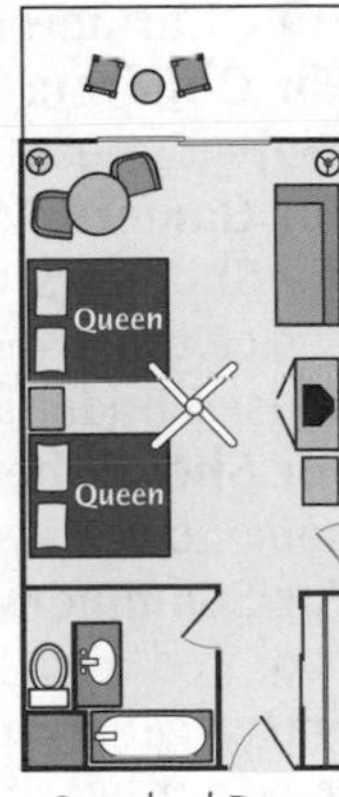

*Standard Room Layout*

DINING & LOUNGING

Paradise offers bounty in food, too. Two table-service restaurants (see page 230) are **Kona Cafe**, offering a filling breakfast and inventive lunch and dinner, and '**Ohana**, serving up food and fun with skewered meats. **Captain Cook's Snack Company** is a good place for a quick breakfast and light meals. Typical items are Mickey waffles ($5.69), Aloha pork sandwich ($6.99), and kids' chicken strips ($4.29). Refillable mugs are available for $12. A family-style **character breakfast** is served at 'Ohana, too. And let's not forget the Spirit of Aloha dinner show (page 237). **Tambu**, the lounge by 'Ohana, serves snacks and drinks, **Kona Island** is a coffee bar in the mornings, and the poolside **Barefoot Bar** has drinks.

# Using the Amenities at Disney's Polynesian Resort

PLAYING & RELAXING

*Jennifer enjoys a spacious standard room at the Polynesian*

**For Athletes**: Boaters rent Sea Raycers and sailboats at the marina. Joggers enjoy the Walk Around the World that partially encircles the Seven Seas Lagoon, and a 1.5-mile path winds through the resort.
**For Charmers**: The Grand Floridian Spa is nearby (see page 64).
**For Children**: The Never Land Club is a childcare club (see page 255)—it's next to the arcade. A playground is near the main pool.
**For Gamers**: Moana Mickey's Arcade offers many video games.
**For Shoppers**: On the first floor, BouTiki has Polynesian-themed gifts and clothing and Wyland Galleries has collectibles. The second floor houses Trader Jack's (souvenirs and sundries) and Samoa Snacks.
**For Show-Goers**: Tucked in the back of the resort is Luau Cove, home to Polynesian-style dinner shows. More details on page 237.
**For Swimmers**: The Nanea Volcano themed pool features a large pool "fed" by a spring, a water slide, warm water areas, and a zero-entry section (pool wheelchair available). There's also a kids' play fountain, beach for sunbathing, and leisure pool, but no spa (hot tub).

GETTING ABOUT

A **monorail** shuttles you to the Magic Kingdom (see chart below for in-transit times), the Grand Floridian, and the Contemporary, as well as the Transportation and Ticket Center (TTC). A **boat** also goes to the Magic Kingdom. To reach Epcot, walk to TTC and board the monorail. To reach other parks and Downtown Disney, take **direct buses** (see map on page 74 for the bus stop). To reach most resorts, take a monorail to the Magic Kingdom and transfer to a resort bus (daytime), or bus to Downtown Disney and transfer to a resort bus (evening).

| Magic Kingdom | Epcot | Disney's Hollywood Studios | Disney's Animal Kingdom | Downtown Disney |
|---|---|---|---|---|
| monorail/boat ~10/~5 min. | walk + monorail ~10+10 min. | direct bus ~15 min. | direct bus ~15 min. | direct bus ~25 min. |

*Approximate time you will spend in transit from resort to destination during normal operation.*

# Making the Most of Disney's Polynesian Resort

TIPS

On the beach in front of the Hawaii and Tahiti longhouses are several **bench swings** and **hammocks**. Not only are these heaven after a long day, they make ideal spots to watch the fireworks.

A **night stroll** here is sublime. A very secluded spot over the rise on the beach's point (Sunset Point) is pure magic—it's where we (your authors) were married in 2004—see pages 256–257 for photos.

The **Electrical Water Pageant** passes right by the Polynesian around 9:00 pm. If you don't have a water-view room, take a stroll down to the beach or to the end of the dock near the marina.

The resort's guest rooms recently got a **facelift** with new designer bedding in tropical colors, new furniture (including a desk that can be extended out), and large flat-screen TVs (see photo on previous page). The public areas also received a fresh, new treatment.

NOTES

Families love the Polynesian and it may get a bit **noisy** in the pool areas (near Samoa, Niue, Hawaii, Rarotonga, and Tokelau).

Walk to the Transportation and Ticket Center for the **Epcot monorail**. The monorail around the lagoon adds 20 minutes otherwise.

The Polynesian Resort shares **bus routes** with the Contemporary and Grand Floridian resorts, picking up/dropping off guests at the Contemporary first and Grand Floridian last.

**Daily activities** are available for kids of all ages, such as coconut races, torch lightings, and hula lessons. Inquire at Lobby Concierge.

**Check-in time** is 3:00 pm. Check-out time is 11:00 am.

RATINGS

*Ratings are explained on page 26.*

| Our Value Ratings: | | Our Magic Ratings: | | Readers' Ratings: |
|---|---|---|---|---|
| Quality: | 8/10 | Theme: | 9/10 | 62% fell in love with it |
| Accessibility: | 9/10 | Amenities: | 7/10 | 29% liked it well enough |
| Affordability: | 3/10 | Fun Factor: | 8/10 | 7% had mixed feelings |
| **Overall Value:** | **7/10** | **Overall Magic:** | **8/10** | 2% were disappointed |

| The Polynesian is enjoyed by... | (rated by both authors and readers) | |
|---|---|---|
| Younger Kids: ♥♥♥♥ | Young Adults: ♥♥♥♥♥ | Families: ♥♥♥♥♥ |
| Older Kids: ♥♥♥♥♥ | Mid Adults: ♥♥♥♥♥ | Couples: ♥♥♥♥♥ |
| Teenagers: ♥♥♥♥ | Mature Adults: ♥♥♥♥♥ | Singles: ♥♥♥ |

# Finding Your Place at Disney's Polynesian Resort

## POLYNESIAN RESORT MAP

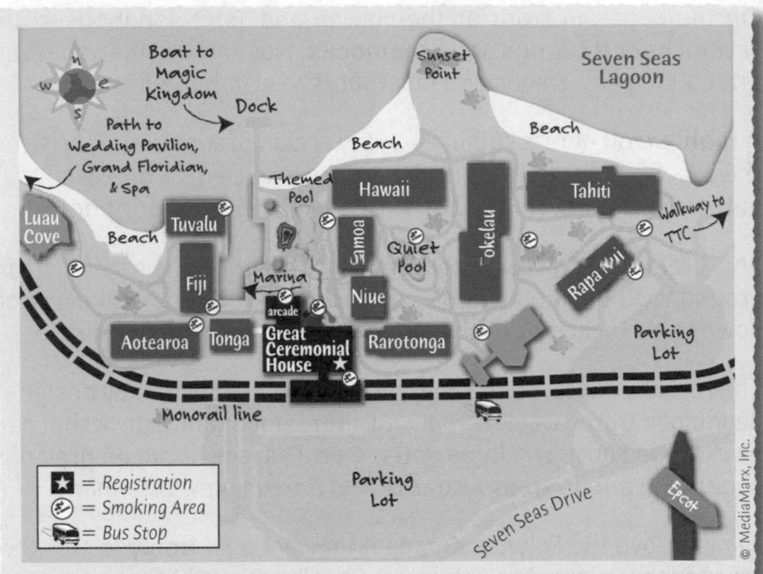


## BEST LOCATIONS

All **first-floor rooms** have patios, and all **third-floor rooms** have balconies. Most **second-floor rooms** have no balconies, with the exception of Tahiti, Rapa Nui, Tokelau, and Tonga, which do. Particularly nice water views can be found in Tuvalu, Hawaii, Tahiti, and Fiji. The first-floor rooms in Tahiti facing away from the water have pleasant, secluded patios, as do those in Rapa Nui and Rarotonga. If you opt for a garden view, we recommend Aotearoa with beautiful landscaping and an up-close view of the monorail. For added **privacy**, request a room on the top floor.

## RATES

**2008 Sample Room Rates** *Seasons are noted on page 14.*

| Room Type | Value | Regular | Peak | Holiday |
|---|---|---|---|---|
| Garden View | $340-$360 | $399-$419 | $465-$485 | $535-$555 |
| Lagoon View | $440-$460 | $500-$520 | $585-$615 | $650-$670 |
| Garden View Concierge (Club) | $480-$500 | $545-$565 | $640-$670 | $720-$740 |
| Lagoon View/Suite Concierge | $590-$610 | $670-$690 | $765-$795 | $840-$860 |
| One-Bedroom Suite Concierge | $780-$800 | $890-$910 | $1,105-$1,045 | $1,135-$1,155 |

*12.5% tax is not included in the above. One-bedroom suites start in the low $700s. Higher rates in price ranges are for weekends and holiday periods (see page 29).*

## INFO

**Disney's Polynesian Resort**
1600 Seven Seas Drive, Lake Buena Vista, FL 32830
Phone: 407-824-2000 Fax: 407-824-3174
For reservations, call Central Reservations: 407-939-6244

# Disney's Pop Century Resort

Auld acquaintance shall be remembered at Pop Century, the Walt Disney World Resort's newest value-priced resort. By the time the final phase of construction is done (no date is projected at press time), each of the 20th century's decades will be immortalized for its contribution to popular culture. Pop Century Resort is located in the Epcot area (use the blue tab at the top of the page for parks and eateries in the vicinity) on the northeast corner of Osceola Parkway and Victory Way.

AMBIENCE

Whether you're 8 or 80, a **blast from your past** awaits at Pop Century. In what will actually be twin-sister resorts when complete, Pop Century Classic Years and Pop Century Legendary Years surround a 33-acre lake and are connected by a scenic bridge (called the "Generation Gap"). Go from the quaint days of Main Street U.S.A. "to infinity and beyond" in eye-popping style with a uniquely themed check-in lobby, food court/shop/lounge, and pool bar. Outside, giant cultural icons fill the senses, including a monumental Rubik's Cube®, a billboard-sized laptop computer, and the biggest Big Wheel® ever parked in a front yard. The themes continue with six imaginative themed pools. Each guest lodge building is festooned with cultural icons and "groovy" catch phrases.

RESORT LAYOUT & ROOMS

The 2,880 guest rooms that are open in Pop Century Classic Years are situated in five differently themed areas encompassing a total of 10 guest lodges. **Pop Century Classic Years** celebrates the decades of the 1950s, '60s, '70s, '80s, and '90s. Opening at some undetermined date, **Pop Century Legendary Years** will take us back to the 1900s, '10s, '20s, '30s, and '40s. Themed courtyards are formed between two or more of the ten T-shaped guest lodges. Each decade's theme is reflected in the guest room decor, but rich, wood-grain furniture adds elegance to the fun. Rooms have either two double beds or one king bed, a large TV with remote, a small table with two chairs, and a roomy chest of drawers. Rooms hold up to four guests plus one child under three in a crib (a folding crib is available on request). Rooms are small—about 260 sq. ft.—but as with the All-Star Resorts, furnishings allow adequate floor space. Rooms have no private balconies or patios, but each offers climate controls. Amenities include soap, housekeeping, large in-room safe, table-side modem jack, iron and ironing board, and voice mail. Inquire at check-in about renting a small refrigerator for $10/night.

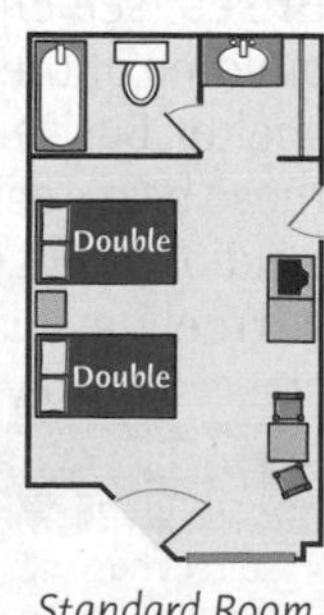

*Standard Room Layout*

# Using the Amenities at Disney's Pop Century Resort

## EATING & DRINKING

Reflections of the '80s

Pop Century Classic Years has a large **food court** with a variety of food stations, plus a lounge. The eatery is open daily for breakfast, lunch, and dinner. Typical menu items include a breakfast platter ($5.99), a double cheeseburger ($6.89), and vegetable lo mein ($6.59). Purchase a mug for $12 and get unlimited refills from the beverage bar (which includes frozen Cokes). A pizza delivery service is available in the afternoons and evenings, along with seasonal snack carts.

## PLAYING & RELAXING

**For Athletes**: The 12' wide lakeside path is ideal for walks and jogs. The lake does not offer a marina, but we hear that surrey bikes may be available for jaunts around the lake when the resort is done.
**For Children**: A quiet playground and play fountain is located within the resort (see map on page 78 for locations).
**For Gamers**: An arcade is located in the resort's main building.
**For Shoppers**: The resort offers a large shop with Disney logo merchandise, clothing, sundries, and some snack foods.
**For Swimmers**: Cool off in the main pool with a wading pool, and two smaller themed pools. Classic Years' pools are shaped like a bowling pin, a flower, and a computer; Legendary Years' pools (not yet open) will resemble a crossword puzzle, soda bottle, and highway sign. There are no spas (hot tubs) at this resort.

## GETTING ABOUT

**Buses** (see chart below for in-transit times) are outside the main building of the resort. Stops are well-marked and offer benches and shelter. Bus service is prompt and efficient. Destinations other than those below can be reached by changing buses at Disney's Hollywood Studios or Epcot (daytime) or Downtown Disney (evening). Parking is freely available, though you should study the map to find the closest lot to your room.

| Magic Kingdom | Epcot | Disney's Hollywood Studios | Disney's Animal Kingdom | Downtown Disney |
|---|---|---|---|---|
| direct bus ~25 min. | direct bus ~20 min. | direct bus ~15 min. | direct bus ~15 min. | direct bus ~20 min. |

*Approximate time you will spend in transit from resort to destination during normal operation.*

# Making the Most of Disney's Pop Century Resort

TIPS

The **33-acre lake** between these resorts is an added perk for a value resort—the equivalent All-Star Resorts have no ponds, lakes, or rivers. The lakeside promenade and Generation Gap bridge are a total delight. Frequent park benches line the path, and "roadside" signs note landmark cultural events of each era. Note, however, that you cannot yet walk all the way around the lake.

Epcot's **IllumiNations** fireworks are visible across the lake. Best views are from the '50s B and C buildings—try the fourth floor!

Food court patrons are treated to a **dance routine** performed by the resort's cast members at breakfast and dinner! They do the Twist at 8:00 am and the Hustle at 6:00 pm. Be there or be square!

While Mom or Dad checks in, the kids can enjoy a **big-screen video** theater. Be sure to take in the memorabilia exhibits, too.

A **children's pop-jet fountain** is tucked away in a corner between the '60s and '70s—look for a statue of Goofy and a red Corvette.

Plan to either **carry your own luggage** or wait a while (perhaps 45–60 minutes) for the resort's luggage service to drop it off at your building. Arrangements to pick up luggage on your departure day should be made the night before.

NOTES

**Coin-operated laundries** are located near each pool. Bring lots of quarters—wash loads and dry cycles are $2.00 each.

We've heard that the Legendary Years section may open its guest rooms as "**family suites**" similar to All-Star Music (see page 37).

**Check-in time** is 4:00 pm. Check-out time is 11:00 am.

RATINGS

*Ratings are explained on page 26.*

| Our Value Ratings: | | Our Magic Ratings: | | Readers' Ratings: |
|---|---|---|---|---|
| Quality: | 6/10 | Theme: | 6/10 | 63% fell in love with it |
| Accessibility: | 5/10 | Amenities: | 4/10 | 18% liked it well enough |
| Affordability: | 9/10 | Fun Factor: | 4/10 | 11% had mixed feelings |
| **Overall Value:** | **7/10** | **Overall Magic:** | **5/10** | 8% were disappointed |

| Pop Century is enjoyed by... | | (rated by both authors and readers) |
|---|---|---|
| Younger Kids: ♥♥♥♥♥ | Young Adults: ♥♥♥♥ | Families: ♥♥♥♥ |
| Older Kids: ♥♥♥♥♥ | Mid Adults: ♥♥♥ | Couples: ♥♥ |
| Teenagers: ♥♥♥ | Mature Adults: ♥♥ | Singles: ♥♥♥ |

# Finding Your Place at Disney's Pop Century Resort

## POP CENTURY RESORT MAP

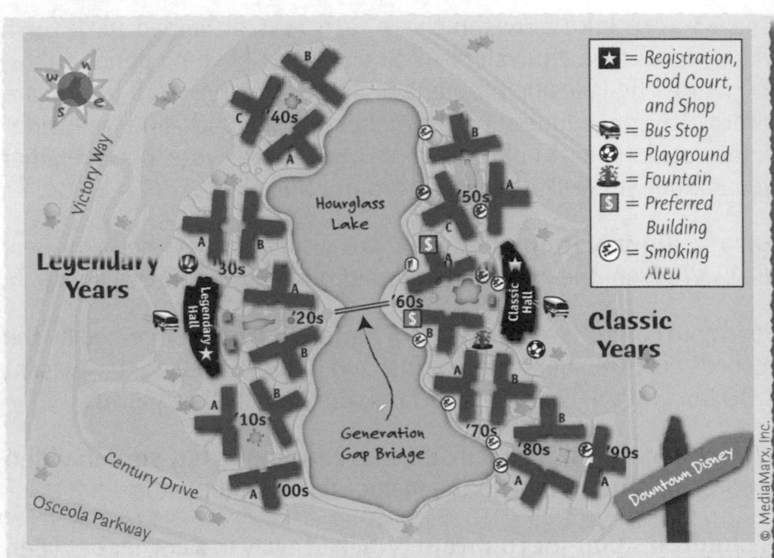

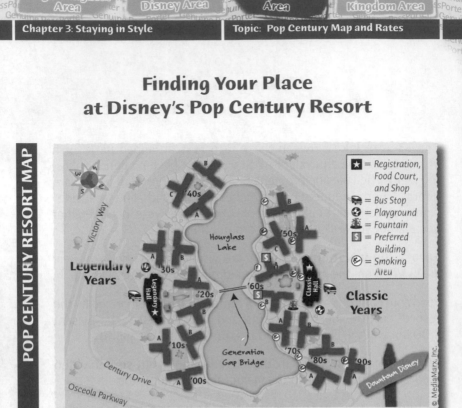

## BEST LOCATIONS

Rooms at Pop Century **vary only by location** within the resorts and floor level. For convenience, we recommend the '50s, '60s, or '70s (Classic Years)—they are closest to pools, food, and transportation. Our personal pick is the '70s (at Classic Years) as it is relatively quiet and has good views from most windows. Note that several buildings offer excellent views of Hourglass Lake, notably '50s B & C, '60s, and '70s A. If you seek quiet, request a room on the third or fourth floors. While the Legendary Years buildings are not yet open, when they are, we recommend the '10s, '20s, and '30s.

## RATES

### 2008 Sample Room Rates

*Seasons are noted on page 14.*

| Room Type | Value | Regular | Summer | Peak | Holiday |
|---|---|---|---|---|---|
| Standard Room | $82 | $99–$109 | $109–$124 | $119–$134 | $129–$139 |
| Preferred Room | $94 | $111–$121 | $121–$136 | $131–$146 | $141–$151 |

*12.5% tax is not included in above rates. Preferred rooms are in the guest lodges closest to the main buildings (the '60s at Classic Years). There is a $10 per person charge for the third and fourth adult in a room, but no extra charge for children under 18. Rooms may face parking lots, pools, the lake, or courtyards. Higher rates in price ranges are for weekends and holiday periods (see page 29).*

## INFO

### Disney's Pop Century Resort

1050 Century Drive, Lake Buena Vista, FL 32830

Phone: 407-938-4000 Fax: 407-938-4040

For reservations, call Central Reservations: 407-939-6244

# Disney's Port Orleans Resort

In 2001, sister resorts Port Orleans and Dixie Landings merged into one resort known as Port Orleans. The large, moderately priced resort is located along the banks of the Sassagoula River, north of Downtown Disney (use the blue tab at the top of the page for other places in the same vicinity). Port Orleans is popular with young couples, families, and children, both for its value and for its fun atmosphere.

AMBIENCE

The romance of the Old South awaits you at Port Orleans. The resort is divided into two separate districts: the French Quarter (the smaller district and the original Port Orleans) and Riverside (the former Dixie Landings). The **French Quarter** recaptures the feeling and flavors of historic New Orleans as it prepares for Mardi Gras. The Mint is your first stop in the French Quarter, a large building with wrought ironwork details and a soaring glass atrium that safeguards the district's front desk, Lobby Concierge, and shop. A step outside reveals narrow cobblestone lanes, complete with "gas" lamps, wrought iron benches, and grand magnolia trees. A leisurely 10-minute walk along the Sassagoula River takes you over to **Riverside**. Banjo music and southern hospitality greet you as you enter Riverside's Sassagoula Steamboat Company, a replica of an old riverboat depot. The depot is the crossroads of this quaint settlement, housing the district's front desk and services. Venture out along meandering paths and wooden bridges to antebellum mansions in one direction or the quaint bayou dwellings in the other.

RESORT LAYOUT

The resort's 3,056 guest rooms are scattered among the two districts, with 1,008 in the French Quarter and 2,048 in Riverside. Rooms in the French Quarter are housed in seven large buildings (see map on page 83), each designed to resemble **rows of townhouses** with differing architectural styles, varying rooflines, and facades bricked or painted in shades of blue, cream, or peach. Most buildings have their own yards and gardens in front, which are charmingly fenced with wrought iron. Down the Sassagoula in Riverside you'll find 1,024 rooms gracing "Gone With the Wind," plantation-style mansions in an area called **Magnolia Bend**. These three-storied, elegant buildings are situated majestically along the Sassagoula River. An equal number of rooms are housed within crackerbox-style dwellings in the **Alligator Bayou** section. These two-storied, rough-hewn dwellings peek through the trees, with quaint paths winding through the "bayous" interspersed among them. Alligator Bayou has a more intimate feel to it than its neighbor, Magnolia Bend.

# Lodging and Dining at Disney's Port Orleans Resort

## RESORT ROOMS

Rooms are 314 sq. ft. in size and **decorated in three styles**. In the French Quarter, you find faux French Provincial furniture, gilt-framed mirrors, and Venetian blinds. In Riverside's Magnolia Bend, antebellum rooms delight with cherry furniture and brocade settees. Riverside's Alligator Bayou rooms sport beds made of hewn "logs" and patchwork quilts. All rooms accommodate up to four and come with either two extra-long double beds or one king bed (king bed rooms are located on building corners); 963 Alligator Bayou rooms house up to five guests by offering a complimentary trundle bed in rooms with double beds (trundle beds slide out from under the double bed and fit a child or small adult). Rooms include a TV, armoire, table and chairs, ceiling fan, and a separate vanity area with double pedestal sinks and privacy curtain. Every room has a window (corner rooms have two), but none have private balconies. Amenities include toiletries (soap and shampoo only), hair dryers, coffeemakers, housekeeping, limited room service, in-room safe (most rooms), refrigerator, and voice mail.

*Allie watches TV at Port Orleans French Quarter*

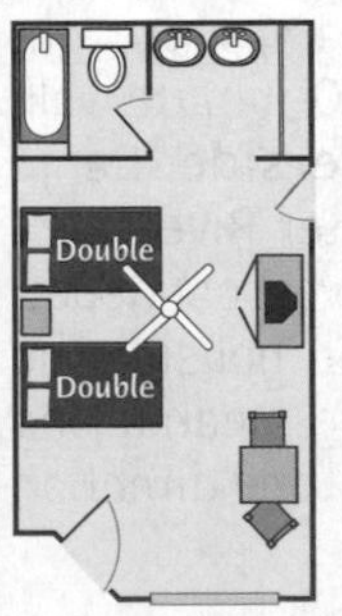

*Standard Room Layout*

## DINING & LOUNGING

Port Orleans plays host to one of the more popular resort eateries: **Boatwright's Dining Hall**. This table-service restaurant in the Riverside district offers breakfast and dinner—see page 231. Two large food courts—**Sassagoula Floatworks and Food Factory** in the French Quarter and the **Riverside Mill** at Riverside—offer breakfast, lunch, and dinner. Typical menu items are croissants ($2.29), French toast with eggs ($5.99), cheesecake ($3.89), grilled chicken sandwich ($6.49), create-your-own-pasta ($8.99), and kids' chicken nuggets ($3.99). Purchase a mug for $12 and get free refills at both food courts. The French Quarter's **Scat Cat's Club** is a full-service bar with live music on the weekends, while **Mardi Grogs** pool bar has drinks and snacks. In Riverside, the **River Roost** offers specialty drinks, appetizers, and music in the evenings, and **Muddy Rivers Pool Bar** has drinks and snacks. **Limited room service**.

# Using the Amenities of Disney's Port Orleans Resort

PLAYING & RELAXING

**For Athletes**: The Dixie Levee marina in Riverside rents pedal boats, rowboats, canopy boats, and bikes (including surrey bikes). Be sure to check the rental hours early on to avoid disappointment later. Both districts offer plenty of paths for walkers and joggers, too.
**For Fishers**: An old-fashioned fishin' hole on Ol' Man Island in Riverside lets you hang a cane pole over a pond stocked with catfish, perch, bass, and bluegill (catch and release only). For more adventure, you can book a fishing excursion down the Sassagoula.
**For Children**: Two playgrounds are near the two themed pools.
**For Gamers**: South Quarter Games (French Quarter) has plenty of video games, as does the Medicine Show Arcade (Riverside).
**For Romantics**: Enjoy a relaxing, private carriage ride for $35.
**For Shoppers**: Jackson Square Gifts & Desires (French Quarter) and Fulton's (Riverside) stock sundries, souvenirs, and snacks.
**For Swimmers**: The French Quarter's Doubloon Lagoon is a moderately sized themed pool with a huge dragon housing the water slide (you slide right down its tongue). A Mardi Gras band of crocodiles shoots water at unsuspecting swimmers. The French Quarter also has a wading pool for the young ones and a hot tub (spa) nearby. In Riverside, Ol' Man Island offers a particularly nice "swimmin' hole" with a large free-form pool, complete with a water slide, a waterfall cascading from a broken sluice, and a fun geyser. A hot tub and kids' wading area are also here. Riverside also has five quieter pools spread throughout the resort.

GETTING ABOUT

Direct **buses** to the major theme parks and Downtown Disney stop regularly (see chart below for in-transit times). Buses usually pick up guests at French Quarter's single bus stop first, then go on to the four stops in Riverside. To get to other resorts and destinations, take a bus to Epcot (daytime) or to Downtown Disney (evening), and transfer to the appropriate bus. A **boat** also picks up guests from Riverside and the French Quarter and goes to and from Downtown Disney Marketplace until 11:00 pm (weather permitting). Boats run about once an hour until 4:00 pm and every 15 minutes thereafter. The trip is leisurely and relaxing. A **shuttle boat** also operates between the French Quarter and Riverside on a frequent basis, especially at meal times. Parking is available throughout the resorts.

| Magic Kingdom | Epcot | Disney's Hollywood Studios | Disney's Animal Kingdom | Downtown Disney |
|---|---|---|---|---|
| direct bus ~10 min. | direct bus ~10 min. | direct bus ~15 min. | direct bus ~15 min. | direct bus/boat ~15/~20 min. |

*Approximate time you will spend in transit from resort to destination during normal operation.*

# Making the Most of Disney's Port Orleans Resort

TIPS

The two **spas** (hot tubs) near the themed pools are heavenly after a long day at the parks. The spa in the French Quarter is a bit of a walk from the pool and quite secluded (look near the laundry), but large enough for several people to soak comfortably (and sociably).

Explore the **resort's grounds** for the quaint parks and gardens scattered throughout. The French Quarter's street and park names are a treat unto themselves, with names like Mud du Lac Lane and Beaux Regards Square. An evening stroll in the French Quarter when the "gas" lamps are lit is particularly magical.

Enjoy an **evening carriage ride** through the two sister resorts. Carriages depart from in front of Boatwright's in Riverside between 6:00 pm and 9:00 pm. Cost is $35 for a 30-minute ride for up to four adults or two adults and two to three children.

Small **refrigerators** are available in your room. Roll-away/trundle beds are also free of charge—request these at reservation time.

NOTES

The **beds** are pretty high off the floor. Watch young ones so they don't fall out, or request complimentary bed rails from housekeeping. If you are concerned, note that some rooms in Alligator Bayou at Riverside come with a pullout trundle bed, which you can request upon reservation and check-in. In fact, this trundle bed allows for a fifth person, making Port Orleans the only moderately priced resort to accommodate five people. Do note that the trundle is small and is really intended for a child or very short person.

Due to the resort merger, Port Orleans has **two front desks**, one in each district. Refer to your reservation to know whether to check-in at French Quarter or Riverside.

**Check-in time** is 3:00 pm. Check-out time is 11:00 am.

RATINGS

*Ratings are explained on page 26.*

| Our Value Ratings: | | Our Magic Ratings: | | Readers' Ratings: |
|---|---|---|---|---|
| Quality: | 7/10 | Theme: | 8/10 | 65% fell in love with it |
| Accessibility: | 7/10 | Amenities: | 6/10 | 22% liked it well enough |
| Affordability: | 8/10 | Fun Factor: | 6/10 | 4% had mixed feelings |
| **Overall Value:** | **7/10** | **Overall Magic:** | **7/10** | 9% were disappointed |

| Port Orleans is enjoyed by... | | (rated by both authors and readers) |
|---|---|---|
| Younger Kids: ♥♥♥ | Young Adults: ♥♥♥♥♥ | Families: ♥♥♥♥ |
| Older Kids: ♥♥♥♥♥ | Mid Adults: ♥♥♥♥ | Couples: ♥♥♥♥♥ |
| Teenagers: ♥♥♥ | Mature Adults: ♥♥♥ | Singles: ♥♥♥ |

# Finding Your Place at Disney's Port Orleans Resort



FRENCH QUARTER MAP

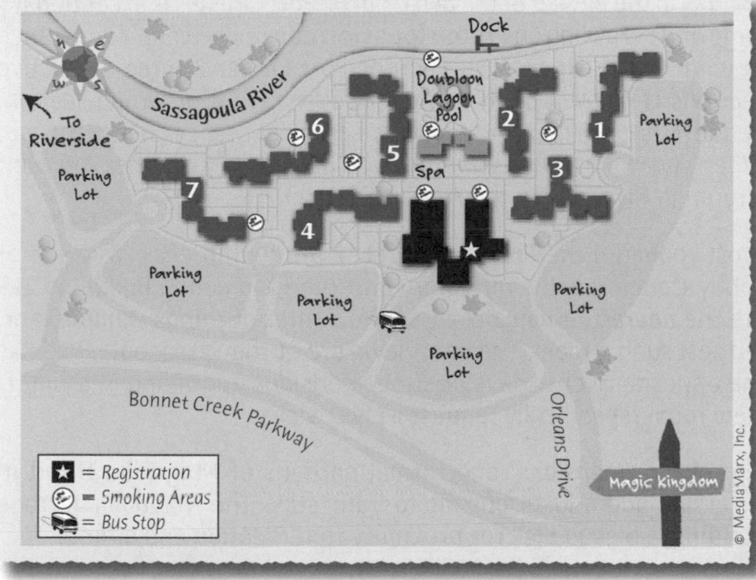

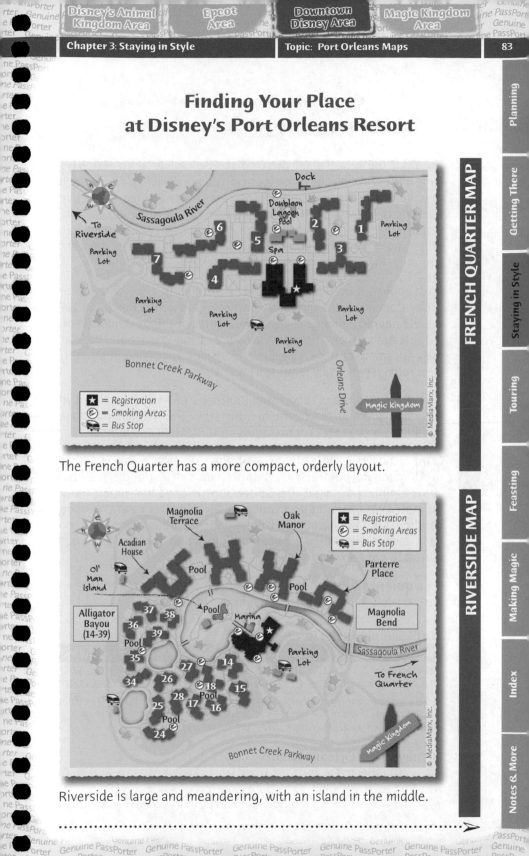

The French Quarter has a more compact, orderly layout.

RIVERSIDE MAP

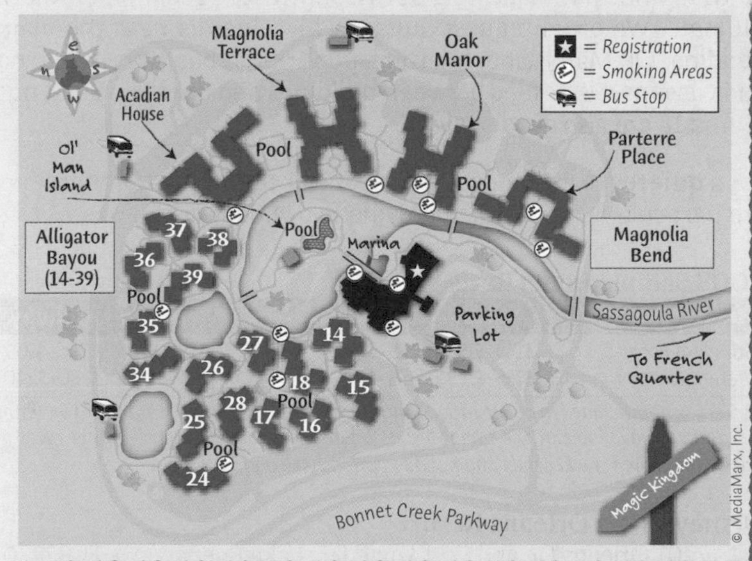


Riverside is large and meandering, with an island in the middle.

# Choosing Your Room at Disney's Port Orleans Resort

BEST LOCATIONS

Thanks to the merger of the two resorts, Port Orleans is exceptionally large and sprawling and **room location** can really make a difference in your resort experience. Each of Port Orleans' three distinctive sections is beloved by its fans. There's no right or wrong section. Request the style that suits you best—don't let Disney choose for you. When you make your reservation, you can specify whether you want a room in Riverside or the French Quarter.

Most rooms in the **French Quarter** are within easy distance of Lobby Concierge, the gift shop, and the food court. Buildings 2–5 are the nearest. If being close to the center of things is important, request such a room. The best views are of the Sassagoula River, as the opposite river bank is pristine—consider upgrading to a water-view room (specifically request a river view).

The grand "mansions" and formal gardens of **Magnolia Bend** in Riverside add a luxurious air to your stay. The Magnolia Terrace building is a good pick for proximity to recreation and dining.

Our personal favorite is **Alligator Bayou** in Riverside. The buildings in Alligator Bayou are smaller (only two stories) and have lush landscaping that make this sprawling resort seem much more intimate. We often request building 14, which is near the main building, Ol' Man Island, a leisure pool, and a bus stop—it has no bad views as it is nestled between buildings and the river. Buildings 15 and 18 are also good choices.

For a **quieter** room, request the second or third floor. Corner rooms are particularly nice as they provide two windows.

RATES

## 2008 Sample Room Rates

*Seasons are noted on page 14.*

| Room Type | Value | Regular | Summer | Peak | Holiday |
|---|---|---|---|---|---|
| Standard Room | $149-$159 | $165-$175 | $179-$194 | $189-$204 | $205-$215 |
| Preferred, Water, or King | $165-$175 | $185-$195 | $199-$214 | $215-$230 | $230-$240 |

*12.5% tax not included in above rates. King-bed rooms come in both standard or water view and are available at the same rate as a water-/pool-view room. Higher rates in price ranges are for weekends and holiday periods (see page 29).*

INFO

## Disney's Port Orleans Resort

2201 Orleans Dr. and 1251 Dixie Dr., Lake Buena Vista, FL 32830
Phone: 407-934-5000 (French Quarter) or 934-6000 (Riverside)
Fax: 407-934-5353 (French Quarter) or 934-5777 (Riverside)

# Disney's Saratoga Springs Resort and Spa

The largest of Disney's Deluxe Villa Resorts is just across the lake from Downtown Disney. Opened in May 2004 and completed in 2007, Disney's Saratoga Springs Resort and Spa offers deluxe villas for Disney Vacation Club members and nightly rental for everyone.

**AMBIENCE**

Saratoga Springs stretches out over 65 acres of the former Disney Institute, adjacent to the Lake Buena Vista Golf Course and across Village Lake from Downtown Disney. This **Victorian-styled resort** is modeled on the historic vacation escape in Upstate New York. The fashionable elite of New York City journeyed up the Hudson on Commodore Vanderbilt's railroad to sip the health spa's waters, stroll its shady byways, and cheer their race horses to victory. Disney's architects soaked up the town's Arts and Crafts atmosphere to bring its essence (minus the horses) to Walt Disney World. Saratoga Spring's 18 lodges cluster around the resort's lakes in five districts—Congress Park, The Springs, The Paddock, The Carousel, and The Grandstand—representing the resort's theme of history, health, and horses. Other buildings survive from the former Disney Institute, including The Carriage House check-in and hospitality building, which also offers dining and shopping.

**RESORT LAYOUT & ROOMS**

Studio villas (355 sq. ft.) accommodate up to four guests with one queen bed, a sofa bed, sink, microwave, and a small refrigerator. The one-bedroom (714 sq. ft.) and two-bedroom (1,075 sq. ft.) villas hold up to 4 or 8 guests each and offer master suites with king beds and whirlpool tubs, DVD players, sofa beds, full kitchens, and washers/dryers. The Grand Villas (2,113 sq. ft.) sleep up to 12 on two levels and feature three bedrooms—the living room, dining room, and master suite (with its whirlpool tub) are on the first level, and on the second level are two more bedrooms with queen beds and private baths. All villas have a laptop-sized safe, and high-speed Internet access is available for $9.95/24-hour period.

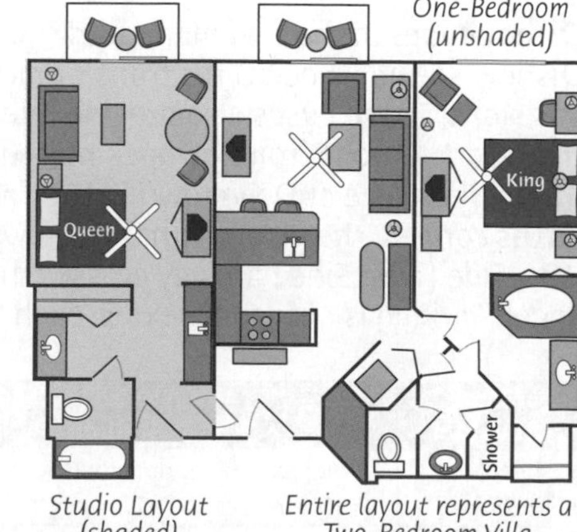


Studio Layout (shaded)

Entire layout represents a Two-Bedroom Villa

# Using the Amenities at Disney's Saratoga Springs Resort

## DINING & LOUNGING

Hungry? The renovated **Turf Club Bar & Grill** is a full-service restaurant (see details on page 231). **The Artists' Palette** is an eatery and market resembling an artist's loft. Open all day, it has pizzas, salads, sandwiches, bakery items, meals, groceries, gifts, and sundries. **The Rocks** and **Backstretch** pool bars are open daily.

*Allie and Jennifer relax in their one-bedroom villa at Saratoga Springs*

## PLAYING & RELAXING

**For Athletes**: Rent surrey bikes at Horsing Around Rentals. There are also two clay tennis courts, basketball, shuffleboard, jogging path, and golf at the Lake Buena Vista Golf Course.
**For Charmers**: Saratoga Springs Spa (formerly The Spa at the Disney Institute) has a fitness center and a full range of spa treatments.
**For Children**: Organized activities are offered at Community Hall. Children's playground. "Pop-jet" play fountains are by the main pool and The Grandstand pool. Board games are in The Turf Club.
**For Gamers**: Win, Place, or Show Arcade games in Community Hall.
**For Romantics**: Enjoy a relaxing, 25-minute carriage ride for $35.
**For Shoppers**: Visit The Artists' Palette for groceries and sundries.
**For Swimmers**: The High Rock Spring themed pool features a zero-entry/children's wading area, a 125-foot-long water slide, two free-form hot-tub spas, and an adjoining kids' play area. There are also three leisure pools with spas (hot tubs).

## GETTING ABOUT

**Direct buses** to the four major parks, water parks, and Downtown Disney (see chart below for transit times) stop at the resort's four bus stops. These buses also provide internal transportation within the resort. A **boat** from the dock near the Carriage House goes to the Marketplace at Downtown Disney and Old Key West. **Walking paths** connect the resort with Downtown Disney Marketplace and West Side (West Side pathway crosses the footbridge near the boat dock). Parking is available next to each lodge building.

| Magic Kingdom | Epcot | Disney's Hollywood Studios | Disney's Animal Kingdom | Downtown Disney |
|---|---|---|---|---|
| direct bus ~25 min. | direct bus ~10 min. | direct bus ~15 min. | direct bus ~20 min. | walk/bus/boat ~15/10/7 min. |

*Approximate time you will spend in transit from resort to destination during normal operation.*

# Making the Most of Disney's Saratoga Springs Resort

TIPS

The **Main Street Railroad Station** at Magic Kingdom was modeled on the former station in Saratoga Springs, New York. The Carriage House, theater, and other nearby buildings recycled from the Disney Institute were originally modeled on the architecture of another historic Upstate New York resort, Chautauqua.

Want to **relax**? Barbecue pavilions, lakeside pavilions, formal gardens, and gazebos/fountains for "taking the waters" all add to the relaxed resort atmosphere.

A **refillable mug** ($12) is available for purchase at The Artists' Palette—you can refill it here and also at the pool bars.

In July 2006, the **Turf Club** reopened as a full-service "bar and grill" serving creatively prepared American favorites such as crab cakes ($10.49), reuben sandwich ($9.99), angus cheeseburger ($11.49), and sirloin steak ($19.99). Kids meals are $6.99. Seating is available inside and out. Hours are from noon to 9:00 pm.

NOTES

The classroom and meeting areas of the old Disney Institute are now the **main sales offices** and show-villas for Disney Vacation Club.

The **remaining villas** from the old Disney Institute won't be offered to the public. The Fairway Villas and Grand Villas were demolished. We also hear the Treehouse Villas may be removed, but nothing new can be built in its wetland protected area.

**Check-in time** is 4:00 pm. Check-out time is 11:00 am.

RATINGS

*Ratings are explained on page 26.*

| Our Value Ratings: | | Our Magic Ratings: | | Readers' Ratings: |
|---|---|---|---|---|
| Quality: | 6/10 | Theme: | 6/10 | 67% fell in love with it |
| Accessibility: | 6/10 | Amenities: | 6/10 | 18% liked it well enough |
| Affordability: | 6/10 | Fun Factor: | 5/10 | 10% had mixed feelings |
| **Overall Value:** | **6/10** | **Overall Magic:** | **6/10** | 5% were disappointed |

| Saratoga Springs is enjoyed by... | | (estimated by the authors) |
|---|---|---|
| Younger Kids: ♥♥♥♥ | Young Adults: ♥♥♥♥ | Families: ♥♥♥♥♥ |
| Older Kids: ♥♥♥♥ | Mid Adults: ♥♥♥♥♥ | Couples: ♥♥♥ |
| Teenagers: ♥♥♥ | Mature Adults: ♥♥♥♥♥ | Singles: ♥♥ |

# Finding Your Place at Disney's Saratoga Springs Resort

## SARATOGA SPRINGS RESORT MAP

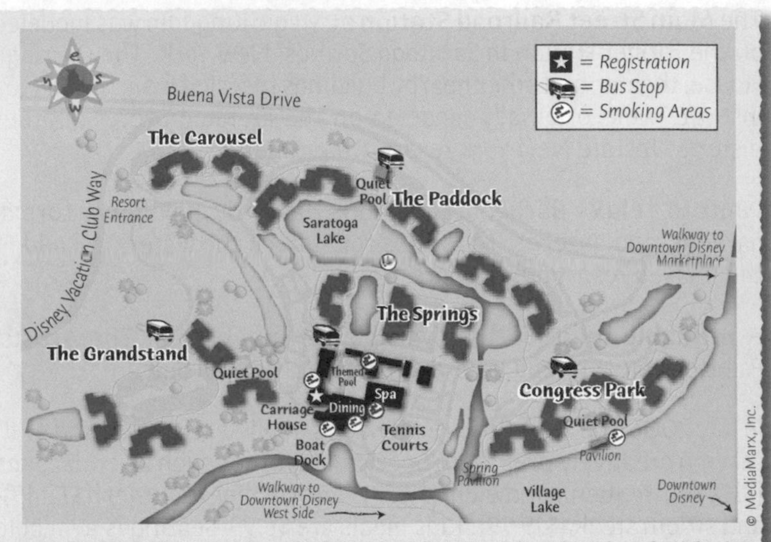


## BEST LOCATIONS

Rooms in **Congress Park** have views of Downtown Disney and/or gardens and offer a short walk to the Downtown Disney Marketplace and a moderate walk to The Carriage House. Some garden views include parking lots. **The Springs** offers closest proximity to The Carriage House and themed pool, with views of Saratoga Lake or gardens/parking. **The Paddock** and **The Carousel** are the most spread out and distant from other facilities. Request to be close to the leisure pool and/or footbridge (to The Carriage House) if that's important. **The Grandstand** may be nicest of all, as it is close to the main facilities and has a superior pool area. Requests for particular locations are honored when possible.

## RATES

**2008 Sample Villa Rates**

*Seasons are noted on page 14.*

| Room Type | Value | Regular | Peak | Holiday |
|---|---|---|---|---|
| Studio Villa | $285 | $315 | $370 | $410 |
| One-Bedroom Villa | $380 | $430 | $500 | $575 |
| Two-Bedroom Villa | $530 | $630 | $765 | $875 |
| Grand Villa | $1,170 | $1,305 | $1,475 | $1,645 |

*12.5% tax is not included in the above rates.*

## INFO

**Disney's Saratoga Springs Resort & Spa**

1960 Broadway, Lake Buena Vista, FL 32830

Phone: 407-827-1100 Fax: 407-827-1151

For reservations, call Central Reservations: 407-934-7639

*Looking for Shades of Green? Page 98. Swan Resort? Page 99.*

# Disney's Wilderness Lodge and Villas Resort

The Wilderness Lodge and Villas are nestled in a dense forest of pines on Bay Lake, accessible by waterway from the Magic Kingdom (use the blue tab at the top of the page for parks and eateries in the area). The Lodge and Villas were inspired by the U.S. National Park lodges built in the 1900s.

## AMBIENCE

Ah, wilderness! Rustic log buildings, swaying pines, babbling brooks, and the faintest whiff of wood smoke from the crackling fireplace. The Wilderness Lodge pays homage to the **grand log lodges** of the Pacific Northwest, with its towering lobby, 55-foot totem poles, and deluxe rooms. The Villas at Wilderness Lodge offer Disney's Deluxe Villa accommodations for Disney Vacation Club members (see pages 102–103) and all other guests. Architecturally, the Villas represent an earlier era than the main Lodge building and draw influences from the lodges created by America's railroad workers.

## RESORT LAYOUT & ROOMS

The Wilderness Lodge and the Villas offer varying accommodations, ranging from 340 to 1,071 sq. feet. The **Lodge** houses 728 guest rooms and suites, with some encircling the cavernous lobby but most in the two wings. The cozy Lodge rooms are outfitted with new furniture and bed spreads with Hidden Mickeys. Most Lodge rooms have two queen beds, but some offer a bunk bed in place of the second bed. The **Villas** feature 136 studios and one- and two-bedroom suites, each with a kitchenette or full kitchen, DVD player, and washer and dryer. All rooms have a balcony or patio, a small table and chairs, TV, double sinks, toiletries, in-room safe, refrigerator, turndown service (on request), newspaper delivery, voice mail, and valet parking.

*Standard Lodge Room Layout*

## DINING

As you would expect from a Lodge, the food here is served in hearty, healthy portions. The two table-service restaurants (see page 232) are **Artist Point** for fine dining in the evening and **Whispering Canyon Cafe** for a fun, western-style adventure serving all-you-can-eat meals throughout the day. **Roaring Fork Snack Shop** is a self-service cafe serving breakfast foods, burgers, sandwiches, and snacks—purchase a refillable mug here for $12 and get free self-serve refills. Typical menu items include breakfast platter ($5.99), smoked turkey sandwich ($6.49), cheeseburger with fries ($6.89), and grilled chicken salad ($7.99). **Miss Jenny's In-Room Dining** is available for limited room service at breakfast and dinner.

# Using the Amenities at Disney's Wilderness Lodge and Villas Resort

LOUNGING

**Territory Lounge**, a saloon adjacent to Artist Point, serves up beers, wines, spirits, and snacks. The **Trout Pass Pool Bar** offers cocktails and light snacks you can enjoy at tables overlooking the main pool and Bay Lake. Beer and wine are also available from the resort shop.

© MediaMarx, Inc.

*The Wilderness Lodge courtyard at twilight is breathtaking*

PLAYING & RELAXING

**For Athletes**: Rent watercraft and bicycles at Teton Boat & Bike Rentals. A bike and jogging path extends about a mile to Fort Wilderness. A health club, Sturdy Branches, is available.
**For Children**: The Cub's Den is a supervised program for kids ages 4–12 (see page 255). A playground is located near the beach.
**For Gamers**: Buttons and Bells arcade, across from Cub's Den.
**For Shoppers**: The large Wilderness Lodge Mercantile in the Lodge carries clothing, sundries, foodstuffs, newspapers, and gifts.
**For Swimmers**: Cleverly designed to seem like part of Silver Creek, a free-form swimming pool is nestled among craggy rocks and waterfalls. A water slide and wading pool, as well as two hot tubs, are also available nearby. A leisure pool and another hot tub are located near the Villas. The white sand beach here on Bay Lake is ideal for relaxing upon, but swimming is not permitted.

GETTING ABOUT

You can take a direct **boat** to the Magic Kingdom (see chart below for in-transit times). Boats also ferry you to Fort Wilderness and the Contemporary. **Buses** take you directly to Epcot, Disney's Hollywood Studios, Disney's Animal Kingdom, Downtown Disney, and the water parks. To reach other resorts, go to the Magic Kingdom (daytime) or Downtown Disney (evening), and then transfer to a resort bus. Fort Wilderness and Wilderness Lodge share many of their bus routes, so travel to and from Fort Wilderness for the Hoop-Dee-Doo show (see page 236), horseback riding, etc., is quite convenient.

| Magic Kingdom | Epcot | Disney's Hollywood Studios | Disney's Animal Kingdom | Downtown Disney |
|---|---|---|---|---|
| boat ~8 min. | direct bus ~10 min. | direct bus ~15 min. | direct bus ~15 min. | direct bus ~25 min. |

*Approximate time you will spend in transit from resort to destination during normal operation.*

# Making the Most of Disney's Wilderness Lodge and Villas Resort

TIPS

Guests staying in the **Villas at Wilderness Lodge** register at the main Lodge registration desk.

For good rainy day activities, ask for a **kids' activity/coloring book** at the bell station or a list of **Hidden Mickeys** at Lobby Concierge. You can also get a list of the resort's music at the Mercantile shop.

**Explore the resort**. Indian artifacts, historic paintings, and survey maps are displayed. Follow Silver Creek from its indoor origin as a hot spring and onward outside as a bubbling brook and waterfall, eventually making its way to Bay Lake (see photo on page 90).

Ask about becoming a **Flag Family**. Each morning, a family is selected to go on the Lodge roof to help raise or lower the flag! This is popular, so inquire at check-in for a better chance.

Inquire about the **"Wonders of the Lodge" tour** at Lobby Concierge. The walking tour explores the architecture, landscaping, totem poles, and paintings. Offered Wednesdays–Saturdays at 9:00 am.

Watch **Fire Rock Geyser**, modeled after Old Faithful, erupt like clockwork every hour on the hour from 7:00 am to 10:00 pm. The **Electrical Water Pageant** is visible from the beach at 9:35 pm.

Courtyard-view rooms can be **noisy** with the sounds of children and rushing water. Opt for a Lodge view if you prefer serenity.

About 37 Lodge rooms with **king beds** double as the barrier-free (handicap-accessible) rooms and have a large shower with no tub.

**Check-in time** is 3:00 pm. Check-out time is 11:00 am.

NOTES

RATINGS

*Ratings are explained on page 26.*

| Our Value Ratings: | | Our Magic Ratings: | | Readers' Ratings: |
|---|---|---|---|---|
| Quality: | 9/10 | Theme: | 10/10 | 79% fell in love with it |
| Accessibility: | 6/10 | Amenities: | 6/10 | 17% liked it well enough |
| Affordability: | 6/10 | Fun Factor: | 8/10 | 3% had mixed feelings |
| **Overall Value:** | **7/10** | **Overall Magic:** | **8/10** | 1% were disappointed |

| Wilderness Lodge is enjoyed by... | (rated by both authors and readers) | |
|---|---|---|
| Younger Kids: ♥♥♥♥ | Young Adults: ♥♥♥♥♥ | Families: ♥♥♥♥ |
| Older Kids: ♥♥♥♥ | Mid Adults: ♥♥♥♥♥ | Couples: ♥♥♥♥♥ |
| Teenagers: ♥♥♥♥ | Mature Adults: ♥♥♥♥ | Singles: ♥♥♥ |

# Finding Your Place at Disney's Wilderness Lodge and Villas Resort

## LODGE AND VILLAS RESORT MAP

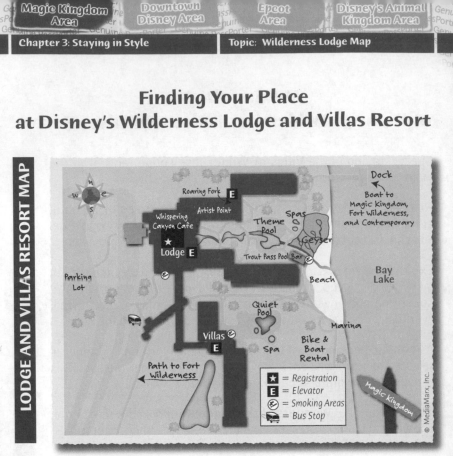

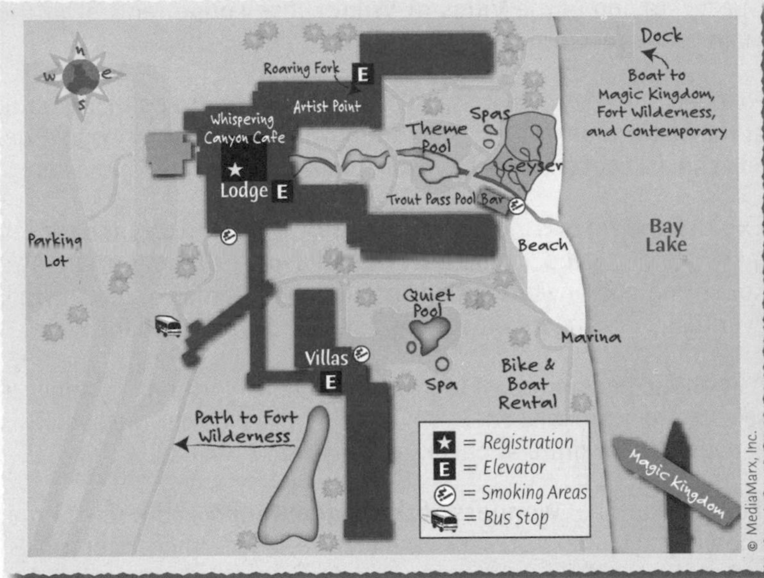

## BEST LOCATIONS

**Standard rooms** overlook the parking areas yet are close to the Lobby. **Lodge views** overlook woods (north side) or the Villas (south side). **Top-floor rooms** facing the woods on the Magic Kingdom (north) side may catch a glimpse of fireworks. Rooms facing the **courtyard or lake** offer panoramic views and cheerful resort sounds. If you seek privacy, consider a **honeymoon suite** at the top of the Lobby or a top-floor room with solid balcony railings. Concierge service is offered for suites and rooms on the seventh floor. **Villas** in the northeast corner offer views of the pool.

## RATES

### 2008 Sample Room and Villa Rates

*Seasons are noted on page 14.*

| Room Type | Value | Regular | Peak | Holiday |
|---|---|---|---|---|
| Standard View | $225-$245 | $275-$295 | $340-$370 | $370-$390 |
| Lodge View (Woods) | $250-$270 | $295-$315 | $370-$400 | $415-$435 |
| Courtyard View | $275-$295 | $330-$350 | $395-$425 | $430-$450 |
| Studio Villa | $315 | $360 | $425 | $480 |
| One-Bedroom Villa | $425 | $485 | $590 | $635 |

*12.5% tax is not included in the above. Suites and concierge start in the high $300s. Higher rates in price ranges are for weekends and holiday periods (see page 29).*

## INFO

**Disney's Wilderness Lodge and Villas Resort**

901 Timberline Drive, Lake Buena Vista, FL 32830

Phone: 407-824-3200 Fax: 407-824-3232

For reservations, call Central Reservations: 407-939-6244

# Disney's Yacht and Beach Club and Villas Resorts

Offering luxury, convenience, and added amenities, the Yacht Club and Beach Club are sister resorts. Both resorts feature a relaxing atmosphere and are located on Crescent Lake within walking distance of Epcot (use the blue tab at the top of the page for parks and eateries in the area).

AMBIENCE

These resorts evoke the charm of **bygone seaside resorts**. The Yacht Club is housed in a dove-gray clapboard building, exuding elegance and grace. The Beach Club atmosphere is casual, bringing to mind sun-filled days you might have found along the eastern seaboard generations ago. Windows in the sky-blue building may gaze out upon the "beach houses" nestled alongside the beach. The Beach Club Villas are housed in a separate building evoking the charm of Cape May, New Jersey. The Villas' clapboard walls are painted in seafoam green with white railings and columns, and gingerbread trim. Colorful pennants flap in the breeze from atop the roofs and turrets, and strings of light bulbs dangle gracefully between old-fashioned street lamps.

RESORT LAYOUT & ROOMS

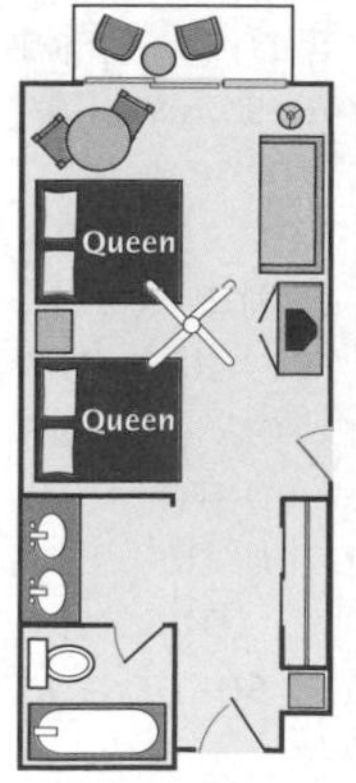

*Standard Room Layout*

Each of the standard rooms at the Yacht and Beach Club is housed within five floors of one deceptively large yet creatively shaped building, while the villas are located within a free-standing addition. Covered walkways connect the Villas to the Beach Club lobby. Well-appointed and understated, the standard rooms are large (380 sq. ft.) and sunny. The 634 **Yacht Club** rooms are outfitted in ocean blues, floral patterns, and antiqued wood. The 580 **Beach Club** rooms are playfully decorated in seafoam greens and cabana-striped pinks. Guest rooms have one king or two queen beds, a daybed, ottoman, double sinks, a make-up mirror, a small table and chairs, an armoire with a TV, and a small refrigerator. Some smaller rooms have a king-size Murphy bed and an extra sink and counter. Many rooms—but not all—have balconies or patios (all Yacht Club guest rooms have balconies). Amenities include room service, hair dryers (most rooms), iron, newspaper delivery, turndown service (on request—not available in the Villas), in-room safe, toiletries, and voice mail. Both the Yacht Club and the Beach Club offer concierge service with slightly larger rooms on the fifth floor. In addition, 40 special suites (20 in each resort) range in size from a junior suite to a two-bedroom suite to the ultimate Presidential Suite.

Planning | Getting There | Staying in Style | Touring | Feasting | Making Magic | Index | Notes & More

# Lodging and Dining at Disney's Yacht and Beach Club Resorts

**VILLAS**

Added in mid-2002 are the 205 Beach Club Villas with studio, one-, and two-bedroom **villas** for Disney Vacation Club members (see pages 102–103) and the public at large. Studios accommodate up to four guests with one queen-size bed, a double-size sofa bed, and a kitchenette (with a sink, microwave, and a small refrigerator). The one- and two-bedroom villas accommodate up to four or eight guests respectively and offer full kitchens, DVD players, king-size beds, delightful whirlpool tubs in the master bathroom, double-size sleeper sofas in the living room, and washers/dryers. All villas are quite homey and feel like a cottage you might have on the beach. Amenities for all villas include room service, iron and ironing board, hair dryer, newspaper delivery, in-room safe, toiletries (shampoo and soap), and voice mail.

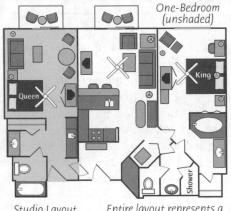

© MediaMarx, Inc.

*Exploring the Beach Club*

One-Bedroom (unshaded)

Queen

King

Shower

Studio Layout (shaded)

Entire layout represents a Two-Bedroom Villa

**DINING**

With the Yacht and Beach Club sharing restaurants, there are more dining options here than at almost any other resort. Table-service options (see page 233) include **Beaches and Cream**, a popular soda fountain; **Cape May Cafe**, a character breakfast and all-you-can-eat clambake; **Yachtsman Steakhouse** for dinner; and the **Yacht Club Galley** for breakfast, lunch, and dinner. The **Crew's Cup** offers a good snack menu. For a quick meal, try **Hurricane Hanna's**, a poolside grill, or the **Beach Club Marketplace**, offering breakfast items, baked goods, sandwiches, salads, gelato, coffee, and beverages (refillable mugs—$12, too) for eat-in or take-out.

# Using the Amenities at Disney's Yacht and Beach Club Resorts

LOUNGING

Several lounges will help you relax after a long day of playing. **Ale & Compass** and **Crew's Cup** in the Yacht Club serve drinks and munchies. At Beach Club, **Martha's Vineyard** features an award-winning wine list and appetizers. **Rip Tide Lounge** is closed at press time, and we're not sure when or if it will reopen. **Hurricane Hanna's** is a pool bar. Room service is always available.

PLAYING & RELAXING

**For Athletes**: The Ship Shape Health Club is a complete fitness club offering a spa, sauna, and massage therapies. The resorts also sport two lighted tennis courts and a sand volleyball court. The Bayside Marina rents watercraft for cruises, including the new "Breathless II," a wooden yacht named after Breathless Mahoney in "Dick Tracy" (see page 252), and surrey bikes to ride around the lake.
**For Charmers**: Periwig's Beauty and Barber Shop is a full-service salon for hair, skin, and nail care.
**For Children**: A playground is near Stormalong Bay. Sandcastle Club offers supervised activities for children ages 4–12 (see page 254).
**For Gamers**: Lafferty Place Arcade has video games.
**For Shoppers**: The Beach Club Marketplace (Beach) and Fittings and Fairings (Yacht) offer sundries and resort wear.
**For Swimmers**: The three-acre Stormalong Bay water park is resort swimming at its best. Three free-form, sandy-bottomed pools create deceptively complex waterways with whirlpools, bubbling jets, "rising sands," a water slide in a shipwreck, and two hot tubs. Stormalong Bay is for Yacht and Beach Club and Villas resort guests only (bring your resort ID). Leisure pools are located at the far ends of the resorts. The Villas has its own leisure pool, called "Dunes Cove," and a hot tub.

GETTING ABOUT

**Boats** (see chart below for in-transit times) depart from the marina for Epcot and Disney's Hollywood Studios. **Buses** outside the lobby go to the Magic Kingdom, Disney's Animal Kingdom, and Downtown Disney. Reach other destinations by transferring at Disney's Hollywood Studios (day) or Downtown Disney (evening). Parking is available, as well as valet parking ($10/day). The BoardWalk, Dolphin, and Swan are all within **walking distance**, as is the International Gateway to Epcot. You could also walk to Disney's Hollywood Studios along the path beside the BoardWalk Villas (see map on page 46).

| Magic Kingdom | Epcot | Disney's Hollywood Studios | Disney's Animal Kingdom | Downtown Disney |
|---|---|---|---|---|
| direct bus ~20 min. | walk/boat ~10/~10 min. | walk/boat ~20/~15 min. | direct bus ~20 min. | direct bus ~15 min. |

*Approximate time you will spend in transit from resort to destination during normal operation.*

# Making the Most of Disney's Yacht and Beach Club Resort

TIPS

Enjoy a **waterfront stroll** around Crescent Lake using the boardwalks and bridges encircling it. This is a very lively place!

Request **turndown service** from housekeeping before you go out for the evening, and return to find your bedcovers turned down with a chocolate. This service is not available in the Beach Club Villas.

A **bank of elevators** near each resort's lobby serves most rooms. If your room is at one of the far ends, look for a **single elevator or stairway** rather than trek down the hallways. If you're going to Epcot, the exit near Beach Club's leisure pool is convenient.

Yacht and Beach Club have **separate entrances** and **front desks**. Beach Club Villas guests check in at the Beach Club's front desk.

Explore the charming **public areas**, such as The Solarium (just off the Beach Club Lobby), The Drawing Room (near the Villas' entrance), and The Breezeway (near the Dunes Cove pool).

NOTES

Bring **resort identification** with you to Stormalong Bay—it will be checked. It can be noisy with the sounds of happy children late into the night, so avoid it and places nearby if you seek peace.

All rooms on the first floor have pleasant patios. Most rooms on the top floor have full **balconies**, as do some on the intervening floors. Be aware that some balconies are standing room only, however. If a full-size balcony is important, request it.

A **conference center**, reminiscent of a town hall, is available.

**Check-in time** is 3:00/4:00 pm (Villas). Check-out time is 11:00 am.

RATINGS

*Ratings are explained on page 26.*

| Our Value Ratings: | | Our Magic Ratings: | | Readers' Ratings: |
|---|---|---|---|---|
| Quality: | 8/10 | Theme: | 8/10 | 55% fell in love with it |
| Accessibility: | 8/10 | Amenities: | 9/10 | 34% liked it well enough |
| Affordability: | 3/10 | Fun Factor: | 6/10 | 7% had mixed feelings |
| **Overall Value:** | **6/10** | **Overall Magic:** | **8/10** | 4% were disappointed |

| Yacht and Beach Clubs are enjoyed by... (rated by both authors and readers) | | |
|---|---|---|
| Younger Kids: ♥♥♥♥ | Young Adults: ♥♥♥♥ | Families: ♥♥♥♥ |
| Older Kids: ♥♥♥♥♥ | Mid Adults: ♥♥♥♥♥ | Couples: ♥♥♥♥♥ |
| Teenagers: ♥♥♥♥ | Mature Adults: ♥♥♥♥♥ | Singles: ♥♥♥ |

# Finding Your Place at Disney's Yacht and Beach Club Resort

RESORT MAP

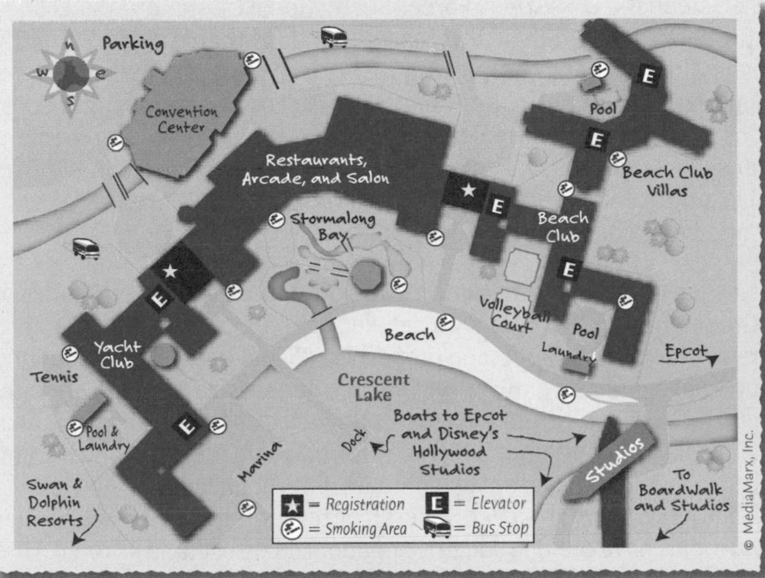


BEST LOCATIONS

Your room location can make or break your experience. We strongly recommend you indulge in a room with a **water view** at either the Yacht or Beach Club. Specifically, try to avoid the standard-view, even-numbered Beach Club rooms between 3662–3726, 4662–4726, and 5662–5726, which overlook an ugly rooftop. You may also want to request a room **closer to the lobby** for easier access. Rooms with a king-size Murphy bed are slightly smaller than other rooms. The slightly larger rooms on the Beach Club's fifth floor are concierge. Rooms at the **Beach Club Villas** have views of Epcot, gardens, or the pool, but rates are the same for all.

RATES

## 2008 Sample Room and Villa Rates

*Seasons are noted on page 14.*

| Room Type | Value | Regular | Peak | Holiday |
|---|---|---|---|---|
| Standard View or Studio Villa | $325-$345 | $370-$390 | $440-$470 | $490-$510 |
| Water View | $395-$415 | $450-$470 | $515-$545 | $560-$580 |
| One-Bedroom Villa | $435 | $495 | $575 | $645 |
| Two-Bedroom Villa | $610 | $795 | $1,005 | $1,140 |

*12.5% tax is not included in the above. Concierge rooms start in the mid-$400's. Higher rates in price ranges are for weekends and holiday periods in non-Villa rooms (see page 29).*

INFO

## Disney's Yacht and Beach Club and Villas Resorts

1700/1800 Epcot Resort Blvd., Lake Buena Vista, FL 32830
Phone: 407-934-7000/8000 Fax: 407-934-3450/3850

# Shades of Green Resort

Shades of Green is a U.S. Armed Forces Recreational Center on Walt Disney World property, located near the Magic Kingdom theme park. Formerly The Disney Inn, this self-supporting resort is exclusively for active and retired military personnel in the Army, Navy, Air Force, Marines, and Coast Guard, as well as those in the Reserves and National Guard. Department of Defense civilians and U.S. Public Health Officers are also eligible. The resort closed for renovations in 2003 and reopened in March 2004 with bigger and better accommodations.

**ROOMS**

Nestled in the woods **between two golf courses**, the new Shades of Green offers 586 rooms with deluxe accommodations. Guest rooms remain among the largest on property at 450 sq. feet, accommodating up to five guests. Features include two queen-size beds, an armoire, and a TV, plus a sitting area with a daybed or sleeper sofa and table and chairs. Rooms have a refrigerator, coffeemaker, iron and ironing board, hair dryer, and an in-room safe. Internet access is available via a dataport (no high-speed access), or through the TV for $9.95/day. All rooms have either a balcony or patio. The resort (and all rooms) are smoke-free (smoking may be allowed on the balcony/patio). Eleven 1–3 bedroom suites are available, sleeping 6–8 guests each.

**AMENITIES**

**Dining choices** include the Garden Gallery family restaurant, Evergreens sports bar, a new specialty Italian restaurant (Mangino's), the new Express Cafe for quick-service meals, and room service. There's also a lounge (Eagles). Resort amenities include two lighted tennis courts, two heated pools, wading pool, playground, exercise room, arcade, and laundry facilities. You can also purchase theme park tickets. Two **buses** are available, and you can walk to the Polynesian and Transportation and Ticket Center. You must show your Shades of Green resort ID or military ID to board their buses. A car is helpful, and a multi-level parking structure is available ($5/day).

**RATES**

Rates are based on rank or pay grade and begin at **$80** for standard rooms and **$90** for pool views. You may reserve up to three rooms. Reserve up to 53 weeks in advance. **Tip**: If the resort is full for your preferred time, inquire about overflow rates and the wait list.

**INFO**

**Shades of Green Resort**
P.O. Box 22789, Lake Buena Vista, FL 32830
Phone: 407-824-3400 Fax: 407-824-3460
For more information, call 888-593-2242 or 407-824-3665
Web site: http://www.shadesofgreen.org

# Walt Disney World Swan and Dolphin Resorts

Crowned by five-story-high sculptures of swans and heraldic dolphins, the recently renovated Walt Disney World Swan and Dolphin resorts tower above nearby Epcot area resorts. Westin and Sheraton, both of which are divisions of Starwood Hotels, jointly manage this pair of luxury hotels popular with business and international visitors.

ROOMS

**Guest rooms** feature either one king-size bed or two double-size beds, separate vanity and bath areas, two 2-line phones, mini-bar, hair dryer, iron, coffeemaker, newspaper delivery, and in-room safe. High-speed Internet is $10.99/day, and use the of health club is $10/person/day (no mandatory resort fees). Some rooms have balconies, and 195 suites offer a bit more room. Guest rooms at both resorts were recently renovated and now sport a modern design by Michael Graves and "Heavenly Beds" with pillow-top mattresses and down comforters (delightful!). The sister resorts offer conference facilities, plus many of the same amenities and benefits found at Disney resort hotels.

AMENITIES

Between the resorts, there are **15 eateries**, including the new Il Mulino, Gulliver's Grill, Kimonos, Shula's Steakhouse, bluezoo (an upscale restaurant by chef Todd English), and Fresh (an innovative market-style buffet)—see pages 231–232 for details. Picabu is a 24-hour quick-service buffet/cafeteria with a whimsical atmosphere. The BoardWalk entertainment district is just a stroll away, as is Fantasia Gardens miniature golf. Free **buses** serve Disney's parks and Downtown Disney, and boats run to Disney's Hollywood Studios and Epcot. Guests receive many of the benefits enjoyed at the Disney-owned resorts, including package delivery, Extra Magic Hours, and the option to purchase park tickets. The only thing guests can't do is charge Disney purchases to their room.

RATES

Rooms begin in the **high $200s**, but discounts and special rates are available—ask about discounts for AAA, Annual Passholders, teachers, nurses, military, and AllEars.net readers. Great rates can be found on Hotwire.com and won on Priceline.com (page 16). Starwood members earn points (see http://www.spg.com).

INFO

**Walt Disney World Swan and Dolphin Resorts**

1200/1500 Epcot Resort Blvd., Lake Buena Vista, FL 32830

Phone: 407-934-4000 Fax: 407-934-4884

For reservations, call 888-828-8850 or 407-934-4000

For more information, visit http://www.swandolphin.com

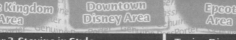

*Looking for more information? Get details on our full-length Disney Cruise guide on page 285.*

# Disney Cruise Line

The Disney Cruise Line set sail in 1998 with the same enthusiasm and energy you find at the Walt Disney World Resort. Each of the two ships (the Disney Magic and the Disney Wonder) have four uniquely themed restaurants, including one for adults only. Experience Broadway-quality productions, first-run and classic Disney movies, and nightclubs. Separate areas of the ship were designed exclusively for adults and children.

**ITINERARY**

Ships depart Disney's own terminal in Port Canaveral at 5:00 pm. Four-night **cruises** spend the next day in Nassau, followed by a day at Castaway Cay, Disney's private island, then a full day at sea. Guests debark at Port Canaveral at 9:00 am the following morning. Three-night cruises follow the same plan, but skip the day at sea. Seven-night cruises offer different itineraries—one to the Eastern Caribbean (with stops at St. Maarten, St. Thomas/St. John, and Castaway Cay), three to the Western Caribbean (with stops at ports like Key West, Grand Cayman, Cozumel, and Castaway Cay), and some special cruises. In summer 2008, the Disney Magic sails to the West coast for Mexican Riviera cruises.

**STATEROOMS**

**Staterooms** range from downright comfortable to out-and-out luxurious. Even the least expensive (there are no "cheap") rooms are decorated in glowing, warm woods and include a television, phone, refrigerator, and in-room safe. The bright and cheery bathrooms include a hair dryer and tub. Deluxe staterooms include a split bathroom, which makes family travel especially comfortable, and 44% of all staterooms offer a verandah. Staterooms that sleep four usually have one queen bed, a single daybed, and a single berth—great for families but not so great for two couples. At the high end, the two-bedroom Walter E. and Roy O. Disney suites are a feast for the eyes, decorated with exotic wood paneling and cut crystal—they include a whirlpool tub!

**RATES**

Many vacationers book seven-day land/sea **packages** that include a three- or four-night cruise and three or four nights at Walt Disney World. 2008 value season packages start at $883/person (for double occupancy) for a standard inside stateroom to more than $5,000/person for a Royal Suite. Third, fourth, and fifth occupants pay much less. Airfare and ground transfers are extra, but the land/sea packages include park admission. Packages with less expensive staterooms include a room at a moderate resort, while the more expensive rate a deluxe resort. Cruise-only vacations start at $423/person.

# Making the Most of the Disney Cruise Line

DINING

Your cruise includes all food onboard (including room service) and lunch at Castaway Cay. Soft drinks are free at meals and at the Deck 9 beverage station. Alcoholic beverages are extra. Each night you'll be assigned to a different dining room. **Triton's** (Wonder) or **Lumiere's** (Magic) is the most formal dining room, which is also open daily to all for full-service breakfast and lunch. **Parrot Cay** is the informal, Caribbean-themed room, and also hosts a breakfast buffet. **Animator's Palate** is an extraordinary room, lined with black and white drawings of famous Disney characters that gradually blossom into full color. **Palo** is the ships' intimate, adults-only restaurant with an elegant Italian menu and marvelous service. You may reserve a table at Palo ($10/person surcharge) in advance online or in person on the afternoon that you board, and seats can go quickly. Breakfast and lunch buffets and snacks are served on Deck 9. Fountain drinks are complimentary from the beverage station on Deck 9.

NOTES

You'll receive your **cruise documentation** listing your stateroom assignment a few weeks before you sail. If you have preferences, state them upon reservation and again a month before you sail.

Around June 2008, passports must be presented by all passengers before boarding. Get your **papers** in order long before you depart.

All shore-side food, transportation, and entertainment in every port of call except Castaway Cay is **at your own expense**. Unless you are especially adventuresome, we suggest you either book a shore excursion (listed in your cruise documentation) or stay onboard.

**Dress** is mostly casual, but have a nice dress or jacket for the Captain's reception, dinner at Triton's/Lumiere's, and Palo.

TIPS

To **save money**, book a cruise-only passage as early as possible. You can still book ground transfers through Disney.

Need to stay connected? Try the **Internet Cafe** or wireless access.

Your day at **Castaway Cay** is short. Be sure to wake up early!

Looking for more information? We have an **entire book** about the Disney Cruise! Visit http://www.passporter.com/dcl/guidebook.htm and see page 285. We also recommend the unofficial Magical Disney Cruise Guide at http://allears.net/cruise/cruise.shtml.

For details, visit http://www.disneycruise.com or call 888-DCL-2500.

# Disney Vacation Club

Can you ever get enough of Walt Disney World? Disney Vacation Club (DVC) members are betting that they can't. DVC is Disney's kinder, gentler version of a vacation timeshare, and offers several enticing twists on the timeshare experience. As with all timeshare offerings, the DVC offers the promise of frequent, reduced-cost Disney vacations in exchange for a significant up-front investment on your part.

**RESORTS**

Disney operates **eight Disney's Deluxe Villa Resorts**: Old Key West (see pages 67–70), Boardwalk Villas (see pages 43–46), Villas at Wilderness Lodge (see pages 89–92), Beach Club Villas (see pages 93–97), Vero Beach (Florida coast), Hilton Head Island (South Carolina), Saratoga Springs (see pages 85–88), and the new Animal Kingdom Villas (see pages 39–42). Studios, one-, two-, and three-bedroom villas with kitchen and laundry facilities are offered (studios have kitchenettes and access to laundry rooms), as well as recreational activities. Housekeeping is limited, with full services every eight days (consider these reduced housekeeping services when you compare the value of a regular hotel to a DVC ownership).

**THE PROGRAM**

With a typical vacation timeshare, you buy an annual one-week (or multiple-week) stay during a particular time period in a specific size of accommodation. DVC uses a novel **point system** that adds far greater flexibility and complexity to the process. You can use your points however you wish to create several short getaways or a single, grand vacation—at any time of the year and at any DVC or other Disney resort. Here's how it works: You buy a certain number of points at the going rate ($104 per point as of July 2007). 160 points is the minimum and a typical purchase—so every year you'd have 160 points to apply toward accommodations. You might need 15 points/night for a one-bedroom at Old Key West weeknights during the off-season. 100 points/night may be needed for a two-bedroom at BoardWalk weekends in peak season. Just as with a regular resort room, rates are affected by size, view, location, season, and day. You also pay annual dues based on the number of points purchased. Rates vary, depending on your "home" resort—from about $4.12 to $5.63 per point—so dues on a 160-point purchase would be about $660–$900. If you compare the combined cost of points and annual membership fees to renting comparable resort rooms at nondiscounted rates, it could take about five years to recover the value of the points purchased. After that, vacations might cost half the prevailing rental rates. Membership contracts at Saratoga Springs Resort expire in 2054; Animal Kingdom Villas contracts expire in 2057; all other contracts expire in 2042.

# Making the Most of the Disney Vacation Club

TIPS

While you can reserve up to eleven months ahead of time at your **home resort**, you can only book seven months in advance at others.

You can **borrow points** from the next year or save unused points until next year. You can buy more points from Disney at the going rate, or buy/sell points on the open market—we heartily recommend DVC By Resale (http://www.dvcbyresale.com, 800-844-4099).

Don't let unused points expire! If you can't use all your points this year or prefer to use them later, you must contact DVC Member Services. Otherwise, those **points expire** at year's end. If you can't use points, bank them or try "renting out" your points (and non-DVC members may consider "renting" points to try out DVC).

Use points to book **at any Disney resort in the world**, Disney Cruise Line, Adventures by Disney, luxury hotels, and adventure travel vacations, or barter points for "swaps" at non-Disney resorts.

DVC members receive many **discounts** on annual passes, resort rooms (based on availability), dining, guided tours, etc.

DVC members staying at a DVC resort on points may purchase the **Disney Dining Plan** for the length of stay (see pages 202–203).

Anyone may **rent Disney Vacation Club points** from a DVC member, and this can be a great money-saver. For more information and folks willing to rent points, visit http://www.mouseowners.com.

NOTES

Vacancies at DVC resorts, now called Disney's Deluxe Villa Resorts, are made available to **nonmembers**—they are booked just like regular Disney resort reservations, and daily housekeeping is included. Thus, it may be very difficult to use your DVC points at a resort if your intended arrival date is 60 days away or less. Plan as far in advance as possible.

Visit our DVC forums at http://www.passporterboards.com/forums/owning-magic-disney-vacation-club/.

INFO

**Disney Vacation Club**

200 Celebration Place, Celebration, FL 34747-9903
Phone: 800-500-3990 Fax: 407-566-3393
DVC information kiosks are at most Disney parks and resorts.
Sales offices and models are at Disney's Saratoga Springs.
http://www.disneyvacationclub.com

# Hotel Plaza Resorts

Each of the following hotels are located on Disney property across from Downtown Disney, but are independently owned and operated. A variety of discounts may be available. Some of the Disney resort hotel benefits mentioned earlier in this chapter do not apply (such as Extra Magic Hour and package delivery). Do note that all the Hotel Plaza Resorts offer scheduled bus transportation to the parks (see sidebar on next page) and are within walking distance of Downtown Disney.

| *Hotel Name (in alphabetical order)* | *Starting Rates* | *Year Built* | *Year Renovated* |
|---|---|---|---|
| **DoubleTree Guest Suites Resort** | **$169+** | **1988** | **1999** |

*This all-suite hotel offers 229 one- and two-bedroom suites. All rooms come with dining areas, kitchenettes (refrigerator, microwave, and coffeemaker), separate living rooms with sofa beds, double-size or king-size beds, three TVs, two phones, in-room safe, hair dryer, iron and ironing board, and toiletries (no balconies). Suites accommodate up to six people (up to four adults). Amenities include a heated pool, wading pool, fitness center, arcade, one restaurant, one lounge, one pool bar, and room service. Look for the freshly baked chocolate chip cookies upon your arrival. Web: http://www.doubletreeguestsuites.com. Call 800-222-8733 or 407-934-1000.*

| **Grosvenor Resort** | **$119+** | **1972** | **1996** |
|---|---|---|---|

*A British-themed resort offering 629 rooms in a 19-story high-rise nestled beside Lake Buena Vista. All rooms come with a VCR and wet bar in addition to the standard two double-size beds or one king-size bed, satellite TV, coffeemaker (with coffee and tea), mini-bar, in-room safe, newspaper delivery, and toiletries (no balconies). Resort amenities include two heated pools, whirlpool spa, two tennis courts (as well as basketball, volleyball, and shuffleboard courts), a European spa, fitness center, arcade, one restaurant (with character breakfasts thrice weekly), one cafe, one pool bar, and room service. The MurderWatch Mystery Theatre is held here on Saturday nights (see page 238). Kids eat free with each paying adult. You can get great rates on Priceline.com. Web: http://www.grosvenorresort.com. Call 800-624-4109 or 407-828-4444.*

| **The Hilton** | **$249+** | **1984** | **2006** |
|---|---|---|---|

*This newly renovated first-class business hotel is located right across the street from the Downtown Disney Marketplace. The 814 rooms are luxurious, each offering "Serenity" beds (two doubles or one king), overstuffed chair, cable TV, two phones, hair dryer, iron and ironing board, coffeemaker, mini-bar, newspapers, high-speed Internet access ($9.95/day), and toiletries (no balconies or in-room safes). Amenities include two heated pools, kids water play area, two whirlpool spas, fitness center, arcade, shopping area, three eateries (one with character meals every Sunday), two cafes, and one lounge, one pool bar, and room service. The Hilton is the only Hotel Plaza Resort to offer the Extra Magic Hour perk (see page 32). Web: http://www.downtowndisneyhotels.com/Hilton.html. Call 800-445-8667 or 407-827-4000.*

| **Holiday Inn** | **$99+** | **1978** | **2007** |
|---|---|---|---|

*With 323 standard rooms and one suite, this renovated 14-story hotel offers clean, basic accommodations. Standard rooms come with two double beds or one king bed, balconies, satellite TV, hair dryer, iron and ironing board, coffeemaker, in-room safe, newspaper delivery, toiletries, and high-speed Internet. Additional amenities include Nintendo games (extra fee), two heated pools, wading pool, whirlpool spa, fitness center, arcade, one restaurant, one cafe, and room service. Web: http://www.downtowndisneyhotels.com/HolidayInn.html. Call 800-223-9930 or 407-828-8888.*

| Hotel Name (in alphabetical order) | Starting Rates | Year Built | Year Renovated |
|---|---|---|---|
| **Hotel Royal Plaza** | **$139+** | **1975** | **2006** |

*This hotel offers 394 standard rooms that each accommodate up to five guests and have a sitting area, balcony or patio, coffeemaker, and phone in addition to the new "Royal Beds" (two double beds or one king bed), daybed, 27" cable TV, in-room safe, hair dryer, iron and ironing board, newspaper delivery, high-speed Internet access, and toiletries. Rooms in the tower are slightly larger and offer upgraded bathrooms. Hotel amenities include a heated pool, whirlpool spa, four tennis courts, arcade, a restaurant (kids 12 and under eat free with a paying adult), a lounge, a pool bar, and room service. Of all the Hotel Plaza hotels, this is the one that gets the most rave reviews from other vacationers. Web: http://www.royalplaza.com. Call 800-248-7890 or 407-828-2828.*

| | | | |
|---|---|---|---|
| **Lake Buena Vista Best Western Resort** | **$128+** | **1973** | **1997** |

*This 18-story, Caribbean-themed hotel is on the shores of Lake Buena Vista. The resort offers 321 standard rooms (345 sq. ft.) and four suites, all of which have balconies. Rooms come with two queen beds or one king bed, satellite TV, hair dryer, iron and ironing board, coffeemaker (with coffee and tea), in-room safe, newspaper delivery, and toiletries. Other amenities include Nintendo games and premium movies for an extra fee, one heated pool, a wading pool, privileges to the DoubleTree fitness center, two eateries, two lounges, and room service. Formerly a Travelodge. Web: http://www.orlandoresorthotel.com. Call 800-348-3765 or 407-828-2424.*

| | | | |
|---|---|---|---|
| **Wyndham Palace Resort & Spa** | **$147+** | **1983** | **1998** |

*A high-rise hotel with 1,014 luxury guest rooms and suites. This is the largest of the hotels on Hotel Plaza Boulevard. It's also the closest hotel to Downtown Disney Marketplace. All rooms feature balconies or patios, two double beds or one king bed, cable TV, cordless phone, coffeemaker (with complimentary coffee and tea), in-room safe, hair dryer, iron and ironing board, newspaper delivery, and toiletries. High-speed Internet access, WebTV, Sony PlayStation games, and premium movies are available for an additional fee. Resort amenities include three heated pools, whirlpool spa, tennis and sand volleyball courts, full-service European-style spa with fitness center and beauty salon, arcade, three restaurants (one with character breakfasts every Sunday), a cafe, two lounges, a pool bar, and room service. Formerly known as Buena Vista Palace. Web: http://www.wyndham.com. Call 407-827-2727.*

## Hotel Plaza Resort Transportation to the Parks

Guests staying at these Hotel Plaza Resorts get free bus transportation to the four major Disney parks, Downtown Disney, and the water parks. Hotel Plaza buses—which differ from the standard Disney buses—run every 30 minutes and typically start one hour before park opening and continue up to two hours after park closing. Note that buses to the Magic Kingdom drop you off at the Transportation and Ticket Center (TTC), where you can take a monorail or boat to the park entrance or transfer to another bus to another Disney destination. Disney's Animal Kingdom buses may operate only once an hour during the slower times of the day. Within walking distance is Downtown Disney, where you can also board Disney buses to other resorts. Those bound for the water parks should check with their hotel for bus schedules. Guests who want to venture off to Universal Studios/Islands of Adventure, SeaWorld, Wet 'n' Wild, or the Belz Outlet Mall can take a shuttle for $12/person round-trip—check with your hotel on pick-up times. Many guests who stay at these hotels recommend you get a rental car—all hotels but the Lake Buena Vista Best Western and Hotel Royal Plaza have a rental car desk.

# Hotels Near Walt Disney World

Below are several hotels and motels near Walt Disney World (but not on Disney property) that either we've stayed in and recommend or at which our readers report good experiences. More hotels are listed on following pages.

| *Hotel Name (in alphabetical order)* | *Starting Rates* | *Year Built* | *Year Renovated* |
|---|---|---|---|
| **Nickelodeon Family Suites** | **$180+** | **1999** | **2005** |

*Besides the resort's close proximity to Walt Disney World (just 3 miles/5 km), the hotel offers unique and very convenient "KidSuites" with a living room, kitchenette, master bedroom, and kids' room. The kids get a bunk bed, TV, game system (fee applies), and a small table and chairs—decorated with SpongeBob SquarePants, Rugrats, The Fairly OddParents, Jimmy Neutron, or Danny Phantom. A three-bedroom KidSuite with an extra adult bedroom is also available. If you don't have kids, you can get a room with a different configuration, such as the Nick@Nite Suite (whirlpool tub and 50" TV) and the Kitchen Suite (full kitchen). A breakfast buffet and Nickelodeon character breakfast are available. The resort also has a huge pool complex with seven water slides, four-story water tower, zero-entry pool, water playground, two hot tubs, and a small miniature golf course. There is a free scheduled shuttle bus to Walt Disney World, but we found it more convenient to drive. Visit http://www.nickhotel.com or call 407-387-5437 or 866-462-6425. Hotel address: 14500 Continental Gateway, Orlando, FL 32821*

| **Radisson Resort Orlando-Celebration** | **$79+** | **1987** | **2005** |
|---|---|---|---|

*We enjoyed our stay at this 718-room, 6-story deluxe hotel just 1.5 miles (2.5 km) from the gates of Walt Disney World. Guest rooms accommodate up to four guests with either one king-size bed or two double-size beds. Recently refurbished rooms come in either pool or courtyard views and feature modern Italian furniture and marble bathrooms. Amenities include a 25" TV, mini refrigerator, in-room safe, coffeemaker, iron and ironing board, hair dryer, make-up mirror, voice mail, data ports, and free high-speed Internet access (most rooms). For a $7 daily service fee, you get enhanced shuttles to attractions, 24-hour access to the fitness center, use of lighted tennis courts, free local and toll calls, and free newspaper delivery. The resort has two pools, a water slide, a wading pool, and two hot tubs, as well as playground, and arcade. Food service includes a full-service restaurant (open for breakfast and dinner), a deli with Pizza Hut items, a sports bar, a pool bar, and room service. Note that kids under 10 eat free when accompanied by a paying adult. For the best rates, visit http://orlando.guestselectresorts.com or call 866-358-5609 or 407-396-7000 and ask for the "Y-PASS" rate code. 2900 Parkway Boulevard, Kissimmee, FL 34747*

| **Sheraton Safari Resort** | **$125+** | **1994** | **1998** |
|---|---|---|---|

*While this isn't equivalent to Disney's Animal Kingdom Lodge, this safari-themed resort is a winner with kids and adults alike. The 489-room, 6-story hotel is located just 1/4 mile (1/2 km) from the Disney property (you can't walk to it, but it is a short drive or ride on the scheduled shuttle). Guest rooms come in standard (one king-size or two double-sized beds), Safari Suites (with kitchenette and separate parlor), and deluxe suites (with full kitchens and large parlors). Standard rooms accommodate up to four guests, or five guests with the rental of a roll-away bed. All rooms have a balcony or patio, TV with PlayStation, two phones with voice mail, dataports, and high-speed Internet access, hair dryer, make-up mirror, coffeemaker, iron and ironing board, and in-room safe. The resort features a large pool with a 79-ft. water slide, wading pool, hot tub, fitness center, and arcade. One full-service restaurant (Casablanca's) offers breakfast and dinner (kids under 10 eat free with paying adults), along with the Outpost Deli (for lunch and dinner), the ZanZibar Watering Hole, and room service (6:30 am–10:00 pm). Visit http://www.sheratonsafari.com or call 407-239-0444 or 800-423-3297. Hotel address: 12205 Apopka-Vineland Road, Orlando, FL 32836*

# Hotels Near Universal Studios

Below are the three on-site hotels at Universal Studios Florida (about 7 miles/11 kilometers from Walt Disney World property). Note that guests staying in these hotels get special privileges at Universal Studios and Islands of Adventure, such as the "Universal Express" ride access system to bypass attraction lines, priority seating at some restaurants, complimentary package delivery, on-site transportation, and more. Each of these hotels accepts pets and offers pet-related services. All of these resorts are operated by Loews Hotels (http://www.loewshotels.com).

| *Hotel Name (in alphabetical order)* | *Starting Rates* | *Year Built* |
|---|---|---|
| **Hard Rock Hotel** | **$259+** | **2001** |

*If you think Hard Rock Cafe is great, this recently-renovated 650-room hotel really rocks. Step inside a rock star's mansion filled to the rafters with a million-dollar rock memorabilia collection. Standard guest rooms (365 sq. ft.) feature two queen beds or one king bed, flat-panel TV, MP3 station, stereos, two-line cordless phones, mini-bar, coffeemaker, in-room safe, hair dryer, bathroom scale, iron and ironing board, and toiletries. There are 14 Kids Suites with a separate sleeping area for the kids. Hotel amenities include a heated pool with a water slide and underwater audio system, wading pool, two whirlpool spas, sand beach, fitness center, two restaurants (including a Hard Rock Cafe with a concert venue), a cafe, a lounge, a pool bar, and room service. Web: http://www.hardrockhotelorlando.com/locations/hotels/orlando. Call 800-BE-A-STAR (800-232-7827) or 407-445-ROCK. Hotel address: 5800 Universal Blvd., Orlando, FL 32819*

| | | |
|---|---|---|
| **Portofino Bay Hotel** | **$279+** | **1999** |

*Stay in this remarkably themed resort and get a big taste of the Italian Riviera. The hotel is a deluxe recreation of the seaside village of Portofino, Italy, developed with the help of Steven Spielberg. There may be cobblestone streets outside, but luxury abounds inside. 750 rooms and suites are available, including several Kids Suites. Standard rooms come with either two queen beds or one king bed and double sofa bed, cable TV, two phones, mini-bar, coffeemaker, in-room safe, hair dryer, iron and ironing board, and toiletries. Deluxe rooms offer a bit more space, an upgraded bathroom, a VCR, CD player, and fax machine. Resort amenities include three heated pools, a water slide, whirlpool spas, a full-service spa, fitness center, a Bocce ball court, four restaurants, three cafes, a lounge, and room service. Web: http://www.portofinobay.com. Call 407-503-1000 or 800-232-7827. Hotel address: 5601 Universal Blvd., Orlando, FL 32819*

| | | |
|---|---|---|
| **Royal Pacific Resort** | **$209+** | **2002** |

*This relatively new hotel is Universal Studio's lowest-priced resort, boasting 1,000 guest rooms with a South Seas theme and lush landscaping. Standard rooms (355 sq. ft.) accommodate up to five guests (four adults) and feature two queen beds or one king bed, cable TV, mini-bar, coffeemaker, in-room safe, hair dryer, iron and ironing board, and toiletries. The Club Rooms add robes, bathroom scales, turndown service, newspaper delivery, continental breakfast, and afternoon beer/wine/snacks. Resort amenities include a huge pool, kids' water play area, wading pool, two whirlpool spas, sand beach, volleyball court, putting green, fitness center, arcade, a supervised children's program, two restaurants, a cafe, a lounge, a pool bar, and room service. Web: http://www.loewshotels.com/hotels/orlando_royal_pacific or http://www.usf.com and click on "Hotels." Call 888-322-5541 or 407-503-3000. Hotel address: 6300 Hollywood Way, Orlando, FL 32819*

→

# More Hotels Outside Disney

You may prefer to stay "off-property" to attend a conference, visit other parks, or pay a bargain rate. Below are several popular hotels, motels, and inns off property. We've included starting rates for standard rooms (off-season), driving distance to Downtown Disney, available transportation to Disney, the year it was built (plus the year it was renovated, if available), if it is a Disney "Good Neighbor Hotel" (able to sell multi-day passes), a short description, web site (if available), and a phone number.

| Hotel/Motel Name (in alphabetical order) | Starting Rates | Distance to WDW | Trans Avail. | Year Built | Good Neighbor |
|---|---|---|---|---|---|
| **AmeriSuites LBV** | $64+ | 3mi/5km | Bus | '00 | |
| *151-suite resort with free breakfast. http://www.amerisuites.com. 407-997-1300* | | | | | |
| **Caribe Royale Resort** | $179+ | 4mi/6km | Bus($) | '97 | ✔ |
| *Ten-story suite hotel with living rooms and wet bars. AAA discount. 407-238-8000* | | | | | |
| **The Celebration Hotel** | $249+ | 8mi/12km | Bus | '99 | ✔ |
| *Upscale business hotel within Disney's town of Celebration. 407-566-6000* | | | | | |
| **DoubleTree Club Hotel** | $101+ | 1.5mi/2km | Bus | '86('99) | ✔ |
| *246 rooms and kid suites. http://www.doubletreeclublbv.com. AAA discount. 407-239-4646* | | | | | |
| **Embassy Suites LBV** | $111+ | 3mi/5km | Bus | '85 | ✔ |
| *All-suite hotel with a Caribbean theme in Lake Buena Vista. 407-239-1144* | | | | | |
| **Gaylord Palms** | $269+ | 1mi/1.5km | Bus | '02 | ✔ |
| *1,406-room luxury resort near Disney. http://www.gaylordpalms.com. 407-586-0000* | | | | | |
| **Hawthorne Suites LBV** | $114+ | 1mi/1.5km | Bus | '00 | ✔ |
| *Rooms and suites, all with free breakfast. http://www.hawthornsuiteslbv.com. 407-597-5000* | | | | | |
| **Holiday Inn Maingate East** | $54+ | 6mi/10km | Bus($) | '73('99) | ✔ |
| *Standard rooms and Kidsuites. Located in Kissimmee. 407-396-4488* | | | | | |
| **Homewood Suites** | $80+ | 6mi/10km | Bus | '91('00) | ✔ |
| *Two-room suites with kitchen, living area, and bedroom. AAA discounts. 407-396-2229* | | | | | |
| **Hyatt Regency Grand Cypress** | $249+ | 3mi/5km | Bus | '84('97) | |
| *750-room hotel with balconies, private lake, nature trails, and golf. 407-239-1234* | | | | | |
| **Marriott Orlando World Center** | $299+ | 4mi/6km | Bus($) | '86('99) | |
| *28-floor, 2,000-room resort with four restaurants and a convention center. 407-239-4200* | | | | | |
| **Quality Suites Maingate** | $79+ | 6mi/10km | Bus | '90('99) | ✔ |
| *One- and two-bedroom suites with living rooms and kitchenettes. 407-396-8040* | | | | | |
| **Red Roof Inn** | $40+ | 5mi/8km | – | '89('97) | |
| *Basic budget lodging with a good reputation. Located in Kissimmee. 407-396-0065* | | | | | |
| **Sheraton's Vistana Resort** | $249+ | 3mi/5km | Bus | '80('97) | |
| *One- and two-bedroom villas. Details at http://www.sheraton.com. 407-239-3100* | | | | | |
| **Staybridge Suites** | $135+ | 2mi/3km | Bus | '93('98) | ✔ |
| *All-suite hotel with one- and two-bedroom suites and free breakfast. 407-238-0777* | | | | | |

Tip: You really need a car when staying at off-property hotels. Even when shuttles to the parks are provided, the schedules and drop-off/pick-up points aren't accommodating. If you are flying to Orlando and staying off-site, be sure to factor in the cost of renting a car.

# Vacation Home Rentals

Another off-property lodging option that can provide excellent value is a vacation home rental. Vacation homes are typically free-standing **houses or condos with several bedrooms, kitchens, and pool access** ... some vacation homes even have their own private pools and hot tubs. Vacation homes are ideal for large families and groups. Many vacation home rental companies operate near Walt Disney World, and choosing from among them can get confusing. Important points to look for in a vacation home rental company include proximity of homes to Walt Disney World, quality of customer service, prices, and extra fees. We've only tried one rental company—ALL STAR Vacation Homes—but we've been so impressed that we've been back several times. Below is their information, followed by general contact information for some other vacation home companies for which we've received positive reviews from our readers.

**ALL STAR Vacation Homes** really shines in our book. ALL STAR Vacation Homes has a full guest service center near their properties; more than 150 homes within four miles of Walt Disney World (we can see Expedition Everest from the patio of our favorite home at 8009 Acadia Estates); excellent amenities in clean, luxurious homes; and great deals on a wide variety of home sizes. Most homes have computers with Internet, and all guests have free access to their Internet Cafe. Their customer service has always been helpful and friendly, and their vacation homes have secured and gated entrances. Vacation home rentals start as low as $119/night. We could go on and on ... actually, we have in the form of several feature articles (see http://www.passporter.com/asvh.asp). For more information and to make a reservation, phone 888-825-6405 or visit http://www.allstarvacationhomes.com and ask for the PassPorter rate deal (free standard rental car or $125 off a 7-night home rental).

*Relaxing in our ALL STAR Vacation Home*

**Florida Spirit Vacation Homes**—More than 100 vacation homes within six to ten miles of Walt Disney World, which you can pre-select online. http://www.floridaspiritvacationhome.com, 866-357-7474.

**Mouse Pads Vacation Rentals**—Offers homes and townhomes, all with private pools. http://www.mousepadsorlando.com, 866-668-7335.

Electronic, interactive worksheet available– see page 287

# Lodging Worksheet

Use this worksheet to jot down preferences, scribble information during phone calls, and keep all your discoveries together. Don't worry about being neat—just be thorough! Circle your final choices once you decide to go with them (to avoid any confusion) and be sure to transfer them to your Room(s) PassPocket.

Arrival date: ____________ Alternates: ____________

Departure date: ____________ Alternates: ____________

Total number of nights: ______ Alternates: ____________

We prefer to stay at: ______________________

Alternates: ______________________

______________________

Using your preferences above, call Disney's Reservations phone line at 407-939-6244 and jot down resort availabilities in the table on the next page. It works best for us when we write the available days in the far left column, followed by the resort, view/type, special requests, rate, and total cost in the columns to the right. Draw lines between different availabilities. Circle those you decide to use, and then record the reservation numbers, as you'll need them to confirm, cancel, or make changes later. The two columns at the far right let you note confirmations and room deposits so you don't forget and consequently lose your reservation.

**Additional Notes:**

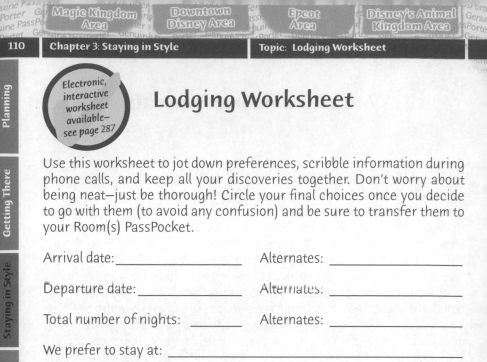

HOTEL

Collect information on lodging in the table below. We've included some sample notes to show you how we do it, but you're welcome to use this space in any way you please.

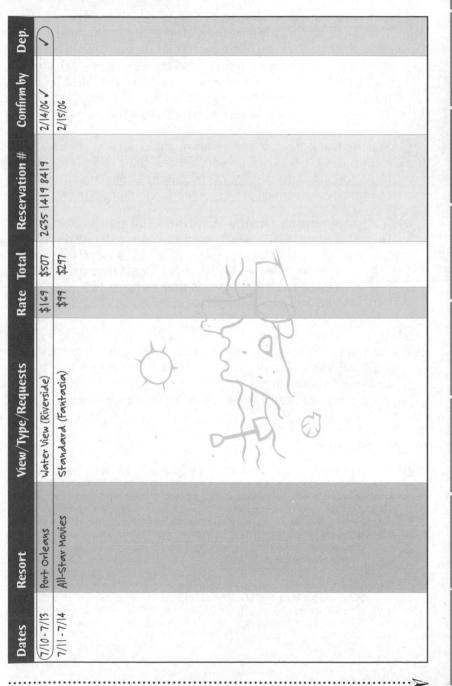

| Dates | Resort | View/Type/Requests | Rate | Total | Reservation # | Confirm by | Dep. |
|---|---|---|---|---|---|---|---|
| 7/10-7/13 | Port Orleans | Water View (Riverside) | $169 | $507 | 2635 1419 8419 | 2/14/06 ✓ | ✓ |
| 7/11-7/14 | All-Star Movies | Standard (Fantasia) | $99 | $297 | | 2/15/06 | |

# The Last Resort

"Schedule some **pool time**, especially if you have young children. This can be particularly refreshing after a long, hot day in the parks. All of the Disney resort pools have great themes. I work at a travel agency and when I ask parents (who have taken their children to Walt Disney World for the first time) what the kids liked best, it is usually the swimming pool ... and the Mickey ice cream bars."
*– Contributed by Barbara Hargrove, a winner in our 2007 Lodging Tip Contest*

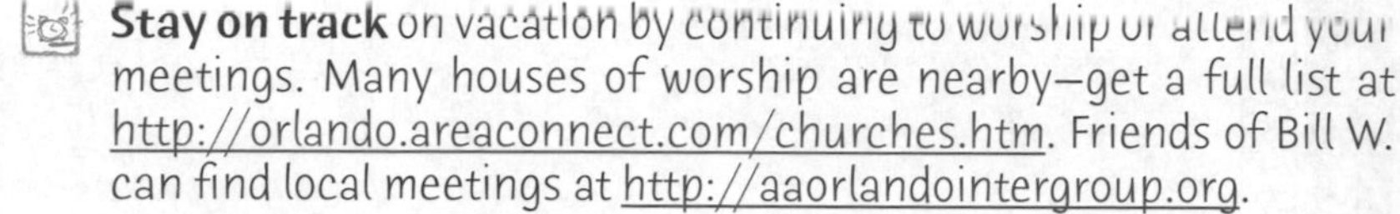

**Stay on track** on vacation by continuing to worship or attend your meetings. Many houses of worship are nearby—get a full list at http://orlando.areaconnect.com/churches.htm. Friends of Bill W. can find local meetings at http://aaorlandointergroup.org.

"Consider **renting Disney Vacation Club points** to stay at a Disney's Deluxe Villa Resort for the price of a moderate resort. This tip saved us money and allowed us to stay at a much nicer resort in a much nicer room than we otherwise would have been able to." *[See information on Disney Vacation Club on pages 102–103.]*
*– Contributed by Matt Riker, a winner in our 2007 Lodging Tip Contest*

"To put into **perspective** just how vast Walt Disney World really is, the cities of Buffalo, New York City, Grand Rapids, Miami, Newark, and San Francisco are all smaller. In fact, Walt Disney World is larger than the countries of Nauru and San Marino combined! Things are not just around the block here." *– Contributed by Tom Anderson*

## Magical Memory

*"Before we left for Walt Disney World, I prepared a set of tip envelopes for Mousekeeping (Disney Housekeeping)—one per night of our stay. I had my preschooler, Sammy, help me decorate each with stickers and drawings of his favorite Disney friends, and a short thank-you note. Then we placed tip money in each envelope. Each morning as we left for the parks, I let Sammy choose a tip envelope and set it out for the housekeeper. This was a great project to help him feel involved with the planning of the trip and get him excited about Disney World. It also helped me, as I didn't have to scrounge around for tip money each morning!"*

*...as told by Disney vacationer Bonnie M.*

*Tip: You can download free "Mousekeeping" envelope templates at a fellow PassPorter reader's web site, Eileen's Mouse House, located at http://www.remleml.com/mouse/. You'll find many other fun and useful Disney-related items here to download, including luggage tags, touring cards, and "fun jar" labels for loose change! Well worth a visit!*

# Touring the "World"

GET
where you
want to go
with ease


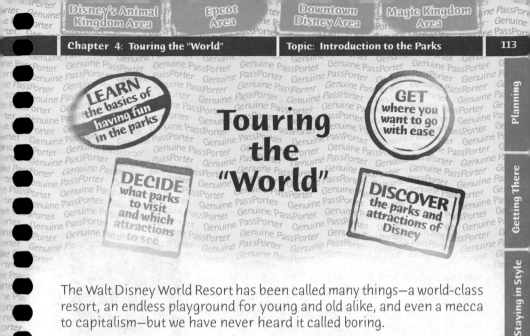

DECIDE what parks to visit and which attractions to see

The Walt Disney World Resort has been called many things—a world-class resort, an endless playground for young and old alike, and even a mecca to capitalism—but we have never heard it called boring.

The "World" (as it is known to insiders) began in 1971. Opening on October 1st of that year, it offered a small fraction of what we enjoy today: the Magic Kingdom park and the Contemporary, Polynesian, and Fort Wilderness resorts. It was the dream of an All-American leader, Walt Disney, who didn't live to see opening day. Yet his legacy flourished, becoming the 43-square-mile wonderland we know and love today.

One of the things that makes the Walt Disney World Resort so special is the attention to detail and service. It takes tens of thousands of people, known as "cast members," working together to stage the "show" we see as "guests." You'll notice that Disney often uses special words to describe their unique services and attractions. There's nothing mundane here.

To help you recognize these terms, we begin with Park Passwords, defining the "Disneyese" you'll hear and read, such as the much-touted "FASTPASS" ride reservation system. We then move on to practical matters, such as transportation and admission to the parks. Next come our detailed attraction descriptions for the four major theme parks, along with the largest theme park maps you'll find in any Disney guidebook. (They fold out!) Descriptions and maps of the smaller parks follow, along with hints, tips, and a Touring Worksheet to help you decide what to do. Don't overlook our at-a-glance attraction lists and theme park touring plans.

October 1, 2007, marked Epcot's 25th birthday. While no celebratory plans had been announced at press time, the rumors abound! You can read more about Epcot's 25th birthday later in this chapter. We also include information on the upcoming additions to Disney-MGM Studios, which changes its name to Disney's Hollywood Studios on January 1, 2008.

So let's go around the "World" in 86 pages!

# Park Passwords

**Admission Media**—Park passes (tickets). See pages 116–117 for pass details and rates.

**Attraction**—An individual ride, show, or exhibit.

**Baby Care Centers**—Special centers are found in each of the major parks. All restrooms (men's included) support diaper changing.

**Cast Member**—All Disney employees are "cast members"—they wear white name tags with their names.

**Disney Dollars and Gift Cards**—Disney's own currency, good throughout the Walt Disney World Resort.

**ECV**—Electric Convenience Vehicle. You can rent these four-wheeled scooters at the parks and elsewhere. See page 34.

**Extra Magic Hour**—Resort guests can enjoy certain parks earlier or later on certain days. See page 32 for details.

**FASTPASS**—Disney's ride "reservation" system (see below).

*Splash Mountain FASTPASS*

## Making the Most of FASTPASS

Tired of waiting in long lines? Disney's FASTPASS system reduces the amount of time you spend in line—and it's free to all park guests! Just slip your park pass into a machine near an attraction with FASTPASS. Out pops your pass and a printed ticket (see sample below) that promises you a ride during a particular period some time later in the day. Depending on how many tickets have been issued to other guests, you may be able to return in 25 minutes, or hours later. When you receive your FASTPASS, look for the time you can get your next FASTPASS (you can usually get another immediately after the return time of your current pass, or in two hours, whichever comes first). The FASTPASS ticket now also shows important information, such as height restrictions. When your FASTPASS return time arrives, walk up to the attraction's "FASTPASS Return" entrance, show your FASTPASS to the cast member, and walk on in. There's usually still a short wait, and you'll experience most or all "pre-show" activities. Every FASTPASS attraction has a "Standby" line, which is the regular wait-in-line queue—the wait time for the Standby queue is typically half as long as the FASTPASS return time.

We recommend you get your first FASTPASS early in the day for one of the more popular rides, as FASTPASS tickets can run out on busy days. Our attraction descriptions later in this chapter indicate if an attraction has FASTPASS (look for the FP icon), and our touring plans give recommendations on which FASTPASSes to get throughout a day. Note that FASTPASS isn't always available, especially later in the day when all tickets have been issued. **Tip**: Enjoy the same ride twice! Get a FASTPASS, then get in the Standby queue. By the time your ride is over, your FASTPASS may be ready to use. Note that the FASTPASS system may be used for special events, such as during Star Wars Weekend.

**Sample FASTPASS**

Return Anytime Between
**9:45 am**
and
**10:45 am**
Riders must be at least 40" (102cm) to experience Splash Mountain

Another FASTPASS® ticket will be available after 9:45 am
**SUN JUN 17**
6/17/2007 8:49

*Actual size: 2" x 3 ½"*

**First Aid**—First aid stations are at the four theme parks and two water parks (see maps).

**Guest Relations**—An information desk, located both inside and outside the front gates of all four major parks. Lobby Concierge at resorts provides a similar range of services.

**Guidemaps**—Free maps available at the parks. See also "Times Guide."

**Land**—An area of a park organized around a common theme.

**Lockers**—Available for a fee ($7 + $2 deposit) in each park and at the Transportation and Ticket Center. Save your receipt for a new locker at another park on the same day.

**Lost & Found**—Lost items or children can be claimed at a central location in each park. Consult a guidemap or a cast member. Also see page 251.

**Money**—Pay with Disney Dollars, Disney Gift Cards, cash, traveler's checks, American Express, MasterCard, Visa, Discover, JCB, Diner's Club, and Disney Visa Reward Vouchers. Disney Dollars and Gift Cards are sold at parks, resorts, and most U.S. Disney Stores. ATMs are in the parks, resorts, and Downtown Disney. Disney resort guests can charge to their room.

**Packages**—Purchases can be delivered and held for pick-up near the park exit at all major parks, and Disney resort guests can have packages delivered to their resort the next afternoon free of charge. Inquire about package delivery before purchasing.

**Park**—Disney's recreational complexes requiring admission, which include the four major parks (Magic Kingdom, Epcot, Disney's Hollywood Studios, and Disney's Animal Kingdom) and five minor parks (Blizzard Beach, Typhoon Lagoon, Pleasure Island, Wide World of Sports, and DisneyQuest). Descriptions begin on page 121.

**Parking**—Fee is $10 per day for cars, $11 for camper/trailers, and $14 for bus/tractor trailers. Parking is free to Disney resort guests; Swan/Dolphin, Shades of Green, and The Hilton guests; and Annual Passholders. Disney Dining Experience members park free after 5:00 pm. Tip: Save your receipt to park free at another park on the same day.

**PhotoPass**—This service lets you view all photos taken by Disney's photographers at http://www.disneyphotopass.com. No more waiting in long queues to view/buy photos.

**Queue**—A waiting area or line for an attraction or character meet.

**Re-Entry**—Guests may exit and re-enter the same park on the same day. Be sure to hold on to your pass and bring photo ID. Disney now uses a safe finger scan (biometrics) rather than handstamps when you enter and re-enter a park (see photo).

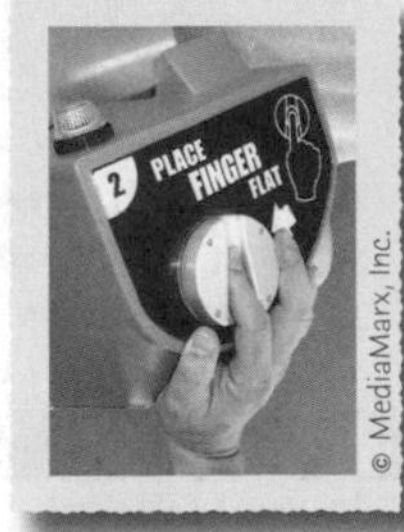

*All guests get a finger scan upon park entry*

**Security**—All bags are searched before entering parks.

**Shopping**—Shops sell Disney and themed items. We list the best shops in this chapter.

**Smoking**—Prohibited in resorts, buildings, queues, and parks, except in designated smoking areas (see park maps).

**Strollers & Wheelchairs**—Strollers ($10/single stroller, $18/double stroller, $8–$16/day for length-of-stay rental), wheelchairs ($10/day—no deposit, $8/day for length-of-stay rental), and ECVs ($35/day + $5 deposit) can be rented at the parks. Limited availability—arrive early, bring your own, or rent elsewhere (see page 34). You can save your receipt for a free rental at another park on the same day, but there is no guarantee a rental will be available.

**Tax**—Florida and county sales tax totals 6.5%.

**Times Guide**—Free listing of attraction hours and showtimes. Times Guides are available when you enter the parks.

# Park Passes

It's safest to budget **$76**/day for ages 10+ (**$64**/kids ages 3-9), the single-day/single-park base price with tax for the major parks (based on the last price increase in August 2007). The "Magic Your Way" multi-day passes deliver flexibility and savings (especially for stays of five days and longer), so you can do more at a lower price. The prices below include tax). Estimate a 6%–12% increase when rates go up again (sometime in mid-2008?).

### Magic Your Way Tickets — *Actual 2007-2008 Rates*

*Magic Your Way tickets are available for 1-10 days. Guests can stick to basic admission or add one or more options at the time of purchase (see explanations below). Magic Your Way replaces single-day passes and all varieties of Park Hopper passes. A Magic Your Way* ***Base Ticket*** *($76-$240) is good for entry to a single major park (Magic Kingdom, Epcot, Disney's Hollywood Studios, or Disney's Animal Kingdom) for each day of the ticket. Multiday Base Tickets bring substantial discounts (see chart on the next page), so it pays to buy your admission all at once. Multiday Base Tickets expire 14 days after the first use, but they do not have to be used on consecutive days. Buy only as much admission as you'll actually need for your visit to Disney. Note that multiday Base Tickets are imprinted with the guest's name, so they are not transferable. The* ***Park Hopping*** *option (add $47.93) lets you visit more than one major park on the same day, for the length of your ticket. Available with any Base Ticket, this option is costly unless you spend four or more days at the parks, but it's indispensible if you plan to visit all four parks in fewer than four days, and it can maximize the enjoyment of any longer stay. The Magic Your Way* ***Water Parks Fun and More*** *option (add $53.25) adds a limited number of single-day, single-park admissions for the minor parks (Blizzard Beach, Typhoon Lagoon, Pleasure Island, DisneyQuest, and Wide World of Sports) to any Base Ticket. Each Water Parks Fun and More option is worth $10–$38, depending on where you use it. Purchase this feature with 1-day Base Tickets and you receive two Water Parks Fun and More options, while 2- to 10-day Base Tickets receive the same number of options as there are days on the pass. Regardless of how many options you receive, the cost to add this feature is always the same. As long as you make a minimum of two visits to the more costly minor parks, you'll get your money's worth. The* ***Premium*** *option (add $101) is a combination of a Base Ticket, Park Hopping, and Water Parks Fun and More options (but at no additional savings). The* ***No Expiration*** *option (add $15–$180) is best suited for those who plan to save the unused portion of a multiday ticket for a future vacation. The 14-day life span of a Base Ticket is generally enough for any one vacation. Prices for the various tickets are listed in the comparison chart on the next page.*

### Annual Pass — *Actual 2007-2008 Rates*

*Unlimited admission to the four major parks for a full year, plus special privileges. An Annual Pass ($477/$421) costs less than two 3-day Magic Your Way Base Tickets with Park Hopping. Annual Passes also kick in great discounts on resorts (based on availability) and other privileges, such as a newsletter and events. There are also annual passes for the water parks ($106/$86), Pleasure Island ($60), DisneyQuest ($95/$76), and water parks plus DisneyQuest ($137/$105). You cannot share an Annual Pass (or any other multiday pass).*

### Premium Annual Pass — *Actual 2007-2008 Rates*

*A Premium Annual Pass ($617/$543) offers the same privileges as the regular Annual Pass plus unlimited admission to the minor parks (including DisneyQuest) for $140 more. Five minor park visits cover the added cost. A Premium Annual Pass costs less than two 3-day Premium Magic Your Way tickets with a No Expiration option, and it is good for a full year.*

**Old Ticket Media**: If you have an old Park Hopper with unused days on it, you may use those days, but you can no longer upgrade old ticket media if it has been used.

**Upgrades and Exchanges**: Within 14 days of your pass's issue, upgrade or apply the unused value to a better pass. Visit Guest Relations/Lobby Concierge before you go home.

**Advance Purchase Discounts**: Historically Disney offered small discounts if your purchased your pass in advance, but as of August 2007 these discounts were elminated.

**Disney Vacation Club Discounts**: Discounts of about $100 are available on Annual Passes for members of the immediate family residing in the same household.

**AAA**: Members (see page 11) can expect some sort of discount (historically 5%) on some passes. You must purchase tickets directly from AAA to get the discount.

**Florida Resident Discounts**: It pays to live nearby. Florida Resident Seasonal Passes work like Annual Passes, but with blackout dates in busy seasons. There are some other special deals for Florida residents only, including discounted Annual Passes. A new one-day ticket for Florida residents is available with a small, pre-arrival discount–check the Disney World web site for details.

**Military Discounts:** Discounts of roughly 7%–8% may be available on admission–check with your Exchange shop or MWR (Morale, Welfare, and Recreation) office. Some offices may need to pre-order your tickets, so we advise you check with them well in advance. Keep an ear out for special programs for active military personnel–in recent years, Disney offered all active military personnel a free five-day park hopper, with discounted admission for up to five family members or friends. To check on current specials and buy tickets, phone 407-939-4636, or visit Shades of Green (see page 98) upon arrival.

**Online Ticket Brokers**–These folks sell legitimate, unused tickets at excellent rates: http://www.ticketmania.com (877-811-9233), http://www.floridaorlandotickets.net (407-344-0030), or http://www.mapleleaftickets.com (800-841-2837). Be wary of others hawking tickets, including eBay and timeshares.

**Kids Ride Free (Well, Some Do)**: Kids under 3 are admitted into the parks for free (and get a free ride if the ride allows someone that small). Anyone 10 and over is considered an adult in the eyes of the ticket booth. Passes for kids ages 3-9 cost about 20% less than adult passes. Also, the option-filled pass you buy for yourself is usually more than your child needs, especially if you use childcare programs (detailed on pages 254-255).

**Pass Comparison Chart**: Options and prices for your number of days in the parks. *(2007 prices for adult, nondiscounted passes purchased at the gate, including tax.)*

| Pass Type Days: | 1 | 2 | 3 | 4 | 5 | 6 | 7 | 8 | 9 | 10 | 11 | 12 | 13 | 14 |
|---|---|---|---|---|---|---|---|---|---|---|---|---|---|---|
| Base (single day/park) | $76 | $148 | $216 | $225 | $229 | $231 | $233 | $236 | $238 | $240 | | | | |
| Base + No Expiration | | $164 | $238 | $274 | $293 | $300 | $334 | $374 | $402 | $431 | | | | |
| Base + Park Hopping | $123 | $196 | $264 | $274 | $277 | $279 | $281 | $283 | $285 | $288 | | | | |
| Base + Park Hop. + No Exp. | | $212 | $285 | $322 | $341 | $348 | $382 | $422 | $451 | $479 | | | | |
| Base + Water Parks & More | $129 | $201 | $269 | $279 | $282 | $284 | $286 | $289 | $291 | $293 | | | | |
| Base + Water Parks + No. Exp. | | $217 | $291 | $327 | $346 | $354 | $388 | $427 | $456 | $485 | | | | |
| Premium | $177 | $249 | $317 | $327 | $330 | $332 | $334 | $337 | $339 | $341 | | | | |
| Premium + No Exp. | | $265 | $339 | $375 | $394 | $402 | $436 | $475 | $504 | $533 | | | | |
| Annual Pass | | | | | | | | | | | $477 → | | | |
| Premium Annual Pass | | | | | | | | | | | | | $617 → | |

*For more details and updates, visit http://www.passporter.com/wdw/parkpasses.htm.*

# Getting Around the Resort and Parks

The internal **transportation system** at the Walt Disney World Resort is quite extensive, with buses, boats, and the famed monorail all doing their part to shuttle guests around the property. Transportation hubs exist at each major theme park and Downtown Disney, where you can reach nearly any other place in the "World" by bus, monorail, or boat. The Transportation and Ticket Center (TTC) near the Magic Kingdom forms another hub, where you can get the monorail, ferryboat, and various buses. For current route information, see our property transportation chart on the right, check with a transportation cast member, or call 407-WDW-RIDE (407-939-7433).

**Bus service** is the cornerstone of the Walt Disney World transportation system. It is efficient, if occasionally confusing. With a few exceptions, bus routes run every 15 to 20 minutes, from about one hour prior to park opening until about one hour after closing. Bus stops are clearly marked (see photo to right). Travel times vary by route. Be sure to build in extra time for travel. Tip: Special early-morning "character breakfast" buses visit all Disney resorts to pick up guests—ask about it at your resort. Most buses are lift-equipped to accommodate a limited number of wheelchairs and ECVs (usually two at a time).

*Waiting for a bus at the All-Star Sports Resort*

**Monorail** trains run along two circular routes for the Magic Kingdom. The express route visits the park and the Transportation and Ticket Center (TTC), while the resort route also stops at the Contemporary, Polynesian, and Grand Floridian resorts. A separate line connects the TTC to Epcot. Monorails run from 7:00 am until 90 minutes after park closing.

If you **drive**, you'll find ample parking at the parks. Use the map on the back flap of your PassPorter to get around the "World." **Tip:** Jot the row number and name of your parking lot in your PassPorter so you don't forget where you parked. Also, if you intend to take advantage of Extra Magic Hour (EMH) mornings (see page 32), we recommend you avoid driving to the Magic Kingdom—it may be difficult to get into the park early enough. If you do drive, the gates at the TTC generally open between 7:15 am and 7:30 am on EMH mornings.

From several locales, **boats** (also known as launches, ferries, cruisers, and Friendships) usher guests to the Magic Kingdom, Epcot, Disney's Hollywood Studios, and Downtown Disney and between some resorts. Boats generally depart every 15–30 minutes. At the Magic Kingdom, large ferries transport guests from the TTC to the gates, and a **railroad** encircles the park. Small boats run between the Magic Kingdom and the nearby resorts. At Epcot, "**Friendship**" boats shuttle you between points in the World Showcase.

By far the most reliable and common method of transportation within the "World" is **walking**. You can't walk between most parks and resorts—it's too far and there are few sidewalks, making it unsafe. You will, however, walk a lot around the parks, the resorts, and even between some parks and resorts. Bring comfortable, broken-in, walking shoes!

# Disney Property Transportation Chart

*Note: TTC = Transportation and Ticket Center (see previous page)*

| To get to the Magic Kingdom from... | Take the... |
|---|---|
| Polynesian or Grand Floridian | Monorail or boat |
| Contemporary | Monorail or walk |
| Wilderness Lodge or Fort Wilderness | Boat |
| All other resorts | Bus |
| Disney's Hollywood Studios or Animal Kingdom | Bus to TTC, then monorail or boat |
| Epcot | Monorail to TTC, then monorail or boat |
| **To get to Epcot from...** | **Take the...** |
| Polynesian | Monorail (or walk) to TTC, then monorail |
| Contemporary or Grand Floridian | Monorail to TTC, then monorail |
| BoardWalk, Yacht/Beach Club, Swan/Dolphin | Boat or walk (to World Showcase) |
| All other resorts | Bus (to Future World) |
| Disney's Hollywood Studios or Animal Kingdom | Bus (or boat/walk from Studios) |
| Magic Kingdom | Monorail or boat to TTC, then monorail |
| **To get to Disney's Hollywood Studios from...** | **Take the...** |
| BoardWalk, Yacht/Beach Club, Swan/Dolphin | Boat or walk |
| All other resorts | Bus |
| Epcot or Disney's Animal Kingdom | Bus (or boat/walk from Epcot) |
| Magic Kingdom | Monorail or boat to TTC, then bus |
| **To get to Disney's Animal Kingdom from...** | **Take the...** |
| All resorts | Bus |
| Disney's Hollywood Studios or Epcot | Bus |
| Magic Kingdom | Monorail or boat to TTC, then bus |
| **To get to Downtown Disney/Typhoon Lagoon from...** | **Take the...** |
| Port Orleans | Boat *(DD Marketplace only)* or bus |
| Old Key West or Saratoga Springs | Boat *(DD Marketplace only)*, bus, or walk |
| All other resorts | Bus |
| All parks (except Magic Kingdom) | Bus, boat, monorail to a resort, then bus |
| Magic Kingdom | Monorail to Grand Floridian, then bus |
| **To get to Blizzard Beach/Winter Summerland from...** | **Take the...** |
| Disney's Animal Kingdom | Any resort bus going to Blizzard Beach |
| All resorts (or other theme parks) | Bus (or take resort bus and transfer) |
| **To get to Fantasia Gardens from...** | **Take the...** |
| All resorts *(guests at Swan, Dolphin, BoardWalk, and Yacht & Beach Club can walk)* | Travel to Disney's Hollywood Studios, take a bus to Swan, then walk |
| **To get to Wide World of Sports from...** | **Take the...** |
| All resorts | Go to Disney's Hollywood Studios, then bus |
| **To get to Hoop-Dee-Doo Revue from...** | **Take the...** |
| Magic Kingdom, Wilderness Lodge, or Contemporary | Boat to Fort Wilderness |
| Any other park | Bus to Fort Wilderness |
| Any other resort | Go to Magic Kingdom, then boat |
| **To get to a Disney Resort Hotel from...** | **Take the...** |
| Any resort *(Swan, Dolphin, BoardWalk, Yacht & Beach Club are in walking distance of each other)* | Go to nearby theme park or Downtown Disney, then bus, boat, or monorail |

# Park Tips and Ratings

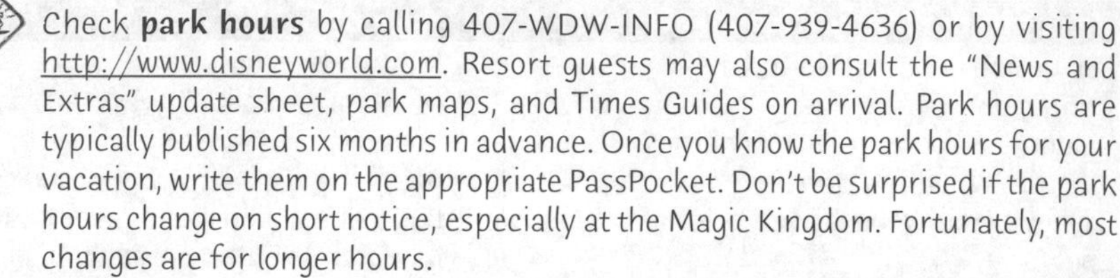

Check **park hours** by calling 407-WDW-INFO (407-939-4636) or by visiting http://www.disneyworld.com. Resort guests may also consult the "News and Extras" update sheet, park maps, and Times Guides on arrival. Park hours are typically published six months in advance. Once you know the park hours for your vacation, write them on the appropriate PassPocket. Don't be surprised if the park hours change on short notice, especially at the Magic Kingdom. Fortunately, most changes are for longer hours.

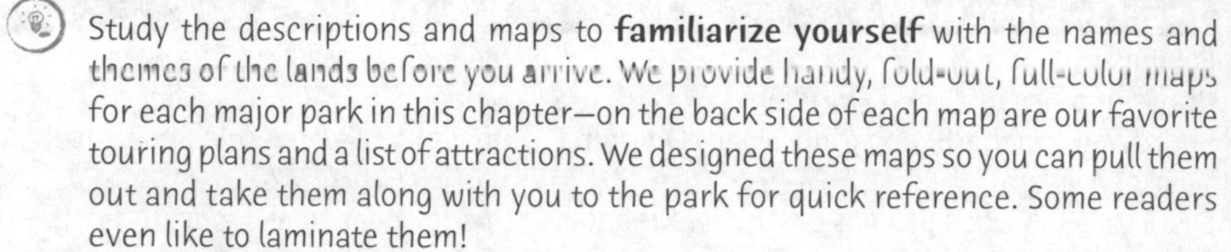

Study the descriptions and maps to **familiarize yourself** with the names and themes of the lands before you arrive. We provide handy, fold-out, full-color maps for each major park in this chapter—on the back side of each map are our favorite touring plans and a list of attractions. We designed these maps so you can pull them out and take them along with you to the park for quick reference. Some readers even like to laminate them!

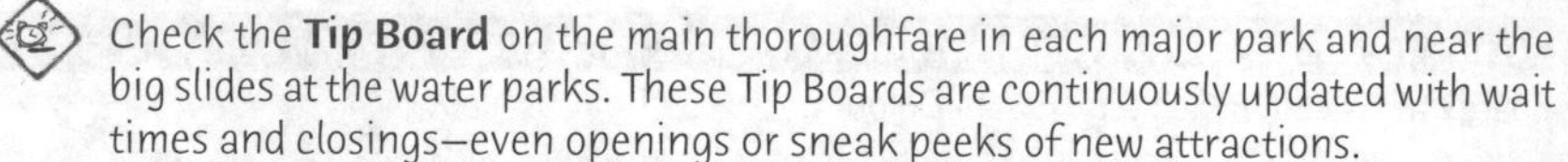

Check the **Tip Board** on the main thoroughfare in each major park and near the big slides at the water parks. These Tip Boards are continuously updated with wait times and closings—even openings or sneak peeks of new attractions.

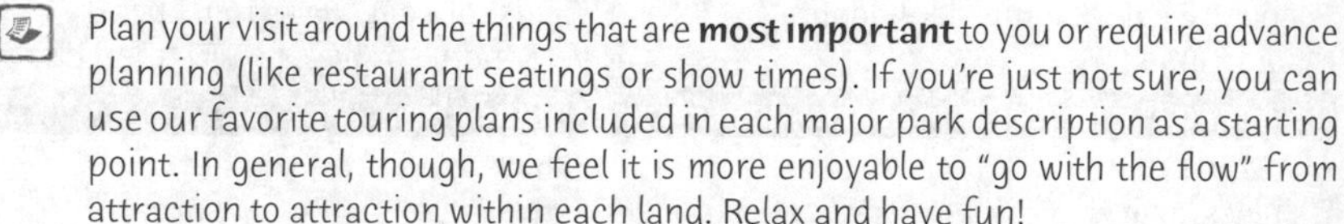

Plan your visit around the things that are **most important** to you or require advance planning (like restaurant seatings or show times). If you're just not sure, you can use our favorite touring plans included in each major park description as a starting point. In general, though, we feel it is more enjoyable to "go with the flow" from attraction to attraction within each land. Relax and have fun!

## Park Ratings

We rate each park to help you make the best decisions. Even so, our ratings may differ from your opinions—use the ratings as a guide only.

**Value Ratings** range from 1 (poor) to 10 (excellent) and are based on **quality** (cleanliness, maintenance, and newness); **variety** (different types of things to do); and **scope** (quantity and size of things to do)—**overall value** represents an average of the above three values. **Magic Ratings** are based on **theme** (execution and sense of immersion); **excitement** (thrills, laughs, and sense of wonder); and **fun factor** (number and quality of entertaining activities)—**overall magic** represents an average of the above three values. We use a point accumulation method to determine value and magic ratings.

**Readers' Ratings** are calculated from surveys submitted by vacationers at our web site (http://www.passporter.com/wdw/rate.htm).

**Guest satisfaction** is based on our and our readers' experiences with how different types of guests enjoy the park:

❤❤❤❤❤=love it ❤❤❤❤=enjoy it ❤❤❤=like it
❤❤=tolerate it ❤=don't like it

# Magic Kingdom

The Magic Kingdom is a true fantasyland, playfully painted in bold strokes upon the canvas of the imagination. This is quintessential Disney and often the first park guests visit. It is located the farthest north of all parks, on the shore of the Seven Seas Lagoon.

## AMBIENCE

The Magic Kingdom conjures up fantasy, nostalgia, youth, and most of all, **magic**. One thing it does especially well is blend the ordinary with the unusual, enhancing both to make it all seem better than reality. This giant, 107-acre playground attracts people of all ages to its bygone boulevards, tropical gardens, western landscapes, living cartoons, and yesterday's vision of tomorrow. All roads lead to Cinderella Castle, the crown of the Kingdom.

## PARK LAYOUT AND HIGHLIGHTS

Five "lands" radiate like spokes from the hub of Cinderella Castle, located in the center of the park, with two more lands added on for good measure (see the fold-out map on page 124). Below are the lands in clockwise order, along with descriptions and headline attractions. See page 123a&b for our favorite itineraries and an at-a-glance list of attractions, and pages 128–136 for attraction details.

| | |
|---|---|
| **Main Street, U.S.A.** *Headline Attraction:* | An early 1900s Main Street bustles with shops, eateries, a barbershop quartet, and City Hall. *Walt Disney World Railroad* |
| **Adventureland** *Headline Attractions:* | Walk to the beat of jungle drums in a paradise filled with pirates, parrots, crocs, and camels. *Pirates of the Caribbean, Tiki Room, Jungle Cruise, Aladdin* |
| **Frontierland** *Headline Attractions:* | Journey back to the American Frontier, complete with a fort and "mountain range." *Splash Mountain, Big Thunder Mountain Railroad* |
| **Liberty Square** *Headline Attractions:* | Step back in time to Colonial America with her presidents, riverboats, and a haunted house. *The Haunted Mansion, The Hall of Presidents* |
| **Fantasyland** *Headline Attractions:* | An enchanted, brightly colored "small world" where elephants fly and teacups spin. *Winnie the Pooh, Dumbo, Mickey's PhilharMagic, Peter Pan* |
| **Mickey's Toontown Fair** *Headline Attractions:* | Walk through a cartoon world to Goofy's farm, Mickey and Minnie's homes, and Donald's Boat. *Mickey's Country House, The Barnstormer at Goofy's Farm* |
| **Tomorrowland** *Headline Attractions:* | The future as imagined in the 1930s, complete with space flights, aliens, and time travel. *Space Mountain, Buzz Lightyear, Stitch's Great Escape!* |

# Entertainment and Shopping at the Magic Kingdom

Fold out the next page for touring plans and a handy attraction chart →

## ENTERTAINMENT

Fun and excitement surround you in the Magic Kingdom. Live entertainment fills the streets with parades, performers, bands, and fireworks. Every afternoon, the 20-minute-long **Disney Dreams Come True Parade** highlights favorite Disney moments (see the parade route on page 124). We like to watch the parade from Frontierland or Liberty Square. The dazzling **Wishes fireworks show** is generally held whenever the park is open after dark. Stand in front of Cinderella Castle to see Tinker Bell as she flies toward Tomorrowland during the 12-minute show. Mickey's Toontown Fair, Tomorrowland (near Indy Speedway), and Liberty Square are good viewing locations, too. Fantasyland is also possible, but it is very loud. Cinderella Castle is the backdrop for live musical stage shows such as the Dream Along With Mickey stage show. The **SpectroMagic** evening parade (if showing) adds lights and music to the fun and follows the same route (in reverse) as the day parade. Disney characters make appearances throughout the park, especially at park opening and after some shows. See the Times Guide for showtimes or visit Steve Soares' unofficial entertainment site at http://pages.prodigy.net/stevesoares.

*"We wants the redhead!" Allie gives her best stony-faced impression of a pirate at Pirates of the Caribbean*

## SHOPPING

Sure stops for general Disney merchandise include much of Main Street, U.S.A.—shops here are open for 30–60 minutes after park closing. Here are some of our favorite **themed shops**:

| Shop | Land | What makes it special |
|---|---|---|
| The Chapeau | Main Street, U.S.A. | Hats with embroidered names |
| Disney Clothiers | Main Street, U.S.A. | Upscale yet casual Disney clothes |
| Agrabah Bazaar | Adventureland | Themed, open-air marketplace |
| Plaza del Sol Caribebazaar | Adventureland | Pirate clothing and decor |
| Briar Patch | Frontierland | Great theme, Pooh and friends |
| Tinker Bell's Treasures | Fantasyland | Disney costumes and dolls |
| Mickey's Star Traders | Tomorrowland | Sci-fi toys and gadgets |

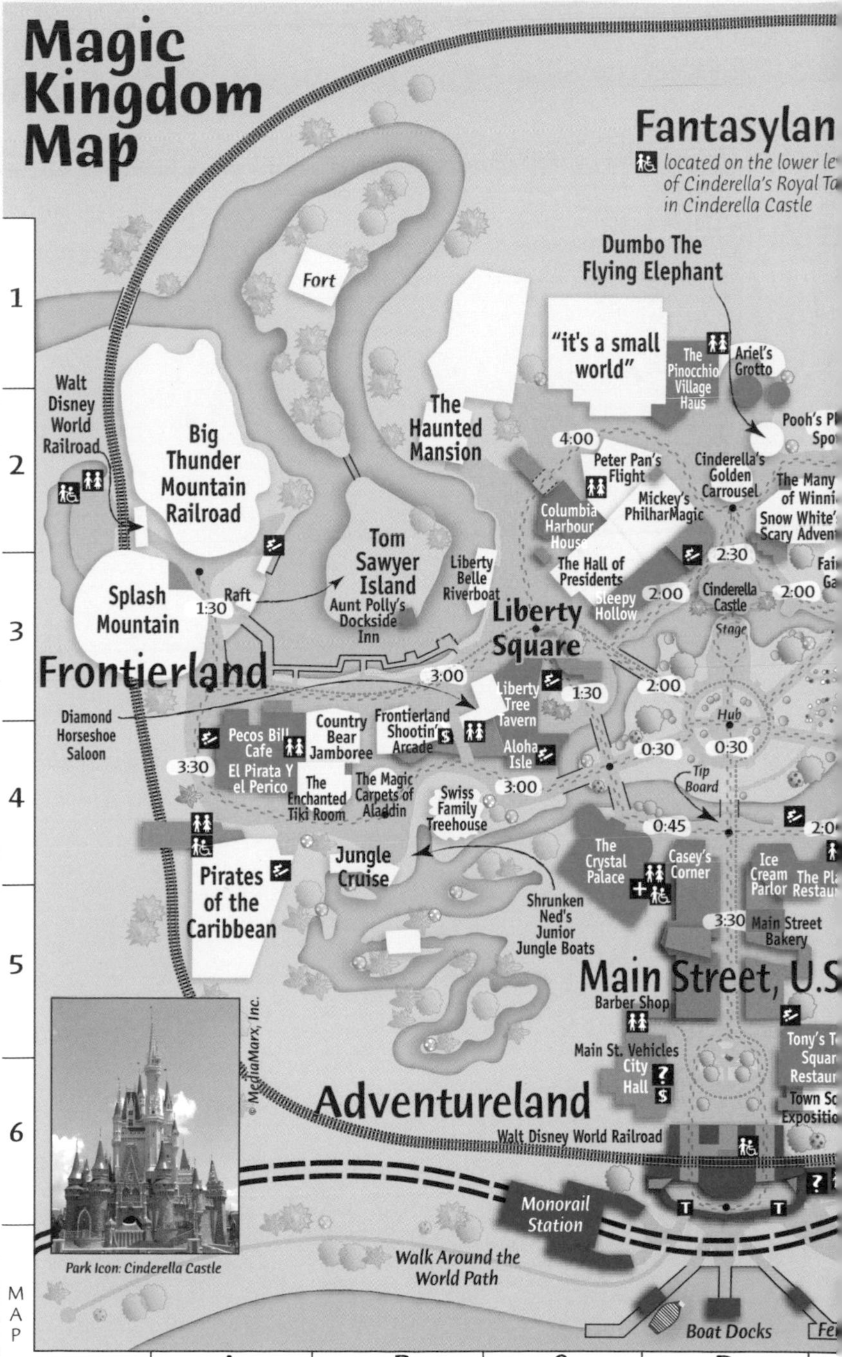

# Magic Kingdom Map

Fantasylan

located on the lower le
of Cinderella's Royal Ta
in Cinderella Castle

Dumbo The Flying Elephant

Fort

"it's a small world"

The Pinocchio Village Haus

Ariel's Grotto

Pooh's Pl Spo

The Haunted Mansion

Walt Disney World Railroad

Big Thunder Mountain Railroad

4:00

Peter Pan's Flight

Cinderella's Golden Carrousel

The Many of Winni

Mickey's PhilharMagic

Columbia Harbour House

Snow White's Scary Adven

Tom Sawyer Island

Liberty Belle Riverboat

The Hall of Presidents

2:30

Fai Ga

Splash Mountain

1:30

Raft

Aunt Polly's Dockside Inn

Liberty Square

Sleepy Hollow

2:00

Cinderella Castle

2:00

Stage

Frontierland

3:00

Liberty Tree Tavern

1:30

2:00

Hub

Diamond Horseshoe Saloon

Pecos Bill Cafe

Country Bear Jamboree

Frontierland Shootin' Arcade

Aloha Isle

0:30

0:30

3:30

El Pirata Y el Perico

The Enchanted Tiki Room

The Magic Carpets of Aladdin

Swiss Family Treehouse

3:00

Tip Board

0:45

2:0

Pirates of the Caribbean

Jungle Cruise

The Crystal Palace

Casey's Corner

Ice Cream Parlor

The Pla Restau

Shrunken Ned's Junior Jungle Boats

3:30

Main Street Bakery

Main Street, U.S

Barber Shop

© MediaMarx, Inc.

Main St. Vehicles

City Hall

Tony's T Squar Restaur

Adventureland

Town Sq Expositi

Walt Disney World Railroad

Park Icon: Cinderella Castle

Monorail Station

Walk Around the World Path

Boat Docks

Fe

1 2 3 4 5 6

MAP COORDINATES A B C D

# Magic Kingdom Attractions At-A-Glance

*(alphabetical order)*

| Attraction | Type | Allow | Page |
|---|---|---|---|
| ☐ Ariel's Grotto [D-2] | Playground | 30–60 | 132-Fa |
| ☐ Astro Orbiter [F-4] | Ride | 20+ | 135-T |
| ☐ Barnstormer at Goofy's Farm [F-2] | Coaster | 30+ | 134-TT |
| ☐ Big Thunder Mountain Railroad [A-2] | Coaster | 50+ | 130-Fr |
| ☐ Buzz Lightyear [F-4] | Track Ride | 30+ | 135-T |
| ☐ Carousel of Progress [F-4] | Show | 30+ | 135-T |
| ☐ Cinderella's Golden Carrousel [D-2] | Ride | 15+ | 132-Fa |
| ☐ Country Bear Jamboree [B-4] | Show | 30+ | 130-Fr |
| ☐ Diamond Horseshoe Saloon [B-3] | Pavilion | 20+ | 131-LS |
| ☐ Donald's Boat [G-1] | Playground | 20+ | 134-TT |
| ☐ Dumbo The Flying Elephant [D-2] | Ride | 30+ | 132-Fa |
| ☐ Fairytale Garden [E-3] | Live Show | 30+ | 132-Fa |
| ☐ Frontierland Shootin' Arcade [B-4] | Arcade | 15+ | 130-Fr |
| ☐ Galaxy Palace Theater [F-5] | Live Show | 30–60+ | 135-T |
| ☐ Hall of Presidents, The [C-3] | Show | 30+ | 131-LS |
| ☐ Haunted Mansion, The [B-2] | Track Ride | 30+ | 131-LS |
| ☐ "it's a small world" [C-2] | Boat Ride | 25+ | 132-Fa |
| ☐ Jungle Cruise [B-4] | Boat Ride | 40+ | 129-A |
| ☐ Liberty Belle Riverboat [B-3] | Boat Ride | 30+ | 131-LS |
| ☐ Mad Tea Party [E-2] | Ride | 20+ | 132-Fa |
| ☐ Magic Carpets of Aladdin [B-4] | Ride | 30+ | 129-A |
| ☐ Main Street Vehicles [D-5] | Vehicles | 30+ | 128-MS |
| ☐ Mickey's Country House [F-1] | Walk-thru | 60+ | 134-TT |
| ☐ Mickey's PhilharMagic [D-2] | 3-D Show | 40+ | 133-Fa |
| ☐ Minnie's Country House [F-1] | Walk-thru | 20+ | 134-TT |
| ☐ Monsters, Inc. Laugh Floor [E-4] | Show | 45+ | 135-T |
| ☐ Peter Pan's Flight [C-2] | Track Ride | 40+ | 133-Fa |
| ☐ Pirates of the Caribbean [A-4] | Boat Ride | 30+ | 129-A |
| ☐ Pooh's Playful Spot | Playground | 20+ | 133-Fa |
| ☐ Shrunken Ned's Jr. Jungle Boats [B-4] | Arcade | 10+ | 129-A |
| ☐ Snow White's Scary Adventures [D-2] | Track Ride | 20+ | 133-Fa |
| ☐ Space Mountain [G-3] | Coaster | 40+ | 136-T |
| ☐ Splash Mountain [A-3] | Coaster | 60–90+ | 130-Fr |
| ☐ Stitch's Great Escape! [E-4] | Show | 50+ | 136-T |
| ☐ Swiss Family Treehouse [B-4] | Walk-thru | 30+ | 129-A |
| ☐ Tiki Room, The Enchanted [B-4] | Show | 20+ | 129-A |
| ☐ Tom Sawyer Island [A-3] | Playground | 60+ | 130-Fr |
| ☐ Tomorrowland Arcade [G-3] | Arcade | 20–40+ | 136-T |
| ☐ Tomorrowland Indy Speedway [F-3] | Ride | 50+ | 136-T |
| ☐ Tomorrowland Transit Authority [F-4] | Track Ride | 10+ | 136-T |
| ☐ Toon Park [F-1] | Playground | 15+ | 134-TT |
| ☐ Toontown Hall of Fame [F-1] | Pavilion | 40+ | 134-TT |
| ☐ Town Square Exposition Hall [D-6] | Exhibit | 20+ | 128-MS |
| ☐ Walt Disney World Railroad [D-6, A-2, G-1] | Train Ride | 30+ | 128-MS |
| ☐ Winnie the Pooh, Many Adv. [E-2] | Track Ride | 30+ | 133-Fa |

*See page 139b for an explanation of this chart.*

# Our Favorite Touring Plans for the Magic Kingdom

NOTES

While we don't believe in the "commando" approach to fun, relaxing vacations, we realize that you may want guidance. Use these touring plans, which focus on the highest-rated attractions, as a starting point. You can do these plans in one day if you start by 9:00 am. If you can start earlier or stay later, add in additional attractions. The plans work best if you go in the same order, but feel free to re-order based on showtimes and wait times. Vacationers with infants and toddlers, or thrill-shy adults, may prefer to skip all attractions in blue.

ITINERARIES

## Touring With Adults

**Enter Tomorrowland**
Get FASTPASS for Buzz Lightyear or Space Mountain
Visit Buzz Lightyear
Visit Stitch's Great Escape!
Visit Space Mountain
**Enter Adventureland**
Get FASTPASS for Jungle Cruise
Visit Enchanted Tiki Room
Visit Pirates of the Caribbean
Visit Jungle Cruise
**Enter Frontierland** (and have a snack)
Get FASTPASS for Splash Mountain
Visit Big Thunder Mountain
Visit Splash Mountain
**Eat lunch** at Liberty Tree Tavern or Columbia Harbour House (*about 4 hours after entering park)*
**Enter Liberty Square**
Visit Haunted Mansion
Visit Hall of Presidents
Watch parade from Sleepy Hollow
**Enter Fantasyland** (and have a snack)
Get FASTPASS for Peter Pan's Flight
Visit Mickey's PhilharMagic
Visit Peter Pan's Flight
**Enter Mickey's Toontown Fair**
Visit Barnstormer at Goofy's Farm
Take Walt Disney World Railroad from Toontown Fair to Main Street, U.S.A.
*If the park is still open, do the following:*
**Eat dinner** at Crystal Palace, Tony's Town Square, or Plaza Restaurant (*about 8 1/2 hours into your day*)
Watch nighttime parade from Main Street, Cinderella Castle, or Liberty Square
Watch fireworks from same spot
*(Tour duration: About 10 1/2 hours)*

## Touring With Kids

**Enter Fantasyland**
Visit Dumbo the Flying Elephant
Visit Peter Pan's Flight
Get FASTPASS for Mickey's PhilharMagic
Visit Winnie the Pooh
Visit Mickey's PhilharMagic
Watch Dream Along With Mickey (if showing)
**Eat lunch** at Pinocchio Village Haus
**Enter Mickey's Toontown Fair**
Visit Barnstormer at Goofy's Farm
Visit Minnie's Country House
Take the WDW Railroad to Frontierland
**Enter Frontierland**
Get FASTPASS for Splash Mountain or Big Thunder Mountain Railroad
**Enter Adventureland**
Visit Pirates of the Caribbean
**Enter Frontierland**
Visit Splash Mountain or Big Thunder Mtn.
**Enter Adventureland** (and have a snack)
Get FASTPASS for Jungle Cruise
Visit Magic Carpets of Aladdin
Visit Jungle Cruise
**Enter Liberty Square**
Watch parade from Sleepy Hollow
Visit Haunted Mansion
**Enter Tomorrowland**
Get FASTPASS for Buzz Lightyear
Visit Stitch's Great Escape!
Visit Monsters, Inc. Laugh Floor
Visit Space Mountain
Visit Buzz Lightyear
**Eat dinner** at Tony's Town Square, Crystal Palace, or Cosmic Ray's (*about 8 hours after entering park*)
Watch nighttime parade from Main Street
Watch fireworks from hub or Liberty Square
*(Tour duration: About 10 1/2 hours)*

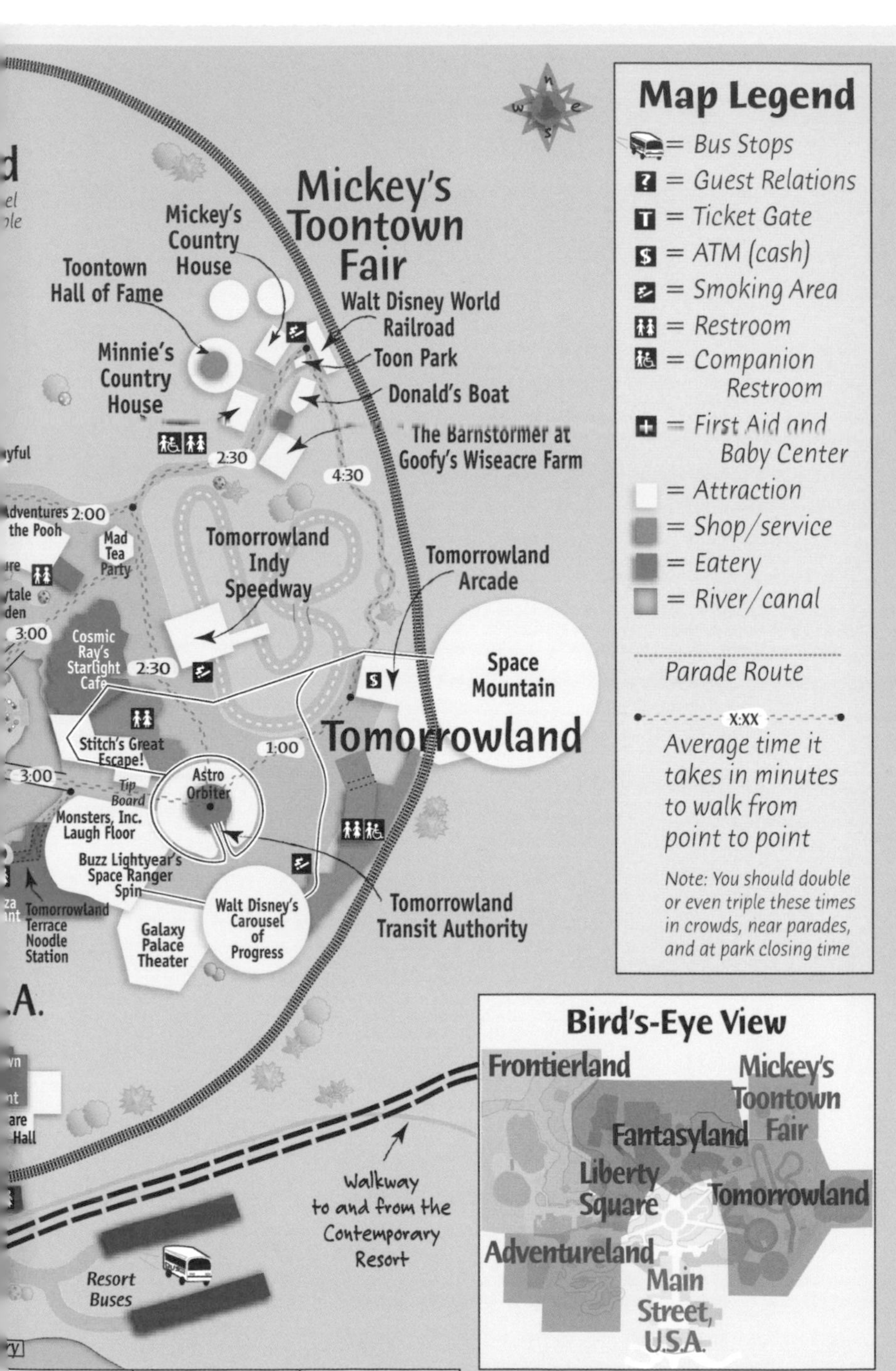
Mickey's Toontown Fair
Mickey's Country House
Toontown Hall of Fame
Minnie's Country House
Walt Disney World Railroad
Toon Park
Donald's Boat
The Barnstormer at Goofy's Wiseacre Farm
2:30
4:30
2:00
Adventures the Pooh
Mad Tea Party
Tomorrowland Indy Speedway
Tomorrowland Arcade
3:00
Cosmic Ray's Starlight Café
2:30
Space Mountain
Tomorrowland
Stitch's Great Escape!
1:00
3:00
Tip Board
Astro Orbiter
Monsters, Inc. Laugh Floor
Buzz Lightyear's Space Ranger Spin
Tomorrowland Terrace Noodle Station
Galaxy Palace Theater
Walt Disney's Carousel of Progress
Tomorrowland Transit Authority
Walkway to and from the Contemporary Resort
Resort Buses
E
F
G
Map Legend
= Bus Stops
= Guest Relations
= Ticket Gate
= ATM (cash)
= Smoking Area
= Restroom
= Companion Restroom
= First Aid and Baby Center
= Attraction
= Shop/service
= Eatery
= River/canal
Parade Route
X:XX
Average time it takes in minutes to walk from point to point
Note: You should double or even triple these times in crowds, near parades, and at park closing time
Bird's-Eye View
Frontierland
Mickey's Toontown Fair
Fantasyland
Liberty Square
Tomorrowland
Adventureland
Main Street, U.S.A.
Map © MediaMarx, Inc.

# Making the Most of the Magic Kingdom

Take a **spin around the park** when you first arrive by boarding the train at the Walt Disney World Railroad station in Main Street, U.S.A. The 20-minute journey is a great introduction to the park.

Consider a **guided tour**. Four Magic Kingdom tours are currently offered. For tour details and information on making advance reservations, see Backstage Passes on pages 244–245.

Need a trim? You can get a **haircut** at the Harmony Barber shop on Main Street. Try some colored hair gel and watch out for the pixie dust confetti! You may even be serenaded by a barbershop quartet. Young 'uns can get their very first haircut done here (see photo).

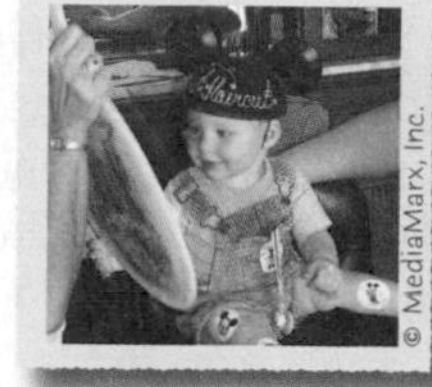

© MediaMarx, Inc.

Want a hairdo? The new **Bibbidi Bobbidi Boutique** inside Cinderella Castle offers fancy do's for girls and boys ages 3 and up. Open from 8:00 am–7:00 pm—reserve up to 180 days at 407-WDW-STYLE.

Make time for the **Flag Retreat** in the Main Street town square, usually at 5:00 pm or 5:30 pm daily. A color guard takes down the American flag, and most days a band plays as well. Veterans may inquire at City Hall about assisting in the flag lowering, too.

**Dining options** abound, although table-service isn't as prevalent as at Epcot. There are five table-service restaurants and many counter-service cafes and carts. See pages 207–209 for details.

If you have **young kids**, consider visiting other theme parks first—nothing else quite lives up to the wonder of the Magic Kingdom.

**Main Street, U.S.A.** closes a half hour later than the rest of the park. So while other folks fight the crowds in the parking lot, feel free to linger. Note that the stores are extremely busy at the end of the day.

**No alcohol** is served within the Magic Kingdom. If you want an adult beverage, ride the monorail to the Contemporary, Polynesian, or Grand Floridian resorts, where there are several lounges.

Need a **good place to meet**? The covered patio near Ariel's Grotto and the waterside seating across from the Plaza Restaurant are good choices. We recommend you avoid setting Cinderella Castle as your meeting point as it is sometimes inaccessible due to shows.

TIPS

NOTES

# Getting to the Magic Kingdom

**BEST TIMES TO GO**

The park tends to be the **busiest on Saturdays and Sundays**, and any day there are Extra Magic Hours scheduled (see page 32). We recommend you check the Extra Magic Hour schedule on Disney's web site and avoid those days if you prefer fewer crowds. Popular attractions such as Space Mountain and Splash Mountain are best done first thing in the morning to avoid long lines. Visit lands on the west (left) side of the park **earlier in the day**. Parents of young children are best off doing Fantasyland (particularly Dumbo) or Mickey's Toontown Fair first as they get busier later in the day. If you go to Splash Mountain and/or Big Thunder Mountain **during parade times**, note that the area can be very congested—use the riverside boardwalk or railroad instead. **Shop in the afternoon** to avoid crowds (ask about sending packages to the park exit or your resort).

**GETTING THERE**

**By Monorail**—From the Contemporary, Polynesian, or Grand Floridian resorts, take the monorail directly to the park. From Epcot, take the monorail to the Transportation and Ticket Center (TTC) and transfer to a Magic Kingdom express monorail or boat.

**By Boat**—From the TTC, boats ferry guests to and from the Magic Kingdom. Guests at the Polynesian, Grand Floridian, Wilderness Lodge and Villas, and Fort Wilderness also have a boat service.

**By Bus**—From all other resorts, buses take you directly to the Magic Kingdom. From Disney's Hollywood Studios or Disney's Animal Kingdom, bus to the TTC and transfer to monorail or boat. From Downtown Disney, bus to the Polynesian and then take the monorail.

**By Car**—Take I-4 to exit 67 (westbound) or exit 62 (eastbound) and continue about four miles to the toll plaza. All-day parking is $10 (free to resort guests and annual passholders) and the pass is valid at other parks' lots on the same day. Park, take a tram to the Transportation and Ticket Center, and monorail or boat to the park.

**By Foot**—You can walk from the Contemporary Resort.

**RATINGS**

*Ratings are explained on page 120.*

| Our Value Ratings: | | Our Magic Ratings: | | Readers' Ratings: |
|---|---|---|---|---|
| Quality: | 7/10 | Theme: | 7/10 | 82% fell in love with it |
| Variety: | 9/10 | Excitement: | 10/10 | 15% liked it well enough |
| Scope: | 7/10 | Fun Factor: | 7/10 | 2% had mixed feelings |
| **Overall Value:** | **8/10** | **Overall Magic:** | **8/10** | 1% were disappointed |

| Magic Kingdom is enjoyed by... | | (rated by both authors and readers) |
|---|---|---|
| Younger Kids: ♥♥♥♥♥ | Young Adults: ♥♥♥♥ | Families: ♥♥♥♥♥ |
| Older Kids: ♥♥♥♥♥ | Mid Adults: ♥♥♥ | Couples: ♥♥♥♥ |
| Teenagers: ♥♥♥♥ | Mature Adults: ♥♥♥ | Singles: ♥♥♥ |

# Understanding and Using the Attraction Descriptions and Ratings

PassPorter's custom-designed attraction charts include background, trivia, tips, restrictions, queues, accessibility details, enhanced ratings, and much more! We've organized this wide array of information into a consistent format so you can find what you need at a glance. Below is a key to our charts, along with notes and details. Enjoy!

## Description Key

Icons[4] | Ratings[5]

| 1 Attraction Name [D-3[2]] (Bar Color[3]) FP ⛹ A-OK! | # # # |
|---|---|
| *An overview of the attraction, what to expect (without giving too much away), historical background, trivia and "secrets," our suggestions for the best seating/viewing/riding, tips and tricks, waiting/queue conditions (e.g., covered, outdoor, etc.), wheelchair and stroller access, height/age restrictions, and* **Alex's ToddlerTips** *(ages 1-3), Allie's KidTips (ages 7-10),* **Allie's TweenTips** *(ages 11-12), and* **Allie's TeenTips** *(ages 13-15)—hints and tips by kids for kids!* | **Type[6]**<br>Scope[6]<br>Ages[7]<br>Thrill Factor[8]<br>Avg. Wait[8]<br>Duration[8] |

[1] Each chart has an empty **checkbox** in the upper left corner—use it to check off the attractions you want to visit (before you go) or those you visited during your trip.

[2] **Map coordinates** are presented as a letter and a number (i.e., A-5). Match up the coordinates on the park's map for the attraction's location within the park.

[3] The **bar color** indicates the attraction's target audience, as follows:

| Thrill Seekers | Family Friendly | Loved by Little Kids | Everything Else |
|---|---|---|---|

[4] Icons indicate when an attraction has FASTPASS (FP) or a height/age restriction (⛹).

[5] Our **ratings** are shown on the far right end. An A-OK! indicates that an attraction is approved as little kid-friendly by our kids Allie and Alexander Marx. The three boxes on the right side show ratings on a scale of 1 (poor) to 10 (don't miss!). The first is **Jennifer's** rating, the second is Dave's, and the third is our Readers' ratings. We offer our personal ratings to show how opinions vary, even between two like-minded people. You can also use our ratings as a point of reference—Jennifer appreciates good theming and dislikes sudden spins or drops, while Dave enjoys live performances and thrills. We both appreciate detail-rich attractions where we can learn something new.

[6] The boxes on the right below the numeric ratings give basic information. The first box is **attraction type**. The second box is always **attraction scope**, which we rate as follows:

- E-Ticket Headliner attraction; the ultimate; expect long lines
- D-Ticket Excellent fun, not-to-be-missed
- C-Ticket Solid attraction that pleases most guests
- B-Ticket Good fun, but easily skipped in a pinch
- A-Ticket A simple diversion; often overlooked

[7] **Age-appropriate ratings**. For example, we may say "All Ages" when we feel everyone, from infant on up, will get something out of the experience. More common is "Ages 4 & up" or "Ages 8 & up" for attractions we think will be best appreciated by vacationers who are at least 4 or 8. This is only our guideline and not a Disney rule.

[8] **Thrill/scare factor, average wait**, and **duration** follow the age ratings, though we eliminate these if they don't apply or expand them if deserving. We did our best to format this information so you can understand it without having to check this key, too!

# Charting the Attractions at Main Street, U.S.A.

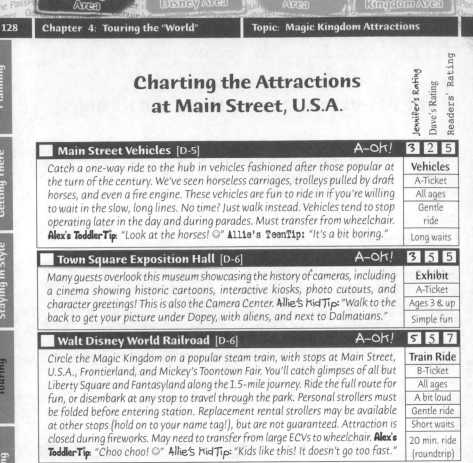

Jennifer's Rating | Dave's Rating | Readers' Rating

## Main Street Vehicles [D-5]

A-OK! 3 2 5

*Catch a one-way ride to the hub in vehicles fashioned after those popular at the turn of the century. We've seen horseless carriages, trolleys pulled by draft horses, and even a fire engine. These vehicles are fun to ride in if you're willing to wait in the slow, long lines. No time? Just walk instead. Vehicles tend to stop operating later in the day and during parades. Must transfer from wheelchair.* **Alex's ToddlerTip:** *"Look at the horses! ☺"* **Allie's TeenTip:** *"It's a bit boring."*

**Vehicles** | A-Ticket | All ages | Gentle ride | Long waits

## Town Square Exposition Hall [D-6]

A-OK! 3 5 5

*Many guests overlook this museum showcasing the history of cameras, including a cinema showing historic cartoons, interactive kiosks, photo cutouts, and character greetings! This is also the Camera Center.* **Allie's KidTip:** *"Walk to the back to get your picture under Dopey, with aliens, and next to Dalmatians."*

**Exhibit** | A-Ticket | Ages 3 & up | Simple fun

## Walt Disney World Railroad [D-6]

A-OK! 5 5 7

*Circle the Magic Kingdom on a popular steam train, with stops at Main Street, U.S.A., Frontierland, and Mickey's Toontown Fair. You'll catch glimpses of all but Liberty Square and Fantasyland along the 1.5-mile journey. Ride the full route for fun, or disembark at any stop to travel through the park. Personal strollers must be folded before entering station. Replacement rental strollers may be available at other stops (hold on to your name tag!), but are not guaranteed. Attraction is closed during fireworks. May need to transfer from large ECVs to wheelchair.* **Alex's ToddlerTip:** *"Choo choo! ☺"* **Allie's KidTip:** *"Kids like this! It doesn't go too fast."*

**Train Ride** | B-Ticket | All ages | A bit loud | Gentle ride | Short waits | 20 min. ride (roundtrip)

*Attraction descriptions and ratings are explained on page 127.*

## What Is and Isn't an Attraction?

We defined an "attraction" on page 114 as an individual ride, show, or exhibit. These are the destinations at the park and almost invariably come with a queue. We cover virtually all the attractions that Disney lists in their own guidemaps, plus a few that aren't listed but we still think are deserving of the "attraction" title (such as Ariel's Grotto). Like Disney, we don't consider things like talking trash cans (yes, they exist!) to be attractions as they rarely need a queue. We also don't consider outdoor stage shows, parades, or fireworks to be attractions, either—we cover these in the Entertainment sections in the park introduction pages of your PassPorter. Character greeting areas are less straightforward—if Disney considers one to be an attraction (such as the Toontown Hall of Fame) or we feel it offers more than simple character greetings, we include a description of it. For a list of character greeting locations, refer to the guidemap and Times Guide available upon your arrival. We also list popular spots to find favorite characters at Disney's Hollywood Studios on page 153b. For more specific information or hard-to-find characters, ask at Guest Relations in any of Disney's parks. Also check out our new *Disney Character Yearbook*—details on page 286.

*Alexander finds attractions everywhere*

# Charting the Attractions at Adventureland

Jennifer's Rating | Dave's Rating | Readers' Rating

**"The Enchanted Tiki Room–Under New Management"** [B-4] A-OK! 7 7 6

*A perfectly cool place to sit and rest while Audio-Animatronics creatures sing and cavort above you. The Enchanted Tiki Room has been a Disney fixture for many childhoods. Now those famous fowl–Iago (Aladdin) and Zazu (The Lion King)–have stepped in to jazz it up. This is a fun musical revue, which grew from Walt Disney's notion for an unusually entertaining Chinese restaurant. Don't miss the brief pre-show in the outdoor, covered queue area. Best views are on the left side. Wheelchair friendly. Assistive listening devices.* **Alex's ToddlerTip:** ☺ **Allie's KidTip:** *"Look for the Tiki gods."* **TeenTip:** *"It may seem lame, but it's not!"*

Show | D-Ticket | All ages | Dark, loud, angry gods | Short waits | 2 min. intro 9 min. show

**Jungle Cruise** [B-4] FP A-OK! 6 6 7

*See the sights along the "rivers of the world" in the company of a silly skipper. You and your fellow explorers will go chug-chugging up river in an open-air, awning-covered river boat inspired by the "African Queen." Every skipper tells a slightly different tale. Audio-Animatronics animals and "natives" liven things up. You may get damp. After-dark cruises are particularly fun. Outdoor, covered queue–lines can be deceptively long. Transfer from ECV to wheelchair.* **Alex's ToddlerTip:** ☺ **Allie's KidTip:** *"Lions, and tigers, and King Cobra!"* **TweenTip:** *"One of my favorites!"*

Boat Ride | D-Ticket | Ages 3 & up | Corny jokes | FASTPASS or long waits | 10 min. ride

**The Magic Carpets of Aladdin** [B-4] A-OK! 5 6 5

*Take a spin through a whole new world. Colorful, rider-controlled carpets go around, up, and down–sit in the front to control the height, or sit in the back to tilt forward and back. Similar to Dumbo (see page 132). Water-spitting camels add to the fun. Transfer from ECV to wheelchair.* **Alex's ToddlerTip:** *"Wow! ☺"* **Allie's KidTip:** *"Sit in the front so you can zoom up and get sprayed by camels."*

Ride | D-Ticket | Ages 3 & up | Med. waits | 1½ min. ride

**Pirates of the Caribbean** [A-4] A-OK! 8 7 9

*"Yo ho, yo ho!" The ride that inspired the movies is a slow, dark cruise through a subterranean world of Audio-Animatronics pirates (including Jack Sparrow and Barbossa) and the townsfolk they plunder. Enjoy scene after riotous scene and fun special effects. Lines can be long, especially on hot days because you get to wait in a cool cellar. Take the left line–it's shorter. You aren't likely to get wet, but the seats can be damp. Transfer from ECV to wheelchair and transfer from wheelchair. http://www.disneyparkpirates.com.* **Allie's TeenTip:** *"Very cool! I love Jack!"*

Boat Ride | E-Ticket | Ages 6 & up | Gentle drop, dark, scary to young kids | 9 min. ride

**Shrunken Ned's Junior Jungle Boats** [B-4] 3 4 3

*Steer small, remote-controlled craft resembling the Jungle Cruise boats around a lagoon sporting fountains and river gods. $1 for 2 minutes.* **Allie's KidTip:** *"Steering was very stubborn. When I did something right it still didn't work."*

Arcade | A-Ticket | Ages 6 & up

**Swiss Family Treehouse** [B-4] 5 5 4

*Walk through the home of the shipwrecked family from the Disney classic "Swiss Family Robinson." The branches of the huge (and very fake) banyan tree, known affectionately as "Disneyodendron eximus," cradle the family's heirlooms and contraptions. The treehouse has multiple levels that you need to climb. Thus, this attraction is not wheelchair or stroller accessible, and it can be tiring for some. The line of guests winds through slowly.* **Allie's KidTip:** *"This is boring."*

Walk-thru | B-Ticket | Ages 4 & up | Lots of stairs | Allow 15–30 min. to tour

# Charting the Attractions at Frontierland

Jennifer's Rating | Dave's Rating | Readers' Rating

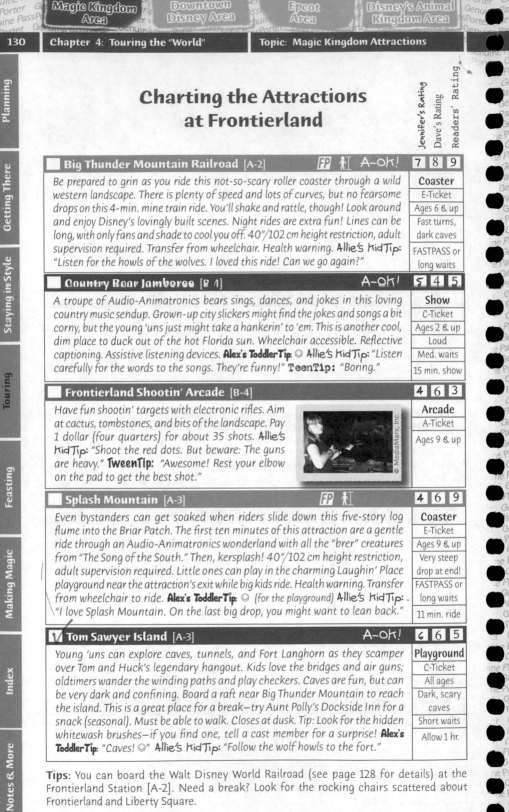

## Big Thunder Mountain Railroad [A-2] — FP — A-OK! — 7 8 9

*Be prepared to grin as you ride this not-so-scary roller coaster through a wild western landscape. There is plenty of speed and lots of curves, but no fearsome drops on this 4-min. mine train ride. You'll shake and rattle, though! Look around and enjoy Disney's lovingly built scenes. Night rides are extra fun! Lines can be long, with only fans and shade to cool you off. 40"/102 cm height restriction, adult supervision required. Transfer from wheelchair. Health warning.* **Allie's KidTip:** *"Listen for the howls of the wolves. I loved this ride! Can we go again?"*

Coaster | E-Ticket | Ages 6 & up | Fast turns, dark caves | FASTPASS or long waits

## Country Bear Jamboree [B-4] — A-OK! — 5 4 5

*A troupe of Audio-Animatronics bears sings, dances, and jokes in this loving country music sendup. Grown-up city slickers might find the jokes and songs a bit corny, but the young 'uns just might take a hankerin' to 'em. This is another cool, dim place to duck out of the hot Florida sun. Wheelchair accessible. Reflective captioning. Assistive listening devices.* **Alex's ToddlerTip:** ☺ **Allie's KidTip:** *"Listen carefully for the words to the songs. They're funny!"* **TeenTip:** *"Boring."*

Show | C-Ticket | Ages 2 & up | Loud | Med. waits | 15 min. show

## Frontierland Shootin' Arcade [B-4] — 4 6 3

*Have fun shootin' targets with electronic rifles. Aim at cactus, tombstones, and bits of the landscape. Pay 1 dollar (four quarters) for about 35 shots.* **Allie's KidTip:** *"Shoot the red dots. But beware: The guns are heavy."* **TweenTip:** *"Awesome! Rest your elbow on the pad to get the best shot."*

© MediaMarx, Inc.

Arcade | A-Ticket | Ages 9 & up

## Splash Mountain [A-3] — FP — 4 6 9

*Even bystanders can get soaked when riders slide down this five-story log flume into the Briar Patch. The first ten minutes of this attraction are a gentle ride through an Audio-Animatronics wonderland with all the "brer" creatures from "The Song of the South." Then, kersplash! 40"/102 cm height restriction, adult supervision required. Little ones can play in the charming Laughin' Place playground near the attraction's exit while big kids ride. Health warning. Transfer from wheelchair to ride.* **Alex's ToddlerTip:** ☺ *(for the playground)* **Allie's KidTip:** *"I love Splash Mountain. On the last big drop, you might want to lean back."*

Coaster | E-Ticket | Ages 9 & up | Very steep drop at end! | FASTPASS or long waits | 11 min. ride

## Tom Sawyer Island [A-3] — A-OK! — 6 6 5

*Young 'uns can explore caves, tunnels, and Fort Langhorn as they scamper over Tom and Huck's legendary hangout. Kids love the bridges and air guns; oldtimers wander the winding paths and play checkers. Caves are fun, but can be very dark and confining. Board a raft near Big Thunder Mountain to reach the island. This is a great place for a break—try Aunt Polly's Dockside Inn for a snack (seasonal). Must be able to walk. Closes at dusk. Tip: Look for the hidden whitewash brushes—if you find one, tell a cast member for a surprise!* **Alex's ToddlerTip:** *"Caves! ☺"* **Allie's KidTip:** *"Follow the wolf howls to the fort."*

Playground | C-Ticket | All ages | Dark, scary caves | Short waits | Allow 1 hr.

**Tips**: You can board the Walt Disney World Railroad (see page 128 for details) at the Frontierland Station [A-2]. Need a break? Look for the rocking chairs scattered about Frontierland and Liberty Square.

# Charting the Attractions at Liberty Square

Jennifer's Rating | Dave's Rating | Readers' Rating

## Diamond Horseshoe Saloon [B-3] – – –

*The Diamond Horseshoe Saloon is serving light refreshments—and little else—at press time. This attraction has had difficulty finding its place in recent years, and we wouldn't be surprised if it changes in the near future. Let's hope they bring back a live show. If it's open, it should remain wheelchair accessible.*

Pavilion
A-Ticket

## The Hall of Presidents [C-3] 5 4 6

*Ladies and gentlemen, the Presidents of the United States! The show begins with a 180° film presenting a patriotic, stirring view of our past. Every U.S. President is represented in full Audio-Animatronics glory—including President George W. Bush, who has a speaking part. A red brick colonial hall houses the 700-seat theater, a cool, quiet hideaway. Wheelchair accessible. Reflective captioning. Assistive listening devices. Shows are every half hour.* **Allie's KidTip:** *"You might like the movie—it talks about freedom."* **TeenTip:** *"I'd rather do something else."*

Show
C-Ticket
Ages 10 & up
Dark theater
Short waits
23 min. show

## The Haunted Mansion [B-2] A-OK! 9 8 9

*Another movie-inspiring attraction! Go for a gore-free ride through a world of 999 grinning ghosts in this recently renovated attraction. The spooky visual effects are astounding, but the scares are served up with a wink and lots of chuckles. There's a new storyline, added special effects, and enough delicious detail here that you'll ride again and again. Just be sure to leave room in your two- to three-person "doom buggy" for hitchhiking ghosts! May be too intense for young kids (even though Allie liked it, she was a bit scared). Transfer from wheelchair to ride. Visit http://www.doombuggies.com for more details.* **Allie's KidTip:** *"Can you find the dog skeleton? Hint: It's on a cliff in the graveyard."*

Track Ride
E-Ticket
Ages 6 & up
Mild scares, very dark
Medium waits
3 min. intro
7 min. ride

## Liberty Square Riverboat [B-3] 5 6 5

*Take a cruise on a steam-driven sternwheeler, refurbished in 2006. Mark Twain narrates your spin around Tom Sawyer Island, but the real joy is the attention to detail. The boat and its steam power plant are more interesting than the scenery—be sure to tour the decks. Dodge the sun in the middle deck salon. The "Liberty Belle" replaced the "Richard F. Irvine" in 1996. Wheelchair accessible. Adult supervision. Departs on the hour and half-hour.* **Allie's KidTip:** *"Boring."*

Boat Ride
C-Ticket
All ages
Gentle rides
Med. waits
20 min. ride

*Attraction descriptions and ratings are explained on page 127.*

### Strollers: To Bring or Rent

*See page 115 for more on rentals.*

If you bring your own stroller (a boon for the airport and travel to and from the buses/parking lot), we recommend a compact, umbrella stroller, as it's easy to tote about. If you prefer to bring a larger, folding stroller (the kind with cup holders and serious cargo capacity), try to travel the buses at off-hours, when the stroller won't prevent you from getting onboard due to crowded conditions. Rentals are good for kids who only need an occasional ride and weigh less than the 70-lb. weight limit. All rental strollers are now either "jogging style" or molded plastic (see photo).

© MediaMarx, Inc.

# Charting the Attractions at Fantasyland

Jennifer's Rating | Dave's Rating | Readers' Rating

## ☐ Ariel's Grotto [D-1] A-OK! 3 3 3

Little mermaids love to meet Ariel at this character meet-and-greet and fountain play area. Fountains may be turned off in droughts, but even so, kids enjoy having a place to frolic while the long line of parents wait patiently. Wheelchair accessible. **Allie's KidTip:** "You can play here even without water."

Playground · A-Ticket · All ages · Long waits

## ☐ Cinderella's Golden Carrousel [D-2] A-OK! 5 5 6

This colorful, lovingly maintained carrousel painted with scenes from Cinderella sits at the center of Fantasyland. Many of the 84 horses were rescued from a historic New Jersey carousel, but you'd have a hard time telling which ones. The horses closer to the perimeter tend to rise higher. A recently added chariot (an original) holds six. Disney tunes make it a joy for the ears! Enchanting in the evening. Must transfer from wheelchair to board. Adult supervision of children required. **Alex's ToddlerTip:** ☺ **Allie's KidTip:** "Sit carefully on the horse."

Ride · B-Ticket · Ages 2 & up · High horses can be scary · Short waits · 2 min. ride

## ☐ Dumbo The Flying Elephant [D-2] A-OK! 5 5 5

Every child wants to ride around, up, and down on Dumbo. Two-seater flying elephants take you all for a short, fast spin. Show your child how to lift the control lever to go higher. Grown-ups will enjoy the pachyderm's-eye view. The lines are long and hot—the queue area offers some shade and diversions. Adults must ride with small children, and you know the kids will want to ride again—do this ride first thing in the morning. Must transfer from wheelchair. **Alex's ToddlerTip:** ☺ **Allie's KidTip:** "If you ride with a grown-up, pick someone who isn't too big."

Ride · D-Ticket · All ages · Spins high in the air · Long waits · 2 min. flight

## ☐ Fairytale Garden [E-3] A-OK! 6 6 5

Meet characters such as Belle (from "Beauty and the Beast") in this quaint garden created in 1999. Sit on stools and benches among the rose bushes and listen to Belle read a story at various times throughout the day. Belle takes volunteers from the audience to help tell her tale. Arrive about ten minutes early to get a seat. No shade. Character meet and greet, too. Wheelchair friendly. **Allie's KidTip:** "You might want to be in the show because it could be fun!!!"

Live Show · B-Ticket · All ages · Happy ending · 15 min. story

## ☑ "it's a small world" [C-2] A-OK! 5 6 6

"It's a world of laughter, a world of tears..." Yes, these are Disney's famous singing and dancing dolls, who first debuted their act at the 1964–65 New York World's Fair. Their catchy song adapts to the local surroundings as your boat floats sedately past scenes depicting the world's continents and cultures. Must transfer from ECV to wheelchair to ride. **Alex's ToddlerTip:** ☺ **Allie's KidTip:** "Ask your grown-ups for a seat at the end of a row so you can see more."

Boat Ride · C-Ticket · All ages · Short to med. waits · 11 min. cruise

## ☐ Mad Tea Party [E-2] A-OK! 2 3 6

Spin and spin and spin some more inside a giant teacup. Young kids love to get dizzy, so this ride draws them like a magnet. Turn the metal wheel at the center of your teacup to make it spin even faster. You'll be as dizzy as the Mad Hatter. This is one ride that lasts a bit longer than you'd like. Sit this one out if you're prone to dizziness. Adult supervision of children under 7. Must transfer from wheelchair to ride. **Alex's ToddlerTip:** "I want to ride the 'teacups' again ... and again! ☺" (this is his favorite ride!) **Allie's KidTip:** "Look for the dormouse!"

Ride · C-Ticket · Ages 4 & up · Scares adults · Short waits · 2 min. spin

➢

# Charting the Attractions at Fantasyland

*(continued)*

Ratings: Jennifer's Rating | Dave's Rating | Readers' Rating

## The Many Adventures of Winnie the Pooh [E-2] FP A-OK! 6 5 7

*Take a gentle ride through the world of that fabulously popular bear. Blow through the Blustery Day, bounce along with Tigger, dream of Heffalumps and Woozles, and float away in a mighty spring flood, all in a four-seat "honey pot" that moves along an indoor track. Pooh fans will exit feeling warm and fuzzy—the better you know Pooh's tales, the more you'll get from your tour through the cartoon cutout scenery. The covered queue winds through pages blown away from a huge storybook. Lines can be long—we suggest you get a FASTPASS soon after the park opens. Transfer from ECV to wheelchair.* **Alex's ToddlerTip:** *"Tigger and Pooh! ☺"* **Allie's KidTip:** *"Sit in the front."*

Track Ride | D-Ticket | All ages | Kid-friendly; dark could be slightly scary | FASTPASS or long waits | 3 min. ride

## Mickey's PhilharMagic [D-2] FP A-OK! 8 9 9

*Trouble's brewing in Fantasyland in Disney's latest 3-D movie experience, when Donald "borrows" (and loses) Mickey's sorcerer hat. The audience, assembled in front of a giant, 150-foot-wide screen in PhilharMagic Concert Hall, awaits a concert conducted by Mickey. Donald, naturally, gets into deep trouble. Soon he's scurrying through scenes from Disney classic films, trying to regain the lost hat. Along the way he meets Simba, Peter Pan, Lumiere, Aladdin, Ariel, and other favorite Disney characters. Look for Donald at the "end." The 3-D movie effects and sensations are kid-friendly. Best seats in middle or back of theater. Covered queue. Wheelchair accessible. Assistive listening devices. Reflective captioning.* **Alex's ToddlerTip:** ☺ **Allie's TeenTip:** *"Wow! Good for all ages."*

3-D Show | E-Ticket | All ages | Intense effects may be scary | FASTPASS or med. waits | 10 min. show

## Peter Pan's Flight [C-2] FP A-OK! 6 6 8

*Climb aboard a flying, three-seat pirate ship that twists and turns sedately through the clouds. Follow Peter Pan and the Darling children from London to Neverland. Scenes featuring the Lost Boys, mermaids, Captain Hook's ship, and the crocodile unfold below, then you're safely home. Very dark, 4-minute ride. Covered queue area. Transfer from wheelchair to ride.* **Alex's ToddlerTip:** ☺ **Allie's KidTip:** *"Can you find the mermaids? One of them looks like Ariel!"*

Track Ride | D-Ticket | Ages 3 & up | Dark, heights | FASTPASS or long waits

## Pooh's Playful Spot [E-2] A-OK! 6 5 5

*Kids love the chance to burn off some steam at this playground across from The Many Adventures of Winnie the Pooh. The Hundred Acre Woods-themed play area has a slide, hollow logs, playhouse, and interactive pop-jet fountains (parents, be sure to bring a swimsuit or at least a change of clothes). The playground is in part of the former 20,000 Leagues Under the Sea lagoon. Watch for character greetings with Pooh and friends here, too!* **Alex's ToddlerTip:** *"Yay! ☺ ☺ ☺"*

Playground | B-Ticket | Ages 2–5 | Med. waits | Allow 15–30 minutes

## Snow White's Scary Adventures [D-2] A-OK! 4 6 5

*What's the most underappreciated ride in all of Fantasyland? Snow White! Your wooden mining car carries you though scene after scene from Disney's classic animation. The Wicked Witch provides the scares, but just when things get too gloomy you'll be transported into the welcome arms of the Seven Dwarfs and Prince Charming. Kids' legs fit best in the front seat, which is lower. May be too intense for young children. Must transfer from wheelchair to ride.* **Alex's ToddlerTip:** ☺ **Allie's KidTip:** *"Look for the name on the front of your car!"*

Track Ride | C-Ticket | Ages 5 & up | Dark, scary for kids | Short waits | 3 min. ride

*Attraction descriptions and ratings are explained on page 127.*

# Charting the Attractions at Mickey's Toontown Fair

Jennifer's Rating | Dave's Rating | Readers' Rating

## The Barnstormer at Goofy's Wiseacre Farm [F-2] A-OK! 7 7 6

*It's tough to find a finer "kiddie" coaster than The Barnstormer. Even grown-up coaster fans love this fast, swooping flight through (and we do mean "through") one of the goofiest barnyards you'll ever see. The queue is a delight, too, as you get to inspect Goofy's crops and livestock. Long lines move quickly through the uncovered queue. Cars may be small for big/tall adults. Closes often during inclement weather. Transfer from wheelchair.* **Alex's ToddlerTip:** *"I like Goofy's plane! ☺"* **Allie's KidTip:** *"Lift your hands in the air! You'll want to go on it again and again!"*

**Coaster** | D-Ticket | Ages 2 & up (35" and up) | Fast turns | Med. waits | 1 min. flight

## Donald's Boat [G-1] A-OK! 4 3 4

*Your little ducklings will have a hoot splashing about in Uncle Donald's fountains and exploring his boat. Bring suits and towels (change at the Service Station restrooms beside Minnie's House). Fountains may be off in droughts. Wheelchair accessible.* **Alex's ToddlerTip:** ☺ **Allie's KidTip:** *"Pull the horn and bell!"*

**Playground** | A-Ticket | All ages | No wait

## Mickey's Country House and Judge's Tent [F-1] A-OK! 5 5 6

*Mickey's house is chock-full of chuckles and "tchochkes" (knick-knacks). Look closely at his decorating—there are enough sight gags and delights to turn anyone into a gleeful kid. Long, slow lines snake in the front door, out the back, and through his garden, because Mickey himself is waiting to greet you in the Judge's Tent next door. If the house and garden are enough, exit through Mickey's garage. Wheelchair accessible.* **Allie's KidTip:** *"Meet Mickey afterwards!"*

**Walk-thru** | B-Ticket | All ages | Long waits | Allow 20 min. to 1 hour

## Minnie's Country House [F-1] A-OK! 6 5 6

*Walk through Minnie's in-home studio and office for a fascinating glimpse into the talents of this fabled celebrity. Her painting, sculpting, and quilting talents are remarkable, and her kitchen is a wonder (look in the fridge and oven). Minnie's not at home to greet you, but that also means the lines move faster than they do at Mickey's. Wheelchair accessible.* **Alex's ToddlerTip:** *"Bake a birthday cake! ☺"* **Allie's KidTip:** *"Look for things you can play with in the house, like the popcorn."*

**Walk-thru** | B-Ticket | All ages | No scares | Med. waits | Allow 20 min.

## Toon Park [F-1] A-OK! 5 5 6

*Toddler playground with lots of pint-sized slides, tunnels, and playhouses. Soft padded ground. Restricted to kids 40" and under.* **Alex's ToddlerTip:** ☺ ☺ ☺

**Playground** | A-Ticket

## Toontown Hall of Fame [F-1] A-OK! 3 2 6

*Meet Minnie and many other Disney characters in three separate greeting areas located on the right-hand side of this big, candy-striped "tent" that doubles as a store. Lines, not surprisingly, are long. Wheelchair accessible.* **Alex's ToddlerTip:** *"Princess kisses! ☺"* **Allie's KidTip:** *"Bring your autograph book!"*

**Pavilion** | A-Ticket | All ages | Long waits

## Walt Disney World Railroad [G-1] A-OK! 5 5 7

*Toontown Fair Station! All out for Mickey's Toontown Fair, Fantasyland, and Tomorrowland. Next stop, Main Street, U.S.A. See page 128. This is a fun shortcut when you're heading for the exit. Large ECVs may need to transfer to wheelchair.*

**Train Ride** | B-Ticket | All ages

**Tip**: To get from Mickey's Toontown Fair to Tomorrowland faster, take the path that starts at the railroad station in Mickey's Toontown Fair and ends beside the Tomorrowland Arcade.

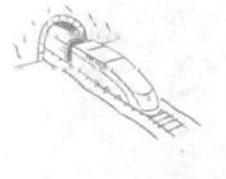

# Charting the Attractions at Tomorrowland

Jennifer's Rating | Dave's Rating | Readers' Rating

## Astro Orbiter [F-4] A-OK! 1 3 3

Go for a short, fast spin in a two-seat rocket high above Tomorrowland. Often mistaken for a futuristic sculpture, the fanciful planets of Astro Orbiter go into motion with each launch. Think "Dumbo" with small, silvery space ships. Pull back on the stick to "soar" high. Get a dizzying view as your ship whirls. Must ride an elevator to board. Motion sickness warning. Outdoor, covered queue. Adults must accompany kids under 7. Transfer from wheelchair to ride. **Allie's Kid Tip:** "You can get a great view of the park." **TweenTip:** "Faster than Dumbo and Aladdin."

Ride | C-Ticket | Ages 5 & up | Heights | Long waits | 1½ min. flight

## Buzz Lightyear's Space Ranger Spin [F-4] FP A-OK! 8 8 8

All right, Space Rangers, it's time to help Toy Story's Buzz Lightyear defeat the evil Emperor Zurg! Buzz himself briefs new cadets before you're sent into battle in a Day-Glo, comic book world of planets and space creatures. Your two-seat space vehicle (an "XP-37 Space Cruiser") is equipped with a pair of "ion cannons" (laser pointers) mounted on the dashboard. Aim and shoot the electronic targets to accumulate points (aim for the higher targets for more points). Move the joystick to make your vehicle spin and home in on your targets. Compare your score at the end. Covered queue area is mostly indoors. Wheelchair accessible. **Alex's ToddlerTip:** ☺ **Allie's Kid Tip:** "Check your score. I made Space Cadet!"

Train Ride | D-Ticket | Ages 2 & up | Mild "space flight" effects | FASTPASS or med. waits | 4 min. flight

## Walt Disney's Carousel of Progress [F-4] A-OK! 9 6 6

See the march of modern technology through the eyes of an American family. Each of the four scenes in this Audio-Animatronics show highlights another 20 years (or so) of progress in the 20th century. When the scene changes, the entire theater moves around to the next stage. One of Walt Disney's favorite attractions. (Jennifer loves it, too!) Limited hours. Outdoor, covered queue. Wheelchair accessible. Assistive listening devices. Closed captioning (pre-show only). **Allie's Kid Tip:** "Rover is cute."

Show | C-Ticket | Ages 6 & up | No scares | Short waits | 22 min. show

## Galaxy Palace Theater (seasonal) [F-5] A-OK! 4 5 4

This outdoor, partially covered theater plays host to a variety of live shows and entertainment throughout the year, such as the "Galaxy Search" talent show or "Mickey's 'Twas the Night Before Christmas" show. Most Tomorrowland visitors don't even know it exists, and much of the time the theater is "dark." Check your Magic Kingdom Times Guide for current show listings. Wheelchair accessible. Assistive listening devices. **Allie's Kid Tip:** "Sounds like fun!"

Live Show | B-Ticket | All ages | Showtimes vary (seasonal)

## Monsters, Inc. Laugh Floor [E-4] A-OK! 6 7 7

This new Monsters, Inc. theme show opened in early 2007. The show picks up where the movie left off, inviting guests into a comedy club to collect their laughter and power Monstropolis. The fun show uses the same cool technology from "Turtle Talk with Crush" (see page 145), meaning the monsters onscreen like Mike Wazowski can interact with audience members. Expect some good natured ribbing, and some audience members may appear on screen. Indoor queue. Guests sit on hard plastic benches in the 458-seat theater. Wheelchair/ECV accessible. Assistive listening. Handheld and video captioning for portions of show.

Show | D-Ticket | All ages | Dark, playful monsters | 12 minute show

*Attraction descriptions and ratings are explained on page 127.*

# Charting the Attractions at Tomorrowland

*(continued)*

Ratings: Jennifer's Rating / Dave's Rating / Readers' Rating

## Space Mountain [G-3] FP — 6 8 9

*Blast off into the blackness of space on the Magic Kingdom's most exciting roller coaster. This fast, indoor ride has sudden turns and short drops, but no big, stomach-in-your-throat drops. The darkness makes it scarier than it really is. The indoor queue and ride loading areas are rich with visual detail—pay attention while you're waiting. There are two slightly different coasters—go left for one, right for the other when you reach the loading area. Single rider queue (when available) can cut wait time. Transfer from ECV to wheelchair, then transfer from wheelchair to ride. 44"/112 cm height restriction. Adult supervision. Health warning.* **Allie's KidTip:** *"I loved it! But it is bumpy. Try to sit in the middle. Ride it again if you can!"*

Coaster | E-Ticket | Ages 8 & up | Dark, rough, jerky, fast | FASTPASS or long waits | 2½ min. flight

## Stitch's Great Escape! [E-4] FP — 6 5 6

*Guests are recruited by the Grand Councilwoman, Captain Gantu, and Pleakley to guard "Experiment 626" (Stitch), and mischief ensues when that wily captive escapes into the theater. Even Skippy, from this attraction's previous incarnation, has a part. Animation, Audio-Animatronics, surround sound, lighting, and tactile effects combine to make an immersive experience. Alas, restrictive shoulder restraints, periods of total darkness, and a barrage of fire from "laser cannon" leave Stitch with too many scare factors and too little charm. Outdoor, covered queue. 40"/102 cm minimum height. Handheld captioning. Assistive listening. Wheelchair and ECV accessible.* **Allie's TweenTip:** *"I love it when the power goes out!"*

Show | E-Ticket | Ages 7 & up | Could be scary for young kids | FASTPASS or long waits | 12 min. show

## Tomorrowland Arcade [G-3] A-OK! — 3 2 3

*Play the latest in video games, as well as some old classics, in this large, very loud arcade at the exit of Space Mountain. Spending money is required. Wheelchair accessible.* **Allie's KidTip:** *"Try to play a Disney dancing game here and win!"*

Arcade | A-Ticket | Ages 6 & up

## Tomorrowland Indy Speedway [F-3] A-OK! — 4 3 4

*Every kid wants a chance to drive, and when they're tall enough they can at this popular attraction. Experienced drivers won't be as thrilled. Guide rails, shock-absorbing bumpers, and a low top speed (7 mph maximum) make these gas powered "race cars" safe. Family members can cheer from an enclosed grandstand (the entrance is to the right). Shortest waits are early in the morning. Covered outdoor queue. Transfer from wheelchair to ride. 52"/132 cm height restriction to drive solo. Health warning. Adult supervision required.* **Allie's KidTip:** *"Even if you're tall enough, make sure your feet can touch the pedals before you drive."*

Ride | C-Ticket | Ages 4 & up | Cars may bump yours from behind | Long waits | 4 min. drive

## Tomorrowland Transit Authority [F-4] A-OK! — 6 6 6

*Take a grand tour of Tomorrowland on an elevated, automated people mover. The four-seat vehicles move sedately along a route that takes you through Space Mountain and past nearly every other attraction in Tomorrowland. Along the way you can look down upon Tomorrowland's crowds and view a scale model of Progress City (formerly of Disneyland's Carousel of Progress). It makes a great introduction to Tomorrowland. Outdoor, mostly covered queue. Must be ambulatory to ride.* **Allie's KidTip:** *"This is ok, but not one of my top ten. Look for the stars when you go through Space Mountain."*

Track Ride | B-Ticket | All ages | Dark | Short waits | 12 min. grand tour

**Tip**: Ever hear a talking trash can? Look for one called "PUSH" outside Mickey's Star Traders shop in Tomorrowland.

# Epcot

Triple the size of the Magic Kingdom, Epcot opened its doors (and many minds) in 1982. Epcot is the ultimate world's fair, showcasing a future where technology improves our lives, the countries of the world live in peace, and dreams really can come true.

AMBIENCE

Striving to educate and inspire as well as entertain, Epcot introduces millions to new **technological and international frontiers**. Epcot began as Walt Disney's dream of an "Experimental Prototype Community of Tomorrow;" it's a far cry from the ordinary communities where most of us live. The first of two "worlds," Future World greets you with its awe-inspiring, 180-foot-tall, geodesic sphere (Spaceship Earth). Streamlined structures and broad vistas transport you into the future of today's hopes and dreams. Beyond Future World is World Showcase, offering an inspiring glimpse into faraway lands, different customs, and exotic peoples.

PARK LAYOUT AND HIGHLIGHTS

The two worlds of Epcot offer a variety of attractions, all housed in "pavilions"—nine in Future World and eleven in the World Showcase (see the fold-out map on page 140). Below are the headline attractions in the west and east sides of Future World and World Showcase. See pages 139a&b for our favorite itinerary and an at-a-glance list of attractions, and pages 143–149 for attraction details.

| | |
|---|---|
| **Future World East** | Science and technology take center stage with an up-close look at space travel, vehicle testing, communications, and energy. |
| *Headline Attractions:* | *Mission: SPACE, Test Track, Spaceship Earth, Universe of Energy* |
| **Future World West** | Explore the nature of the world on land and in the sea, and the nature of imagination and perception in the recesses of our minds. |
| *Headline Attractions:* | *Soarin', The Seas with Nemo & Friends* |
| **World Showcase East** | Cruise a river in Mexico, experience a maelstrom in Norway, see the wonders of China, celebrate in Germany and Italy, and explore the heritage of the American adventure. |
| *Headline Attractions:* | *Maelstrom, Gran Fiesta Tour, Reflections of China* |
| **World Showcase West** | Hear drummers in Japan, view treasures in Morocco, see the sights in France, tour gardens in the United Kingdom, and explore the wonders of Canada. |
| *Headline Attractions:* | *Impressions de France, O Canada!* |

Fold out the next page for a touring plan and a handy attraction chart

# Entertainment and Shopping at Epcot

## ENTERTAINMENT

Epcot presents a rich medley of sounds and sights for the strolling visitor. Guests may encounter acrobats, dancers, actors, and musicians—more than **two dozen groups** in all. Most shows last about 10–20 minutes. Favorites include the Voices of Liberty and fife and drum corps at The American Adventure, Celtic rock and bagpipes in Canada, Beatles look-alikes in the United Kingdom, brass bands in Germany, and a fun mariachi band in Mexico. You'll flip for China's acrobats, and Japanese and African drummers set your pulse pounding. The spectacular **Fountain of Nations** dances in time to the music (see page 144). Beyond casual entertainment, check your Times Guide for the open-air **America Gardens Theatre**, which offers half-hour performances, plus the Flower Power concerts in the spring, Eat to the Beat concerts in autumn, and Candlelight Processional in December (see page 259). Crowds throng the World Showcase every evening at park closing for the popular **IllumiNations** fireworks and light show (see page 150 for details).

© MediaMarx, Inc.

*Epcot's Imagination Pavilion*

## SHOPPING

The World Showcase makes Epcot the center for unusual shopping, too. A wide array of **international gifts and crafts** grace every pavilion, from British woolens and Japanese silks to German cut crystal and Moroccan leather. Here are our favorite shops:

| Shop | Location | What makes it special |
|---|---|---|
| Art of Disney | Near Innoventions | Collectibles and animation cels |
| Disney Traders | World Showcase | Disney-themed merchandise |
| MouseGear | Future World | Huge store with clothes and gifts |
| ImageWorks | Imagination! | Unique photos and photo gifts |
| Plaza de Los Amigos | Mexico | It just feels good to shop here! |
| Yong Feng Shangdian | China | Huge store with a wide variety |
| Mitsukoshi Dept. Store | Japan | Authentic Japanese gifts, snacks |
| Tangier Traders | Morocco | Open-air, exotic shopping |
| La Maison du Vin | France | Two words: wine tastings! |
| The Crown and Crest | United Kingdom | Family name histories |

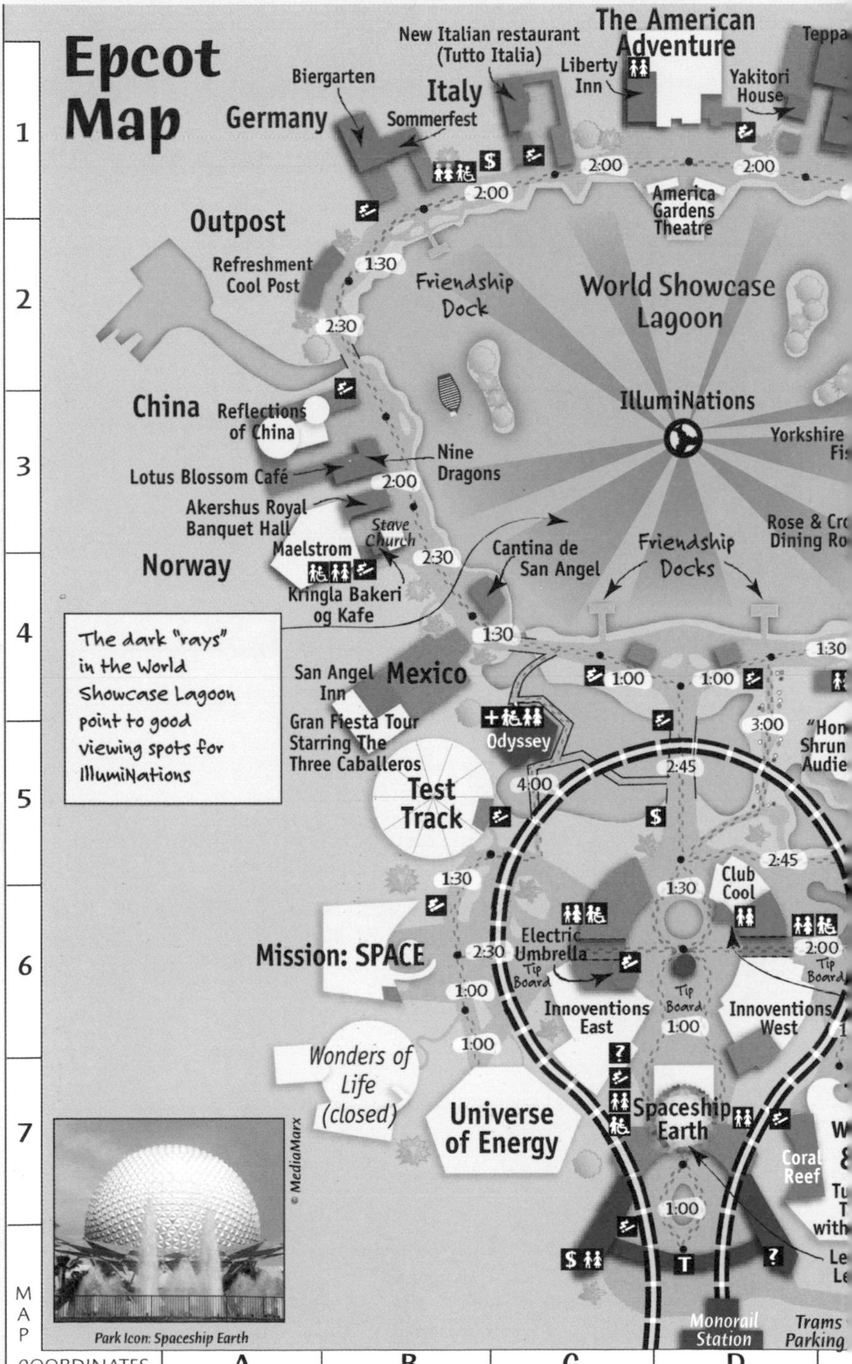

# Epcot Map

Germany
Biergarten
Sommerfest
Italy
New Italian restaurant (Tutto Italia)
The American Adventure
Liberty Inn
Yakitori House
America Gardens Theatre
Outpost
Refreshment Cool Post
Friendship Dock
World Showcase Lagoon
IllumiNations
China
Reflections of China
Nine Dragons
Lotus Blossom Café
Akershus Royal Banquet Hall
Stave Church
Maelstrom
Norway
Kringla Bakeri og Kafe
Cantina de San Angel
Friendship Docks
Yorkshire Fi...
Rose & Cr... Dining Ro...
San Angel Inn
Mexico
Gran Fiesta Tour Starring The Three Caballeros
Odyssey
Test Track
"Hon... Shrun... Audie..."
Club Cool
Mission: SPACE
Electric Umbrella
Tip Board
Innoventions East
Innoventions West
Wonders of Life (closed)
Universe of Energy
Spaceship Earth
Coral Reef
Monorail Station
Trams Parking

The dark "rays" in the World Showcase Lagoon point to good viewing spots for IllumiNations

Park Icon: Spaceship Earth

© MediaMarx

MAP COORDINATES: 1, 2, 3, 4, 5, 6, 7; A, B, C, D

# Epcot
# Attractions At-A-Glance
*(alphabetical order)*

| Attraction | Type | Allow | Page |
|---|---|---|---|
| ☐ America Gardens Theatre [D-1] | Show | 30–40+ | 148-WS |
| ☐ The American Adventure [D-1] | Pavilion | (80+) | 148-WS |
| ☐ The American Adventure Show [D-1] | Show | (50+) | 148-WS |
| ☐ Canada [E-4] | Pavilion | 30–40+ | 149-WS |
| ☐ China [B-3] | Pavilion | (35+) | 147-WS |
| ☐ Club Cool [D-6] | Walk-thru | 15-20+ | 145-FW |
| ☐ The Circle of Life [F-6] | Film | 15-20+ | 145-FW |
| ☐ France [F-2] | Pavilion | 30–40+ | 149-WS |
| ☐ Germany [B-1] | Pavilion | (15–30+) | 148-WS |
| ☐ Gran Fiesta Tour [B-4] | Boat Ride | 20+ | 147-WS |
| ☐ Honey, I Shrunk the Audience [E-5] | 3-D Film | 25–45+ | 146-FW |
| ☐ ImageWorks [E-5] | Playground | 20–30+ | 146-FW |
| ☐ Impressions de France [F-2] | Film | 20–25+ | 149-WS |
| ☐ Innoventions East [C-6] | Playground | 40–60+ | 143-FW |
| ☐ Innoventions West [D-6] | Playground | 40–60+ | 145-FW |
| ☐ Italy [C-1] | Pavilion | (15–30+) | 148-WS |
| ☐ Japan [D-1] | Pavilion | 15–30+ | 148-WS |
| ☐ Journey Into Imagination [E-5] | Track Ride | 15-20+ | 146-FW |
| ☐ The Land [E-6] | Pavilion | (90+) | 145-FW |
| ☐ Living With the Land [F-6] | Boat Ride | 30–40+ | 146-FW |
| ☐ Maelstrom [B-3] | Boat Ride | 25–40+ | 147-WS |
| ☐ Mexico [B-4] | Pavilion | (25+) | 147-WS |
| ☐ Mission: SPACE [B-6] | Thrill Ride | 40–90+ | 144-FW |
| ☐ Morocco [E-1] | Pavilion | 20–30+ | 149-WS |
| ☐ Norway [B-3] | Pavilion | (45+) | 147-WS |
| ☐ O Canada! [E-4] | Film | (20–25+) | 149-WS |
| ☐ Reflections of China [A-3] | Film | 25–30+ | 147-WS |
| ☐ The Seas with Nemo & Friends [E-7] | Pavilion/Ride | 40–60+ | 145-FW |
| ☐ Soarin' [F-5] | Simulator | 60–75+ | 146-FW |
| ☐ Spaceship Earth [D-7] | Track Ride | 30–40+ | 143-FW |
| ☐ Test Track [B-5] | Thrill Ride | 40–90+ | 144-FW |
| ☐ Turtle Talk with Crush [E-7] | Show | 30–40+ | 145-FW |
| ☐ United Kingdom [F-3] | Pavilion | 15–30+ | 149-WS |
| ☐ Universe of Energy [B-7] | Film/Ride | 40–60+ | 143-FW |

*The Allow column gives the amount of time (in minutes) you should allow for an attraction, assuming you do not have a FASTPASS and there are no ride breakdowns. Times in parentheses are approximate totals for all attractions in that pavilion—component times for that pavilion's attractions are also in the attraction list.*

*The letters after the page numbers stand for the first two letters of the land in which that attraction is located: FW for Future World and WS for World Showcase.*

Touring

# Our Favorite Touring Plan for Epcot

NOTES

Epcot is so large it's really difficult to do in one day, and we don't recommend it if at all possible. We recognize that many families may only have one day for Epcot, however, so we're sharing our best, one-day touring plan (which assumes entry by 9:00 am). If you can enter earlier, spend that extra time in Future World. Those lucky enough to have more time to spend at Epcot probably don't need a touring plan at all. But if you'd like to use ours anyway, you can easily split Future World and World Showcase into two days—just add in all the optional attractions and plan to sleep in on the day you do World Showcase (as it opens later than Future World). As with our other touring plans, you can skip items in blue if you're with young kids or sedate adults.

ITINERARY

## Touring With Adults and/or Kids

**Enter Future World East**
Get FASTPASS for Mission: SPACE
Visit Test Track
Visit Mission: SPACE
Visit Spaceship Earth
Visit Club Cool
**Enter The Land (Future World West)**
Get FASTPASS for Soarin'
**Enter The Seas with Nemo & Friends**
Visit The Seas with Nemo & Friends
See Turtle Talk with Crush
**Enter The Land**
Visit Living With the Land
(Optional: Visit The Circle of Life)
**Eat lunch** at The Garden Grill or Sunshine Seasons (*estimate lunch time at about two hours after you enter the park*)
Visit Soarin'
**Enter Imagination!**
Visit Honey, I Shrunk the Audience
Visit Journey Into Imagination with Figment
**Enter Canada**
Browse Canadian pavilion
**Enter United Kingdom**
Browse United Kingdom pavilion
**Enter France**
Browse French pavilion
Visit Impressions de France
**Enter Morocco**
Browse Moroccan pavilion
Have a snack in World Showcase East (try a baklava in Morocco or Kaki Gori in Japan)
**Enter Japan**
Browse Japanese pavilion
**Enter American Adventure**
Visit The American Adventure
**Eat dinner** in World Showcase East. Try San Angel Inn or Cantina de San Angel in Mexico, or Akershus Royal Banquet Hall in Norway (*estimate time at 7½ hours after you enter the park*)
**Enter Mexico**
Visit Gran Fiesta Tour Starring The Three Caballeros
Enjoy any extra "free time" at the World Showcase
(Optional: Visit Maelstrom—if you decide to do this, you may want to get a FASTPASS for it earlier.)
Find an IllumiNations viewing spot (the terrace of Cantina de San Angel can be good—see pages 150 and 252 for tips)
Watch IllumiNations

*(Tour duration: About 11 hours)*

## Touring With Kids

Start at The Land or The Seas with Nemo & Friends rather than Mission: SPACE (be sure to see Turtle Talk with Crush). Proceed with the plan, omitting those items in blue that won't appeal to your kids. The extra time you gain can be used at the Epcot Character Spot or Kidcot stations around the World Showcase.

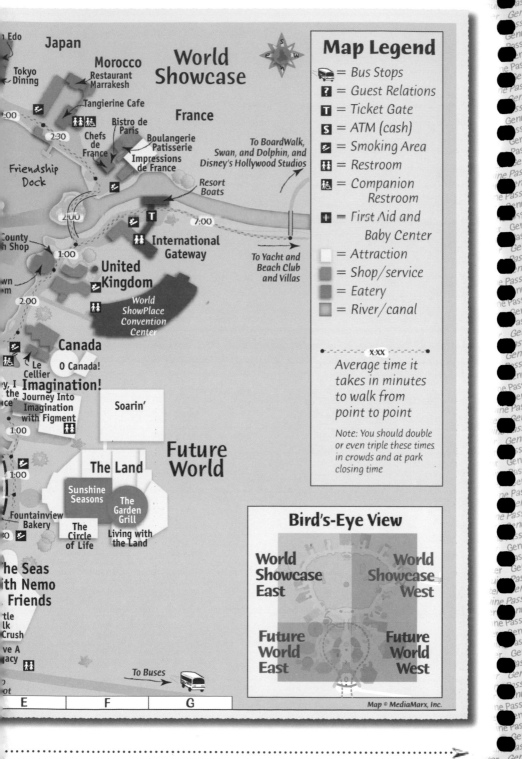

Japan
Morocco
Restaurant Marrakesh
Tokyo Dining
Tangierine Cafe
World Showcase
France
Bistro de Paris
Chefs de France
Boulangerie Patisserie
Impressions de France
Friendship Dock
To BoardWalk, Swan, and Dolphin, and Disney's Hollywood Studios
Resort Boats
International Gateway
United Kingdom
To Yacht and Beach Club and Villas
World ShowPlace Convention Center
Canada
Le Cellier
O Canada!
Imagination!
Journey Into Imagination with Figment
Soarin'
Future World
The Land
Sunshine Seasons
The Garden Grill
Fountainview Bakery
The Circle of Life
Living with the Land
The Seas with Nemo & Friends
To Buses

## Map Legend

- = Bus Stops
- = Guest Relations
- = Ticket Gate
- = ATM (cash)
- = Smoking Area
- = Restroom
- = Companion Restroom
- = First Aid and Baby Center
- = Attraction
- = Shop/service
- = Eatery
- = River/canal

X:XX Average time it takes in minutes to walk from point to point

Note: You should double or even triple these times in crowds and at park closing time

## Bird's-Eye View

World Showcase East | World Showcase West
Future World East | Future World West

E | F | G

Map © MediaMarx, Inc.

# Making the Most of Epcot

TIPS

If you arrive at Epcot via the **monorail**, you get a wonderful aerial view of Future World and a glimpse of World Showcase—this is how we snapped the photo on page 138.

Little ones adore the **Kidcot Fun Stops** at each World Showcase pavilion as well as Innoventions West, Test Track, The Land, and The Seas with Nemo & Friends. Cast members offer kids masks to color and decorate with beads and cutouts—there's something different to add to the mask at each country. Alexander loves it! Kids also love the play fountains on the promenade between Future World and the World Showcase, and behind Innoventions East. Come prepared with suits under clothing and/or dry clothes and shoes.

Looking for **characters** at Epcot? Check out the new Epcot Character Spot in Future World West, near Innoventions West.

*Allie at Club Cool*

Consider an Epcot **guided tour**, such as Around the World (on a Segway!) or Undiscovered Future World. See pages 244–245.

On your way out of the park in the evening, glance down at the path as you pass Innoventions—you'll discover **fiber-optic lights** embedded in the pavement that make beautiful patterns.

Epcot is the dining capital of the "World." Nearly all the good stuff encircles the lagoon in an **international dining extravaganza**, offering everything from the upscale Bistro de Paris to tacos at Cantina de San Angel. Future World offers less table-service dining, but it has some counter-service opportunities. See pages 210–216.

NOTES

"**Friendships**" (boats) convey you to different points within World Showcase. You can usually get there faster if you walk, however.

The **Epcot wand** on Spaceship Earth was removed in mid-2007.

Good viewing locations for **IllumiNations** go quickly. See page 150 for hints on getting the best possible view of the action.

After IllumiNations ends, step aside and wait for the crowds to thin. Take a **leisurely stroll** around the lagoon. Enjoy the music and the lights—you'll have a nice, quiet walk with very few people around. As a bonus, you'll miss the traffic in the parking lot and bus queues.

# Getting to Epcot

**BEST TIMES TO GO**

The **best time to visit World Showcase** is when it first opens at 11:00 am, as most guests are still in Future World. It follows then that the **best time to tour Future World** is in the late afternoon and during dinner time (note that many attractions in Future World close at about 7:00 pm). World Showcase becomes congested in the evenings due to the many restaurants and IllumiNations show. Because of the focus on dining at Epcot, traditional lunch and dinner times are better spent at the attractions while others are eating. Along the same vein, you will find restaurants less busy and noisy if you dine before or after the normal lunch and dinner hour. **IllumiNations** is held nightly at park closing (usually 9:00 pm)—for a good view, start looking about one hour prior (see page 150). If you've already seen IllumiNations, consider **dining during it** for a quieter experience.

**GETTING THERE**

**By Monorail**—From the Magic Kingdom, Contemporary, Polynesian, or Grand Floridian, take the monorail to the Transportation and Ticket Center (TTC) and transfer to the Epcot monorail.
**By Boat**—From Disney's Hollywood Studios, Swan/Dolphin, BoardWalk, and Yacht & Beach Club, boats go to Epcot's International Gateway.
**By Bus**—From other resorts, Disney's Hollywood Studios, or Disney's Animal Kingdom, buses take you directly to Epcot. From Downtown Disney, take a bus to a nearby resort and transfer to an Epcot bus, boat, or walk. (Tip: Bus to BoardWalk and walk/boat to Epcot.)
**By Car**—Take I-4 to exit 67 (westbound) or exit 62 (eastbound) and continue on to the Epcot toll plaza. All-day parking is available for $10 (free to resort guests and annual passholders).
**By Foot**—From the BoardWalk Inn & Villas, Yacht & Beach Club and Villas, Swan & Dolphin, and Disney's Hollywood Studios, Epcot is within walking distance. Follow the paths toward International Gateway—it emerges between United Kingdom and France. Walk through United Kingdom and Canada to reach Future World.

**RATINGS**

*Ratings are explained on page 120.*

| Our Value Ratings: | | Our Magic Ratings: | | Readers' Ratings: |
|---|---|---|---|---|
| Quality: | 8/10 | Theme: | 8/10 | 58% fell in love with it |
| Variety: | 8/10 | Excitement: | 8/10 | 34% liked it well enough |
| Scope: | 10/10 | Fun Factor: | 6/10 | 7% had mixed feelings |
| **Overall Value:** | **9/10** | **Overall Magic:** | **7/10** | 1% were disappointed |

**Epcot is enjoyed by...** **(rated by both authors and readers)**

| | | |
|---|---|---|
| Younger Kids: ♥♥♥ | Young Adults: ♥♥♥♥ | Families: ♥♥♥♥ |
| Older Kids: ♥♥♥ | Mid Adults: ♥♥♥♥♥ | Couples: ♥♥♥♥♥ |
| Teenagers: ♥♥♥ | Mature Adults: ♥♥♥♥♥ | Singles: ♥♥♥♥♥ |

# Charting the Attractions at Future World (East)

Jennifer's Rating | Dave's Rating | Readers' Rating

## Spaceship Earth [D-7] A-OK! 9 7 8

**Track Ride** | E-Ticket | Ages 3 & up | Dark, steep incline, but gentle | Short waits | 15 min. ride

*Go inside the huge geodesic sphere that towers above Epcot for a look at the development of communication technologies from cave paintings through the space age. Four-seat "time machine" vehicles take you up into the huge sphere past dozens of Audio-Animatronics reenacting milestones in communication. This attraction was closed for renovations at press time, but when it re-opens in late 2007/early 2008, expect new ride scenes, changes to existing scenes, and an interactive touchscreen in the "time machine" vehicle. At the end of the ride, you'll exit into a new post-show exhibit, Project Tomorrow, sponsored by Siemens. Here you can "build a body" in 3-D, experience a driving simulation game, and check out an illuminated globe with a collage of futuristic images. Adults should accompany and sit beside children. We suggest you visit at park opening or in the evening for shorter waits. Outdoor queue is mostly covered. Guests must transfer from wheelchair.* **Alex's ToddlerTip:** ☺ **Allie's KidTip:** *"You'll love all the lights. And it's good for learning."* **Allie's TeenTip:** *"Really boring."*

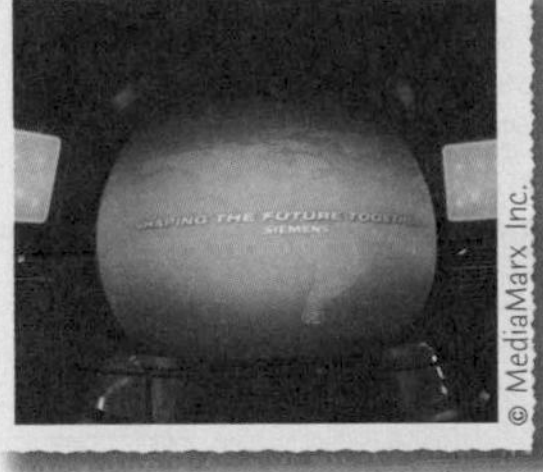
© MediaMarx, Inc.

*Project Tomorrow post-show*

## Innoventions East [C-6] A-OK! 7 5 6

**Playground** | B-Ticket | All ages | Noisy | Short waits | Allow about 1 hour to explore

*If gee-whiz technology pushes your buttons, pay a visit to Innoventions—Epcot's two-part, high-tech, hands-on trade exhibit. Innoventions East exhibits on Internet activities (send electronic and video e-mail back home), UL product testing (test the limits of products like a real UL engineer), the House of Innoventions (see inventive products available today), the Fantastic Plastics Works exhibit (design your own plastic robot—rumor has it this exhibit could be closing soon), and the Kim Possible Kidcot area (see page 141 for information about Kidcot). Short queues in some exhibits. Wheelchair accessible.* **Allie's TeenTip:** *"Video e-mail is fun."*

## Universe of Energy (Ellen's Energy Adventure) [B-7] A-OK! 5 6 7

**Film/Ride** | E-Ticket | Ages 4 & up | Dark, loud, dinosaurs | Med. waits | 8 min. intro 37 min. ride

*Join Ellen DeGeneres for a humorous crash course in energy, the stuff that powers our world. Widescreen films, thunderous sound effects, and gigantic Audio-Animatronics dinosaurs help tell the tale. Ellen's cast includes Bill Nye the Science Guy, Jamie Lee Curtis, and Alex Trebek. Shows start every 17 minutes. Indoor queue with uncovered, outdoor, overflow queue. The queue moves quickly once the show begins. Effects may be too intense for small kids and some adults. ECV must transfer to wheelchair. Wheelchair accessible. Assistive listening. No flash photo or video lights.* **Alex's ToddlerTip:** *"Dinosaurs roar! ☺"* **Allie's KidTip:** *"Dinosaurs!!! Oh, and it has a movie about energy, too. May be loud."* **Allie's TeenTip:** *"It's still cool to me, and a fun way to learn."*

© MediaMarx, Inc.

*Dinosaur topiaries outside*

*Attraction descriptions and ratings are explained on page 127.*

# Charting the Attractions at Future World (East)

*(continued)*

Jennifer's Rating | Dave's Rating | Readers' Rating

## Mission: SPACE [B-6]

FP

Ratings: 9 | 9 | 8

*Prepare for space flight at the International Space Training Center. As a civilian "astronaut," you board a four-person training centrifuge to experience the sensations of liftoff and zero gravity. Guests can choose between the original, high-intensity version (Orange Team) or a low-intensity experience (Green Team). In the high-intensity version, sensations are intense—the simulator spins rapidly and you may get queasy. If you go for the full-octane experience, heed the warnings and don't close your eyes or look to the side during the ride. If you'd rather not take the chance of getting sick, try the milder version—it's the same ride but without the spinning. Save time to enjoy the post-show exhibits. Young kids enjoy the Space Base playground. Indoor, themed queue. 44"/112 cm height restriction. Young kids must be with an adult. Health and motion sickness warnings.* **Allie's TweenTip:** *"It feels like you're actually taking off into space!* **TeenTip:** *"One of my favorite attractions of all time! Do not miss it!"*

**Thrill Ride**
E-Ticket
Ages 8 & up
Disorienting
FASTPASS or long waits
7 1/2 min. pre-show
5 min. ride

## Test Track [B-5]

FP A-OK!

Ratings: 8 | 8 | 9

*Do you feel the need for speed? How does 65 miles per hour in a rapidly accelerating six-seat, open-air test vehicle on a tightly banked track sound? Learn how GM tests (and tortures) new vehicles and experience some of those tests. Wait in an incredibly noisy, slow queue and watch test gear whack auto parts. Get a FASTPASS early in the day, or use the "single-rider queue" on the left for the shortest wait. Front seat offers more leg room. Indoor/outdoor queue. 40"/102 cm height restriction. Young children must be accompanied by adult. Health warning. Must transfer from wheelchair to ride. Assistive listening. Closed captioning.* **Allie's KidTip:** *"Sit in the middle so you don't get sprayed!"* **TeenTip:** *"I love the end of the ride when you go SUPER fast!"*

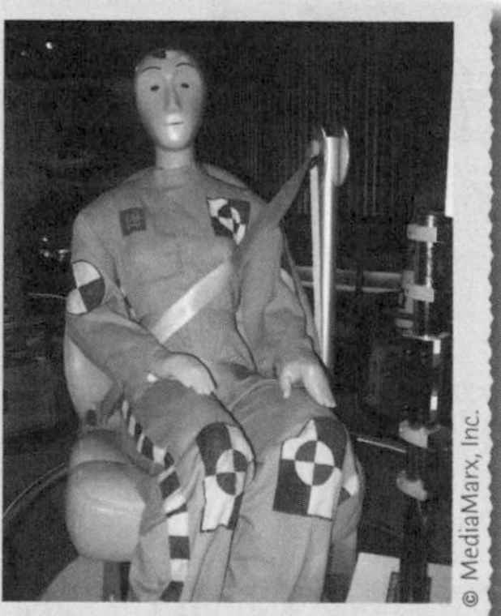

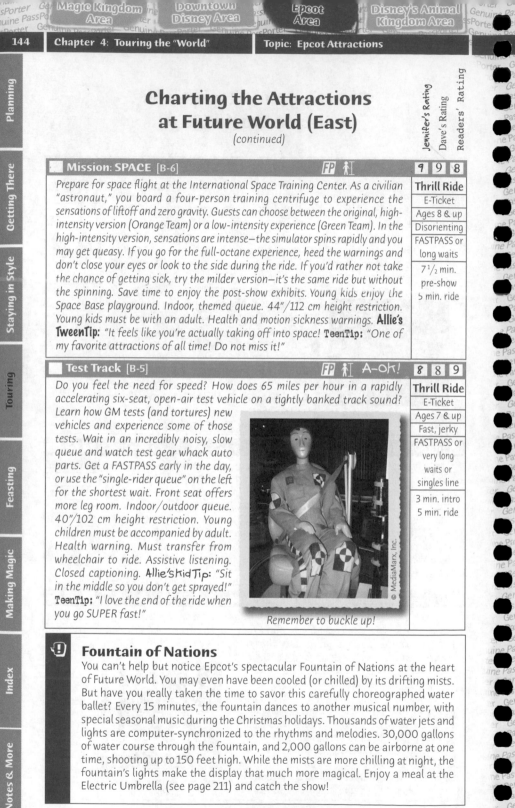

© MediaMarx, Inc.

*Remember to buckle up!*

**Thrill Ride**
E-Ticket
Ages 7 & up
Fast, jerky
FASTPASS or very long waits or singles line
3 min. intro
5 min. ride

### Fountain of Nations

You can't help but notice Epcot's spectacular Fountain of Nations at the heart of Future World. You may even have been cooled (or chilled) by its drifting mists. But have you really taken the time to savor this carefully choreographed water ballet? Every 15 minutes, the fountain dances to another musical number, with special seasonal music during the Christmas holidays. Thousands of water jets and lights are computer-synchronized to the rhythms and melodies. 30,000 gallons of water course through the fountain, and 2,000 gallons can be airborne at one time, shooting up to 150 feet high. While the mists are more chilling at night, the fountain's lights make the display that much more magical. Enjoy a meal at the Electric Umbrella (see page 211) and catch the show!

# Charting the Attractions at Future World (West)

Jennifer's Rating | Dave's Rating | Readers' Rating

## Club Cool [D-6] — 7 | 6 | 8

Sample free Coke beverages from other countries at this "clubby" diversion. This is a fun place to cool off and enjoy a soft drink, including an unusual aperitif called Beverly. You can purchase Coke merchandise here, including a frozen Coke "Build a Cup" station with Disney cup toppers ($8/cup). Wheelchair accessible. **Allie's TeenTip:** "The drink from Japan is the best!"

**Walk-thru** | A-Ticket | Ages 2 & up | Noisy, sticky floor

## Innoventions West [D-6] — 5 | 5 | 6

This is the other half of Innoventions (see page 143). Exhibits include the Welcome Center featuring Segway (guests ages 16 and older and less than 250 lbs. can test-drive the two-wheeled transportation device—see photo to right), exhibits on computing and high-speed Internet technologies, e-mail postcards, Disney's interactive games, home theater demos, and a fire safety exhibit with an interactive game house. Some short queues. Wheelchair accessible. **Allie's TeenTip:** "Video games are cool."

© MediaMarx, Inc.

**Playground** | B-Ticket | Ages 6 & up | Noisy | Short waits | Allow one hr.

## The Seas with Nemo & Friends (The Living Seas) [E-7] A-OK! — 6 | 7 | 6

Board "Clamobiles" and explore the world's largest saltwater aquarium tank and artificial coral reef. New technology allows your favorite characters from "Finding Nemo" to swim among the real marine life in the aquarium. View dolphins, sharks, manatees, and thousands of sea creatures. Check with a cast member for a demo schedule. For programs that explore the aquarium in more depth, see page 247. After the tame ride, don't miss Turtle Talk with Crush (see below). Indoor queue. Wheelchair accessible. Assistive listening. Reflective captioning. Closed captioning. **Alex's ToddlerTip:** "I found Nemo! ☺" **Allie's KidTip:** "I love the dolphins."

**Pavilion/Ride** | D-Ticket | All ages | Sharks! | Med. waits | Allow about one hour

## ✓ Turtle Talk with Crush [E-7] A-OK! — 9 | 9 | 9

State-of-the-art technology allows guests to interact with Crush (the sea turtle from "Finding Nemo")—he can see and hear you, and talk back! This animated, interactive experience engages kids and impresses adults. Encourage young kids (ages 3-8) to sit up front for the best experience. Inside The Living Seas pavilion. Wheelchair accessible. **Alex's ToddlerTip:** ☹ (bored) **Allie's TeenTip:** "Totally awesome, dude! It's so cute to hear the little kids' questions and answers."

**Show** | D-Ticket | Ages 3 & up | Long waits | 12 min. film

## The Land [E-6] A-OK! — 7 | 6 | 7

Agriculture and the environment take center stage, hosted by Nestlé. Rides, film, food court, and restaurant. "Behind the Seeds" guided greenhouse tour.

**Pavilion** | D-Ticket

## The Circle of Life [F-6] A-OK! — 6 | 5 | 6

Timon and Pumbaa from The Lion King set out to build the Hakuna Matata Village Resort—without regard to their ecosystem. Simba reminds them (and us) how important it is to protect the environment. Great photography. Indoor queue with benches. Inside The Land pavilion. Wheelchair accessible. Assistive listening. Reflective captioning. **Alex's ToddlerTip:** "Simba! ☺" **Allie's KidTip:** "Simba tells us about the earth and how to take care of it." **TeenTip:** "Great for everyone!"

**Film** | C-Ticket | Ages 3 & up | Short waits | 12 min. film

Attraction descriptions and ratings are explained on page 127.

# Charting the Attractions at Future World (West)

*(continued)*

Jennifer's Rating | Dave's Rating | Readers' Rating

## Soarin' [F-6] — FP — 10 | 9 | 9

*Soar over California's awesome scenery in a stunning copy of the headline ride at Disney's California Adventure park. Guests are strapped into oversized porch swings and rise from the floor for a simulated hang glider tour of the Golden State. An eye-filling, IMAX-quality movie screen, gentle motion, stirring music, and scented breezes combine for an exhilarating journey that ends with fireworks over Disneyland. Queue is indoors and offers fun games to play while waiting. Inside The Land pavilion. 40"/102 cm height restriction. Transfer from wheelchair to ride. Closed captioning.* **Allie's TeenTip:** *"Wow!"*

**Simulator** | E-Ticket | Ages 7 & up | Heights | FASTPASS or very long waits | 5 min. ride

## Living With the Land [F-6] — FP — A-OK! — 7 | 6 | 7

*Learn how modern agriculture serves the needs of a hungry world and protects the environment. Your boat cruises through a multimedia exhibit and Disney's amazing experimental hydroponic greenhouses. See veggies that may be served for dinner upstairs (more than 30 tons are produced annually). Flash photos are only allowed in the greenhouses. Indoor queues. Inside The Land pavilion. Must transfer from ECV to wheelchair. Wheelchair accessible.* **Alex's ToddlerTip:** ☺ **Allie's KidTip:** *"They have American Alligators!"* **TeenTip:** *"Boring but educational."*

**Boat Ride** | D-Ticket | Ages 4 & up | Dark | FASTPASS or med. waits | 13 min. ride

## Honey, I Shrunk the Audience [E-5] — FP — A-OK! — 8 | 8 | 8

*Get shrunk by Dr. Wayne Szalinski (Rick Moranis) when a demonstration of his world-famous shrinking/enlarging machine goes awry. A funny story and spectacular visual and special effects make this a must-see show for those who aren't terrified by snakes, mice, and dogs. There's no need to sit up front. An indoor/outdoor queue leads to a pre-show film sponsored by Kodak. This may be too intense for children and some adults. Wheelchair accessible. Assistive listening. Reflective captioning.* **Alex's ToddlerTip:** ☺ **Allie's KidTip:** *"It's scary. Take off your glasses when you get scared and just watch the TV."*

**3-D Film** | E-Ticket | Ages 8 & up | Loud, intense | FASTPASS or long waits | 5 min. intro 13 min. film

## Journey Into Imagination with Figment [E-5] — A-OK! — 5 | 5 | 3

*Figment, the cute purple dragon, comes roaring back to Epcot in a reenergized version of Journey Into Your Imagination. Figment and Dr. Nigel Channing (Eric Idle) team up to stimulate our imaginations with sight, sound, smell, a bit of whimsy, and music from Disney legends Richard and Robert Sherman. Highlights include Figment's House and the final rendition of the theme song, One Little Spark. The ride still doesn't rate an "A," but you'll be charmed and tickled. Riders exit into the ImageWorks interactive playground. Indoor queue with outdoor overflow queue. Effects too intense for some children. Wheelchair accessible.* **Alex's ToddlerTip:** *"Ride again, please! ☺"* **Allie's TeenTip:** *"It's pretty lame!"*

**Track Ride** | C-Ticket | Ages 5 & up | Portions are very dark, loud, with bright flashes | Med. waits | 6 min. ride

## ImageWorks: Kodak "What If" Labs [E-5] — A-OK! — 6 | 6 | 7

*Hands-on sound and image exhibits and a gift shop, at the exit to Journey Into Imagination with Figment. Digital portraits (which can be sent via e-mail), inventive photo gifts, and a unique Kodak photo lab. "Backdoor" entrance through shop.* **Allie's KidTip:** *"It's cool! Check out the floor piano!"*

**Playground** | B-Ticket | All ages | Allow 30 min.

# Charting the Attractions at World Showcase

(clockwise order)

Jennifer's Rating | Dave's Rating | Readers' Rating

## Mexico [B-4] A-OK! 7 6 8

*Enter Mexico's Mayan pyramid to find yourself in a magical, twilit village plaza with a volcano smoking ominously in the distance. Enjoy a fine exhibit of art and artifacts, eateries, a ride (see below), shops, and musicians.* **Allie's Kid Tip:** *"Don't worry, that's not a real volcano. Looks like it, though!"*

**Pavilion** | D-Ticket | All ages | Low light

## Gran Fiesta Tour Starring The Three Cabelleros [B-4] A-OK! 6 5 5

*Tour Mexico in this revamped boat ride (formerly El Rio del Tiempo) featuring Audio-Animatronics, music, and short film/animation clips with the Three Caballeros (Donald Duck, Jose Carioca, and Panchito Pistoles). Jose and Panchito fly through Mexico in search of Donald for the big show. Don't miss the cool fiber-optic fireworks display. Your boat floats past diners at the San Angel Inn restaurant. Some call this ride the Mexican version of "it's a small world," complete with dancing dolls. Indoor queue inside the Mexico pavilion. Transfer from ECV to wheelchair to ride. Wheelchair accessible.* **Alex's Toddler Tip:** *"Ride again! ☺" (his new favorite!)* **Allie's Kid Tip:** *"Be sure to look up and see the fireworks!"*

**Boat Ride** | C-Ticket | All ages | Dark, but very tame | Short waits | 7 minute cruise

## Norway [B-3] A-OK! 6 6 7

*This taste of Norway features a Viking ship, shops, the Maelstrom ride (see below), eateries, and an ancient wooden church. Tours available. Peek inside the church for a history of the Vikings.* **Allie's Kid Tip:** *"If you see a troll, rub its nose for luck. It's too bad you can't play in the Viking ship anymore."*

**Pavilion** | C-Ticket | All ages | Allow 30 min.

## Maelstrom [B-3] FP A-OK! 6 5 7

*Board a boat for a refreshing ride through the Norway of fact and fancy. Trolls, Vikings, and a North Sea storm are all part of a fanciful ride that is much tamer than the name implies. The few "drops" are little more than a bounce. The Viking boats deposit you in an attractive indoor fishing village, prior to viewing a filmed travelogue. A new film is in production, set to debut sometime in the future—walk right through the theater if you decide to skip the film. Indoor queue. Must transfer from wheelchair to ride. Assistive listening. Reflective captioning (movie).* **Allie's Kid Tip:** *"Don't be scared of the life-size polar bears."*

**Boat Ride** | D-Ticket | Ages 5 & up | Small drops and dark | FASTPASS or med. waits | 15 min. ride

## China [B-3] A-OK! 4 5 6

*Explore China through a film (see below), art and photography exhibits, gardens, eateries, and the Yong Feng Shangdian department store. Visit a half-scale model of Beijing's Temple of Heaven. Acrobats and gymnasts perform.* **Allie's Kid Tip:** *"When you walk into the temple to see the movie, look up."*

**Pavilion** | C-Ticket | All ages | Allow 20 min.

## Reflections of China [A-3] 7 6 7

*Experience marvels of China in a sweeping, 360° motion picture. Grand scenes of the Great Wall, the Yangtze Gorge, and Beijing's Forbidden City alternate with views of bustling cities. The film—previously called "Wonders of China"—was improved in 2003 with vibrant new footage of modern China including Macao and Hong Kong. You must stand to view. Indoor waiting area with wooden benches. Wheelchair accessible. Assistive listening devices. Reflective captioning.* **Allie's Kid Tip:** *"Don't sit down or you'll miss part of the movie."*

**Film** | C-Ticket | Ages 6 & up | Could cause dizziness | Short waits | 13 min. show

*Attraction descriptions and ratings are explained on page 127.*

# Charting the Attractions at World Showcase

*(continued in clockwise order)*

Jennifer's Rating / Dave's Rating / Readers' Rating

### Germany [B-1] — 3 4 7

*Steep-roofed stone buildings, oompah bands, eateries, and shops evoke a quaint German square. Look for the model railroad, and listen for the glockenspiel that chimes on the hour.* **Allie'sKidTip:** *"Find the train set in the toy shop."*

Pavilion | C-Ticket | All ages

### Italy [C-1] — 5 4 6

*Disney faithfully captures the spirit and architecture of Venice in this Italian piazza. Eateries, shops, jugglers, music, and entertainers in a Mediterranean garden set the scene at this pavilion. Look closely at the angel atop the 83-foot-tall bell tower—it is covered in real gold leaf. The tower itself is a replica of the Campanile in St. Mark's Square, Venice. While there are no rides or movies at this pavilion, it's still worth a visit.* **Allie'sKidTip:** *"Make a good wish at King Neptune's fountain."*

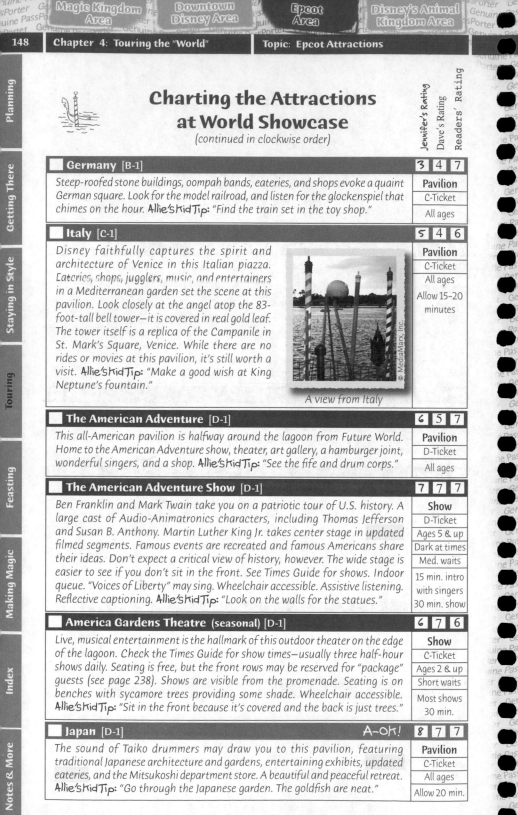

© MediaMarx, Inc.
*A view from Italy*

Pavilion | C-Ticket | All ages | Allow 15-20 minutes

### The American Adventure [D-1] — 6 5 7

*This all-American pavilion is halfway around the lagoon from Future World. Home to the American Adventure show, theater, art gallery, a hamburger joint, wonderful singers, and a shop.* **Allie'sKidTip:** *"See the fife and drum corps."*

Pavilion | D-Ticket | All ages

### The American Adventure Show [D-1] — 7 7 7

*Ben Franklin and Mark Twain take you on a patriotic tour of U.S. history. A large cast of Audio-Animatronics characters, including Thomas Jefferson and Susan B. Anthony. Martin Luther King Jr. takes center stage in updated filmed segments. Famous events are recreated and famous Americans share their ideas. Don't expect a critical view of history, however. The wide stage is easier to see if you don't sit in the front. See Times Guide for shows. Indoor queue. "Voices of Liberty" may sing. Wheelchair accessible. Assistive listening. Reflective captioning.* **Allie'sKidTip:** *"Look on the walls for the statues."*

Show | D-Ticket | Ages 5 & up | Dark at times | Med. waits | 15 min. intro with singers | 30 min. show

### America Gardens Theatre (seasonal) [D-1] — 6 7 6

*Live, musical entertainment is the hallmark of this outdoor theater on the edge of the lagoon. Check the Times Guide for show times—usually three half-hour shows daily. Seating is free, but the front rows may be reserved for "package" guests (see page 238). Shows are visible from the promenade. Seating is on benches with sycamore trees providing some shade. Wheelchair accessible.* **Allie'sKidTip:** *"Sit in the front because it's covered and the back is just trees."*

Show | C-Ticket | Ages 2 & up | Short waits | Most shows 30 min.

### Japan [D-1] — A-OK! — 8 7 7

*The sound of Taiko drummers may draw you to this pavilion, featuring traditional Japanese architecture and gardens, entertaining exhibits, updated eateries, and the Mitsukoshi department store. A beautiful and peaceful retreat.* **Allie'sKidTip:** *"Go through the Japanese garden. The goldfish are neat."*

Pavilion | C-Ticket | All ages | Allow 20 min.

# Charting the Attractions at World Showcase

(continued in clockwise order)

Jennifer's Rating | Dave's Rating | Readers' Rating

## Morocco [E-1] — A-OK! — 7 | 6 | 7

*Morocco's Moorish architecture, art exhibits, exotic cuisine, live entertainers, and crafts beckon to the adventuresome traveler. Much is hidden from the casual visitor—take the free "Treasures of Morocco" tour for a better look (ask a cast member for details). You'll find a character meet-and-greet area virtually hidden across from Restaurant Marrakesh, plus artisans and cultural representatives scattered throughout. Excellent shopping opportunities.* **Allie's KidTip:** *"You'll feel like you want to go to Africa. I like the entertainers here, too."*

Pavilion | C-Ticket | All ages | No scares | Allow about 20-30 min. to explore

## France [F-2] — A-OK! — 7 | 7 | 7

*The Eiffel Tower, cobblestone streets, eateries, shops (including a new Guerlain boutique), street performers, and a film (see below) evoke the essence of France.* **Allie's TeenTip:** *"I want to go to Paris, and this is almost as good."*

Pavilion | D-Ticket | All ages

## Impressions de France [F-2] — A-OK! — 9 | 9 | 7

*The beauty and romance of France's villages, cities, and countryside come to life in a breathtaking film. Fabulous scenery, wonderful 200° widescreen photography, and the best musical soundtrack at Walt Disney World (great French classical tunes) make this one of our favorites. Cool, dark theater offers seating and welcome relief. Shows on the hour and half-hour. Wrought-iron benches and small exhibits make even the indoor, air-conditioned queue enjoyable. Wheelchair accessible. Assistive listening. Reflective captioning.* **Alex's ToddlerTip:** ☹ *(bored)* **Allie's KidTip:** *"You get to see Notre Dame, like in 'Hunchback of Notre Dame.'"*

Film | D-Ticket | Ages 5 & up | Dark theater, loud music | Short waits | 18 min. film

## United Kingdom [E-3] — A-OK! — 7 | 6 | 7

*This is Florida's British Colony, full of quaint shops, gardens, a restful park with live entertainment (check the Times Guide for The British Invasion band—they're excellent!), a busy pub, and deliciously British eateries. Well-themed.* **Allie's KidTip:** *"You gotta play in the hedge maze! And there's really cool music."*

Pavilion | C-Ticket | All ages will enjoy

## Canada [E-4] — 5 | 5 | 7

*The architecture and natural beauty of Canada are captured in a 360° movie (see below), nifty waterfall, gardens, shops, eateries, and live music.*

Pavilion | C-Ticket

## O Canada! [E-4] — A-OK! — 7 | 5 | 6

*Experience the natural and manmade wonders of Canada in an updated Circle-Vision 360 film. Swooping aerials and dramatic scenery highlight this tour encompassing the Rockies and old-world Montreal. The updated film includes about 50% new footage and features Martin Short and Eva Avila. Shows start every 20 minutes. Stand to view. Indoor queue. Wheelchair accessible. Assistive listening. Reflective captioning.* **Alex's ToddlerTip:** ☹ *(bored)* **Allie's KidTip:** *"I got tired of standing for so long."*

© MediaMarx, Inc.

*Looking out at Canada*

Film | C-Ticket | Ages 5 & up | Dark, a little dizzying | 14 min. film

*Attraction descriptions and ratings are explained on page 127.*

# Making the Most of IllumiNations

**IllumiNations: Reflections of Earth** brings every night to a spectacular close. Brilliant fireworks and a rousing, original musical score fill Epcot's World Showcase Lagoon every evening at park closing, heralding the creation of Earth. A shower of sparkling comets paves the way, a huge globe glides across the lagoon to take center stage, and a pageant of breathtaking scenery, wildlife, and the peoples of the earth plays across a giant video display covering the continents of the globe. Lasers, blazing torches, and more fireworks tumble forth as the music builds to a rousing climax. Although the show is visible anywhere around the lagoon, there are definitely **better viewing sites**. You can judge a viewing site well in advance of the show as you stroll around the lagoon, or check our map on page 140. A clear view of the water at the center of the lagoon is critical, as is a clear view of the sky (watch those tree limbs). It also helps if the wind is to your back or side (to avoid fireworks smoke). The bridge between France and the United Kingdom is a prime (and popular) location. Italy and Norway are other good viewing spots. Or try for a 7:30 pm priority seating at the Rose & Crown. Check in at the podium early and request a patio table. You may get lucky with a great view. If not, enjoy your meal anyway—diners are invited outside to stand and enjoy the show. Another place to stay seated is at Cantina de San Angel in Mexico. Arrive at least 90 min. early for a lagoon-side table. We also highly recommend the excellent views from the lagoon-side patios in the United Kingdom and France, if they aren't already occupied by private parties.

*IllumiNations finale*

### PhotoPass

Disney's parks are awash in official photographers these days, now that Disney's PhotoPass has hit the scene. PhotoPass has added new convenience to having professional photos taken in the parks. When you have your first photo taken, the photographer will give you a PhotoPass card—it looks just like a credit card. At the next photo op, hand your card to the photographer and he/she will slide it through a card reader. Later, whether at a photo shop in the park, or at the PhotoPass web site (http://www.disneyphotopass.com), all your photos will be together in one place. Order prints, or get a CD with all the shots from your vacation. Keep using the same card on every visit, or combine the photos from several cards into a single account. The best thing, as far as we're concerned, is that you don't have to wait in long lines at the park's photo shop to get your pictures. Visit http://www.stitchkingdom.com/photopass/ for an unofficial guide to PhotoPass!

# Disney's Hollywood Studios
## *(formerly Disney-MGM Studios)*

Disney-MGM Studios' name changes to Disney's Hollywood Studios on January 1, 2008. This park's 154 acres spotlight the golden era of Hollywood and the glamorous silver screen. It's located southwest of Epcot and is connected to Epcot by Friendship boats and walkways.

### AMBIENCE

Tinseltown never looked so good. All the glamour, glitz, and pageantry of Hollywood come out to greet you at Disney's Hollywood Studios. Disney's rendition of Hollywood Boulevard is done up in 1930s art deco architecture, and an old-fashioned water tower (complete with Mickey ears) sets the stage. And you can't miss the 122-foot-tall version of **Mickey's Sorcerer's Hat**, representing the magic of show business and Disney animation. Disney's Hollywood Studios gives you a behind-the-scenes glimpse at movie-making as well as an opportunity to get involved in shows and tours. Celebrities may put in live appearances at Disney's Hollywood Studios as well, complete with a procession down Hollywood Boulevard and a handprint ceremony. There may also be chances to see upcoming movies being filmed on the actual soundstages that make their home here. The whole effect is of being a special guest at a major movie studio in the heart of Hollywood.

### PARK LAYOUT AND HIGHLIGHTS

Unlike other parks, Disney's Hollywood Studios' layout is free-form, much like Hollywood's artistic personalities (see park map on page 154). See pages 153a&b for daily touring itineraries and an attractions-at-a-glance list, and pages 157–160 for attraction details.

| | |
|---|---|
| **Hollywood Boulevard Area**<br>*Headline Attraction:* | Stroll among the stars—this is the "main street" of Tinseltown in its heyday.<br>*The Great Movie Ride* |
| **Sunset Boulevard Area**<br>*Headline Attractions:* | Step back in time to the Hollywood that never was on this famous, palm-lined boulevard.<br>*Rock 'n' Roller Coaster, Tower of Terror, Beauty and the Beast* |
| **Echo Lake Area**<br>*Headline Attractions:* | Learn the magic behind spectacular stunts and effects, and go for a journey into outer space.<br>*Star Tours, Indiana Jones Epic Stunt Spectacular* |
| **Streets of America Area**<br>*Headline Attractions:* | Visit a movie set evoking famous urban skylines. It even has "towering" skyscrapers!<br>*Muppet*Vision 3-D; Lights, Motors, Action! Extreme Stunt Show* |
| **Mickey Avenue Area**<br>*Headline Attractions:* | Peek behind the scenes in soundstages, the "backlot," and animation exhibits.<br>*Voyage of the Little Mermaid, One Man's Dream* |

Fold out the next page for touring plans and a handy attraction chart

# Entertainment and Shopping at Disney's Hollywood Studios

## ENTERTAINMENT

Entertainment is simply a matter of course at Disney's Hollywood Studios. The unique **"streetmosphere"** performers make their home along famous boulevards of Hollywood and Sunset, as well as Echo Lake. Dressed in 1940s-style garb, they're responsible for all sorts of on-the-street shenanigans. The afternoon parade prior to spring 2008 is "**Disney Stars and Motor Cars**," showcasing more than 60 Disney characters. Come spring, the "**Block Party Bash**" parade from Disney's California Adventure debuts, featuring Disney-Pixar pals in an interactive experience. The parade route is marked on the map on page 154. Be sure to stake out your viewing spot along the parade route about 30 min. in advance. If you're a fan of *High School Musical*, check out the **High School Musical Pep Rally** on a traveling stage. Come evening, it's Mickey versus villains in **Fantasmic!** at the Hollywood Hills Amphitheater. Fantasmic! is a spectacular mix of live action, music, and fireworks. The huge outdoor amphitheater seats 6,900 at this nightly show. Fantasmic! may be held more often during busy seasons (later shows have shorter waits and better seating). Fantasmic! is popular, though we can take it or leave it. A Fantasmic! Meal Package may be available with special seating—see page 219.

© MediaMarx, Inc.

*The Sorcerer's Hat icon at night*

## SHOPPING

**General merchandise** shopping is on Hollywood and Sunset Boulevards. Many major attractions have a **themed shop**, too. All shops can be entered without going on a ride. Here are our favorites:

| Shop | Location | What makes it special |
|---|---|---|
| Crossroads of the World | Hollywood Blvd. | Guidemaps, Times Guides, ponchos |
| Sid Cahuenga's | Hollywood Blvd. | One-of-a-kind movie memorabilia |
| Celebrity 5 & 10 | Hollywood Blvd. | Custom embroidery and engraving |
| Keystone Clothiers | Hollywood Blvd. | Quality Disney clothes |
| Villains in Vogue | Sunset Blvd. | Disney Villain clothing and gifts |
| Stage One Company Store | Streets of America | Quirky shop with Muppets! |
| Writer's Stop | Streets of America | Books! (We can't resist 'em!) |
| Tatooine Traders | Echo Lake | Star Wars items, fun theme |
| Hollywood Tower Hotel | Sunset Blvd. | Scary stuff and Tower of Terror gifts |

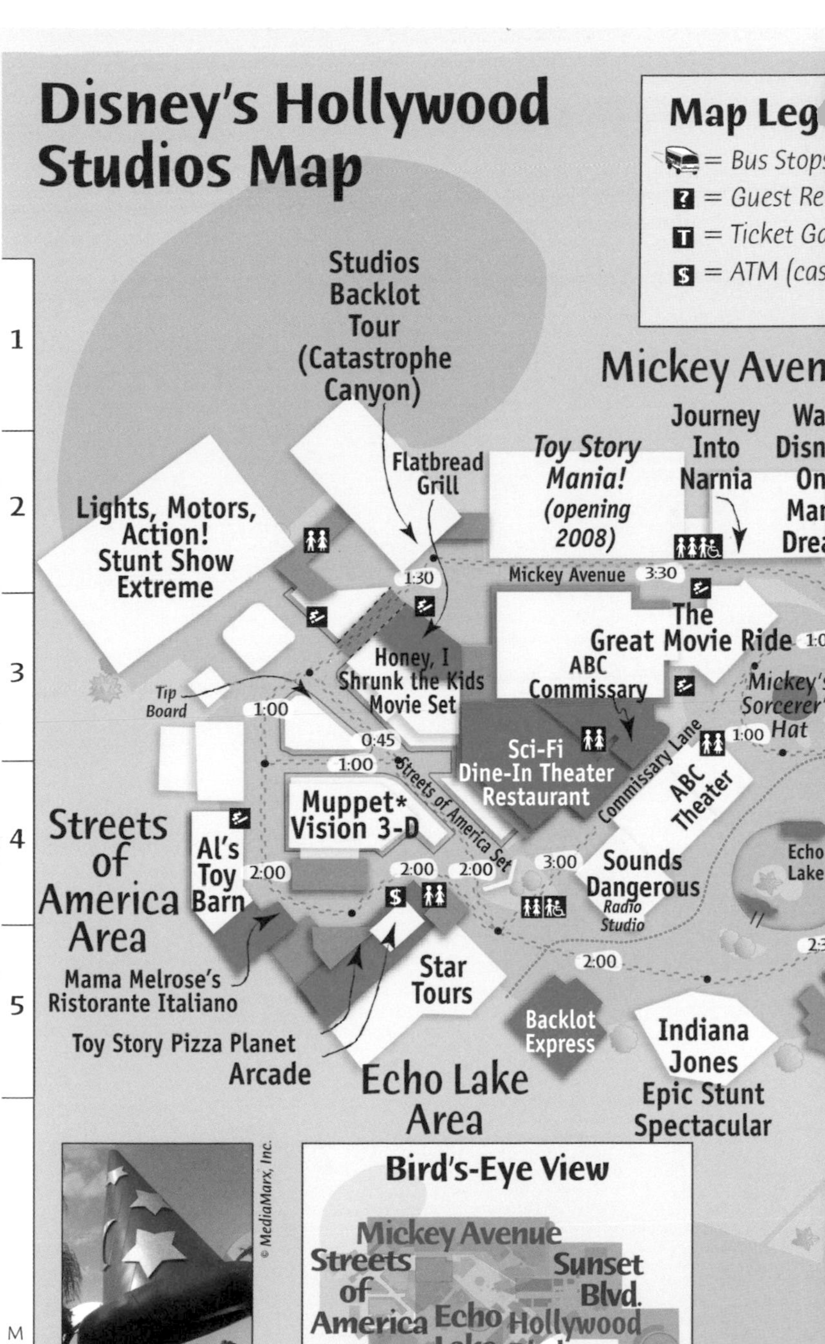

Disney's Hollywood Studios Map
Map Leg
= Bus Stops
= Guest Rela
= Ticket Gat
= ATM (cash
Studios Backlot Tour (Catastrophe Canyon)
Mickey Avenu
Journey Into Narnia
Walt Disne One Man': Drear
Toy Story Mania! (opening 2008)
Flatbread Grill
Lights, Motors, Action! Stunt Show Extreme
Mickey Avenue
The Great Movie Ride
Honey, I Shrunk the Kids Movie Set
ABC Commissary
Mickey's Sorcerer's Hat
Tip Board
Sci-Fi Dine-In Theater Restaurant
Commissary Lane
ABC Theater
Muppet* Vision 3-D
Streets of America Set
Streets of America Area
Al's Toy Barn
Sounds Dangerous Radio Studio
Echo Lake
Star Tours
Mama Melrose's Ristorante Italiano
Toy Story Pizza Planet Arcade
Backlot Express
Indiana Jones Epic Stunt Spectacular
Echo Lake Area
Bird's-Eye View
Mickey Avenue
Streets of America
Sunset Blvd.
Echo Lake
Hollywood Blvd.
© MediaMarx, Inc.
Park Icon: Mickey's Sorcerer's Hat
MAP COORDINATES
A
B
C
D
1
2
3
4
5

# Disney's Hollywood Studios Attractions At-A-Glance

*(alphabetical order)*

| Attraction | Type | Allow | Page |
|---|---|---|---|
| ☐ Beauty and the Beast [G-4] | Live Show | 40–55+ | 160-HS |
| ☐ The Great Movie Ride [D-3] | Film/Ride | 25–45+ | 160-HS |
| ☐ Honey, I Shrunk the Kids [B-3] Movie Set Adventure | Playground | 20–30+ | 158-SA |
| ☐ Indiana Jones Epic Stunt [D-5] | Live Show | 40–50+ | 157-EL |
| ☐ Journey Into Narnia [D-2] | Walk-thru | 35–55+ | 159-MA |
| ☐ Lights, Motors, Action! Extreme Stunt Show [A-2] | Live Show | 45–60+ | 158-SA |
| ☐ Magic of Disney Animation [F-2] | Walk-thru | 40–60+ | 159-MA |
| ☐ Muppet*Vision 3-D [B-4] | 3-D Film | 30–40+ | 158-SA |
| ☐ One Man's Dream [D-2] | Walk-thru | 30–40+ | 159-MA |
| ☐ Playhouse Disney [E-3] | Live Show | 20–30+ | 159-MA |
| ☐ Rock 'n' Roller Coaster [G-3] | Coaster | 20–45+ | 160-HS |
| ☐ Sounds Dangerous [C-4] | Film | 15–25+ | 157-EL |
| ☐ Star Tours [B-5] | Thrill Ride | 20–40+ | 157-EL |
| ☐ Streets of America Set [B-4] | Walk-thru | 20–30+ | 158-SA |
| ☐ Studios Backlot Tour [B-2] | Tram Ride | 30–40+ | 159-MA |
| ☐ Toy Story Mania [D-2] | Ride | 45–60+ | 159-MA |
| ☐ Toy Story Pizza Planet [B-5] | Arcade | 15–20+ | 158-SA |
| ☐ Twilight Zone Tower of Terror [H-4] | Thrill Ride | 25–60+ | 160-HS |
| ☐ Voyage of the Little Mermaid [E-2] | Live Show | 25–40+ | 159-MA |

*The Allow column gives the amount of time (in minutes) you should allow for an attraction, assuming you do not have a FASTPASS and there are no ride breakdowns. The letters after the page numbers stand for the first one or two letters of the land in which that attraction is located: EL=Echo Lake, SA=Streets of America, MA=Mickey Avenue, and HS=Hollywood/Sunset Blvds.*

## Finding the Stars at Disney's Hollywood Studios

Disney's Hollywood Studios is the perfect star-gazing spot. The chart below shows typical locations of popular Disney characters.

| Star(s) | Location(s) |
|---|---|
| ☐ Various characters | Near Sorcerer's Hat/Great Movie Ride |
| ☐ Toy Story friends | Al's Toy Barn |
| ☐ Monsters, Inc. characters | Across from the ABC Commissary |
| ☐ The Incredibles, Remy | Magic of Disney Animation |
| ☐ JoJo, Handy Manny | Animation Courtyard |
| ☐ Cars, Kim Possible | Streets of America |
| ☐ Power Rangers | Streets of America |

*Note: Greeting locations and characters vary (check your guidemap), but Mickey Avenue, Hollywood Boulevard near the Chinese Theater, Animation Courtyard, and Al's Toy Barn are the likely locations.*

# Our Favorite Touring Plan for Disney's Hollywood Studios

NOTES

While Disney's Hollywood Studios has fewer attractions than the Magic Kingdom and Epcot, it's harder to see everything you want to visit due to show times and lengths. It is important to check your Times Guide or the Tip Board (on the corner of Hollywood and Sunset Boulevards) and note showtimes. We recommend you jot down these showtimes on this page once you know them—you'll find a fill-in-the-blank line for those attractions/events with specific showtimes. The plans work best if you go in the same order, but you should feel free to skip an attraction or two (and return to it later) if it makes sense for you. You should be able to accomplish either of these plans in one day if you start by 9:00 am. Those with infants and toddlers, or thrill-shy adults, may prefer to skip all attractions in blue.

ITINERARIES

## Touring With Adults

**Enter Sunset Boulevard**
Visit Rock 'n' Roller Coaster
Visit Tower of Terror
**Enter Echo Lake Area**
Get FASTPASS for Star Tours
**Enter Streets of America Area**
Visit Lights, Motors, Action! @ _____
Visit Muppet*Vision 3-D
**Enter Echo Lake Area**
Visit Star Tours
Visit Indiana Jones @ _____
**Eat lunch** at Studio Catering, Sci-Fi Dine-In, Backlot Express, '50s Prime Time, or Hollywood & Vine (*about 3 hours after you enter the park*)
**Enter Streets of America Area**
Visit Streets of America Set
**Enter Mickey Avenue Area**
Get FASTPASS for Voyage of the Little Mermaid @ _____ (if open)
Visit One Man's Dream or Magic of Disney Animation @ _____
Visit Voyage of the Little Mermaid (if open) or watch the afternoon parade @ _____
**Eat dinner** at Hollywood Brown Derby, Hollywood & Vine, '50s Prime Time, or Catalina Eddie's (*about 7 1/2 hours after you enter the park*)
Watch Fantasmic! @ _____
*(Tour duration: About 10 hours)*

## Touring With Kids

**Enter Echo Lake Area**
Visit Star Tours
Get FASTPASS for Indiana Jones
**Enter Streets of America Area**
Visit Lights, Motors, Action! @ _____
Visit Muppet*Vision 3-D
**Enter Echo Lake Area**
Visit Indiana Jones @ _____
**Enter Mickey Avenue Area**
Visit Playhouse Disney @ _____
**Eat lunch** at Hollywood & Vine, '50s Prime Time, ABC Commissary, or Backlot Exp.
Visit Studios Backlot Tour (*about 3 1/2 hours after you enter the park*)
**Enter Streets of America Area**
Visit Honey, I Shrunk the Kids Movie Set Adventure
Visit Al's Toy Barn Character Greeting
**Enter Echo Lake Area**
Watch the afternoon parade @ _____ and have a snack
**Enter Mickey Avenue**
Get FASTPASS for Voyage of the Little Mermaid (if open)
**Enter Hollywood Boulevard Area**
Visit Great Movie Ride
**Enter Mickey Avenue**
Visit Voyage of the Little Mermaid @ _____
**Eat dinner** at Hollywood & Vine, '50s Prime Time, or Catalina Eddie's (*about 7 1/2 hours after you enter the park*)
Watch Fantasmic! @ _____
*(Tour duration: About 10 hours)*

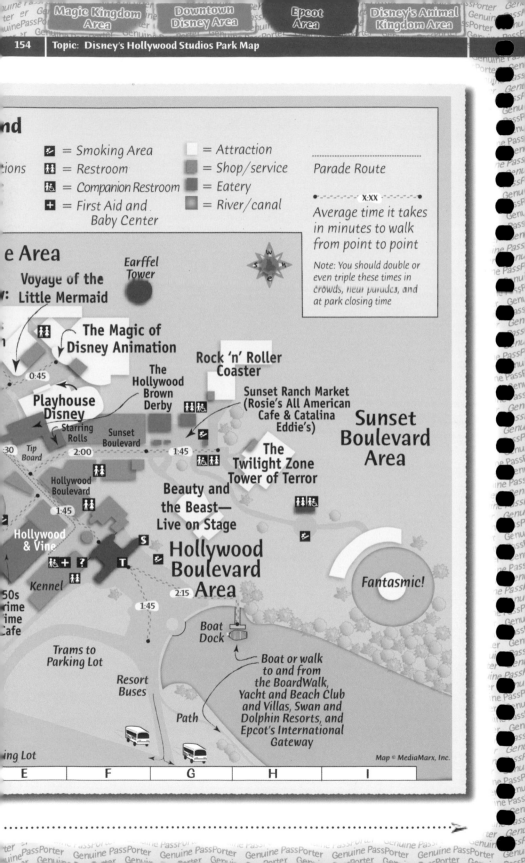

nd
= Smoking Area
= Restroom
= Companion Restroom
= First Aid and Baby Center
= Attraction
= Shop/service
= Eatery
= River/canal
Parade Route
X:XX
Average time it takes in minutes to walk from point to point
Note: You should double or even triple these times in crowds, near parades, and at park closing time
e Area
Earffel Tower
Voyage of the Little Mermaid
The Magic of Disney Animation
Rock 'n' Roller Coaster
The Hollywood Brown Derby
0:45
Playhouse Disney
Sunset Ranch Market (Rosie's All American Cafe & Catalina Eddie's)
Sunset Boulevard Area
Starring Rolls
Sunset Boulevard
Tip Board
2:00
1:45
The Twilight Zone Tower of Terror
Hollywood Boulevard
Beauty and the Beast—Live on Stage
1:45
Hollywood & Vine
Hollywood Boulevard Area
Kennel
2:15
Fantasmic!
50s Prime Time Cafe
1:45
Boat Dock
Trams to Parking Lot
Boat or walk to and from the BoardWalk, Yacht and Beach Club and Villas, Swan and Dolphin Resorts, and Epcot's International Gateway
Resort Buses
Path
ing Lot
Map © MediaMarx, Inc.
E F G H I

# Making the Most of Disney's Hollywood Studios

TIPS

If you're interested in the **live shows**, check the Times Guide for showtimes and plan accordingly to avoid long waits or mad dashes.

**Autograph seekers**, be prepared! Characters come out in force for meet-and-greets throughout the park. See page 153b for a "star" chart, and see page 248 for autograph tips.

Look for the **well** near Indiana Jones Epic Stunt Spectacular (when you're facing the attraction entrance, it's located to the left). Just don't pull the rope. (You've been warned!)

Some of the shows involve **audience participation**. If you like this sort of thing, volunteer enthusiastically for the fun!

If you love **Walt Disney and his legacy of animation**, plan to immediately follow your visit to Walt Disney: One Man's Dream (pages 157 and 159) with The Magic of Disney Animation (page 159). The two attractions complement one another very well.

**Seniors** won't want to rush through Disney's Hollywood Studios—make enough time to slow down and enjoy the ambience of the park.

Disney's Hollywood Studios has several **unique restaurants** and cafes, and many participate in a Fantasmic! Meal Package. See pages 217–219 for dining and package details.

NOTES

The focus at this park is on **independent shows and rides** rather than on a never-ending stream of entertainment. Be prepared for walking and waiting. Your reward is longer, lovingly produced shows, more intense rides, and fascinating backstage glimpses.

The pavement in front of Grauman's Chinese Theater (The Great Movie Ride) is full of **celebrity footprints** and handprints.

*< Allie with Walt at One Man's Dream*

# Getting to Disney's Hollywood Studios

**BEST TIMES TO GO**

Disney's Hollywood Studios can be enjoyed in one day, although it is best to **visit the most popular attractions earlier** to avoid long lines. Arrive before the scheduled opening time for the best advantage. The most popular attractions—Rock 'n' Roller Coaster and The Twilight Zone Tower of Terror—generate very long lines. Make a beeline for these rides first thing, unless you've just eaten breakfast. Several of the shows have **limited seating capacity** (such as Voyage of the Little Mermaid) and can require a lengthy wait if busy. Whenever possible, get a FASTPASS! Check the entertainment schedule in the park Times Guide for show times. Take the length of show times into account when planning your route and keep in mind that several shows take a considerable amount of time. Many attractions and restaurants empty immediately before and during the parade, affording shorter lines or the chance to get a table without advance dining arrangements.

**GETTING THERE**

**By Boat**—From Epcot's International Gateway, BoardWalk Inn & Villas, Yacht & Beach Club & Villas, and Swan & Dolphin, take the Friendship boat.

**By Bus**—Take a direct bus from all other resorts, Epcot's main entrance, and Disney's Animal Kingdom. From the Magic Kingdom, catch a bus at the Transportation and Ticket Center (TTC). From Downtown Disney, Typhoon Lagoon, or Blizzard Beach, take a bus or boat to a resort and transfer to a Disney's Hollywood Studios bus.

**By Car**—Take I-4 to exit 67 (westbound) or exit 62 (eastbound) and continue on to Disney's Hollywood Studios parking. All-day parking is available for $10 (free to resort guests and annual passholders).

**By Foot**—You can walk from the BoardWalk, Swan & Dolphin, and Yacht & Beach Club, and even Epcot's International Gateway. Follow the marked pathways along the canal beside the BoardWalk Villas (see resort map on page 46 for path location).

**RATINGS**

*Ratings are explained on page 120.*

| Our Value Ratings: | | Our Magic Ratings: | | Readers' Ratings: |
|---|---|---|---|---|
| Quality: | 8/10 | Theme: | 8/10 | 64% fell in love with it |
| Variety: | 7/10 | Excitement: | 9/10 | 33% liked it well enough |
| Scope: | 6/10 | Fun Factor: | 7/10 | 2% had mixed feelings |
| **Overall Value:** | **7/10** | **Overall Magic:** | **8/10** | 1% were disappointed |

**Disney's Hollywood Studios is enjoyed by... (rated by both authors and readers)**

| | | |
|---|---|---|
| Younger Kids: ♥♥♥♥ | Young Adults: ♥♥♥♥♥ | Families: ♥♥♥♥♥ |
| Older Kids: ♥♥♥♥ | Mid Adults: ♥♥♥♥♥ | Couples: ♥♥♥♥♥ |
| Teenagers: ♥♥♥♥♥ | Mature Adults: ♥♥♥♥♥ | Singles: ♥♥♥♥ |

*Looking for The Great Movie Ride on Hollywood Boulevard? See page 160.*

# Charting the Attractions in the Echo Lake Area

*(in clockwise order starting from the left side of the park)*

Jennifer's Rating | Dave's Rating | Readers' Rating

## Indiana Jones Epic Stunt Spectacular [D-5] FP A-OK! 7 6 8

*The Indiana Jones films set the stage for an action show of epic proportions. Disney has built a huge indoor/outdoor set to demonstrate the stuntperson's craft, including the famous rolling boulder, an Egyptian marketplace, and a flaming German airplane. Adults may be picked to join the show—arrive early and show enthusiasm if this interests you. Theater opens 25 minutes before the show and guests sit in a covered, outdoor theater. Loud explosions and hot flames may scare young children. Wheelchair accessible. Assistive listening.* **Alex's ToddlerTip:** ☹ **Allie's KidTip** *and* **TweenTip:** *"It's a good show, but it's loud."*

Live Show | E-Ticket | Ages 4 & up | Loud, fire, violence | FASTPASS or med. waits | 30 min. show

## Sounds Dangerous [C-4] 4 6 6

*Yes, it sounds dangerous, but you'll emerge totally unscathed from this entertaining sound effects demonstration hosted by comedian Drew Carey. Drew cooks up a detective mystery to demonstrate the art of sound effects. There's no audience participation—just sit back, put on the headphones, and enjoy the show. When you exit, be sure to try the SoundWorks hands-on exhibits—the Sound Station booths are a fine place to relax and cool off. You can enter via the SoundWorks back door if you'd rather skip the show. Outdoor queue is covered. Wheelchair accessible. Assistive listening.* **Alex's ToddlerTip:** ☹ **Allie's KidTip:** *"If you don't like it, take off the headset. I didn't like it—too loud."*

Film | C-Ticket | Ages 7 & up | Total darkness and very loud noises | Short waits | 12 min. film

## Star Tours [B-5] FP A-OK! 8 8 8

*Take a flight to a galaxy far, far away in this "must ride" for all Star Wars fans. Although the flight simulator at the heart of this ride never really goes anywhere, you'll find it hard to believe as your StarSpeeder dives, banks, and speeds toward the Moon of Endor with a rookie pilot at the helm. But that doesn't mean the ride isn't rough. The roughest seats are in the back row, as we learned from riding it 27 times in a row. Indoor queue offers many visual delights, including R2D2 and C-3PO. Overflow queue outdoors is uncovered. 40"/102 cm height restriction. Young children should be accompanied by an adult. Health warning. Must transfer from ECV to wheelchair. Must transfer from wheelchair to ride. Closed captioning. Non-moving rides available for ECV-bound and motion-sensitive—ask a cast member.* **Allie's KidTip:** *"This is good, but hold on tight!"* **TeenTip:** *"The back seats really are the best."*

Thrill Ride | E-Ticket | Far-out fun | Rough, rocky, may cause motion sickness | FASTPASS or long waits | 3 min. intro 5 min. flight

*Attraction descriptions and ratings are explained on page 127.*

### Studio Gossip

The gossip never stops at Disney's Hollywood Studios. Last year's rumored "film"—Toy Story Mania—opens this year, and it won't evict Narnia or One Man's Dream. But will Mickey Avenue be re-released as Pixar Place? Which attraction gets a rewrite when the next Narnia film debuts? Block Party Bash is in the wings to replace the Disney's Stars and Motor Cars Parade in spring 2008, but there's no news on a Jack Skellington-hosted Halloween party or a Tower of Terror upgrade. Star Tours is on our minds, thanks to the now-permanent Jedi Training Academy show and hints from C-3PO of a new ride film. The often-unused ABC Studios Theater may soon house a new show. And Indiana Jones has a narrow escape, thanks to the 2008 release of another Indy film.

# Charting the Attractions in the Streets of America Area

Jennifer's Rating | Dave's Rating | Readers' Rating

## Honey, I Shrunk the Kids Movie Set Adventure [B-3] A-OK! 6 5 6

Kids climb, cavort, and caper amidst huge plants, insects, and spider webs in this playground based on the popular movies and TV show. Keep cool with various water sprays (it gets very hot here) and slide down giant rolls of film and leaves. Officially kids must be at least 4 years old to play, and adults must be with a child to enter. Wheelchair accessible. **Allie's Kid Tip:** "Get wet by the giant Super Soaker!"

**Playground** | B-Ticket | Ages 4 & up | Giant bugs | Short waits

## Lights, Motors, Action! Extreme Stunt Show [A-2] FP 7 8 8

You'll be wowed by an epic display of the stuntperson's art in this show from Disneyland Paris. Villains in cars and motorcycles roar across the set in pursuit of the hero, as filmmakers shoot scenes for a spy movie. Giant video screens show how special effects action is turned into movie magic. A 5,000-seat partially shaded grandstand offers metal bench seats. With only 2–3 shows daily, plan to arrive early. FASTPASS offered in peak seasons. Brief, hot flames can make the front rows uncomfortable. Assistive listening. Wheelchair accessible. Unshaded queue.

**Live Show** | E-Ticket | Ages 3 & up | Loud! | Long waits or FASTPASS | 25 minutes

## Muppet*Vision 3-D [B-4] A-OK! 7 7 9

Your 3-D glasses get a real workout as Kermit and his pals show you around the Muppet Labs. The Muppets are at their zany, pun-filled best in a frenetic good time that was Jim Henson's last production. The multiscreen videos and hilarious props shown in the pre-show area deserve your full attention. The theater is large and air-conditioned, with comfy seats. There's no need to sit in front to get a good view. Some effects may be scary for young kids. Indoor queue is fun. Wheelchair accessible. Assistive listening. Closed captioning. Reflective captioning. **Alex's Toddler Tip:** "I like Kermit! ☺" **Allie's Kid Tip:** "Keep your 3-D glasses on."

**3-D Film** | E-Ticket | Ages 4 & up | Intense, loud, some violence | Med. waits | 15 min. intro 17 min. film

## Streets of America Movie Set [B-4] 6 6 6

Whether or not you've been to the big city, you'll enjoy the movie set-style renditions of New York, San Francisco, and Chicago, among other cities. The buildings are all facades, of course, but the detail is rich. You'll find familiar bits of Chinatown and a London street, too. Disney characters may appear on the Plaza Hotel-like steps for photos and autographs. Wheelchair accessible.

**Walk-thru** | A-Ticket | All ages | Few waits | Unlimited

## Toy Story Pizza Planet Arcade [B-5] A-OK! 2 3 6

This is a spacious, pleasantly themed arcade adjacent to the Pizza Planet cafe with a typical selection of video games and try-to-hoist-a-toy games. There's a depressing lack of Toy Story-themed arcade games, however. Tokens are needed to play. Most games require 2 to 4 tokens, and the tokens are 25 cents each. Not very magical. Wheelchair accessible. **Allie's Kid Tip:** "Fun games."

**Arcade** | A-Ticket | Ages 5 & up | No scares | Few waits

### Osborne Family Spectacle of Lights

Jennings Osborne's Christmas lights were too much for his Arkansas neighbors, so Disney invited him to the studio backlot, where his lights became a Thanksgiving through New Year's tradition. The lights went dark in 2003 to make room for the Extreme Stunt Show, but the Osborne spirit cannot be dimmed! The five million lights returned in 2004 and moved to the city, gracing the Streets of America Set, hopefully for many holiday seasons to come.

# Charting the Attractions in the Mickey Avenue Area

Jennifer's Rating | Dave's Rating | Readers' Rating

## ☐ The Magic of Disney Animation [F-2] A-OK! 6 | 7 | 8

*Animation fans enjoy this renovated tour with hands-on exhibits. The "Drawn to Animation Theater" features Mulan's Mushu (Eddie Murphy) and a live animator. "Animation Academy" has 38 easels where an animator teaches you to draw favorite characters. This is also a permanent character greeting spot, currently hosting characters from "The Incredibles" and "Ratatouille."* **Allie's KidTip:** *"The part with Mushu is funny!"* **TeenTip:** *"It sounds boring, but it's fun inside."*

**Walk-thru** | D-Ticket | Ages 4 & up | No scares | Med. waits | Allow 45 min.

## ☐ Journey Into Narnia [D-2] 5 | 6 | 6

*Enter the wardrobe from "The Chronicles of Narnia" to see the movie's props, scenes, a short film, and the White Witch. Outdoor queue. Wheelchair accesible.*

**Walk-thru** | B-Ticket

## ☐ Walt Disney: One Man's Dream [D-2] 8 | 8 | 8

*This attraction illustrates Walt's impact on his company and the world. Follow Walt's imaginings as they grow and learn how his boyhood experiences affected his lifelong accomplishments. Hundreds of priceless and never-before-seen artifacts are on display. Showing of "One Man's Dream" at end. Wheelchair accessible.*

**Walk-thru** | D-Ticket | Ages 10 & up | Allow 30 min.

## ☐ Playhouse Disney–Live on Stage! [E-3] A-OK! 7 | 6 | 8

*Costumed characters and puppets gives a live version of Disney Channel favorites. An update in early 2008 will introduce characters from "Mickey Mouse Clubhouse," "Little Einsteins," and "Handy Manny." Seating is on a carpeted floor. Outdoor, covered queue. Wheelchair access.* **Alex's ToddlerTip:** *☺ "Bubbles!"*

**Live Show** | C-Ticket | All ages | 20 min. show

## ☐ Studios Backlot Tour [B-2] A-OK! 6 | 6 | 7

*This is the park's backstage movie magic blockbuster. See how sea battles and storms are stirred up, tour Disney's backlot, and brave Catastrophe Canyon, a special effects tour de force. Stand in long lines not once, but twice. Outdoor queue is covered. Wheelchair accessible. Closed captioning. 6 min. intro.* **Allie's KidTip:** *"Sit on the left side to get wet!"* **TweenTip:** *"At the end you can view movie costumes." (Backdoor entry to costume exhibit via AFI Showcase Shop.)*

**Tram Ride** | D-Ticket | Ages 6 & up | Fires, floods | Long waits | 17 min. ride

## ☐ Toy Story Mania (opening 2008) [D-2] – | – | –

*This new dark ride opening in 2008 will be based on Pixar's Toy Story, offering a family-friendly addition to Mickey Avenue. It will be Disney's first interactive 3-D ride, using digital sets, effects like wind and water spray, and souped-up laser pointers to shoot targets. Look for hidden targets to get extra points and receive different levels of play. Vehicles will seat eight guests each (four groups of two). We also hear there will be an interactive Mr. Potato Head in the queue!*

**3-D Ride** | E-Ticket | Ages and times unknown

## ☐ Voyage of the Little Mermaid [E-2] FP A-OK! 8 | 7 | 8

*Enjoy your favorite tunes while live action, puppets, falling water, and laser effects bring Ariel and her friends to life onstage, making you feel as if you're truly under the sea! Cool theater offers comfy seats. Middle rows are best for view of stage and effects. Stand to right during 5-min. pre-show for up-front seating. No flash photos or video lights. Covered outdoor queue. Wheelchair accessible. Assistive listening. Reflective captioning.* **Alex's ToddlerTip:** *"Ariel is here! ☺"* **Allie's KidTip:** *"I love this! Look up!"* **Allie's TeenTip:** *"Boring!"*

**Live Show** | E-Ticket | Ages 3 & up | Dark, strobe | FASTPASS or long waits | 17 min. show

# Charting the Attractions in the Hollywood and Sunset Boulevard Areas

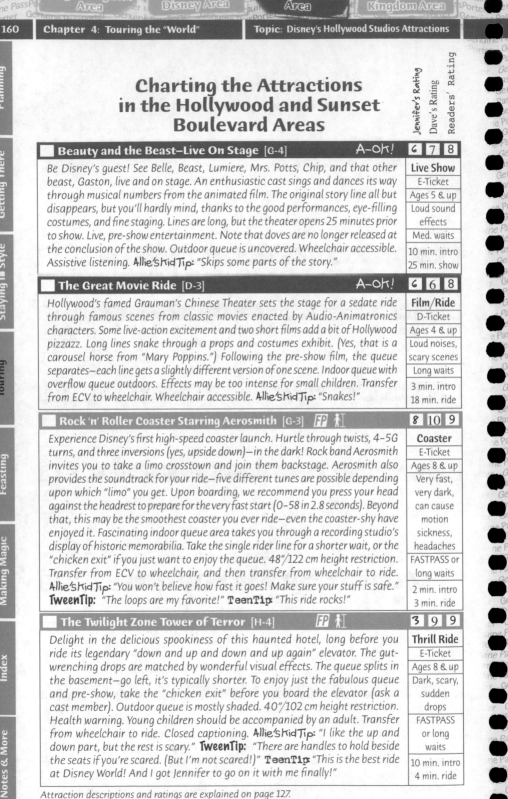

Jennifer's Rating | Dave's Rating | Readers' Rating

## Beauty and the Beast–Live On Stage [G-4] A-OK! 6 7 8

| | |
|---|---|
| *Be Disney's guest! See Belle, Beast, Lumiere, Mrs. Potts, Chip, and that other beast, Gaston, live and on stage. An enthusiastic cast sings and dances its way through musical numbers from the animated film. The original story line all but disappears, but you'll hardly mind, thanks to the good performances, eye-filling costumes, and fine staging. Lines are long, but the theater opens 25 minutes prior to show. Live, pre-show entertainment. Note that doves are no longer released at the conclusion of the show. Outdoor queue is uncovered. Wheelchair accessible. Assistive listening.* **Allie's KidTip:** *"Skips some parts of the story."* | **Live Show**<br>E-Ticket<br>Ages 5 & up<br>Loud sound effects<br>Med. waits<br>10 min. intro<br>25 min. show |

## The Great Movie Ride [D-3] A-OK! 6 6 8

| | |
|---|---|
| *Hollywood's famed Grauman's Chinese Theater sets the stage for a sedate ride through famous scenes from classic movies enacted by Audio-Animatronics characters. Some live-action excitement and two short films add a bit of Hollywood pizzazz. Long lines snake through a props and costumes exhibit. (Yes, that is a carousel horse from "Mary Poppins.") Following the pre-show film, the queue separates–each line gets a slightly different version of one scene. Indoor queue with overflow queue outdoors. Effects may be too intense for small children. Transfer from ECV to wheelchair. Wheelchair accessible.* **Allie's KidTip:** *"Snakes!"* | **Film/Ride**<br>D-Ticket<br>Ages 4 & up<br>Loud noises, scary scenes<br>Long waits<br>3 min. intro<br>18 min. ride |

## Rock 'n' Roller Coaster Starring Aerosmith [G-3] FP 8 10 9

| | |
|---|---|
| *Experience Disney's first high-speed coaster launch. Hurtle through twists, 4–5G turns, and three inversions (yes, upside down)–in the dark! Rock band Aerosmith invites you to take a limo crosstown and join them backstage. Aerosmith also provides the soundtrack for your ride–five different tunes are possible depending upon which "limo" you get. Upon boarding, we recommend you press your head against the headrest to prepare for the very fast start (0–58 in 2.8 seconds). Beyond that, this may be the smoothest coaster you ever ride–even the coaster-shy have enjoyed it. Fascinating indoor queue area takes you through a recording studio's display of historic memorabilia. Take the single rider line for a shorter wait, or the "chicken exit" if you just want to enjoy the queue. 48"/122 cm height restriction. Transfer from ECV to wheelchair, and then transfer from wheelchair to ride.* **Allie's KidTip:** *"You won't believe how fast it goes! Make sure your stuff is safe."* **TweenTip:** *"The loops are my favorite!"* **TeenTip:** *"This ride rocks!"* | **Coaster**<br>E-Ticket<br>Ages 8 & up<br>Very fast, very dark, can cause motion sickness, headaches<br>FASTPASS or long waits<br>2 min. intro<br>3 min. ride |

## The Twilight Zone Tower of Terror [H-4] FP 3 9 9

| | |
|---|---|
| *Delight in the delicious spookiness of this haunted hotel, long before you ride its legendary "down and up and down and up again" elevator. The gut-wrenching drops are matched by wonderful visual effects. The queue splits in the basement–go left, it's typically shorter. To enjoy just the fabulous queue and pre-show, take the "chicken exit" before you board the elevator (ask a cast member). Outdoor queue is mostly shaded. 40"/102 cm height restriction. Health warning. Young children should be accompanied by an adult. Transfer from wheelchair to ride. Closed captioning.* **Allie's KidTip:** *"I like the up and down part, but the rest is scary."* **TweenTip:** *"There are handles to hold beside the seats if you're scared. (But I'm not scared!)"* **TeenTip:** *"This is the best ride at Disney World! And I got Jennifer to go on it with me finally!"* | **Thrill Ride**<br>E-Ticket<br>Ages 8 & up<br>Dark, scary, sudden drops<br>FASTPASS or long waits<br>10 min. intro<br>4 min. ride |

*Attraction descriptions and ratings are explained on page 127.*

# Disney's Animal Kingdom

Disney's Animal Kingdom is the newest and largest park (580 acres) at the Walt Disney World Resort. Part zoological park and part theme park, Disney's Animal Kingdom charms, delights, and thrills guests with a uniquely Disney look at the wild world. Disney's Animal Kingdom is located the farthest west of all the parks on the Walt Disney World property.

## AMBIENCE

The Tree of Life towers above Disney's Animal Kingdom, reminding us of the wonder, glory, and fragility of nature's creations. This is the quietest of the parks out of respect to the animals who make their home here, but "quiet" doesn't mean "boring." Adventure awaits, as discoveries lurk around every bend. Like Epcot, Disney's Animal Kingdom is a place to explore with open eyes and eager minds. Lace up your boots, grab your safari hat, and load your camera—the adventure is about to begin!

## PARK LAYOUT AND HIGHLIGHTS

To set the tone for the day, all guests pass through **The Oasis**, a lush jungle teeming with exotic wildlife, sparkling waters, and rocky crags. Then, standing on Discovery Island at the center of the park, the **Tree of Life** binds the four lands of Disney's Animal Kingdom in a circle of life (see map on page 164). The Tree of Life also hosts the popular attraction, "It's Tough to be a Bug!" See pages 163a&b for our favorite itineraries for touring Disney's Animal Kingdom and a list of attractions, and pages 167–170 for attraction details.

| | |
|---|---|
| **Camp Minnie-Mickey**<br>*Headline Attraction:* | Hike into an evergreen forest reminiscent of Adirondack fishing camps, catching "critters" like Mickey Mouse for hugs and autographs.<br>*Festival of the Lion King* |
| **Africa and Rafiki's Planet Watch**<br>*Headline Attractions:* | Come together in the port town of Harambe, complete with thatched huts and baobab trees, and set off on safaris, treks, and adventures.<br>*Kilimanjaro Safaris, Pangani Forest Exploration Trail* |
| **Asia** <br>*Headline Attractions:* | Step into the mythical kingdom of Anandapur (meaning "place of all delights") to experience the beauty, wonder, and peace of Asia.<br>*Kali River Rapids, Maharajah Jungle Trek, Expedition Everest* |
| **DinoLand, U.S.A.**<br>*Headline Attractions:* | Get tourist-trapped in the wacky world of an old dinosaur dig site, scattered with dino bones and evidence of the paleontology team's pranks, then meet the "real" dinosaurs on a thrilling ride.<br>*Dinosaur, Primeval Whirl, "Finding Nemo—The Musical"* |

Fold out the next page for touring plans and a handy attraction cha[rt]

# Entertainment and Shopping at Disney's Animal Kingdom

ENTERTAINMENT

The best entertainment at Disney's Animal Kingdom is its themed live **theater shows**, described in detail on pages 167–170. Roving entertainers take a back seat to the wildlife, of course. Fireworks shows don't fit in here, either—they would just scare the animals. **Mickey's Jammin' Jungle Parade** features your favorite Disney characters as they set out "on expedition." The parade's "party animals" put on a wild street celebration and encourage guests to join in the action along the way! Other entertainment includes **The Adventure Begins** show, which starts 15 minutes before park opening every day—Minnie, Pluto, and Goofy arrive in a safari truck to start your adventure! In Africa's Harambe Village, **live bands** and acrobats keep the Dawa Bar and Tusker House's outdoor tables hopping. Visitors to Rafiki's Planet Watch may get lucky and catch **live animal acts** on the outdoor stage! Also be on the lookout for **DiVine**, a ten-foot-tall, towering and wandering "vine."

*Jennifer and Alexander at "Finding Nemo—The Musical"*

SHOPPING

The best shopping at Disney's Animal Kingdom can be found in two places: Discovery Island around the Tree of Life and Africa's Village of Harambe. Of the two, Harambe offers more in the way of handcrafted and **imported goods**, while Discovery Island offers themed **Disney merchandise**. Here are our favorite shops:

| Shop | Location | What makes it special |
|---|---|---|
| Outpost | Outside park entrance | Guidemaps, hats, sunglasses |
| Garden Gate Gifts | Inside park entrance | Film, stroller/wheelchair rentals |
| Beastly Bazaar | Discovery Island | Safari hats, logowear |
| Island Mercantile | Discovery Island | Disney-themed gifts |
| Disney Outfitters | Discovery Island | Upscale clothing, decorative items |
| Mombasa Marketplace | Africa | Crafts demonstrations |
| Out of the Wild | Rafiki's Planet Watch | Conservation-themed items |
| Chester & Hester's | DinoLand U.S.A. | Kitschy, quirky gifts (and junk!) |

# Making the Most of Disney's Animal Kingdom

Disney's Animal Kingdom is a paradise, where delightful and often subtle details can work their magic if you **take the time** to notice. This is not a do-it-all-in-a-day-or-die park. Slow down, revel in the beauty, wonder at the animals, and enjoy yourselves!

**Trails** lead off in all directions—don't be afraid to explore them. A bridge and path connects DinoLand and Asia (see map on page 164). It's the perfect way to dodge afternoon parade crowds.

This park is one big photo op! Bring plenty of **memory cards/film** and **batteries**, and even **binoculars** for viewing animals.

**Dining options** here are have seen some recent changes. A new full-service and counter-service restaurant (Yak & Yeti) opened in Asia in late 2007. Also, Tusker House converted to a character buffet breakfast in November 2007. See the listings on pages 220–221.

The outdoor, sheltered **seating** by Flame Tree Barbecue is a wonderful spot, whether you want to dine or simply rest. Tables and dining pavilions are set amidst lush tropical gardens.

Not all **animals** can be seen all the time. On the plus side, you'll often see new ones each time, making subsequent visits unique.

**Beverages** sold in Disney's Animal Kingdom generally do not come with lids and straws, for the animals' safety. Consider bringing your own covered mug or bottle if you want to keep drinks.

It always seems **hotter** at Disney's Animal Kingdom than at any other park, possibly because there are so few attractions with air-conditioning. Be prepared with hats, sunglasses, sunscreen, and ways to keep yourself cool, like plenty of cold water and/or a personal misting fan ($16). Take advantage of the mist-spraying fans throughout the park when you need relief. Take frequent breaks in air-conditioned spots—try the eateries, shops, or attractions like It's Tough to be a Bug!, Festival of the Lion King, or Rafiki's Planet Watch.

**Seniors** should go carefully when touring this park due to the heat. Nearly every attraction is outdoors, which means there's limited air-conditioning. There's plenty of shade while you stand around or watch the shows, though. An ECV is particularly helpful at this park if you have any difficulty with walking or stamina.

# Getting to Disney's Animal Kingdom

**BEST TIMES TO GO**

Most guests arrive in the morning and leave in the afternoon, making **late afternoon** the best time to visit. Not only are the crowds thinner, but the park's animals prefer the cooler temperatures found in the earlier and later parts of the day, so you're more likely to see them. If possible, take advantage of Extra Magic Hours, especially in the cool of the evening. You may have more luck spotting animals during and after a rainstorm, too. When you **first arrive**, head for Expedition Everest or Kilimanjaro Safaris to pick up a FASTPASS (or just go ahead and ride if the wait is short enough). Another strategy is to ride one of the popular attractions early and then immediately get a FASTPASS for another attraction. Check the **Times Guide** for show times and durations, and plan your day accordingly—these shows can chew up more time than you'd expect. You can use our touring plans on page 163a to give you an idea of what you can expect to do in one day. Finally, if your park pass allows it, consider spreading out your visit over a **couple of days** rather than packing it all into one. Midday is best avoided due to the big crowds, the intense heat/sun, and sleeping animals.

**GETTING THERE**

**By Bus**—All resorts, Epcot, and Disney's Hollywood Studios have buses that take you directly to Disney's Animal Kingdom. From the Magic Kingdom, take the boat or monorail to the Transportation and Ticket Center (TTC) and catch a bus. From Downtown Disney, take a bus to an Epcot-area resort and catch a Disney's Animal Kingdom bus. **By Car**—From I-4, take exit 65 (eastbound or westbound) and follow signs to Disney's Animal Kingdom parking. All-day parking is available for $10 (free to resort guests with resort ID and annual passholders). The parking lot is some distance from the entrance. You'll appreciate the free trams to the front gate.

*Note: There is no boat, path, or monorail access to this theme park.*

**RATINGS**

*Ratings are explained on page 120.*

| Our Value Ratings: | | Our Magic Ratings: | | Readers' Ratings: |
|---|---|---|---|---|
| Quality: | 8/10 | Theme: | 9/10 | 44% fell in love with it |
| Variety: | 7/10 | Excitement: | 7/10 | 33% liked it well enough |
| Scope: | 6/10 | Fun Factor: | 6/10 | 15% had mixed feelings |
| **Overall Value:** | **7/10** | **Overall Magic:** | **7/10** | 8% were disappointed |

**Animal Kingdom is enjoyed by... (rated by both authors and readers)**

| | | |
|---|---|---|
| Younger Kids: ♥♥♥♥♥ | Young Adults: ♥♥♥♥ | Families: ♥♥♥♥♥ |
| Older Kids: ♥♥♥♥ | Mid Adults: ♥♥♥♥ | Couples: ♥♥♥♥ |
| Teenagers: ♥♥♥♥ | Mature Adults: ♥♥♥♥ | Singles: ♥♥♥♥ |

# Charting the Attractions at The Oasis, Discovery Island, and Camp Minnie-Mickey

Jennifer's Rating | Dave's Rating | Readers' Rating

## The Oasis [C-6] — A-OK! — 7 | 6 | 7

All guests pass through this lush jungle habitat of gurgling waters and exotic plants on their way in and out of the park. Many of the paths lead to small animal exhibits. Look for shady seats in a rocky grotto. Wheelchair accessible. **Allie's KidTip:** "Can you spot camouflaging lizards anywhere here?"

Walk-thru | A-Ticket | All ages | Allow 20 min.

## Camp Minnie-Mickey Character Greeting Trails [A-5] — A-OK! — 4 | 4 | 6

Meet Mickey, Minnie, and other Disney characters in the shade of four rustic, open-air pavilions—each character has his/her own queue. Low-key atmosphere. Bring your autograph book and have your camera handy. Wheelchair accessible. **Alex's ToddlerTip:** ☺ **Allie's KidTip:** "Don't be shy."

Pavilion | A-Ticket | All ages | Med. waits

## Festival of the Lion King [A-6] — A-OK! — 8 | 8 | 9

This colorful, dynamic pageant set to music from "The Lion King" features singers, dancers, acrobats, and floats, and really sets your hands to clapping! The 1,000-seat theater-in-the-round affords many great vantage points, but arrive early to sit down front. Try the first or last shows for shortest waits. Lots of audience participation and lots of fun! This theatre is fully air-conditioned. Outdoor queue is uncovered. No external video lights. Wheelchair accessible. Assistive listening. **Alex's ToddlerTip:** ☺ **Allie's KidTip:** "If you sit in the front you might get asked to play music!" **TweenTip:** "Try to make the animal sounds."

Live Show | E-Ticket | Ages 2 & up | Long waits (check showtimes in Times Guide) | 30 min. show

## Pocahontas and Her Forest Friends [B-6] — A-OK! — 4 | 2 | 4

Pocahontas and Grandmother Willow are featured in a conservation-themed live animal show. Seating is outdoors with light shade. First three center rows of seats reserved for kids under 11 (no parents), and volunteers are chosen. Brief glimpses of animals. Doors open 15 minutes before show. Check Times Guide for shows. Outdoor queue is uncovered. Wheelchair accessible. Assistive listening. **Allie's KidTip:** "If you're not too shy, sit with the kids in the front."

Live Show | C-Ticket | Ages 3 & up | Live animals and birds | 13 min. show

## ✓ It's Tough to be a Bug! [D-4] — FP — A-OK! — 8 | 8 | 9

Long lines snake around the Tree of Life on Discovery Island for a humorous show hosted by Flik from "A Bug's Life" and featuring a pint-sized cast of animated and Audio-Animatronics characters. 3-D effects, creepy sensations, and yucky smells can terrify the bug-wary. Queue offers close-up views of the tree's animal sculptures. Look for hilarious movie posters in the "lobby." Air-conditioned, 430-seat theater. Outdoor queue is uncovered. Special effects may be too intense for some. Wheelchair accessible. Assistive listening. Reflective captioning. The entrance is marked on the map on page 164. **Allie's KidTip:** "Sit between two grown-ups in case you get scared."

3-D Show | E-Ticket | Ages 6 & up | Dark, smells, bug noises, "stings" | FASTPASS or med. waits | 8 min. show

## The Tree of Life and Discovery Island Trails [C-3] — 6 | 5 | 8

Tropical gardens and exotic animals surround the Tree of Life at the center of the park. Walk the winding paths, and get a close-up view of the tree, too. How many animals can you see in the trunk and roots? (Hint: 366, including a "hidden Mickey.") Wheelchair accessible. **Allie's KidTip:** "The animals are cool."

Walk-thru | A-Ticket | All ages | Allow 30 min.

*Attraction descriptions and ratings are explained on page 127.*

# Charting the Attractions at Africa and Rafiki's Planet Watch

Jennifer's Rating | Dave's Rating | Readers' Rating

## Kilimanjaro Safaris [B-1]

FP A-OK! 8 8 9

*Board a safari truck to explore 100 acres of African habitat with lions, giraffes, crocodiles, ostriches, gazelle, and many other live animals. Wildlife may be plentiful or scarce, since it's free to roam. Disney also includes a story line in case the animals are feeling shy. The ride gets very bumpy, so hang on tight. We recommend you ride first thing in the morning, late afternoon, or after it rains, when the animals are more active. Sit in outside seats for best views and photos. The safari closes at dusk. Outdoor queue is covered and has overhead monitors. Height restriction for children riding in front two seats. Young children should be accompanied by an adult. Health warning. Transfer from ECV to wheelchair to ride. Wheelchair accessible. Assistive listening. Closed captioning.* **Alex's Toddler Tip:** ☺ **Allie's Kid Tip:** *"Be on the lookout for the baby elephant (Little Red)."* **Tween Tip:** *"Look at the signs in the truck to identify the animals."*

**Ride** | E-Ticket | Ages 4 & up | Bumpy, live birds and animals, "close escapes" | FASTPASS or long waits | 19 min. vehicle ride

## Pangani Forest Exploration Trail [B-1]

A-OK! 6 8 7

*Animal lovers will stroll enthralled through this exhibit of African wildlife in an artfully built natural habitat. African birds, hippos, meerkats, and a troop of gorillas make their home here. Hands-on exhibits in the naturalist's hut add interest. A habitat—the Endangered Animal Rehabilitation Centre—calls attention to the African bushmeat crisis. The meerkat viewing area is especially popular, and plan to spend extra time in the aviary. Walk slowly or sit, and the wonders will unfold. Allow several hours if you love to watch animals. Early morning or late afternoon is the best time to visit. Wheelchair accessible. Closed captioning.* **Allie's Kid Tip:** *"You'll love all the animals and birds!"*

**Walk-thru** | D-Ticket | All ages | Live animals, birds flying overhead | Short waits | Allow at least 30 minutes

## Wildlife Express Train to Rafiki's Planet Watch [C-1]

A-OK! 5 4 5

*All aboard! This train at Harambe station is the only route into or out of Rafiki's Planet Watch (formerly called Conservation Station). Enjoy a ringside glimpse of the park's backstage animal care areas. A guide describes the sights as the train chugs slowly along the track. Note: Everyone must disembark at Rafiki's Planet Watch. As always, Disney's eye for detail shines forth around Harambe Station and onboard the train. The best seats are in the front row. Themed, outdoor queue is mostly covered. Wheelchair accessible. Assistive listening.* **Alex's Toddler Tip:** ☺ **Allie's Kid Tip:** *"Sit in the front row of the train to see better."*

**Train Ride** | B-Ticket | All ages | Glimpses of backstage | Short waits | 15 min. ride (each way)

## Rafiki's Planet Watch [off map]

A-OK! 5 6 5

*This is the park's most remote and most underappreciated attraction, a must-visit for animal lovers of all ages. Formerly called Conservation Station, it was renamed and jazzed up with live animal encounter shows, more hands-on activities, and visits from Rafiki. The 5-min. walk from the train station to Rafiki's Planet Watch is interspersed with fun, conservation-themed exhibits and activities. See short films, use interactive video displays, and relax in darkened rain forest "soundscape" booths. View the park's nursery and veterinary hospital. Enjoy the cleanest, most animal-friendly petting zoo anywhere (it even has a hand-washing fountain at the exit). The Wildlife Express Train from Harambe is the only way into or out of Rafiki's Planet Watch. Wheelchair accessible. Assistive listening.* **Alex's Toddler Tip:** ☺ **Allie's Kid Tip:** *"Look for the fishes, lizards, and frogs. And go to the petting farm!"*

**Exhibit** | C-Ticket | All ages | Backstage, educational fun | Live animals | Short waits | Allow at least 90 minutes for a good exploration

# Charting the Attractions at Asia

Jennifer's Rating | Dave's Rating | Readers' Rating

## Expedition Everest [G-3] FP — 9 | 10 | 9

Disney's newest "mountain" thrill ride takes guests on a rickety tea plantation train up and into 199-foot-tall Forbidden Mountain on the way to Mount Everest. Once inside the chilly mountain interior, you'll have a startling encounter with the fearsome Yeti–part god, part beast–and the largest and most complex Audio-Animatronics figure ever built. Banished, you'll hurtle through darkness and even ride backward. The coaster has several steep drops and sharp turns, and some parts are very intense. The incredibly detailed queue snakes through a Himalayan village filled with artifacts, a museum, and a Yeti shrine. 44"/112 cm. height restriction. Health warning. Must transfer from wheelchair to ride. Visit http://www.disneyeverest.com.

**Coaster** | E-Ticket | Ages 8 & up | Dark, drops, heights | FASTPASS or very long waits | 3 min. ride

## Flights of Wonder [D-2] A-OK! — 7 | 7 | 7

Duck! Owls or hawks may fly right above your head during a show starring more than 20 species of free-flying exotic birds and their talented animal handlers. Guano Joe (or Jane), a tour guide from Anandapur Tours, adds some comic relief to this conservation-themed show. Guests are selected from the audience to join in the action. Afterward, everyone has a chance to come down to ask questions, view the "stars" up close, and take photos. Sit near the aisles for the closest animal encounters. Outdoor, shaded theater. Outdoor queue is uncovered. Theater opens 15 minutes beforehand. No food or drink allowed. Leave strollers at the door. Wheelchair accessible. Assistive listening. **Allie's Kid Tip:** "Volunteer to go on the stage! I'm too shy to do it, but it looks like fun."

**Live Show** | D-Ticket | Ages 3 & up | Live birds overhead | Med. waits (showtimes listed in Times Guide) | 25 min. show

## Kali River Rapids [F-2] FP A-OK! — 8 | 8 | 8

Drift through jungle mists, unexpected geysers, and smoking devastation on a somewhat daring ride in a 12-person raft. The roaring rapids boast one thrilling (albeit tame) drop. Just when you think it's all over, Disney tosses in one last little surprise. You will get wet–possibly damp, more likely soaked–and there's no way to predict (or control) how much. A small storage area is available on board, but it won't keep things very dry. Some guests wisely bring a poncho and a dry change of clothing–plastic ponchos are available for sale nearby. Shoes/sandals must be worn at all times. Long lines are common, but they snake through fascinating Asian architecture rich with fine detail. 38"/97 cm height restriction. Special effects may be too intense for some children and adults. Health warning. Must transfer from wheelchair to ride. **Allie's Kid Tip:** "If you go backward on the drop, be prepared to get soaked." **TweenTip:** "It's good when it's really hot out!"

**Raft Ride** | E-Ticket | Ages 7 & up | Med. drop, flames, geysers, and you will get wet! | FASTPASS or long waits | 5 min. cruise

## Maharajah Jungle Trek [E-1] A-OK! — 6 | 8 | 7

Walk a winding path through ancient ruins in a lush Asian setting. Tigers, tapir, fruit bats, deer, antelope, a Komodo dragon, and a walk-through aviary filled with tropical birds highlight this beautifully designed zoo. Artfully hidden barriers make you feel like you can reach out and touch the animals, but fortunately for them (and us) you can't. Cast members are on hand to enrich your animal-viewing adventure. We think the tigers, aviary, and bats are the highlights, but you'll find your own favorites. Be sure to pick up a guidemap on your way in. Animal lovers may be tempted to spend hours here–bring your camera! Wheelchair accessible. **Allie's Kid Tip:** "Tigers! How many can you find?"

**Walk-thru** | D-Ticket | All ages | Live animals, birds overhead | Short waits | Allow at least 30 minutes

# Charting the Attractions at DinoLand U.S.A.

Jennifer's Rating | Dave's Rating | Readers' Rating

## The Boneyard [F-5]

A-OK! 7 5 6

*Kids can climb, slide, crawl, scamper, excavate, and explore to their hearts' content in a funky dinosaur dig. Parents are welcome, too. One of the places at Disney's Animal Kingdom with a water spray for hot days. Keep an eye on your young ones! Bring a towel and dry clothes. Wheelchair accessible.* **Alex's ToddlerTip:** ☺ **Allie's KidTip:** *"You can get wet here if you are hot. I love this place!"*

**Playground** | B-Ticket | Ages 1 & up | Allow 30 min.

## Dinosaur [E-7]

FP A-OK! 7 7 8

*Intrepid riders are sent back through time to fetch a dinosaur before the dinos (and the riders) become extinct. Be prepared to be bounced, jostled, and scared as your Time Rover vehicle hurtles into the past and races through a dark forest. The "pre-show" and science exhibits in the indoor queue areas make the wait interesting. Front row "outside" seats for maximum thrills, inside seats for the less bold. No flash photography. 40"/102 cm height restriction. Young children should be accompanied by an adult. Effects may be too intense for some. Health warning. Must transfer from wheelchair to ride. Closed captioning (pre-show).* **Allie's KidTip:** *"Cover your eyes in the dark parts if you're scared. Ask your grown-ups to tell you when a dinosaur shows up so you can look."*

**Thrill Ride** | E-Ticket | Ages 7 & up | Dark, loud, very scary, rough and bumpy ride | FASTPASS or long waits | 3.5 min. ride

## "Finding Nemo–The Musical" [G-5]

A-OK! 7 8 8

*This all-new "Finding Nemo" themed stage show features original songs by a Tony Award-winning composer and the theatrical puppetry of the same artist who did the puppets for the Broadway version of "The Lion King." Joining the show are acrobats, dancers, and animated backgrounds. The covered, air-conditioned theater opens 20 minutes before show time. No external video lights. Uncovered outdoor queue. Wheelchair accessible. Assistive listening.* **Alex's ToddlerTip:** ☺ **Allie's KidTip:** *"Cool puppets!"*

**Live Show** | E-Ticket | Ages 4 & up | 30 min. show

## Primeval Whirl [F-6]

FP A-OK! 7 7 8

*Chester and Hester cooked up a dizzy bit of fun for Primeval Whirl, a wild mouse coaster (with style). Your round "time machine" car spins as it goes around tight curves, over mild drops, and even through the jaws of a dinosaur. (What else?) Two identical coasters each boast 13 spinning, four-person ride vehicles. 48"/122 cm height restriction. Health warning. Must transfer from wheelchair to ride.* **Allie's KidTip:** *"The dips aren't as scary as they look."*

**Coaster** | D-Ticket | Ages 7 & up | Fast, drops | FASTPASS | 2.5 min. ride

## TriceraTop Spin [F-6]

A-OK! 5 5 7

*Dumbo morphs into a Dino! Sixteen dinosaur-shaped, four-rider cars swoop around a huge, spinning toy top. Part of Chester & Hester's Dino-Rama! (see below). Must transfer from ECV to wheelchair to ride.* **Alex's ToddlerTip:** ☺ **Allie's KidTip:** *"Sit in the front and make the dinosaur tilt forward or backward."*

**Ride** | C-Ticket | Ages 2 & up | 1.5 min. ride

## Chester & Hester's Dino-Rama!

Chester & Hester, the operators of DinoLand's crazy roadside-style gift shop, have created a roadside "carnival" with two attractions and about a half-dozen games of skill or chance. Play midway games for $2 a pop and maybe win a prize. Games include Mammoth Marathon, Bronto-Score, and Fossil Fueler.

# Typhoon Lagoon Water Park

Typhoon Lagoon is a 56-acre water park with lush foliage, lazy rivers, roaring waterfalls, and a huge surfing "lagoon." The water park is located near Downtown Disney West Side.

**AMBIENCE**

Legend has it that this was once the Placid Palms Resort in Safen Sound, Florida, a tropical hideaway nestled on a sparkling lagoon. Disaster struck when a typhoon raged through the sleepy resort, flooding the lagoon and tossing ships about. In its wake, they discovered sharks in the harbor, a surfboard through a tree, and ships scattered everywhere. Most amazing was the Miss Tilly shrimp boat, impaled on a craggy mountain (Mt. Mayday) that kept trying to dislodge the boat with a huge plume of water. Water was everywhere, forming waterfalls, rapids, pools, and surf. In true Disney form, misfortune was turned into luck and the Typhoon Lagoon water park was born. Or so the story goes.

**PARK LAYOUT**

The park's attractions are arrayed around its focal point, the gigantic, 2½-acre **wave pool** at the foot of Mt. Mayday. The "mountain" offers the advantage of height to several tube and body slides that slither down it. Around the perimeter of the park is a "lazy river" called Castaway Creek, offering a relaxing retreat to swimmers drifting lazily along in inner tubes. Finding your way around the park can be confusing at first—the dense foliage and meandering paths recreate the tropical look quite convincingly. Just keep in mind that one path encircles the park, and you can see Miss Tilly perched atop Mt. Mayday from almost everywhere. This park is worth exploring, too—the lush Mountain Trail on Mt. Mayday presents photo opportunities, and many hidden groves and glens offer quiet getaways.

**EATING**

**Leaning Palms** is the largest of the cafes, offering combo meals with a cheeseburger ($5.89), chili dogs ($6.69), BBQ pork sandwich ($7.49),cheese pizza ($5.59), Caesar salad ($2.59), and ice cream ($2.39). A kids' peanut butter and jelly sandwich meal is $5.19 and includes chips, drink, and a sand pail. **Happy Landings** has ice cream and a fun water play area where you can take aim at the guests drifting by on Castaway Creek. **Typhoon Tilly's Galley & Grog** has fish & chips, snacks, ice cream, and beverages. **Let's Go Slurpin'** offers alcoholic drinks and snacks. **Low Tide Lou's** (seasonal) has sandwiches. **Surf Doggies** offers hot dogs and turkey legs. Look for a cart selling yummy donut holes, too! Three **picnic areas** have shade and tables.

# Charting the Attractions at Typhoon Lagoon

| Attraction | Description | Jennifer's Rating | Dave's Rating | Readers' Rating | Type / Ticket / Notes |
|---|---|---|---|---|---|
| **Typhoon Lagoon Surf Pool** [C-4] A-OK! | *Waves in the world's largest inland wave pool at the base of Mt. Mayday change every half-hour, alternating between gentle bobs and 6-foot waves. Kids enjoy the two Bay Slides to the far left and the small tidal pools near the front. Observe the waves before entering.* **Allie's Kid Tip:** *"Don't scrape yourself on the bottom."* | 8 | 8 | 9 | **Pool**<br>E-Ticket<br>Surfing waves scary to kids |
| **Crush 'N' Gusher** [E-5] | *This new "water roller coaster" has jets of water pushing you up hill, followed by short drops. Three slides: Pineapple Plunger and Coconut Crusher (1–3 riders), Banana Blaster (1–2 riders). 48"/122 cm restriction. Transfer from wheelchair/ECV.* | 6 | 7 | 8 | **Tube Slide**<br>E-Ticket<br>Ages 7 & up |
| **Castaway Creek** [Entry points: A-3, A-4, D-2, D-3, D-5] A-OK! | *Relax on a half-mile, 20-minute circuit around the park on inner tubes. Catch a free tube at one of five entrances. Note where you entered, too!* **Allie's Kid Tip:** *"This is nice and relaxing. Little kids will like the yellow inner tubes the best."* | 9 | 8 | 8 | **Pool**<br>D-Ticket<br>Ages 3 & up |
| **Ketchakiddee Creek** [A-2] | *Several fountains, two body slides, and a 30-sec. tube ride—just for little squirts (48"/122 cm or under). Shady, thatched-roof shelters.* **Alex's Toddler Tip:** ☺ | 6 | 6 | 7 | **Playground**<br>B-Ticket |
| **Keelhaul Falls** [B-1] A-OK! | *A slow, solo tube ride with a surprise! (Warning—ride spoilers ahead.) Rafters plunge unexpectedly into a pitch-black tunnel about half the way down.* **Allie's Kid Tip:** *"The waterfall is fun! You don't get as wet as you think you will."* | 6 | 7 | 7 | **Tube Slide**<br>C-Ticket<br>Ages 7 & up |
| **Mayday Falls** [B-1] A-OK! | *Like Keelhaul Falls, this tube ride is solo. Unlike it, Mayday Falls is fast, twisting and turning through caves and waterfalls.* **Allie's Kid Tip:** *"This is very bumpy!"* | 5 | 6 | 7 | **Tube Slide**<br>C-Ticket |
| **Gang Plank Falls** [B-1] A-OK! | *Bring the family on this three- to five-person raft ride down the mountain. Watch out for waterfalls and those twisty-turny rafts!* **Allie's Kid Tip:** *"This is fun! Hold on tight because you go a little fast, but that's no problem."* | 8 | 6 | 6 | **Raft Slide**<br>C-Ticket<br>Ages 4 & up |
| **Humunga Kowabunga** [C-1] | *This is the ultimate thrill slide, shooting sliders down one of two slides in less than 10 seconds. Viewing bleachers at the bottom. 48"/122 cm height requirement. Health requirement. Ages 9 & up.* **Allie's Kid Tip:** *"It gave me a wedgie."* | 1 | 5 | 7 | **Body Slide**<br>E-Ticket<br>Fast, steep |
| **Storm Slides** [D-1] | *Three body slides (Stern Burner, Jib Jammer, and Rudder Buster) corkscrew through waterfalls and caves. Viewing bleachers at the bottom. Ages 8 & up.* | 5 | 6 | 7 | **Body Slides**<br>E-Ticket |
| **Shark Reef** [E-1] A-OK! | *Line up at Hammerhead Fred's Dive Shop for your snorkel (no charge), shower, 5-minute lesson, then snorkel across the small, chilly, saltwater lagoon. You may see a variety of fish, including three kinds of passive sharks. Bring an underwater camera. Scuba-assisted snorkel (extra fee).* **Allie's Kid Tip:** *"I love the sharks!"* | 9 | 8 | 8 | **Pool**<br>E-Ticket<br>Ages 6 & up<br>Cold, salty |

➤

# Making the Most of Typhoon Lagoon

TIPS

A **refillable mug** ($10) uses barcode scanners so you can refill without cast supervision. You can purchase a new refill barcode ($5) on future visits. A Typhoon Lagoon mug can be used at Blizzard Beach and vice versa as long as you buy the appropriate refill.

© MediaMarx, Inc.

*Catching a kid at Ketchakiddee Creek*

Avoid **two-piece suits** on slides—they may come down the slide at a different speed than you. Also, swimsuits with rivets, buckles, or exposed metal are not permitted. Wear water shoes—the sand and pavement can get quite hot.

Use a single-use, **underwater camera** for great photos.

Get your first taste of **scuba** in a special section of the Shark Reef. Cost is $20 for the first 30 min. and $15 for the rest of your party or for repeat dives. Pay at the booth near the dive shop. Brief lessons are provided, and parents can attend their kids without renting.

NOTES

**Children** under the age of 10 must be accompanied by an adult.

**You can rent lockers** ($5–$7) and towels ($1 each). You may wish to bring hotel towels rather than rent them—they're practically the same size. Changing rooms are also available. Life vests are free (refundable deposit). Some personal flotation devices may be permitted.

**Park hours**: generally open by 10:00 am, closed at 5:00 pm or later. A one-day pass (with tax) is $41.54/adults and $35.15/kids 3–9.

RATINGS

*Ratings are explained on page 120.*

| Our Value Ratings: | | Our Magic Ratings: | | Readers' Ratings: |
|---|---|---|---|---|
| Quality: | 7/10 | Theme: | 8/10 | 76% fell in love with it |
| Variety: | 8/10 | Excitement: | 7/10 | 21% liked it well enough |
| Scope: | 3/10 | Fun Factor: | 7/10 | 3% had mixed feelings |
| **Overall Value:** | **6/10** | **Overall Magic:** | **7/10** | 0% were disappointed |

| Typhoon Lagoon is enjoyed by... (rated by both authors and readers) | | |
|---|---|---|
| Younger Kids: ♥♥♥♥ | Young Adults: ♥♥♥♥♥ | Families: ♥♥♥♥ |
| Older Kids: ♥♥♥♥♥ | Mid Adults: ♥♥♥ | Couples: ♥♥♥ |
| Teenagers: ♥♥♥♥♥ | Mature Adults: ♥♥♥ | Singles: ♥♥♥ |

# Finding Your Way at Typhoon Lagoon

## TYPHOON LAGOON PARK MAP

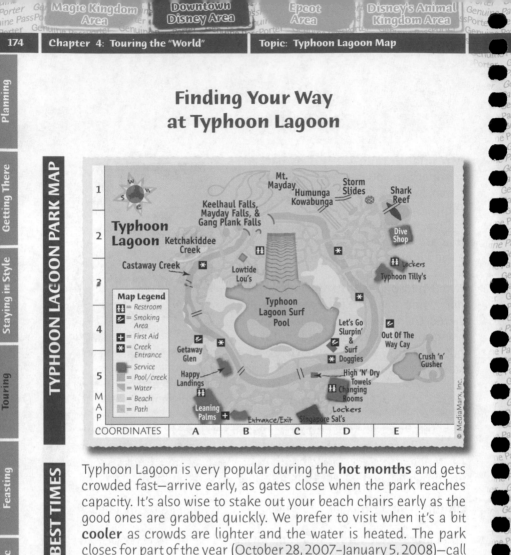

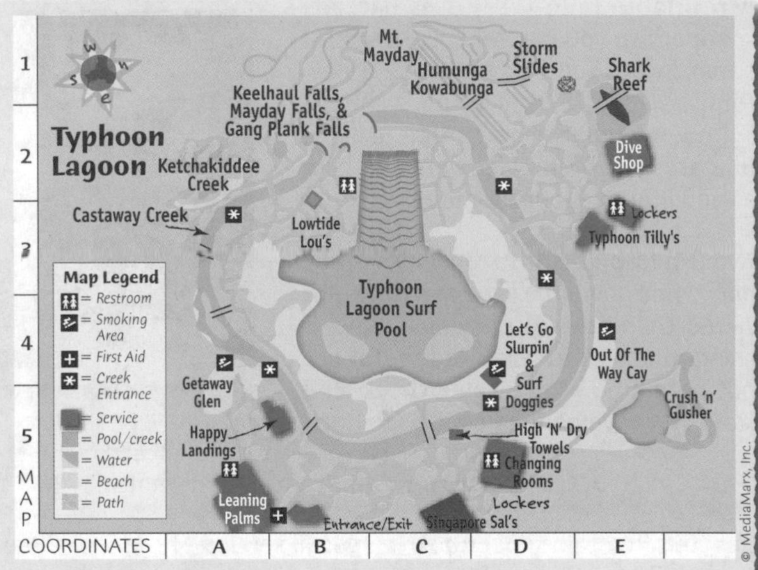


## BEST TIMES

Typhoon Lagoon is very popular during the **hot months** and gets crowded fast—arrive early, as gates close when the park reaches capacity. It's also wise to stake out your beach chairs early as the good ones are grabbed quickly. We prefer to visit when it's a bit **cooler** as crowds are lighter and the water is heated. The park closes for part of the year (October 28, 2007–January 5, 2008)—call 407-560-4141 and confirm that it is open if you intend to visit the park. Beyond that, **weekdays** are better than weekends (locals love to visit the park). Visit in the **late afternoon** when the park empties a bit and the sun is less intense. The park may **close during storms**—when it reopens, it may be nearly empty. If you arrive when there are long lines, bypass them by getting your tickets at the Automated Ticket Vending Machines now available here.

## GETTING THERE

**By Bus**—All Disney resorts have direct buses to Typhoon Lagoon. From Magic Kingdom, Epcot, Disney's Hollywood Studios, and Disney's Animal Kingdom, take a bus or monorail to a nearby resort and transfer to a Typhoon Lagoon bus (which may also be the Downtown Disney bus). Allow about 30–60 minutes if you travel by bus. **By Car**—Take exit 67 off I-4, take the first exit and turn right on Buena Vista Dr.—the park is on the right. From Downtown Disney, turn right to Buena Vista Dr. and the park is on the left. Free parking.

# Blizzard Beach Water Park

Is it a water park, or a ski resort? The Blizzard Beach water park brings the chills and thrills of a Colorado winter to the warm Florida sun. Ski jumps, toboggan rides, and slalom runs zip you past snow that never melts in Disney's most action-oriented water park.

AMBIENCE

Disney's Imagineers scattered magic white stuff over the rocks and pines of towering Mount Gushmore to create a water park that'll make you shiver on the hottest August day. Oh, don't worry, the water is always a warm 80 degrees, but just a look at some of those water slides can freeze your insides. Luckily, Disney never abandons the idea of family fun—even the meekest snow bunny will have a ball!

ATTRACTIONS

Before you "hit the slopes" you'll discover the park's **"base lodge"** facilities—the major food, merchandise, and locker room areas. Then, as you face the mountain, the Tike's Peak children's area will be to your right. Straight ahead are two bridges over Cross Country Creek, the drift-along tube ride that encircles the mountain and most of the fun. Additional lockers can be found close to the action, near Downhill Double Dipper on the left and Ski Patrol on the right. Of course, Mount Gushmore dominates the park in every way. Its slopes are home to nearly two dozen lanes of slides and flumes. Most slides can be seen from the Lodge area, but Runoff Rapids is tucked away on the back slope of the mountain. You can also watch your daredevils in comfort, from shaded grandstands at the bottom of many slides. Three footpaths and a chairlift scale the 90-foot (9-story) mountain. After your first ascent on foot in the hot, Florida sunshine, you'll know why folks wait patiently for the chairlift, which takes you to the top in the comfort of a three-person, umbrella-shaded chair (32"/ 81 cm height restriction; under 48"/122 cm must be with an adult).

EATING

Water park meals are never fancy, which is fine when you're only wearing a swimsuit. **Lottawatta Lodge** serves up cheeseburger combos ($5.89), hot dogs ($5.79), chicken wraps ($7.29), Cobb salads ($6.99), ice cream ($2.30–$2.89), and kosher selections. A kid's meal is $5.19 with a choice of mac & cheese, hot dog, or chicken strips, plus chips, drink, and a toy. **Avalunch** and **The Warming Hut** offer hot dogs, sandwiches, ice cream, and usually close before dinnertime. The thirsty line up at **Frostbite Freddie's Frozen Freshments**, **Polar Pub**, and **The Cooling Hut**. There are also **picnic areas**.

# Charting the Attractions at Blizzard Beach

| Attraction | Jennifer's Rating | Dave's Rating | Readers' Rating | Type |
|---|---|---|---|---|
| **Summit Plummet** [D-2] — *Only the boldest ride the world's highest body slide, which drops 120 feet. Go feet first, cross your arms, and it's over in eight seconds. Be prepared for a steep drop and a wedgie! 48"/122 cm height requirement. Health requirement.* | 2 | 5 | 9 | Body Slide; E-Ticket; Ages 9 & up |
| **Slush Gusher** [D-2] — *Ninety-foot-high double-bump slide is the second-tallest body slide in the park. One-piece suits recommended! 48"/122 cm height requirement. Ages 8 & up.* | 3 | 6 | 8 | Body Slide; D-Ticket |
| **Downhill Double Dipper** [C-2] — *Race head-to-head on a half-enclosed innertube slide. Your race results are flashed on a scoreboard. 48"/122 cm height requirement. Ages 8 & up.* | 5 | 7 | 8 | Tube Slide; D-Ticket |
| **Snow Stormers** [C-2] A-OK! — *Zig and zag your way down this three-flume, family-friendly slalom mat slide. 12-second ride. Allie's Kid Tip: "Fun, but it's a little bumpy." Ages 6 & up.* | 7 | 5 | 8 | Mat Slide; C-Ticket |
| **Toboggan Racers** [D-3] A-OK! — *On your mark, get set, go! Race headfirst down an eight-lane mat slide. 10-second ride. Allie's Kid Tip: "Push yourself off to go down." Ages 6 & up.* | 6 | 5 | 7 | Mat Slide; D-Ticket |
| **Teamboat Springs** [E-3] A-OK! — *Whitewater-loving families can pack up to six in a large, round, river raft for a long, twisting ride—at 1,400 feet it is the longest ride of its kind anywhere. Allie's Kid Tip: "Hold on to the bottom of the raft when you go down."* | 9 | 8 | 9 | Raft Slide; D-Ticket; Ages 4 up |
| **Runoff Rapids** [D-2] — *Ride a tube down this twisty, turny, family-friendly course. Three different open and enclosed slides. Up to two can share a tube on the open slides. Allie's Kid Tip: "Pick up your behind over the bumps, or it won't feel good."* | 8 | 7 | 7 | Tube Slide; C-Ticket; Ages 6 & up |
| **Cross Country Creek** [Entry points: B-4, A-4, B-2, C-1, E-3, D-4] A-OK! — *Float around the park on a moderately flowing creek. Enter and exit at any of six spots around the park. Return to your starting point in 20 minutes. Allie's Kid Tip: "Don't get wet under the freezing waterfalls."* | 8 | 7 | 7 | Pool; D-Ticket; Ages 2 & up |
| **Melt Away Bay** [B-3] A-OK! — *Bob in the sedate waves of a one-acre wave pool. Kids under 10 must be with an adult. Allie's Kid Tip: "The tide pools are cool to play in!" All ages.* | 7 | 6 | 7 | Pool; C-Ticket |
| **Ski Patrol Training Camp** [D-3] A-OK! — *Scaled-down area for kids 12 and under. Try Snow Falls slide, Cool Runners tube slalom, and Thin Ice Training Course—a walk across a field of "ice floes." Allie's Kid Tip: "If an iceberg is far away, lean back to move toward it."* | 8 | 7 | 7 | Playground; D-Ticket; Ages 6–12 |
| **Tike's Peak** [D-5] — *Even the littlest ones have a mini version of the park, with slides, wading pools, and fountains. Must be 48"/122 cm or shorter. Ages 0–6.* **Alex's Toddler Tip:** ☺ | 6 | 5 | 7 | Playground; C-Ticket |

# Making the Most of Blizzard Beach

TIPS

**Save time**—buy your park passes in advance at Guest Relations.

There's **little shade** here—use waterproof sunscreen and cover-ups! Wear water shoes to ward off the heat of the sand and sidewalks.

Play **miniature golf** at Winter Summerland, adjacent to the water park. See page 192 for more on this imaginative mini golf course.

Pick up a **map** on your way in to locate the lockers ($5–$7) and towels ($1). Life jackets are free if you leave an ID card and/or deposit.

You'll find **chaise lounges** wherever you go, but on busy days, follow the path around the back end of the mountain, where you'll find secluded lounging areas and the main entrance to Runoff Rapids.

This is the **"big thrill"** water park, so it draws a young crowd. Typhoon Lagoon is a better choice for families.

If you ride the big slides, bikinis are a very risky fashion statement. You'll have better luck with a **one-piece suit**. Also, swimsuits with rivets, buckles, or exposed metal are not permitted.

NOTES

The **Beach Haus** near the entrance sells just about anything you may have forgotten or lost, from sunscreen to swimsuits.

When the **summer weather** is at its hottest, the parking lots fill up early. Use Disney buses instead, which can always drive in.

**Children** under the age of 10 must be accompanied by an adult.

**Park hours**: generally open by 10:00 am, closed at 5:00 pm or later. A one-day pass (with tax) is $41.54/adults and $35.15/kids 3–9.

RATINGS

*Ratings are explained on page 120.*

| Our Value Ratings: | | Our Magic Ratings: | | Readers' Ratings: |
|---|---|---|---|---|
| Quality: | 7/10 | Theme: | 8/10 | 94% fell in love with it |
| Variety: | 8/10 | Excitement: | 8/10 | 2% liked it well enough |
| Scope: | 4/10 | Fun Factor: | 7/10 | 2% had mixed feelings |
| **Overall Value:** | **6/10** | **Overall Magic:** | **8/10** | 2% were disappointed |

| Blizzard Beach is enjoyed by... | (rated by both authors and readers) | |
|---|---|---|
| Younger Kids: ♥♥♥♥ | Young Adults: ♥♥♥♥♥ | Families: ♥♥♥♥♥ |
| Older Kids: ♥♥♥♥♥ | Mid Adults: ♥♥♥ | Couples: ♥♥♥ |
| Teenagers: ♥♥♥♥♥ | Mature Adults: ♥ | Singles: ♥♥♥♥ |

Planning | Getting There | Staying in Style | Touring | Feasting | Making Magic | Index | Notes & More

# Finding Your Way at Blizzard Beach

BLIZZARD BEACH PARK MAP

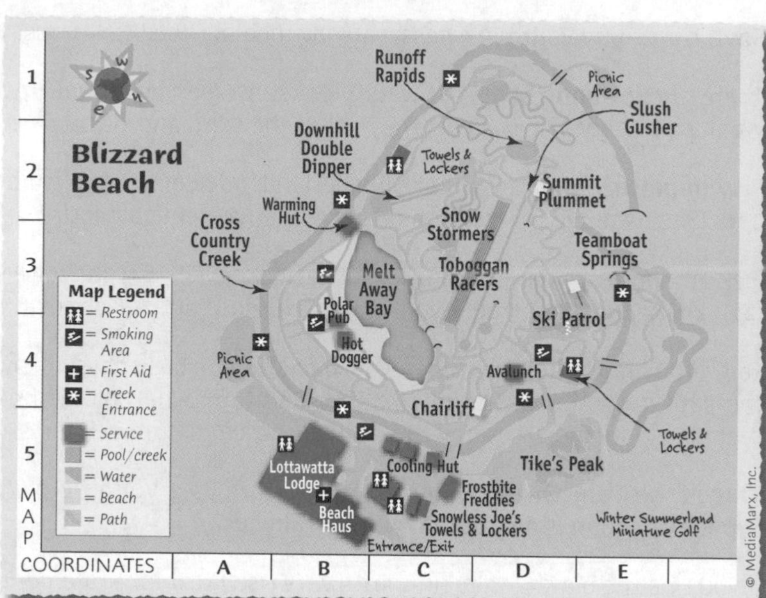


BEST TIMES

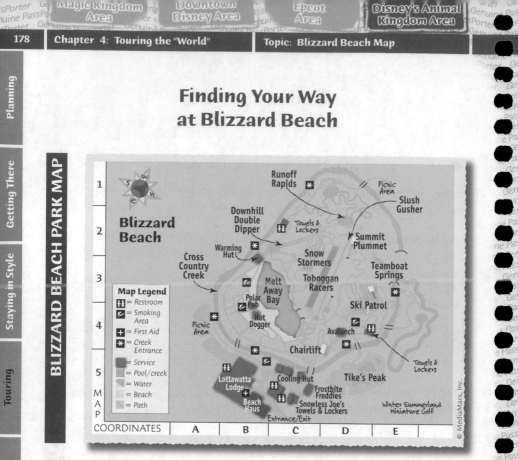

Thanks to the heated waters, you'll be comfortable throughout the **cooler months**, and the sun is kinder. The crowds are thinner, but the days are shorter, and an overcast, rainy winter day can make life miserable. Note that the park may be closed on Fridays and Saturdays in the cooler months. Summer at Blizzard Beach brings **huge crowds** that arrive early in the day. If the park reaches capacity, the gates close to all. By **mid-afternoon**, the crowds have thinned, as those who are worst-wilted have packed it in. That's a good time to arrive, refreshing yourself after a long morning at nearby Disney's Animal Kingdom. Operating hours vary with the season, so check before you trek. The park is closed in early 2008 for its annual refurbishment.

GETTING THERE

**By Bus**—All resorts and Disney's Animal Kingdom have direct buses to Blizzard Beach. From Disney's Hollywood Studios, take the Coronado Springs bus. From Epcot, take the Disney's Animal Kingdom Lodge bus. From the Magic Kingdom and Downtown Disney, take a bus or monorail to a Disney resort and board a bus to Blizzard Beach. We recommend you take Disney transportation when you can, because the parking lot can fill up on busy days.
**By Car**—From westbound or eastbound I-4, take exit 65 (west on Osceola Parkway), exiting at Buena Vista Drive. Free parking.

# Downtown Disney

If "heading downtown" is your idea of rest and recreation, the Walt Disney World Resort's Downtown Disney district is a major treat. From the world's largest Disney Store to mind-boggling Lego sculptures, super dining, and thrilling entertainment, you'll have a ball Downtown.

**AMBIENCE**

Downtown Disney has three unique **districts**. The **Marketplace** is a charming village of shops, **Pleasure Island** thrives on its vibrant night life, and **West Side** is the urban-style shopping, dining, and fun capital of the "World." Downtown Disney's pedestrian-only streets and sprawling layout avoid the "mall" feeling completely. This is one of the brightest, cleanest, and safest downtowns anywhere.

**SHOPPING**

Downtown Disney satisfies the urge to "shop 'til you drop." There's no admission charge here, and you'll find much more than Disney merchandise. The **Marketplace** shops are Wonderful World of Memories (scrapbooking), The Art of Disney, Basin (bath and facial products), Disney's Days of Christmas, Eurospain/Arribas Brothers (crystal shop), Goofy's Candy Co., Once Upon a Toy, Summer Sands (resortwear), Disney's Pin Traders, Lego Imagination Center, Pooh Corner, Team Mickey's Athletic Club, the World of Disney (and its Bibbidi Bobbidi Boutique for little kids), Mickey's Mart (everything under $10), and Disney Tails (pet care and pampering items). **West Side** shopping features Sunglass Icon, Disney's Candy Cauldron, DisneyQuest Emporium, Pop Gallery, Hoypoloi (sculpture gallery), Magnetron (magnets), Mickey's Groove (funky Disney gifts), Harley Davidson, Planet Hollywood on Location, Sosa Family Cigars, Starabilias (collectibles), Virgin Megastore, Wetzel's Pretzels, and shops at House of Blues, Cirque du Soleil, and DisneyQuest. Magic Masters offers top-flight magic gear, demos, and even a hidden room where guests can learn to use their magic tricks. Packages can be delivered to your Disney resort!

**PLAYING**

Downtown Disney builds fun into nearly every shop and restaurant, but four spots put entertainment first. Movie fans flock to the **AMC 24 Theatres Complex**, the Southeast's largest—their theaters sport stadium seating, most with retractable armrests. Tickets are $9.50/adults, $7.50/seniors and students, $6.50/kids ages 2–12. The innovative **Cirque du Soleil** also makes its home Downtown—see page 182. **DisneyQuest**, Disney's indoor "theme park," gets its own write-up and review on pages 183–186, as does **Pleasure Island** on pages 187–190.

# Finding Your Way at Downtown Disney

DOWNTOWN DISNEY MAP

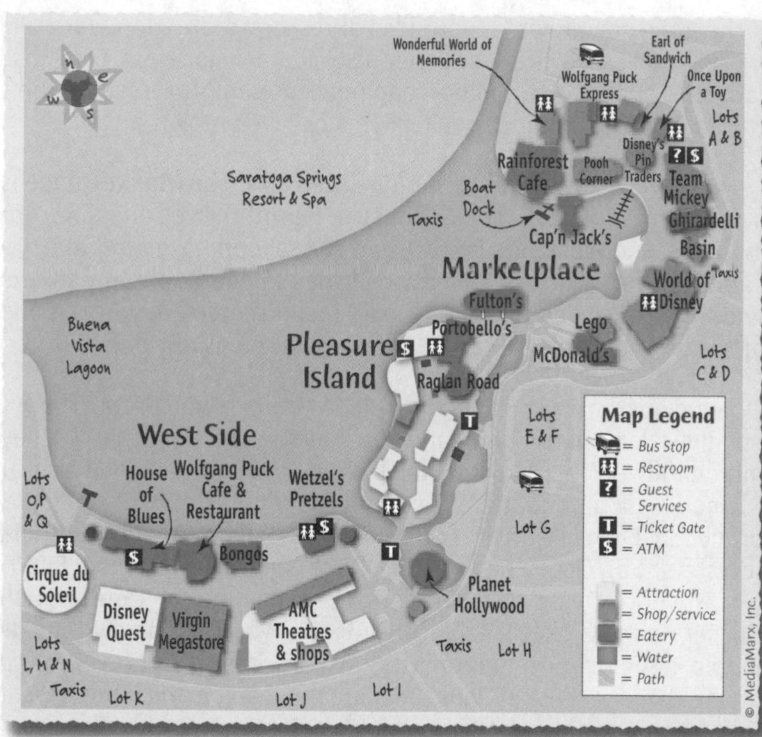


DINING

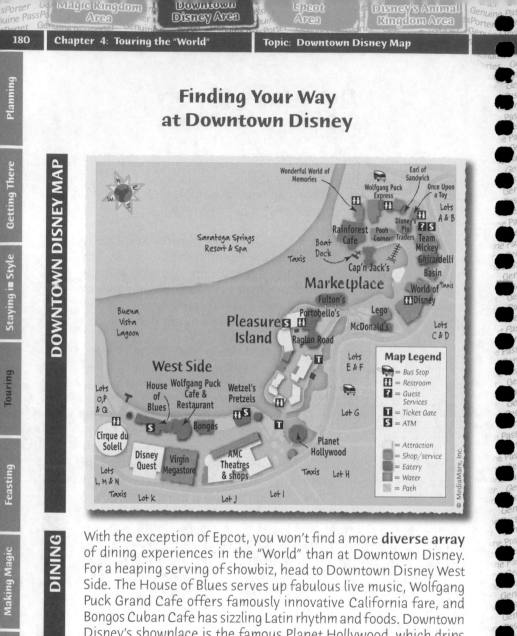

With the exception of Epcot, you won't find a more **diverse array** of dining experiences in the "World" than at Downtown Disney. For a heaping serving of showbiz, head to Downtown Disney West Side. The House of Blues serves up fabulous live music, Wolfgang Puck Grand Cafe offers famously innovative California fare, and Bongos Cuban Cafe has sizzling Latin rhythm and foods. Downtown Disney's showplace is the famous Planet Hollywood, which drips with movie memorabilia. Fulton's Crab House serves upscale seafood on a riverboat, Cap'n Jack's Restaurant does seafood and steaks, and the Rainforest Cafe cooks up imaginative fare. On Pleasure Island, Portobello Yacht Club offers Northern Italian food in a casual atmosphere, while Raglan Road (Irish pub) and Cookes of Dublin offer authentic Emerald Isle fare. A new eatery called T-Rex will arrive here in 2008, too. Busy shoppers like the lighter fare at The Earl of Sandwich, Wetzel's Pretzels, Wolfgang Puck Express, Ghirardelli Soda Fountain & Chocolate Shop, and, of course, "Ronald's Fun House" (McDonald's). Complete descriptions of these eateries begin on page 222.

# Making the Most of Downtown Disney

TIPS

The World of Disney Store houses the popular **Bibbidi Bobbidi Boutique salon**, which offers hair styling and makeover services for both young girls ($45–$225) and boys ($10), ages 3–12. Appointments recommended (407-WDW-STYLE). Tip: Another location recently opened inside Cinderella Castle—see page 125.

**Once Upon A Toy** has amazing decor and unique toys, including make-your-own Tinkertoys, build-your-own light sabers and My Little Pony, and Mr. Potato Head sets with Disney-themed parts.

Kids can **play for free** at the Lego Imagination Center and in the water play fountain near the Marketplace bus stop entrance.

Little-known **discounts and specials** may be available. Be sure to ask! For example, movies at the AMC Pleasure Island 24 are $5 before noon, and $7.50 before 4:00 pm on select days.

Every November, the **Festival of the Masters** at Downtown Disney offers art exhibits, food, performances, and kids' activities.

**Christmas** brings fun activities. There's also a year-round toy train ride (for a fee). Don't forget Disney's Days of Christmas shop, too.

NOTES

Of the eateries here, only Cap'n Jack's is Disney-run, so **reservations policies** differ, although many offer reservations through Disney. Most eateries and shops let you charge to your Disney resort tab.

The Downtown Disney Marketplace and Pleasure Island **parking lots** are often packed. Try the huge West Side parking lot instead.

Most **shops** in the Marketplace open at 9:30 am, while West Side shops open at 10:30 am. Closing is at 11:00 pm, with seasonal variations.

For **more details**, call Downtown Disney at 407-828-3058.

GETTING THERE

**By Bus**—Buses are available from every Disney resort. From the parks, bus or monorail to a nearby resort and transfer.
**By Car**—From I-4, take exit 67, then take the first exit and turn right on Buena Vista Drive. Parking is free.
**By Boat**—Boats may shuttle between the Marketplace and West Side seasonally. Resort guests at Port Orleans, Old Key West, and Saratoga Springs can take a boat to the Marketplace, too.
**By Foot**—Guests at Saratoga Springs and Hotel Plaza Resorts may walk.

# Making the Most of Cirque du Soleil

A circus has come to Walt Disney World, the likes of which you've probably never seen—magical, musical, a little mystical, and poetically graceful. Cirque du Soleil ("Circus of the Sun") from Montreal, Canada, has redefined the concept of "circus" for millions around the world and has a company-in-residence at Downtown Disney West Side.

## SHOWS

Cirque du Soleil weaves its magic with acrobats, clowns, jugglers, dancers, aerialists, lights, original music, and fabulous costumes (and not one animal). The current show, **La Nouba** (from the French "to live it up"), weaves a continuous, dream-like thread. There's a story here, but many guests hardly notice or care. This isn't Big Top-style circus, either. It has as much in common with modern dance as it does with circus. It's not for everyone (Dave likes it, Jennifer doesn't), but it adds yet another dimension to the magic. Note that this show has no intermission.

## INFO

Housed in its own **1,671-seat theater** at the west end of the West Side, Cirque du Soleil offers its 90-min. shows at 6:00 and 9:00 pm, Tues.–Sat. Tickets are $67–$120/adults and $53–$96/kids ages 3–9 depending on category—see chart below. If you are a DVC member or a Florida resident, inquire about possible discounts. Call 407-939-7600 or visit http://www.lanouba.com to reserve up to six months in advance or visit the box office. Seats within categories are assigned based on availability, but you might get your pick at the box office.

## SEATING PLAN

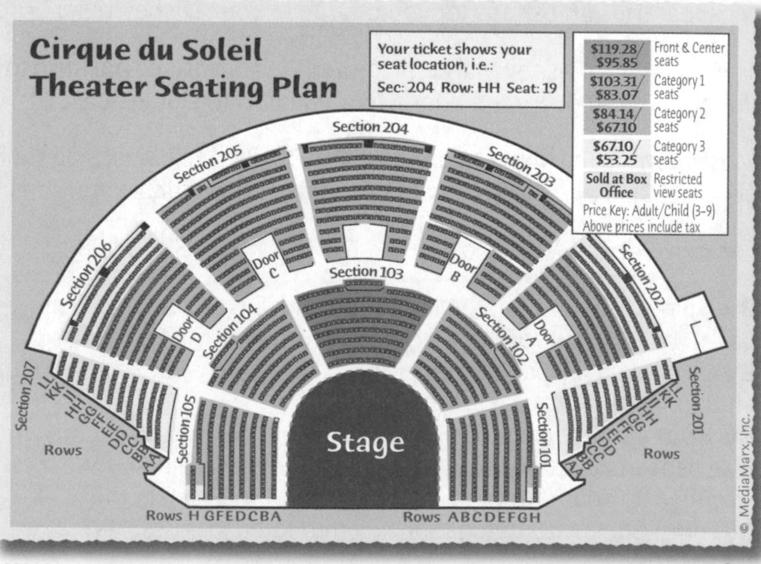

# DisneyQuest

DisneyQuest is an indoor "theme park" housed in a big, blue, five-story building at Downtown Disney West Side. It features ride simulators, high-tech games, and hands-on activities for young and old alike.

LAYOUT

Attractions run the gamut from simple video arcade games to a you-design-it, you-ride-it roller coaster simulator. Take the "Cyberlator" elevator to the Ventureport, where you can enter four zones: **Explore Zone**, **Score Zone**, **Create Zone**, and **Replay Zone**. Each zone organizes the attractions (described below) by theme. Each zone spans at least two floors, with various stairs and walkways linking them. This makes for a bewildering maze—study our map on page 186 to orient yourself before you go.

| **Aladdin's Magic Carpet Ride** [Floor 2] A-OK! | 6 4 6 |
|---|---|
| *Don virtual reality goggles for a wild, 4-min. ride on Aladdin's magic carpet. Swoop through Agrabah and the Cave of Wonder to search for jewels and free the Genie. Motion sickness warning. Explore Zone.* Allie's Kid Tip: *"Make sure your helmet is on tight so it doesn't fall off when you play."* | **Virtual**<br>D-Ticket<br>Ages 6 & up<br>Dizziness |

| **Animation Academy** [Floor 2] A-OK! | 7 7 6 |
|---|---|
| *Take your seat at a computer workstation as an instructor draws out your artistry. Hands-on lessons in drawing and/or animating characters. Several 20-minute lessons are offered. After the class, you can buy your creation. Create Zone.* Allie's Kid Tip: *"Check the schedule for a class that draws a character you like."* | **Hands-on**<br>D-Ticket<br>Ages 6 & up<br>Skill helps |

| **Buzz Lightyear's Astroblasters** [Floor 3] | 7 5 7 |
|---|---|
| *Ride fully enclosed two-person bumper cars mounted with "cannons" that shoot large rubber balls. The driver pilots to scoop up ammo, and the gunner fires on other cars to make them spin out of control. 3-min. game. 51"/130 cm height restriction. Replay Zone.* Allie's Kid Tip: *"Try to hit a lot of cars so they spin around."* | **Vehicles**<br>D-Ticket<br>Ages 9 & up<br>Bumpy |

| **CyberSpace Mountain** [Floor 2] | 9 8 9 |
|---|---|
| *Design and ride your own coaster! Start by choosing a theme and designing the coaster tracks on a computer screen. Then get strapped into a two-person flight simulator to experience your coaster, or choose from a ready-made coaster. Be prepared to be shaken, rattled, and rolled on a ride more dizzying than the real thing. Simulator seats are small. 51"/130 cm height restriction. Create Zone.* Allie's Kid Tip: *"If you feel sick, just hit the red stop button."* | **Simulator**<br>E-Ticket<br>Ages 9 & up<br>Upside-down during inversions |

| **Invasion! An ExtraTERRORestrial Alien Encounter** [Floor 5] A-OK! | 6 7 5 |
|---|---|
| *Dash across the galaxy to rescue Earth colonists from an invading horde in this simulator ride that borrows characters and fun from the former Magic Kingdom attraction. One teammate pilots the rescue vehicle, while three other teammates keep the bad guys at bay. Great pre-show film. Score Zone.* Allie's Kid Tip: *"I think kids will have more fun being a gunner than a pilot."* | **Simulator**<br>E-Ticket<br>Ages 7 & up<br>Violent theme |

*Attraction descriptions and ratings are explained on page 127.*

# Charting the Attractions at DisneyQuest

Jennifer's Rating | Dave's Rating | Readers' Rating

| Attraction | Jennifer's Rating | Dave's Rating | Readers' Rating | Type |
|---|---|---|---|---|
| **Living Easels** [Floor 2] A-OK! — *Draw animated landscapes on a touch-sensitive screen. You can buy print-outs if you like. Create Zone. Allie's Kid Tip: "Use your imagination!" Ages 3 & up.* | 5 | 4 | 4 | Hands-on; B-Ticket |
| **Midway on the Moon** [Floors 4 and 5] A-OK! — *Disney-themed versions of arcade games like Ursula's Whirlpool and traditional games like Skeeball. All games are free play, but prize redemption is no longer offered. Replay Zone. Allie's Kid Tip: "Look at all the games before you play."* | 6 | 8 | 5 | Arcade; A-Ticket; Ages 5 & up |
| **Mighty Ducks Pinball Slam** [Floor 3] — *Use body motion/weight to move a "puck" around a huge screen and "body check" opponents on this simulator. 3-min. game. 48"/122 cm height restriction. Score Zone. Allie's Kid Tip: "If you're tall enough but skinny, it might not work."* | 5 | 4 | 7 | Simulator; D-Ticket; Ages 9 & up |
| **Pirates of the Caribbean: Battle for Buccaneer Gold** [Floor 1] A-OK! — *Yo ho, yo ho! DisneyQuest's newest attraction pits you and up to four shipmates in a 3-D simulated sea battle in quest of pirate gold. Fire virtual cannonballs against your foes, and feel the deck shudder when you take a hit. 35"/89 cm height restriction. Explore Zone. Allie's Kid Tip: "Shoot the ships that you pass!"* | 8 | 8 | 9 | Simulator; E-Ticket; Ages 7 & up; Violent theme |
| **Radio Disney SongMaker** [Floor 2] A-OK! — *Create your own hit song in a soundbooth. Combine styles and lyrics for laughs. You can buy a CD of it. Create Zone. Allie's Kid Tip: "Don't be shy." Ages 4 & up.* | 6 | 6 | 4 | Hands-on; D-Ticket |
| **Ride the Comix** [Floors 4 and 5] — *Swing your laser sword to battle comic strip villains in this 4-min., 3-D virtual reality game. Heavy goggles, sword-play, and motion sickness make this hard to play. Score Zone. Allie's Kid Tip: "The monsters might scare you." Ages 8 & up.* | 2 | 3 | 5 | Virtual; D-Ticket; May feel dizzy |
| **Sid's Create-A-Toy** [Floor 2] — *Create a demented toy from spare toy parts—on a computer screen. You can buy a real version of your creation. Create Zone. Allie's Kid Tip: "Boring." Ages 4 & up.* | 3 | 4 | 5 | Hands-on; B-Ticket |
| **Virtual Jungle Cruise** [Floor 1] A-OK! — *Board a raft, grab a paddle, and take a 4-min. whitewater river cruise back in time on this motion simulator ride. Dr. Wayne Szalinski guides you and your teammates on this riotous journey over waterfalls and into the age of the dinosaurs. You may get a little damp. Explore Zone. Allie's Kid Tip: "Paddle hard."* | 9 | 6 | 6 | Simulator; E-Ticket; Ages 6 & up; Paddling |

**Note**: Magic Mirrors (turn your face into a toon) and Treasure of the Incas (remote-controlled trucks in a maze) are permanantly closed.

**Tip**: DisneyQuest tickets may be sold at a lower price two hours prior to closing time.

# Making the Most of DisneyQuest

DINING

You won't go hungry at DisneyQuest. The Cheesecake Factory operates two satisfying **counter-service eateries**: FoodQuest and Wonderland Cafe. Up on the top floor, FoodQuest (see page 224) offers an appetizing variety of pizzas, salads, burgers, sandwiches, and wraps, plus a few tempting desserts. On the floor below, Wonderland Cafe (see page 225) pleases the sweet tooth with a huge selection of cheesecakes and desserts, and all sorts of luxurious coffee concoctions. And while you sip your latté, you can browse the Internet on limited-use computer terminals.

TIPS

First-time visitors should spend time exploring the entire place before splitting up. While you're at it, choose a **meeting place** and time. The Wonderland Cafe is a good choice with places to sit, and the Ventureport on the third floor is highly visible.

Allow at least **four to five hours** to tour, more if you love arcades.

Be sure to wear a **wristwatch**—it's easy to lose track of time! Also, it's faster to use the stairs to go up or down one level. On the other hand, the elevators are less disorienting than the curving staircases.

The Wonderland Cafe sports tables with **free Internet access**, but the custom browser makes it tough to surf at will.

NOTES

Rumor has it DisneyQuest *may* become an **ESPN Zone** in the future.

**Best times to visit** are during the mornings and afternoons and on the weekends. It gets pretty busy in the evenings, after other parks are closed. Crowds are huge on foul-weather days.

**Discounted admissions** may be available after 10:00 pm.

RATINGS

*Ratings are explained on page 120.*

| Our Value Ratings: | | Our Magic Ratings: | | Readers' Ratings: |
|---|---|---|---|---|
| Quality: | 6/10 | Theme: | 5/10 | 78% fell in love with it |
| Variety: | 4/10 | Excitement: | 5/10 | 22% liked it well enough |
| Scope: | 3/10 | Fun Factor: | 6/10 | 0% had mixed feelings |
| **Overall Value:** | **4/10** | **Overall Magic:** | **5/10** | 0% were disappointed |

| DisneyQuest is enjoyed by... | (rated by both authors and readers) | |
|---|---|---|
| Younger Kids: ♥♥♥♥ | Young Adults: ♥♥♥♥♥ | Families: ♥♥♥♥ |
| Older Kids: ♥♥♥♥♥ | Mid Adults: ♥♥♥ | Couples: ♥♥♥ |
| Teenagers: ♥♥♥♥♥ | Mature Adults: ♥ | Singles: ♥♥♥♥♥ |

## Finding Your Way at DisneyQuest

DISNEYQUEST MAP

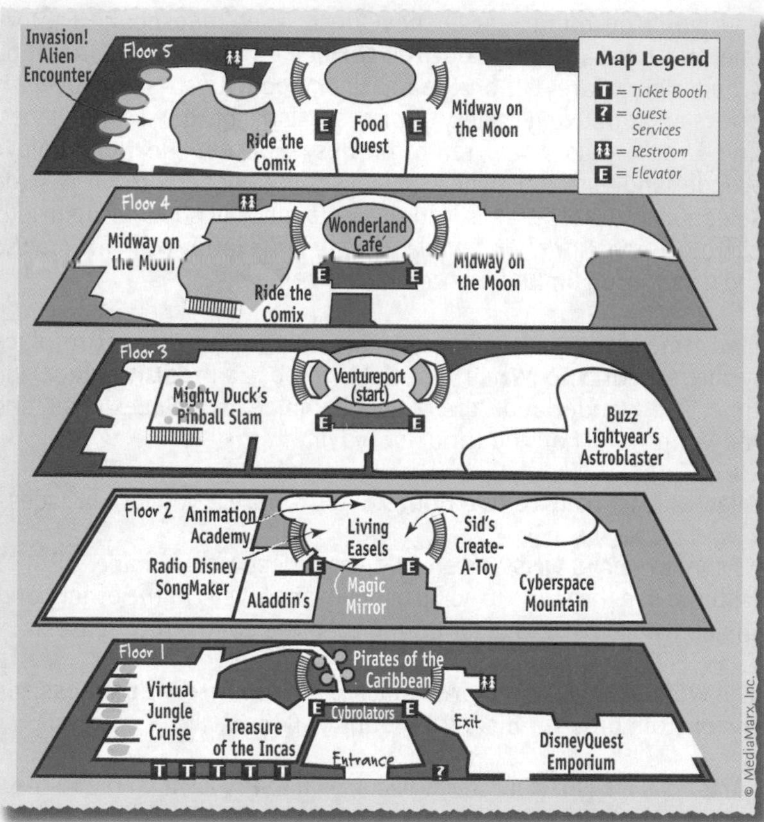


ADMISSION

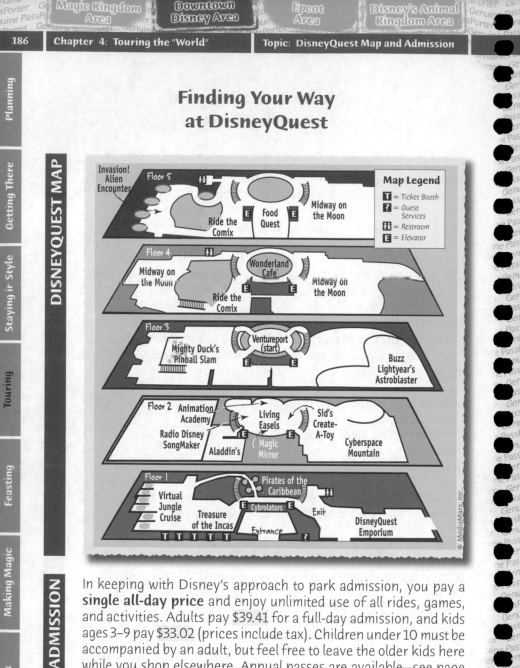

In keeping with Disney's approach to park admission, you pay a **single all-day price** and enjoy unlimited use of all rides, games, and activities. Adults pay $39.41 for a full-day admission, and kids ages 3–9 pay $33.02 (prices include tax). Children under 10 must be accompanied by an adult, but feel free to leave the older kids here while you shop elsewhere. Annual passes are available—see page 116. DisneyQuest **admission is included** in Magic Your Way tickets that have Plus options and Premium Annual Passes. DisneyQuest hours are 10:30 am–11:00 pm Sundays–Thursdays, and 10:30 am–midnight on Fridays and Saturdays.

INFO

For more DisneyQuest **information**, call 407-828-4600 or visit http://www.disneyquest.com. There is also a DisneyQuest kiosk in Downtown Disney Marketplace that offers information.

# Pleasure Island

**AMBIENCE**

Where can you disco down until 2:00 am, laugh it up at a comedy club, and enjoy the camaraderie of a band of intrepid explorers? Pleasure Island! The club's parties start around 7:00 pm and continue up to 2:00 am nightly. There's no cost to stroll through Pleasure Island, but admission to the clubs is required (see page 189). The clubs are described below.

| Club | Description | Ratings / Info |
|---|---|---|
| **8Trax** — 21+ Only | *Disco in all its Saturday Night Fever glory! The sound is classic 70s (Thursday is 80s night), the floor is packed and illuminated, and dancers are enthusiastic!* | 8 5 6 · **Dance** · C-Ticket |
| **Adventurers Club** — A-OK! | *In all ways, this is the most "Disney" of the clubs on Pleasure Island (and our absolute favorite). Be prepared for the unexpected, the quirky, and the hilarious. You'll even encounter some PG-rated adult humor later in the evenings. The walls are encrusted with trophies, mementos, curios, and photos amassed by the club members—intrepid explorers and wannabes all. Look closely—this is Disney, after all! You may be greeted by the club's stoic butler, the matronly Club President, or even a French maid. Different shows are held throughout the night in the Mask Room, Treasure Room, and Library.* **Allie's Kid Tip:** *"The Yakoose moose drools! And they make you sing silly songs!"* | 10 10 8 · **Comedy** · E-Ticket · Shows run continuously from 8 pm to 1 am · Audience participation |
| **BET SoundStage Club** — 21+ Only | *Contemporary music and dancing for guests 21 and over. The club is one of the smaller ones, but the intimate atmosphere can be enjoyable.* | 6 7 4 · **Dance** · C-Ticket |
| **Comedy Warehouse** — A-OK! | *Houses the Who, What and Wherehouse Players, a comedy troupe that delivers hilarious skits, standup acts, improv sketches, and adult humor "Disney-style."* **Allie's Kid Tip:** *"This is funny, but don't sit next to the telephone!"* | 9 7 9 · **Comedy** · D-Ticket · Rib-tickling |
| **Mannequins Dance Palace** — 21+ Only | *Voted the #1 dance club in the Southeast, this is the place for the hottest dance mix and the biggest sound and lighting system. Bouncers in tuxes proof you and let in a few people at a time. Very, very loud.* | 7 6 6 · **Dance** · E-Ticket · Must be 21+ |
| **Motion** — 21+ Only | *A big dance floor and clean, open layout are all that distinguish this large club. Top 40 and alternative dance. Motion replaced the Wildhorse Saloon.* | 2 5 7 · **Dance** · C-Ticket |
| **Rock 'n' Roll Beach Club** — 21+ Only | *Offers fans of classic and modern rock a crowded dance floor, live "cover" bands, and a DJ. You can also play pinball and munch out on nachos.* | 8 7 6 · **Dance** · D-Ticket |

*Are Pleasure Island's clubs good for kids? No—all but two of the clubs are only for adults age 21 and up. If bringing the kids is the only way, kids are allowed in Adventurers Club and Comedy Warehouse and they must be accompanied by a responsible adult.*

➤

# Eating and Playing at Pleasure Island

**SHOPPING & EATING**

Pleasure Island made big changes to become more accessible to more people. As such, many of its shops closed and the stages were removed. Are you hungry? Portobello Yacht Club, Raglan Road Irish pub, and Cookes of Dublin offer decent choices on Pleasure Island. T-Rex will open, perhaps in 2008. Eatery details are on page 223. There's also a new cigar bar—Fuego by Sosa Cigars—with cocktails, coffee drinks, and tobacco products.

© MediaMarx, Inc.

*Dave hoists a cold one at Raglan Road*

**PLAYING**

Most of Pleasure Island's entertainment now takes place inside the clubs. You'll enjoy the loud, straight-ahead **rock bands** at the Rock 'n Roll Beach Club. The Adventurers Club offers a **different kind of fun**: sing-alongs, cabarets, "Fingers" the organ player, and "Balderdash" storytelling! Kungaloosh!

**GETTING THERE**

**By Bus**—Frequent buses are available from Disney resorts. From a park, bus or monorail to a nearby resort and transfer to a Downtown Disney bus. Get off at the second Downtown Disney stop.

© MediaMarx, Inc.

*Competing for the Balderdash Cup at the Adventurers Club*

**By Car**—Follow signs to Downtown Disney. Parking is free. If you intend to drink, please designate a driver. (The designated driver program that existed here is gone.)

**By Boat**—From Port Orleans, Old Key West, and Saratoga Springs, take a boat to the Marketplace and walk. All guests may use the boat between Marketplace and West Side, when it is running. A new boat dock was installed on Pleasure Island itself, too.

# Making the Most of Pleasure Island

TIPS

**Adventurers Club** can seem a little confusing at first, but just wait a while—something's sure to happen wherever you are, when you least expect it. Come with a sense of adventure and be ready to join in. You can be inducted into the club, learn the secret greeting, and sing the club song! The Adventurers Club is one of our favorite places! We recommend the Kungaloosh and Jungle Juice drinks!

If you find the excitement too much, or just want to go somewhere romantic with that special someone, head for our "**hidden patio**." Go down the stairs beside the Adventurers Club.

**Alcoholic beverages** are even served on the streets of Pleasure Island. Adults 21 and older get wristbands to show they can drink. All Pleasure Island clubs are **nonsmoking**.

NOTES

Most Pleasure Island clubs are only for guests **21 years and older**—only the Adventurers Club and Comedy Warehouse allow guests of all ages, but guests under 18 must be accompanied by an adult. You'll need a valid driver's license or state ID (with photo) to enter the clubs. They really do "proof" you at the door. If you bring kids to the Adventurers Club or Comedy Warehouse, be prepared for some good-natured ribbing and adult humor.

Admission is **$11.66/person** to enter a single club (not available for Adventurers Club or Comedy Warehouse). To visit Adventurers Club, Comedy Warehouse, and/or several clubs in one evening, buy a multi-club ticket for **$23.38/person**. You can use a Plus option on a Magic Your Way ticket for admission. Admission is also included with a Premium Annual Pass. Half-price admission is available for Disney Dining Experience members (see page 10). Ask about discounts. Clubs open from 7:00 pm to 2:00 am, though some clubs may open later.

RATINGS

*Ratings are explained on page 120.*

| Our Value Ratings: | | Our Magic Ratings: | | Readers' Ratings: |
|---|---|---|---|---|
| Quality: | 6/10 | Theme: | 6/10 | 48% fell in love with it |
| Variety: | 3/10 | Excitement: | 7/10 | 39% liked it well enough |
| Scope: | 4/10 | Fun Factor: | 7/10 | 9% had mixed feelings |
| **Overall Value:** | **4/10** | **Overall Magic:** | **7/10** | 4% were disappointed |

| Pleasure Island is enjoyed by... | (rated by both authors and readers) | |
|---|---|---|
| Younger Kids: ❤ | Young Adults: ❤❤❤❤❤ | Families: ❤ |
| Older Kids: ❤❤ | Mid Adults: ❤❤❤❤ | Couples: ❤❤❤❤ |
| Teenagers: ❤❤❤❤❤ | Mature Adults: ❤❤ | Singles: ❤❤❤❤❤ |

# Charting Your Route at Pleasure Island

## PLEASURE ISLAND MAP

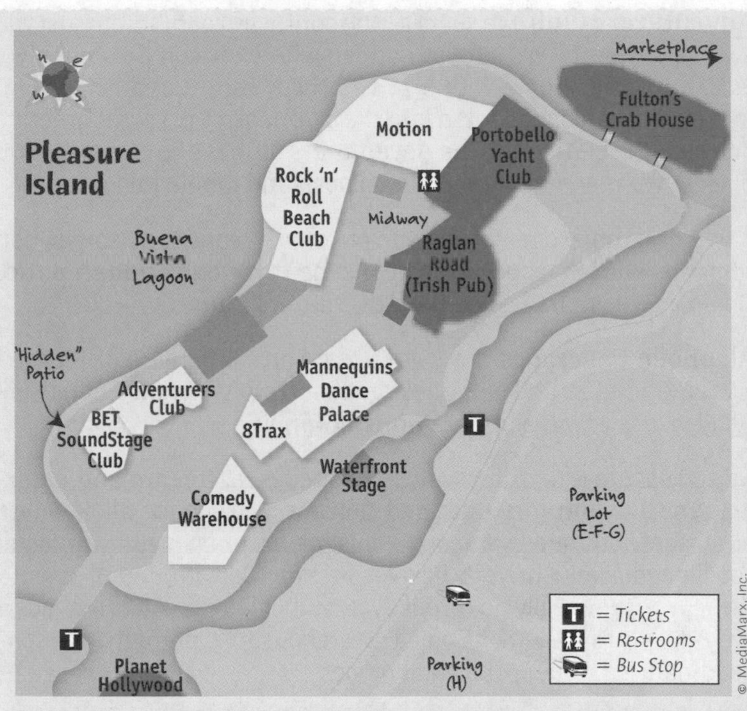

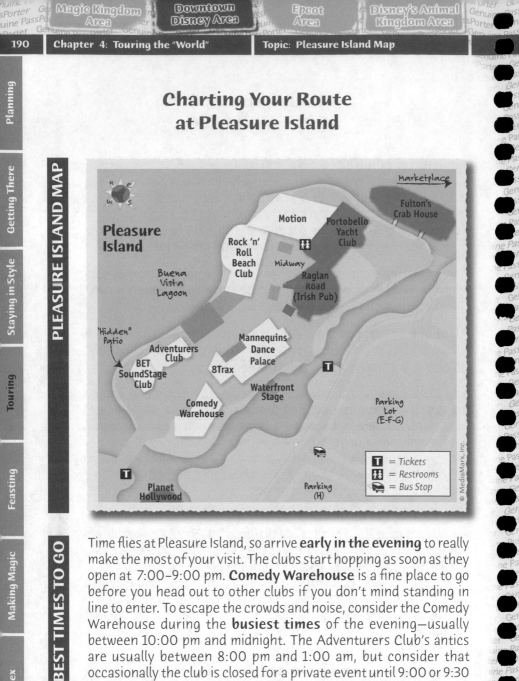

## BEST TIMES TO GO

Time flies at Pleasure Island, so arrive **early in the evening** to really make the most of your visit. The clubs start hopping as soon as they open at 7:00–9:00 pm. **Comedy Warehouse** is a fine place to go before you head out to other clubs if you don't mind standing in line to enter. To escape the crowds and noise, consider the Comedy Warehouse during the **busiest times** of the evening—usually between 10:00 pm and midnight. The Adventurers Club's antics are usually between 8:00 pm and 1:00 am, but consider that occasionally the club is closed for a private event until 9:00 or 9:30 pm. Pleasure Island's streets are admission-free at all times. Stroll through—some clubs may be open for a free "sample." Admission is checked at the club entrances, and tickets can be bought at the ticket booths. Sundays–Thursdays are Cast Member Nights, and now that there are more of them (previously it was just Mondays and Thursdays), they aren't likely to be more crowded than any other night.

# Disney Celebrations in 2008

Nothing adds to a vacation like a **reason to celebrate**, and Disney knows this better than most. If you don't have a celebration of your own, Disney seems to always have one you can "borrow." The 25th anniversary of Walt Disney World in 1996, the Millennium Celebration in 1999/2000, the 100th anniversary of Walt Disney's birth in 2001, the worldwide celebration of Disneyland's 50th birthday, and 2007's Year of a Million Dreams have all given Disney a chance to dress up its parks, introduce new rides and attractions, and give guests even more reasons to come visit. Looking at the calendar, the next anniversary should start before this book is in your hands—Epcot's 25th Anniversary on October 1, 2007. However, as of this writing, there's no word from Disney on what they may do to celebrate, and we doubt Disney will make it the focus of a company-wide party.

The successful "**Year of a Million Dreams**" is being extended through December 31, 2008. This celebration focuses on bestowing more than one million vacation "dreams" and puts a nice "spin" on what is really a huge marketing promotion. The grandest prizes are pretty exciting—for example, every night a very lucky family gets to stay in the Cinderella Castle Suite. Other winners get to visit every Disney park worldwide to be the Grand Marshals in the parks' parades. But the vast majority of these million prizes will require guests to pay their way to a Disney park in order to enjoy them. The most common prize is a "Dream FASTPASS" to Disney's most popular rides. So, it's really all just a huge sweepstakes. How easy is it to win? Let's just say we've spent more than a month total in the parks since it began and we have yet to be bestowed with a prize. Oh well!

So, what about **Epcot's 25th**? The rumor mill is filled with park-lovers' hopes and dreams. This celebration will most likely be low-key and limited to Epcot itself. With the exception of the rehabilitated Spaceship Earth, the new Circle-Vision film at the Canada Pavilion, and the new Italian restaurant to replace Alfredo's, there's not much that's likely to be brand new at Epcot during its anniversary year. Maybe they're just catching their breath after all the other new stuff that has been added over the past few years. We're guessing there may be an update to the IllumiNations fireworks and music show, the possible return of a parade of some sort, and the announcement of one or more new or rehabilitated attractions (something to replace Wonders of Life, an update to Ellen's Energy Adventure, and perhaps a new pavilion for the World Showcase). The glittery "Epcot" sign atop Spaceship Earth (and the adjacent Mickey wand) came down during the summer of 2007 as part of the Siemens-sponsored rehabilitation of the attraction inside the sphere, so if anything, unless they apply lots of decorations to the lamp posts, it seems Epcot will have less glitter and glam during its anniversary, rather than more. Want to know more? Subscribe to our PassPorter newsletter at http://www.passporter.com/news.htm.

# More Places to Play

**BoardWalk**–Pleasure Island doesn't have a monopoly on nightclubs in Walt Disney World–the BoardWalk resort has its own entertainment complex with clubs, restaurants, and entertainment. Jellyrolls is a dueling piano bar that serves drinks and free popcorn ($7 cover, 21 and up, smoking allowed). Atlantic Dance Hall serves specialty drinks while open-request DJ music lures you onto the floor (no cover, 21 and up, open Tuesday–Saturday). ESPN Club (page 226) is a popular sports bar. Midway games and street performers add to the fun. For details and directions to the BoardWalk resort, see pages 43–46.

**Celebration, Florida**–Imagine what would happen if Disney created a real town and you've got the community of Celebration, located just a few miles from the parks. Disney has divested most of its control over the years, but it remains a quaint neighborhood. Visitors may stroll or shop, have a bite in a restaurant, take in a movie at the theater, or stay in the luxury hotel. Others dream of moving to this carefully planned development. For details, call 407-566-2200 or visit http://www.celebrationfl.com.

**Golf**–The Walt Disney World Resort boasts four championship courses and one nine-hole course, and consistently lands on a variety of prestigious "top golf resort" lists. All courses are open to the public and feature full-service facilities, including driving ranges, pro shops, cafes, and lessons. Guests at Disney resort hotels get free transportation to the links for their scheduled tee times. Note: The Eagle Pines course closed in July 2007, but a new course is expected around 2010. For details and tee times, call 407-WDW-GOLF. We recommend the Unofficial Walt Disney World Golf Site at http://www.wdwgolf.com.

**Miniature Golf Courses**–Disney has miniature golf, too! **Fantasia Gardens**, near the Swan Resort, has two 18-hole courses. One course is based on the scenes, characters, and music of Disney's classic animated film, "Fantasia." The other is a "grass" course (Fantasia Fairways) with wildly undulating par-three and par-four holes from 40 to 75 feet long. Waits for tee times for this challenging course are typically double the wait for the Fantasia course, so leave yourself some extra time. **Winter Summerland** is a miniature golf park at Blizzard Beach. It sports two 18-hole courses–one is blanketed in "snow," and the other celebrates the holidays in the tropics. Both are fun, and neither is particularly difficult. Tip: Ask about the "secret hole of the day" after you play at either course–if you get a hole-in-one in the secret hole, you may get a surprise. Cost with tax is $10.75 for adults and $8.50 for kids ages 3–9 (second round is half price), with discounts for Annual Passholders. Hours: 10:00 am to 11:00 pm.

## More Places to Play

*(continued)*

**Fort Wilderness Resort**—Here's another resort with a lot to offer! Fort Wilderness is a respite from the bustle of the parks, offering canoeing, boating, fishing excursions, biking, tennis, horseback trail rides, horse-drawn carriage rides, and wagon rides. And you don't have to spend a penny to visit the petting farm (pony rides cost $3), blacksmith shop, and a nightly campfire program (with character visits and free movies). Jennifer, Dave, and Allie enjoyed their trail ride at the resort's Tri-Circle D Livery. It is a good entry-level horseback riding experience for riders age 9 and up and costs $42. Phone 407-824-2832 for reservations. For more information on Fort Wilderness, see pages 59–62.

**Health Clubs & Spas**—Many of the deluxe resorts have health clubs with exercise equipment—some even offer massage treatments, steam rooms, and saunas. Use of a fitness center (excluding treatments) is complimentary to resort guests or $12/day/person for non-resort guests. If you've got relaxation in mind, we recommend the **Saratoga Springs Spa** and **Grand Floridian Spa & Health Club**. These world-class, full-service centers offer many beauty and wellness treatments, nutrition and fitness counseling, and lots of pampering. Call 407-827-4455 (Saratoga Springs) or 407-824-2332 (Grand Floridian Spa), or visit their web site at http://www.relaxedyet.com.

**Tennis**—Tennis enthusiasts will find tennis courts at most of Disney's deluxe resorts (with the exception of Animal Kingdom Lodge and the Contemporary, which removed its courts recently), Fort Wilderness, Swan and Dolphin, and Shades of Green. For more information, call 407-939-7529.

**Walt Disney World Speedway**—Disney has its own speedway—a one-mile, tri-oval track for **auto racing**. The race track is home to the Richard Petty Driving Experience, in which participants get to drive or ride at speeds up to 145 mph! In July 2002, Dave strapped on his helmet and climbed in the passenger seat of a race car for a "ride around" experience. In a flash, the crew had his seat harness buckled, the photographer snapped his macho image for posterity, and he was headed out of the pit faster than you can say "zero to sixty." Dave's not a racing fan, but you don't really have to be to get a thrill out of this experience. For Richard Petty Experience details, call 407-939-0130 or 800-BE-PETTY, or visit the web site at http://www.1800bepetty.com.

**Disney Nature Reserve**—The Nature Conservancy runs this 12,000-acre hiking haven at the headwaters of the Everglades. For information, visit http://www.nature.org and search on "disney."

# More Places to Play

*(continued)*

**Waterways (Boating, Fishing, etc.)**—Water, water everywhere—and lots of things to do! You can rent boats at nearly every deluxe and moderate resort and Downtown Disney. Probably the most popular rentals craft are little, two-person speed boats called Sea Raycers—the old Water Mice have been replaced by these more up-to-date craft. They're available at most marinas around Disney for $24 per half-hour (must be 12+ to pilot with an adult, or 16+ with a driver's license to pilot alone). Fishing excursions and cane pole rentals are also available in most of those same places. A bass fishing program allows guests to reserve two-hour, guided, catch-and-release bass expeditions at many Disney marinas. All equipment is provided (even a digital camera to document your catch), fishing licenses are not needed thanks to the state-licensed guide on board, and participants even get a free subscription to Bassmaster Magazine. Excursions accommodate up to five guests and cost $200–$230. Kids 6–12 can go on special one-hour excursions for $30. Phone 407-WDW-BASS for info. Tip: Look for money-saving programs at your resort's marina: the Captain's Plan is $125 for four hours of self-drive boat rentals; the Family Plan is $239 and gives up to five resort guests the use of self-drive boats for ten consecutive days.

**Disney's Wide World of Sports Complex**—Disney's state-of-the-art **athletic center** features a 9,500-seat baseball stadium, a 30,000-square-foot fieldhouse, a track & field complex, volleyball, tennis, baseball, softball, football, and more. In 2005, Disney added another 20 acres of baseball, softball, and multi-sport fields under the sponsorship of HESS. The complex already hosts 170 youth, amateur, and professional sporting events annually, and clearly more are on the way. Admission ($11/adults or $8.25/kids 3–9). Note that the Multi-Sport Experience exhibit here has been closed. The 200-acre center is also home to amateur and professional sports, including Atlanta Braves Spring Training and the Tampa Bay Buccaneers training camp. For more information, call 407-828-FANS (recorded information), or 407-939-1500 (to speak with a person), or visit http://www.disneyworldsports.com.

**Walt Disney World Running and Inline Skating Events**—Disney's Wide World of Sports isn't just for spectators. Runners can register for the Walt Disney World Marathon, Half-Marathon, Family Fun Run 5K, and Goofy's Race and a Half Challenge (Jan. 10–12, 2008). The Inline Skating Marathon is May 4, 2008. Visit http://www.disneyworldsports.com to learn more and to register.

# Deciding What To Do

Whew! We bet you're now wondering how in the world (no pun intended) you'll find the time to **fit everything** at Walt Disney World into your vacation. It's simple: You can't do it. Even a month-long stay wouldn't be enough to do and see everything. Rather than try to fit everything into your vacation, make a practical plan.

Naturally, you can't plan everything in advance, nor should you try—spontaneity and discovery are two elements of a great vacation. Yet it is a good idea to get a feeling for the parks, attractions, and activities before you go and to make a note of the ones you simply "must" do. This helps you **create an itinerary** and keeps you from missing the things you've got your heart set on.

First, read the preceding pages carefully to gain a solid idea of what the Walt Disney World Resort is all about. Next, **make a list** of all the things you'd like to see and do. This can be a great family activity. Make it a free-for-all, no-holds-barred event—what we call a "blue-sky session." List everything, no matter how impractical, silly, or expensive. Once you've got a good list, pare it down to the things that are most important and copy them to the worksheet on the next two pages. List the activity, where in the "World" it is located (i.e., which park or resort), its approximate cost, and any notes (including why it's on the list).

When you're done with the list, take a good look at the locations. Are several located in the same park? If so, can you do them all on the same day? Go through the list and note other patterns. With luck, you'll have a better sense of where you're headed. Next, **assign the activities** to specific days of your vacation, using the Day/Date column on the far right. For example, on a recent trip, we wanted to visit Spaceship Earth, race around Test Track, and watch IllumiNations. All those activities are at Epcot, so we grouped them together on our third day. We wrote a "3" next to each of those items, but you could write "Wed" or the date instead. If you've planned too much for one day or place, your Cost and Notes columns may help you decide which activities to keep and which to throw out or schedule for another day.

Not all activities can be decided this way, nor should they. Some choices should be **spur of the moment**. Be sure to "schedule" some free time in your trip—preferably a whole day or two. Use these techniques as a general game plan to a great vacation!

Electronic, interactive worksheet available—see page 287

# Touring Worksheet

Use this worksheet to figure out the things you want to do most on your trip. Match up attractions to determine the parks you want to visit, noting the day/date (you may wish to refer to the Extra Magic Hour schedule on page 32). Fill in the park schedule grid at the bottom of the next page once you've picked days—the park schedule can help you complete your itinerary and choose eateries (in the next chapter).

| Activity | Park | Land | Cost | Notes | Day/Date |
|---|---|---|---|---|---|
| | | | | | |

**Useful Abbreviations**:

*MK (Magic Kingdom)*
*EP (Epcot)*
*DHS (Disney's Hollywood Studios)*
*DAK (Disney's Animal Kingdom)*
*BB (Blizzard Beach)*
*TL (Typhoon Lagoon)*
*BW (BoardWalk)*
*DD (Downtown Disney)*
*DQ (DisneyQuest)*
*PI (Pleasure Island)*
*WWOS (Disney's Wide World of Sports)*
*DS (Disney Speedway)*
*FG (Fantasia Gardens)*
*WS (Winter Summerland)*
*DCL (Disney Cruise Line)*
*VB (Disney's Vero Beach)*
*OFF (Off-site)*
*USF (Universal Studios)*
*IOA (Islands of Adventure)*
*SW (SeaWorld)*
*COVE (Discovery Cove)*
*BG (Busch Gardens)*
*KSC (Kennedy Space Center)*
*CB (Cocoa Beach)*
*FH (Friend/Family's House)*

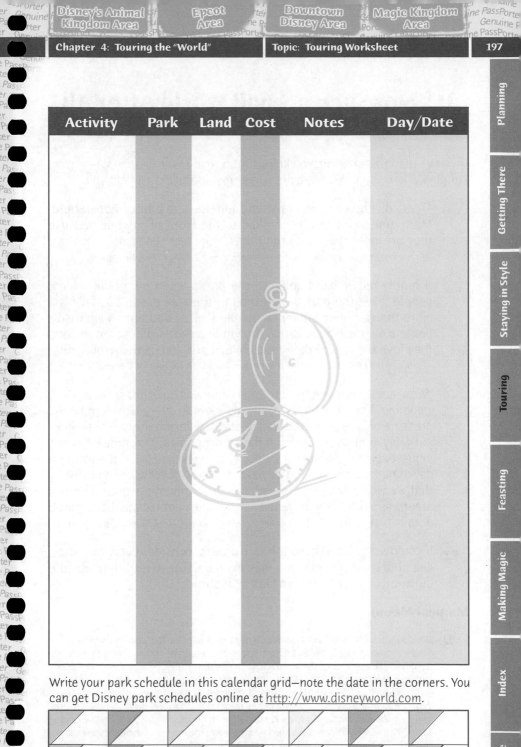

| Activity | Park | Land | Cost | Notes | Day/Date |
| --- | --- | --- | --- | --- | --- |
| | | | | | |

Write your park schedule in this calendar grid—note the date in the corners. You can get Disney park schedules online at http://www.disneyworld.com.

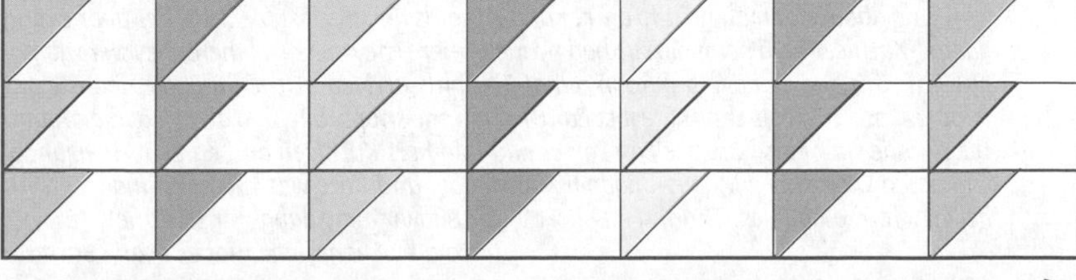

# It's Not Such a Small World After All

If you've read this chapter, you know that touring Walt Disney World is no simple walk in the park. Here are some tips and tricks to help you:

"Try to divide your party to go on each ride as a **pair of two people**. Many times you can be whisked to the front of the line because they are looking for a pair to take up the last two seats."
*–Contributed by Anthony Steeples, a winner in our 2007 Touring Tip Contest*

"I highly recommend going to the parks when it's raining. Most people leave the parks, even though the rain doesn't usually last more than an hour. We rent a double stroller and put an adult-size poncho over it. The kids stay dry while we are walking around and they love the feel of their little cave. It also keeps the stroller dry."
*–Contributed by Celine Johnson, a winner in our 2007 Touring Tip Contest*

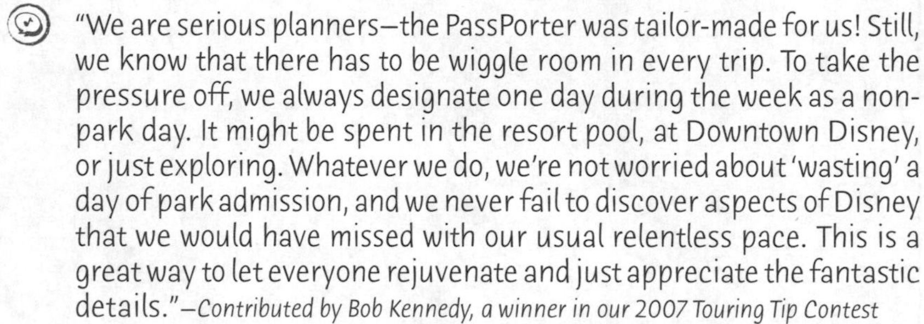

"We are serious planners–the PassPorter was tailor-made for us! Still, we know that there has to be wiggle room in every trip. To take the pressure off, we always designate one day during the week as a non-park day. It might be spent in the resort pool, at Downtown Disney, or just exploring. Whatever we do, we're not worried about 'wasting' a day of park admission, and we never fail to discover aspects of Disney that we would have missed with our usual relentless pace. This is a great way to let everyone rejuvenate and just appreciate the fantastic details."*–Contributed by Bob Kennedy, a winner in our 2007 Touring Tip Contest*

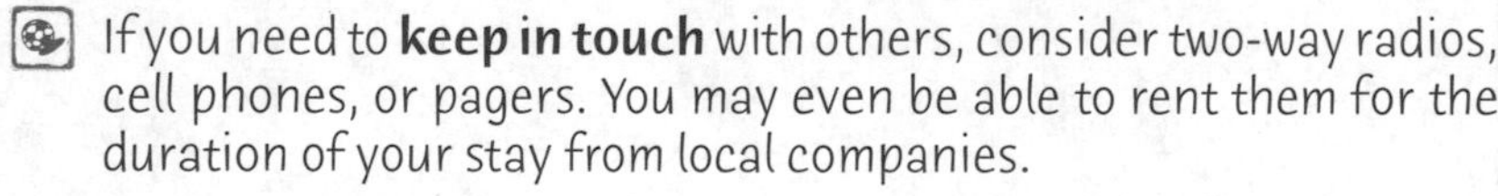

If you need to **keep in touch** with others, consider two-way radios, cell phones, or pagers. You may even be able to rent them for the duration of your stay from local companies.

## Magical Memory

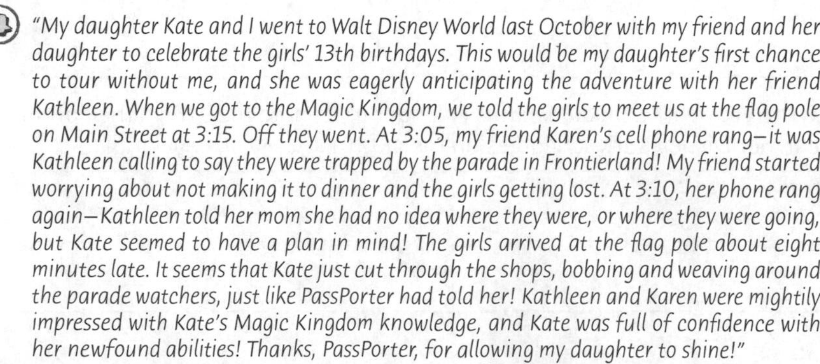

*"My daughter Kate and I went to Walt Disney World last October with my friend and her daughter to celebrate the girls' 13th birthdays. This would be my daughter's first chance to tour without me, and she was eagerly anticipating the adventure with her friend Kathleen. When we got to the Magic Kingdom, we told the girls to meet us at the flag pole on Main Street at 3:15. Off they went. At 3:05, my friend Karen's cell phone rang–it was Kathleen calling to say they were trapped by the parade in Frontierland! My friend started worrying about not making it to dinner and the girls getting lost. At 3:10, her phone rang again–Kathleen told her mom she had no idea where they were, or where they were going, but Kate seemed to have a plan in mind! The girls arrived at the flag pole about eight minutes late. It seems that Kate just cut through the shops, bobbing and weaving around the parade watchers, just like PassPorter had told her! Kathleen and Karen were mightily impressed with Kate's Magic Kingdom knowledge, and Kate was full of confidence with her newfound abilities! Thanks, PassPorter, for allowing my daughter to shine!"*

*...as told by Disney vacationer Diane Barrette*

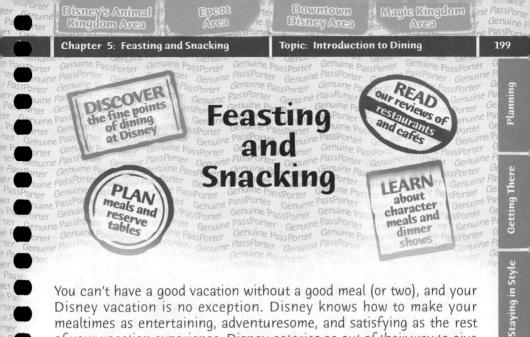

# Feasting and Snacking

PLAN meals and reserve tables

You can't have a good vacation without a good meal (or two), and your Disney vacation is no exception. Disney knows how to make your mealtimes as entertaining, adventuresome, and satisfying as the rest of your vacation experience. Disney eateries go out of their way to give everyone a unique and delicious dining experience, so you'll find that even the most exotic restaurant can please any taste, including the finicky eaters in your family. From the atmosphere to the service to the food itself, it has all been created to fill your imagination as well as your belly.

The choices can be awesome, ranging from basic hot dogs and burgers to once-in-a-lifetime elegance, from ultra-romantic dinners for two to foot-stompin' family hoedowns, and from exotic samplings of far-off places to the magic of a breakfast hug from Winnie the Pooh himself. One thing's for sure—you can't say, "There's nothing to eat around here!"

For us, meal planning is more important than choosing which attractions to visit. It's easier to jump in an unexpectedly short line at Space Mountain than it is to get a table at the better eateries.

The six basic types of Walt Disney World Resort meals are table-service restaurants, counter-service cafes, quick-service snack shops, "special experiences" (such as dinner shows and character meals), room service, and meals you fix yourself. We devote most of the space here to table-service and special dining experiences, which are more costly and require the most planning. We also include details on the counter service and snacks in the parks. Resort counter service and room service is discussed in the "Staying in Style" chapter. We can't say much about your home cooking until we're invited to your villa or campsite, though.

The chapter begins with a meal planning guide, then moves to mealtime tips, park-by-park and resort-by-resort eatery reviews, and the low-down on the big shindigs, and ends with worksheets to plan your meals.

Bon appetit!

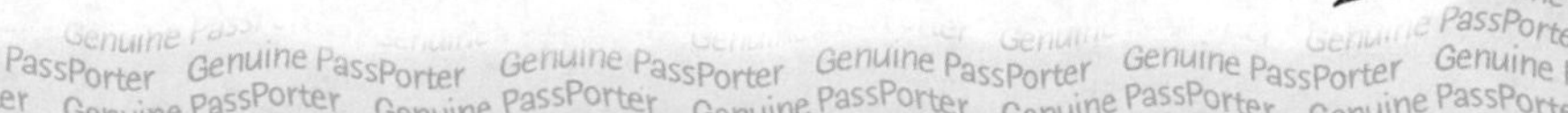

# Deciding on Dining

If you thought selecting a restaurant in your hometown was tough, you haven't seen anything. The Walt Disney World Resort has more than **300 places to eat**. But before you go running for the exit, take heart. We've been to virtually every restaurant on property at least twice (often much more) and we offer easily digestible descriptions and yummy ratings for you in this chapter. Better yet, we have a tried-and-true system for deciding where and when to eat.

First, decide **how often** you want to eat out. Many folks (including ourselves) bring or buy some food for in-room snacks or meals, with light breakfasts being the most practical choice. All resorts can supply a refrigerator (sometimes for an additional fee), some include a coffeemaker, and Disney Vacation Club resorts have kitchen facilities, too. You can, of course, eat out every meal. We like to eat a light breakfast in our room with food we've packed or purchased, such as peanut butter and jelly on English muffins. We then do one or two special breakfasts "out" (such as a character breakfast—see pages 234–235). We often eat lunch and dinner at the parks, resorts, or Downtown Disney. If you're doing the Disney Dining Basic Plan (see pages 202–203), you'll probably do about two meals a day. Some vacationers prefer to eat a big meal mid-morning and another mid-afternoon to save time and money (it's easy to fill up at many restaurants). More money-saving ideas are on page 205.

Once you have an idea of how often you want (and can afford) to eat out, your next task is to decide **when and where**. Revisit your Touring Worksheet (pages 196–197) and check the parks you want to visit—it is much easier to choose a restaurant in or near your day's destination. Every park offers table-service restaurants, counter-service eateries, and snack shops and carts. To help you choose from the overwhelming number of dining choices at Walt Disney World, this chapter offers descriptions of nearly all eateries. Descriptions are organized alphabetically within each park and resort to help you focus on your choices. Pick the eateries that fall within your budget, tastes, and needs—you may find it helpful to highlight or circle those eatery descriptions that interest you.

As you make decisions about your meals and the eateries you want to visit, jot them down on your **Meal Worksheet** at the end of the chapter on page 240. Make note of those table-service eateries for which advance reservations may be made. Continue on to the next page to learn the what, when, and how of advance reservations at the Walt Disney World Resort.

# Advance Reservations

With the popularity of the Disney Dining Plan (see pages 202–203), reservations have become essential at many restaurants. Virtually every table-service restaurant within Disney World allows you to make "Advance Reservations" (formerly known as "priority seating"). Unlike traditional reservations, in which a table would be held for your party at a designated time, Disney's advance reservation system gives you the **first table that becomes available**. The only Disney table-service restaurants that don't accept advance reservations are some Downtown Disney restaurants, Big River Grille (24-hour reservations only), and ESPN Club (see detailed listings in this chapter). Additionally, some restaurants do take traditional reservations, such as Victoria & Albert's, the Swan & Dolphin restaurants (see pages 231–232), and the character meals at Cinderella's Royal Table and Akershus Royal Banquet Hall (see pages 234–235).

Advance reservations can be made **before your arrival** by calling 407-WDW-DINE (407-939-3463). Call up to 180 days ahead of your visit for advance reservations at most restaurants. Tip: Disney resort guests have the advantage of being able to book reservations for the first ten days of their trip at 180 days from their check-in date. We also recommend the Planning Strategy Calculator at http://pscalculator.net for advance reservation details. Arrangements can also be made the same day at the parks, and by touching "*88" on any Disney pay phone or "55" on your Disney resort phone.

When you call, you will be asked to supply the name of your Disney resort, your home phone number, your reservation number, and your date of arrival—you can record this information in your **Advance Reservations Worksheet** on page 241. If you aren't staying at a Disney resort, no problem—simply provide a daytime phone number. Also note that character meals at Cinderella's Royal Table, California Grill, and some special dining experiences (including holiday dining) require a credit card deposit or guarantee. If you are using the Disney Dining Plan for a meal, be sure to note this when you reserve it. You will get a **confirmation number** for each reservation. Record this in your worksheet, and later transfer it to your daily PassPockets. If you decide not to eat at a particular restaurant, just call Disney again and **cancel your reservation**. (In the case of the special dinner shows and those meals that require a credit card guarantee, however, be aware that there are 24- or 48-hour cancellation policies.) If you are unable to get a reservation, call back about one week before the desired date and again on the morning you want to dine.

**Check in at the restaurant's podium 15 minutes before** your seating time. You may also need to wait anywhere from 5 to 30 minutes for a table to become available, depending upon how busy it is. Some restaurants issue a pager, and most have a comfortable waiting area or bar.

➤

# Disney Dining Plan

The hot buzz in recent years is the Disney Dining Plan package. Available as an add-on to a Magic Your Way "package" (see page 30), and sometimes free as part of promotional packages, the Disney Dining Plan has **revolutionized the way many vacationers dine at Disney**. While a hands-down winner in previous years, Disney has made changes for 2008 that make money-saving and maximizing value a challenge.

Starting on January 1, 2008, Disney offers several different Dining Plan packages. The entry level is the **Basic Dining Plan**, which can be added to any Magic Your Way "package" that includes at least one day of park admission. The 2008 add-on price is $37.99 (plus 6.5% tax) for guests ages 10 and up, $9.99 plus tax for ages 3–9. Those under age 3 may share their parent's meal. The Basic Dining Plan provides **three "credits" per person per night of your stay**: one table-service credit, one counter-service credit, and one snack credit. At 2008 pricing, this offers a very small savings over the average cost of dining. **To break even or "win,"** avoid all two-credit dining except for dinner shows and pizza delivery.

New this year is the **Deluxe Dining Plan** for $69.99 (plus tax)/guests ages 10 and up and $19.99 (plus tax)/guests ages 3–9 per night of your stay. The Deluxe Dining Plan includes three meal credits (use for either table or counter service) and two snack credits per person per night, plus one refillable mug per person. Savings and value can be very good on this plan, but you may be exceeding your typical vacation meal budget and calorie count (a real cost of $90–$100/day per adult with gratuities). For the **best value**, choose only one-credit table-service restaurants. Three meals per day too much? Two-credit meals won't destroy your savings on the plan, but don't mix in many counter-service meals.

New also is the **Wine and Dine Plan** for either of the two Dining Plans mentioned above, at $39.99 plus tax per night per room. This plan gives you one bottle of wine per night from a select list (wine at Signature restaurants costs two nights' allowance). We can't judge value, as wine lists were not available at press time.

**How do the credits work?** Table-service credits on the Basic Dining Plan include an entrée, dessert, regular soft drink, and sales tax (the appetizer and 18% gratuity were removed for the 2008 plan, while the package rates are nearly unchanged). Meal credits on the Deluxe Plan add an appetizer. Counter-service meals on either plan provide an entrée, dessert, regular soft drink, and sales tax. Snack credits provide a single item, such as a soft drink, baked item, ice cream, fries, or a Dole Whip (most items under $4 are "snacks"). Disney has affixed little "DDP" icons to its menus to identify snack-credit items. You can use credits at any time, in any combination, for the duration of your stay (beginning at check-in) at more than 100 participating eateries (noted in this chapter), as well as in-room private dining, pizza delivery, and dinner shows (gratuities are included on these last three). All unused credits expire without refund at 11:59 pm on your check-out day.

**How do you get a Dining Plan?** Add the plan to your reservation at least five days prior to your arrival. Disney Vacation Club members can purchase the dining plan when staying "on points"—contact DVC for the details. The biggest "catch" is for Annual Passholders—you can purchase a one-night Magic Your Way package and add on the Dining Plan for the length of your stay, but you'll end up with one day's worth of park admission. The extra admission can be applied toward your next Annual Pass renewal if you remember to save the Key to the World card and bring it with you when you buy that pass. However, rooms booked at Annual Pass rates do not qualify for the dining add-on; you must pay the package rate. If you have an Annual Pass, consider the Disney Dining Experience instead (see page 10).

➢

## Dining Plan Tips:

Use your PassPorter! **It's packed with features** to help you maximize your dining plan. Our eatery descriptions include an "average price" figure that's great for comparing relative meal values on the plan. We also point out Disney Dining Plan participating eateries, as well as "Signature" dining restaurants (which require two table-service credits per meal). Our Meal Worksheet on page 240 includes columns for budgeting the use of your dining credits while you plan, and to keep track of how many are used as you vacation. You can also use the Meals and Snacks section of each PassPocket to keep track of these items.

Consider **sharing meals** to stretch your Dining Plan credits.

The **computed cost** of Basic Dining Plan components is $26.20 (table service), $11.38 (counter service), and $2.37 (snack)—very close to the price you'd pay off the plan. On the Deluxe Dining Plan, the computed cost of each meal is $23.40 (less than on the Basic Plan, and also includes appetizer) and the two snacks are $2.20 each. Using your credits at counter service quickly erodes your savings. On both plans, you get decent "bang" from dinner shows and pizza delivery, as gratuities are also included. The two-credit Cinderella's Royal Table breakfast is a money-waster under either plan.

If you're eating counter service at your resort hotel and have the resort's **refillable mugs** (see page 34), use the soft drink portion of your counter-service credit on a bottled beverage from the Grab-n-Go, and save it for later.

On the 2008 Basic Dining Plan, it matters little if you dine at a la carte or buffet/character table-service meals—the elimination of the appetizer has **equalized relative values**.

Did you choose ice cream for your counter-service dessert? Ask the cashier if you can **get the frozen treat later on** so it won't melt. Generally, they'll mark your receipt so you can claim it later, maybe even until closing time that evening.

Watch your meal credits carefully. Each meal receipt lists the number of credits you have remaining, **but there can be errors**. Your resort's Lobby Concierge can print out a detailed accounting. Note the credits you've used (and plan to use) on our Dining Worksheet.

Your entire travel party's **credits are grouped together by type (adult and child)** so you can use your credits as you wish. You cannot, however, pay for someone else's meal with your credits, nor can you use adult credits for a child and vice versa.

You may **exchange two table-service credits** for selected Grand Gatherings (see page 257), dinner shows, Signature Dining, in-room dining, and pizza delivery—note that one pizza serves two adults. The average values (and quality) of many one-credit table-service restaurants are nearly as high as Signature Dining experiences, which can mean you'll get far **more bang for your buck** by avoiding the Signature establishments altogether.

Eateries participating in the Dining Plan can **change at any time**. You can download the most recent list of eateries at Disney's web site and/or request one at 407-WDW-DINE.

If you have **leftover snack credits** at the end of your trip, use them to buy snacks for the trip home. You cannot use table-service or quick-service credits for snacks, however.

The **Disney Dining Experience** (see page 10) *could* save you more than a dining plan.

Here are some **"secret numbers"** Disney really wishes we wouldn't tell you—these are the average costs of adult meals based on our calculations (remember to add gratuity):

| Meal Type | breakfast | lunch | dinner |
|---|---|---|---|
| Counter-service | $10.11 | $12.37 | $12.37 |
| Table-service - B(asic) Plan | $17.44 | $23.22 | $28.46 |
| Table-service - D(eluxe) Plan | $17.44 | $30.18 | $35.22 |
| Table-service Signature (B/D) | $34.07 | $34.55/ $38.81 | $45.05/$54.42 |

# Restaurant Menu

**Alcoholic Beverages**—Most eateries serve alcoholic drinks, with the notable exception of those in the Magic Kingdom. Bars and lounges are located around the "World." Legal drinking age is 21 and they do check your identification.

**Character Dining**—Dine with Disney characters! See pages 234–235.

**Children's Meals**—Nearly every eatery has a special menu for kids age 3–9. (Note that the age range for kids meals was 3–11 until it was changed in summer 2005 to ages 3–9.) Kid staples like macaroni & cheese and chicken tenders can usually be had at the most exotic of restaurants even when they're not on the menu—ask your server. You may be able to substitute healthy choices such as carrots or fruit in the place of fries, too. Kids also now get free refills on child-size beverages at table-service restaurants, including juice, milk, bottled water, and soda (but not including specialty drinks). All eateries also provide high chairs and booster seats, as needed. As you can imagine, Disney is one of the most kid-friendly places to eat in the world. (Special note to parents of infants and toddlers: Jars of baby food are not available in the eateries, but you can purchase them at the Baby Care Centers of each park if necessary—see page 114.)

**Counter Service**—Most food at Disney is sold fast-food style. The quality does vary—it's generally worse at the Magic Kingdom and best at Disney's Animal Kingdom, the two parks where counter service is most common. At Magic Kingdom, we like Pecos Bill Cafe in Frontierland and Columbia Harbour House in Liberty Square. Disney's Animal Kingdom only has three table-service restaurants, but the counter-service food is several cuts above the ordinary. We especially like Flame Tree Barbecue.

**Coupons/Discounts**—Don't plan on finding coupons for restaurants. We know only of AAA discounts at some Swan/Dolphin eateries. Discounts for annual passholders and Disney Vacation Club members (mostly at lunch) do exist—be sure to ask your server. You may qualify for the Disney Dining Experience (DDE)—see page 10 for details. See the money-saving tips on the following page for more information on available discounts.

**Dietary Requirements**—Low-cholesterol, low-salt, low-fat, and/or vegetarian meals are a regular part of the menu in most restaurants. With 72 hours of advance notice, kosher and other special dietary needs can be met. Cosmic Ray's at Magic Kingdom has a no-advance-notice kosher menu at the check-out (ask for this at other counter-service restaurants, too). Dietary "special needs" are addressed in great detail in the *PassPorter's Open Mouse for Walt Disney World and the Disney Cruise Line* guidebook by Deb Wills and Debra Martin Koma (see page 286).

**Dinner Shows**—Disney offers several dinner shows, combining all-you-care-to-eat meals with live entertainment. See pages 236–238.

**Dress**—Casual clothing is appropriate for most eateries in the "World" except Victoria & Albert's (see page 230), which requires that men wear a jacket. Several spots also require "business casual" dress (sometimes called "resort casual"), which means that men should wear dress slacks, jeans, trousers, dress shorts, collared shirts, and/or t-shirts (jackets are optional) and women should wear skirts, jeans, dress shorts, dresses, blouses, sweaters, and/or t-shirts. Business casual dress code prohibits hats, swimsuits, swim coveralls, tank tops, torn clothing, or flip flops. Business casual restaurants include Artist Point, California Grill, Citricos, Flying Fish, Jiko, Narcoossee's, and Yachtsman Steakhouse.

**Entertainment**—Some restaurants supply entertainment, while others like the Whispering Canyon Cafe and 'Ohana provide activities for kids.

**Menus**—Many menus can be previewed at Guest Services and Lobby Concierge at your resort hotel. Deb Wills' AllEarsNet web site (http://www.allears.net) also has a wonderful collection of up-to-date menus.

**Money**—Cash, Disney Dollars and Gift Cards, traveler's checks, Disney Visa Reward Vouchers, MasterCard, Visa, American Express, JCB, Discover, and Diner's Club. Disney Resort room charge cards are welcomed, even at some of the smallest snack carts. Note that the Disney Resort room charge card is not accepted at the Swan and Dolphin eateries, however. The Shopping & Dining Gift Card, which can be purchased in amounts between $5 and $1,500, is also accepted at select shops and eateries. Sales tax is 6.5%. Gratuities may be applied automatically to large parties (eight or more persons).

**Smoking**—Florida law prohibits smoking in all enclosed restaurants and other indoor public spaces. Only outdoor establishments and freestanding bars (no restaurants or hotel lobbies allowed) can allow smoking, but Disney has chosen to ban smoking at most of these, too.

## Time- and Money-Saving Dining Tips

- ✔ *Inquire with Disney about Dining Plan add-ons (see pages 202–203). In late summer of 2007, Disney offered a free Dining Plan to all guests who booked a Magic Your Way vacation package (and we took advantage of it!). If the Dining Plan is not free, the Basic Dining Plan only offers marginal savings. The Deluxe Dining Plan is a better deal, but only for those who normally eat three table-service meals a day and typically spend at least $90/day per adult.*
- ✔ *At counter-service eateries, there are usually several lines. The line farthest from the entry is often shorter. Look before you leap. Also note that counter-service eateries have lines on both sides of the cash register. If you see a short or nonexistent line on one side of an open register, jump in!*
- ✔ *Consider eating earlier or later than traditional mealtime hours. You'll be more likely to get a seat (if you haven't made reservations) or simply find the restaurant less crowded and noisy.*
- ✔ *Every item at counter-service restaurants can be ordered a la carte. If you don't want fries with that burger "meal," just ask, and you'll pay a reduced price.*
- ✔ *The Rainforest Cafe offers discounts through its Safari Club and an e-mail list—get details at http://www.rainforestcafe.com. It also may offer 10% discounts to annual passholders—ask your server.*
- ✔ *The Disney Dining Experience is for Florida residents and annual passholders. It offers 20% discounts on select restaurants in the parks and resorts, reduced prices on wine tastings, and more. See page 10 for details.*
- ✔ *Resort eateries are frequently less crowded than those in the parks. Consider a visit to a nearby resort restaurant before, during, or after a park visit. The Contemporary, Polynesian, and Grand Floridian resorts are close to the Magic Kingdom, the Yacht & Beach Club, BoardWalk, and Swan & Dolphin restaurants are close to Epcot and Disney's Hollywood Studios, and Disney's Animal Kingdom Lodge is a short drive/bus ride from Disney's Animal Kingdom.*

# Understanding and Using the Eatery Descriptions and Ratings

PassPorter's popular capsule reviews cover all table-service restaurants, as well as counter-service eateries at the parks. Our reviews include all important details, plus ratings. Below is a key to our eatery charts. Dig in!

## Description Key

Ratings[7] ↓

| [1] **Eatery Name** [D-2[2]] (Bar Color[3]) **B $, L $, D $, S**[4] DDPQ[5] [6] | # | # | # |
|---|---|---|---|
| *Description offering an overview of the eatery, including comments on the theming, quality, and menu range. We try to give you an idea of what sort of foods you'll find at a particular eatery, along with typical prices and our recommendations. We also include information on the availability of lighter fare, children's meals, and alcoholic beverages. Whenever possible, we describe the type of seating (tables, booths, etc.) and whether it is indoor or outdoor.* | **Type**[8]<br>Cuisine[8]<br>Noise Factor[9]<br>Reservations[8]<br>Avg. Wait[8]<br>Hours[8] | | |

[1] Each chart has an empty checkbox in the upper left corner—use it to check off the eateries that interest you (before you go) or those at which you ate (after your return).

[2] Map coordinates—match them up to park maps in "Touring the 'World'" for locations.

[3] The **bar color** indicates the eatery's main draw, as follows:

**Gourmet Tastes** | **Eateries for Everyone** | **Fun Food** | **Character Meals**

[4] Meals are indicated by letters: B (breakfast), L (lunch), D (dinner), and S (snack). The dollar figures that follow each meal type represent the average cost of a full adult meal. Table-service meal costs include appetizer, entree, dessert, soft drink, tax, and 18% tip. Average counter-service meal costs include entree, dessert, soft drink, and tax.

[5] The "DDP" symbol indicates that an eatery participates in the Disney Dining Plan (see pages 202–203) at press time. Note that the eateries are subject to change at any time—check with Disney before making plans. The color and letter in the lower right corner shows the type of Dining Plan eatery: blue "S" DDPS is snack, red "Q" DDPQ is quick service (counter service), purple "T" DDPT is table service, and gold "2" DDP2 is signature (because a Signature eatery requires two table-service credits). Verify participation at 407-WDW-DINE.

[6] Eateries with a reasonable selection of healthy items (low-fat/low-sodium/low-calorie) are indicated with a tape measure symbol. These are also friendly to weight watchers!

[7] The three white boxes on the right show ratings on a scale of 1 (poor) to 10 (loved it!). The first rating is **Jennifer's**, the second is **Dave's**, and the third is our **Readers'** rating. We offer our personal ratings to show how opinions vary, even between two like-minded people. You can also use our ratings as a point of reference—Jennifer likes eateries with extensive theming and well-prepared foods that aren't too exotic or spicy. Dave has more cultured tastes, enjoys unusual, spicy, and barbecue dishes, and loves seafood!

[8] The boxes on the right beneath the numeric ratings give basic information: eatery type (Table, Counter, or Buffet), cuisine, noise factor (from quiet to very noisy), seating (if reservations are accepted, needed, suggested, recommended, or required, and how many days in advance you can call), average wait time, and the eatery's hours.

*Kona Cafe*

# Magic Kingdom Eateries

(park map on page 124)

Jennifer's Rating | Dave's Rating | Readers' Rating

## Casey's Corner [D-4] L $10, D $10, S DDPQ 5 4 7

Casey's at the bat, and there's a hot dog at the plate. Old-time stadium foods—hot dogs ($3.99), fries ($1.89), brownies ($1.79), and soft drinks ($2.09 & $2.39). Most seating is outdoors; some indoor grandstands and tables near a big-screen TV.

Counter | American | 11 am-closing

## Cinderella's Royal Table [D-3] B $40, L $44, D $51 DDP2 7 6 8

For Disney magic, you can't beat dining inside Cinderella Castle! The character meals at "Cindy's" are easily the hottest ticket in the Kingdom—breakfast is $32.99 or $22.99/kids 3–9 and lunch is $35.99 or $23.99/kids (see pages 234–235). Dinner is a fixed-price meal ($40.99 or $25.99/kids 3–9) with an appetizer, entree, dessert, and beverage—dinner also includes an appearance by the Fairy Godmother. All meals include a six-print photo package (your photo is taken before you are seated). Meals aren't quite as good as the better resort eateries, but the light through the stained glass windows makes it all worthwhile. If you'll be celebrating a special occasion, mention it at booking. Full payment is required at time of reservation. Note that during Nov. 18–24 and Dec. 16–Jan 5., meal prices are an extra $4/adult and $2/kid.

Table | American | Med. noise | Advance reservations essential | Call 180 days | ~8–10:20 am, Noon–3:00 pm 4 pm–closing

## Columbia Harbour House [C-2] L $13, D $13, S DDPQ 5 6 6

This cozy inn provides cool relief and attractive decor despite the inexpensive menu. Fried chicken strips and fish with fries ($7.09), clam chowder ($4.49), garden salad ($6.99), and sandwiches ($6.49–$6.89) dominate the menu, but several veggie dishes—such as the vegetarian chili ($4.49)—create a rare port in the storm at Magic Kingdom. Kids meals ($3.99) include chilled chicken with cheese and mac & cheese. Quiet, upstairs dining room is usually open.

Counter | American | Med. noise | 11:00 am–1 hour before closing

## Cosmic Ray's Starlight Cafe [E-3] L $15, D $15, S DDPQ 6 5 6

Ray runs the biggest cafeteria at the Magic Kingdom. There's an excellent choice of chicken ($6.69–$7.99), sandwiches ($6–$7), soups ($1.99), burgers ($5.89–$7.39), and salad ($6.99), but not all items are available from all stations. Kids can get mini corn dogs, chicken noodle soup, garden salad, and chicken nuggets ($6.45 each). Toppings bar. Kosher menu, too. We think the 1/2 chicken and BBQ rib combo ($13.99)—see photo—is the best Dining Plan counter-service deal around.

Admiring the big portions

Counter | American | Very noisy | Med. waits | 10:00 am–closing

## The Crystal Palace [C-4] B $24, L $26, D $35 DDPT 6 6 8

Little more than a stone's throw away from Cinderella Castle (but please, don't throw stones), this replica of a Victorian glass conservatory serves character meals all day long. Breakfast is $18.99 ($10.99/kids 3–9), lunch is $20.99 ($11.99/kids), and dinner is $27.99 ($12.99/kids). Winnie the Pooh is your host at this popular buffet. The dinner menu changes weekly, but usually offers carved meats, regional specialties such as arroz con pollo or paella, roasted vegetables, peel-and-eat shrimp, and a wide variety of salads. There's even a separate kids' buffet and an ice cream sundae "bar." Potted and hanging plants and wrought-iron tables and chairs add to the authenticity of the lovely garden setting. See pages 234–235 for details on the character meal.

Buffet | American | Very noisy | Reservations suggested | Call 180 days | Long waits | ~8–10:30 am, 11:30–3:00 pm, 4 pm–closing

# Magic Kingdom Eateries

(continued)

| Eatery | Jennifer's Rating | Dave's Rating | Readers' Rating | Details |
|---|---|---|---|---|
| **El Pirata Y el Perico** [A-4] L $12, D $12, S (DDPQ)<br>*Look to the sign of the Pirate and the Parrot for an informal meal near Pirates of the Caribbean. The brief menu includes tacos ($5.79), veggie taco ($5.49), and taco salad ($6.99). A kid's meal with a quesadilla, carrots, grapes, and a drink ($3.99) is available. The indoor and outdoor themed seating area is shared with Pecos Bill's, so your group has more food choices. May open seasonally.* | 6 | 6 | 7 | **Counter**<br>Mexican<br>Med. noise<br>11:00 am–4:00 pm |
| **Liberty Tree Tavern** [C-3] L $34, D $40 (DDPT)<br>*One if by land, two if by monorail! Disney's elegant, Colonial-styled inn serves a la carte lunches and all-you-can-eat character dinners. At lunch, choose from an assortment of enticing soups and appetizers ($3.99–$7.49), sandwiches ($10.99–$11.49), salads ($3.99–$12.19), seafood ($15.19), turkey ($13.99), and New England Pot Roast ($13.99). Kids' meals are $7.49 including drink and dessert. The character dinner resembles a Thanksgiving feast and comes to the table on platters filled with turkey, flank steak, ham, and all the trimmings for $27.99 (or $12.99/kids). See pages 234–235 for more details on the character meal. The pricey lunch menu is a good choice for an early, moderately priced supper. Seating is at tables and chairs, and the dining rooms are well-themed.* | 6 | 6 | 7 | **Table**<br>American<br>Noisy<br>Reservations suggested<br>Call 180 days<br>Short waits<br>11:30 am–3:00 pm, 4:00 pm–closing |
| **Main Street Bakery** [D-5] B $11, L $11, S (DDPQ)<br>*This favorite Magic Kingdom quick-breakfast and snack shop offers ever-popular fresh-baked cookies, pastries, cakes, ice cream sandwiches, and desserts ($1.49–$5.99), hot breakfast items, and sandwiches, as well as specialty coffees and other beverages. Enjoy your treats in the cute dining area with granite-topped tables and counters, or take it outside to the tables near the Plaza Restaurant.* | 5 | 6 | 6 | **Counter**<br>American<br>Med. noise<br>Med. waits<br>Open all day |
| **Pecos Bill Cafe** [A-4] L $12, D $12, S (DDPQ)<br>*Just the place to rustle up a bowl of chili ($2.99), BBQ pork sandwich ($7.59), or cheeseburger ($5.89–$7.39)—they even have a well-stocked fixins' bar. Chicken wraps and salads ($6.99–$7.59) please the health-conscious. Sit on the covered porch to watch the parade. Themed rooms provide delightful indoor seating. New self-service ordering kiosks are in operation here! El Pirata Y el Perico is next door.* | 7 | 6 | 6 | **Counter**<br>American<br>Very noisy<br>10 am–1 hour before closing |
| **The Pinocchio Village Haus** [D-1] L $13, D $13, S (DDPQ)<br>*Pinocchio's has a popular Italian menu that is nothing to "lie" about. Individual pizzas ($5.59–$6.29),cheese steak sandwich ($7.29), Italian sub ($7.09), and an antipasto salad ($4.99–$6.99) are all on the menu. The Swiss-styled stone building fits perfectly with its surroundings. Sit outside at a patio table for Fantasyland sights; some inside tables have a great view of "it's a small world."* | 6 | 6 | 5 | **Counter**<br>Italian<br>Noisy<br>11 am–1 hour before closing |
| **The Plaza Restaurant** [D-4] L $21, D $21, S (DDPT)<br>*This small Main Street standby has all the old-fashioned ice cream parlor atmosphere you need, offering overstuffed hot and cold sandwiches, including a classic Reuben ($10.79), 6-ounce burgers ($11.49), proper malts and milkshakes ($4.29), Apple Charlotte ($3.99), and fountain sundaes ($3.99–$5.69). A fresh veggie sandwich ($9.39) and the chicken and strawberry salad ($10.29) are offered as "lighter" fare. Kids' meals are $7.49 with drink. Walk-up guests can expect a short wait before being seated. Tables and half-booths.* | 7 | 8 | 7 | **Table**<br>American<br>Med. noise<br>Reservations suggested<br>11 am–1 hour before closing |

# Magic Kingdom Eateries

(continued)

Jennifer's Rating | Dave's Rating | Readers' Rating

## Tomorrowland Terrace Noodle Station [E-4] L $13, D $13, S — 5 | 5 | 6

*Tomorrowland Terrace Noodle Station offers a taste on the Asian side. Menu items include a chicken noodle bowl ($6.99), teriyaki chicken with rice ($6.79), vegetable noodle bowl ($6.79), beef and broccoli with rice ($7.69), iced green teas ($2.39), and a chocolate cake ($3.59). This is a tasty and satisfying addition to the dining lineup. Tables and chairs are in a shaded, open-air (not air-conditioned) terrace that doubles as a shortcut between Main Street and Tomorrowland. The best tables have a panoramic view of the Castle, but the rest are unappealing. This eatery may only be open seasonally.*

**Counter** | Asian | Med. noise | Short waits | 11 am–1 hour before park closing

## Tony's Town Square Restaurant [D-6] L $31, D $47 — 8 | 8 | 8

*Tony's serves Italian cuisine in the heart of Main Street, U.S.A. Familiar dinner entrees include Tony's "special" spaghetti and meatballs from Lady and the Tramp ($18.99) and Grilled Salmon ($23.49). Less familiar but perhaps more interesting is a strip steak with red wine gorgonzola butter ($25.49). Tony's no longer serves breakfast. The lunch menu offers pizzas, sandwiches, and salads ($8.19–$11.19), plus more elaborate entrees ($12.19–$14.19) like baked ziti. Tony's lunch menu is a good choice for an economical, early supper. Kids' meals are around $7.49 and include choices like pasta primavera and vegetable ravioli. This could be the best table-service meal at Magic Kingdom.*

**Table** | Italian | Med. noise | Reservations suggested | Call 180 days | 12–3:00 pm 5:00 pm–closing

*Eatery descriptions and ratings are explained on page 206.*

## Selected Magic Kingdom Snack Shops and Carts

| Name | Land | Specialties |
|---|---|---|
| Plaza Ice Cream Parlor | Main Street, U.S.A. | Hand-dipped ice cream |
| Aloha Isle* | Adventureland | Pineapple Dole Whips (frozen dessert) |
| Sunshine Tree Terrace* | Adventureland | Citrus Swirl, frozen yogurt |
| Aunt Polly's Dockside Inn* | Frontierland | Ice cream, sundaes, pie (seasonal) |
| Frontierland Fries | Frontierland | McDonald's french fries |
| Liberty Square Market* | Liberty Square | Fresh fruit, baked potatoes |
| Sleepy Hollow | Liberty Square | Ice cream, root beer floats, coffee drinks |
| Enchanted Grove* | Fantasyland | Fruit slushes, juices, Strawberry Swirls |
| Village Fry Shoppe | Fantasyland | Fries (of course), carrot cake, jello |
| Mrs. Potts' Cupboard | Fantasyland | Soft-serve ice cream, shakes |
| Scuttle's Landing | Fantasyland | Sweet cream cheese pretzel, soft drinks |
| Toontown Market | Mickey's Toontown Fair | Fresh fruit, yogurt cup, soft drinks |
| Auntie Gravity's | Tomorrowland | Ice cream, smoothies |
| The Lunching Pad | Tomorrowland | Turkey legs, pretzels, frozen drinks |

*Note: Some shops and carts may be seasonal. Eateries marked with an asterisk (*) close as early as 3:00-5:00 pm.*

**Tip**: Remember, opinions vary widely, especially on what constitutes a good meal. If you'd like to read reviews of eateries by other vacationers to gain their unique perspective, we recommend you visit MousePlanet's Walt Disney World Restaurant Resource located at http://www.mouseplanet.com/dtp/wdwrr. Another excellent resource is the PassPorter Message Boards at http://www.passporterboards.com/forums. Click the "Feasting & Snacking" forum and look for messages or post your own!

# Epcot Eateries

(park map on page 140)

Jennifer's Rating | Dave's Rating | Readers' Rating

## Akershus Royal Banquet Hall [B-3] B $29, L $31, D $36 — DDP — 7 8 8

*Enjoy authentic Nordic fare (lunch is $24.99/$13.99 kids ages 3-9, dinner is $28.99/$13.99) in a replica of a rustic Norwegian castle, complete with Disney princesses all day long. Many diners have been happily surprised by food that's both remarkably familiar and somewhat unusual. Cold buffet. Hot specialties are brought to your table. Enjoy meats, cheeses, peel-and-eat shrimp, pasta, braised lamb, pan-seared trout, Kjottkaker, Swedish meatballs (lunch only), and a variety of salads. Kids ($13.99) can get chicken breast, cheese ravioli, meatballs, hot dog, or turkey roll-up. Soft drinks and dessert are included. Breakfast ($22.99/$12.99 kids ages 3-9) offers fruit, pastries, French toast, eggs, bacon, sausage, and hash browns. For character meal details, see pages 234-235.*

**Table** | Norwegian | Med. noise | Reservations recommended | Call 180 days | 8:30-10:10 am, 11:40 am-2:50 pm, 4:20-8:20 pm

## Alfredo di Roma/Tutto Italia [C-1] — DDP — ? ? ?

*Alfredo's closed in summer 2007, reopening as Tutto Italia under the management of the Patina Restaurant Group. Tutto Italia is intended as a temporary eatery—a new, permanent restaurant will debut in fall 2008, also managed by the Patina Restaurant Group, which manages several restaurants at Downtown Disney in California's Disneyland Resort. Due to its opening date, we were unable to evaluate Tutto Italia before this book went to press, but look for a full review on our web site. Chances are good that the beautiful trompe l'oeil murals and elegant setting will remain in its Tutto Italia incarnation. Try for lunchtime seating in the bright and cheery gallery.*

**Table** | Italian | Very noisy | Reservations strongly recommended | Call 180 days | 12-4:15 pm 4:30-closing

## Biergarten [B-1] L $25, D $35 — DDP — 5 8 8

*Willkommen! A Bavarian town square in the midst of Oktoberfest is the setting for a hearty and satisfying German buffet ($23.99/kids $11.99). Wurst (sausages) with weinkraut, pork loin, chicken schnitzel, and rosemary roast chicken reign supreme at lunch. A first-rate sauerbraten and a fish entree are added at dinner. Every dish and side dish is several cuts above the typical German eatery, and each is distinctively seasoned. Musicians in lederhosen are on stage to entertain. Can you say "Gemütlichkeit"? (It roughly translates to "good feeling.") A large salad bar may even please some vegetarians, but this isn't the place for a light meal. Desserts are included; beverages are extra. There's Beck's beer on tap and a good German wine list. Lunch buffet is $19.99/$10.99 ages 3-9.*

**Buffet** | German | Very noisy | Reservations recommended | Call 180 days | Short waits | Noon-3:45 pm, 4:00-8:30 pm

## Bistro de Paris [F-2] D $64 — 7 8 7

*Around the corner, upstairs, and upscale from Chefs de France, this "bistro" serves a limited menu that's anything but informal. Expect a leisurely, quintessentially French meal in mostly quiet and elegant surroundings—a far cry from the bustling restaurant downstairs. The short, classically French menu features escargot ($12) and duck foie gras ($19) appetizers; a roasted lamb loin ($31), seared scallops ($29), a grilled tenderloin of beef ($32), roasted pork tenderloin ($26), and fish of the day (market price). Desserts are outstanding ($6-$8). The wine list is excellent, but the cheapest bottle is $42. Service is generally excellent, but one bad night still sticks in our minds. Ask for a window seat and linger until IllumiNations. No kids menu. No tank tops permitted.*

**Table** | French | Very quiet | Reservations strongly recommended | Call 30 days | Short waits | 6:00 pm-8:45 pm

*Eatery descriptions and ratings are explained on page 206.*

# Epcot Eateries
(continued)

Jennifer's Rating | Dave's Rating | Readers' Rating

| Restaurant | Meals | Ratings | |
|---|---|---|---|
| **Boulangerie Patisserie** [F-2] | L $15, S | 7 7 9 | |
| *A quaint French bakery. Ham and cheese croissants ($3.25), a cheese plate ($5.95) and Quiche Lorraine ($4.95) make a nice, light lunch, while croissants ($1.95–$2.85), eclairs ($3.75), chocolate mousse ($3.35), and fruit tarts ($3.85–$4.25) satisfy sweet tooths. Seating outside and inside Galerie les Halles shop.* | | | **Counter**<br>French<br>Long waits<br>~11 am–closing |
| **Cantina de San Angel** [B-4] | L $13, D $13, S | 6 5 7 | |
| *The partly shaded, open-air patio by the lagoon is the best feature of this taco and burrito stand. Try various platters ($7.29–$8.50), nachos ($7.25), and Mexican chicken salad ($8.50). Try churros ($2.15) for dessert. Vegetarians can make special requests. Enjoy a cold beer or margarita at the bar or watch IllumiNations from a lagoon-side table. Children's platter with drink is $3.99. We hear the cantina may get a new menu and expansion by summer 2008.* | | | **Counter**<br>Mexican<br>Med. noise<br>Med. waits<br>~11 am–closing |
| **Les Chefs de France** [F-2] | L $33, D $54 | 6 7 8 | |
| *Traditional French favorites such as escargot ($9.95), onion soup ($5.95), tomato and goat cheese tart ($9.25), braised lamb shank ($24.95), and grilled beef tenderloin with black pepper sauce ($28.95) carry the imprint of some of France's most famous chefs. The bright, bustling brasserie atmosphere, crowded seating, and overtaxed serving staff can be at odds with the desire for a slow, enjoyable meal. Lighter lunchtime choices such as Salade Niçoise ($14.75), croque monsieur with side salad ($17.95), and Quiche Lorraine ($10.95) will keep things affordable–save the heavier entrees ($15.95–$17.95) until dinnertime, even if they're more expensive then. Kids' meals are $9–$13. Chairs and half-booths. Request a window seat for a great view. Special dietary requests are hit or miss here.* | | | **Table**<br>French<br>Very noisy<br>Reservations strongly recommended<br>Call 180 days<br>Med. waits<br>Noon–3 pm<br>5 pm–closing |
| **Coral Reef** [D-7] | L $47, D $54 | 6 7 7 | |
| *Few restaurants are as breathtakingly beautiful as the Coral Reef–brightly glazed blue mosaic tiles and brushed metal shimmer in the light cast by The Seas with Nemo & Friends aquarium, as fish of all sizes and colors swim by. The inventive seafood menu ($21–$27) covers a variety of international tastes and styles and is generally well-prepared. Meat and veggie lovers will also find foods to enjoy here ($17–$32). If only there was more elbow room, the noise more restrained, and the service more consistent. Tip: Request a tank-side table for the best views. Sweets here are special, especially The Chocolate Wave ($7.99). Kids' meals are $7.49. Enjoy the same view at lunch (entrees $13–$22).* | | | **Table**<br>Seafood<br>Noisy<br>Reservations strongly recommended<br>Call 180 days<br>Noon–3 pm, 4:30–8:00 pm |
| **Electric Umbrella** [C-6] | L $10, D $10, S | 4 4 6 | |
| *If you're looking for basic burgers ($6.89–$7.39) at Epcot, this is the place. It's also decent for healthier fare, like turkey wraps ($6.89) and chicken salad ($6.99)–you can also swap your fries for an apple. The main seating area is noisy–look for quieter seating upstairs, or dine outside on the terrace. Kids meals are $3.99. Toppings bar replaced by unlimited drink station in 2007.* | | | **Counter**<br>American<br>Med. noise<br>Short waits<br>~9 am–9 pm |
| **Fountainview Bakery** [D-6] | B $6, S | 5 6 8 | |
| *How cosmopolitan! Sip a caffe mocha ($3.19) or latte ($3.19) and nibble a croissant ($2.29–4.49), coconut flan ($3.29), or fruit tulip ($3.99) while watching crowds criss-cross Fountain Plaza. Mmmm! Dine inside or out. Noisy. Seasonal.* | | | **Counter**<br>French<br>Hours vary |

# Epcot Eateries
(continued)

| | | Jennifer's Rating | Dave's Rating | Readers' Rating |
|---|---|---|---|---|
| **The Garden Grill Restaurant** [F-6] L $26, D $35, S | DD PT | 8 | 7 | 8 |

*This popular lunch and dinner character dining experience is tucked away in The Land pavilion. Farmer Mickey, Pluto, Chip, and Dale make the rounds of this rotating restaurant. Watch an ever-changing American landscape while you enjoy an updated menu. At lunch ($20.99/$11.99 ages 3–9) and dinner ($27.99/$12.99 ages 3–9), the grown-ups get a soft drink, bread and honey-orange butter, salad (dinner only), rotisserie chicken, catfish, flank steak, potato casserole, and greenhouse vegetables. A "homegrown" salad comes with dinner—veggies are from Disney's hydroponic gardens. Vegetarians can make special requests. Kids ages 3–9 get chicken strips, mac & cheese, fries, and veggies. Dessert is a very berry puff pastry for adults and a make-your-own-cupcake for kids. Soft drinks included. Try for a booth on the lower tier, which is closer to the scenery.*

*Cupcakes in the Garden*

Table | American | Med. noise | Reservations not always needed | Call 180 days | Short waits | 11:00 am–3:30 pm, 4:30 pm–7:00 pm

| | | Jennifer's Rating | Dave's Rating | Readers' Rating |
|---|---|---|---|---|
| **Kringla Bakeri og Kafé** [B-3] L $15, D $15, S | DD PQ | 5 | 6 | 8 |

*This is a must stop for veteran World Showcase visitors. Have a light meal with tasty open-faced sandwiches ($5.89). Or treat yourself to a "kringle" (sweet pretzel-$3.79), schoolbread ($2.49), cloudberry horn (a cream-filled pastry–$3.09), or other desserts ($1.49–$3.99). Kids meals are $3.99. Beer and wine by the glass. Nice outdoor tables. Popular before IllumiNations.*

Counter | Norwegian | Med. noise | Long waits | ~11 am–9 pm

| | | Jennifer's Rating | Dave's Rating | Readers' Rating |
|---|---|---|---|---|
| **Le Cellier** [E-4] L $50, D $53 | DD PT | 7 | 8 | 7 |

*Oh, Canada! This steakhouse-in-a-stone-cellar is one of World Showcase's gems. Warm lighting, brocade upholstery, and stained glass make this the coziest cellar around. The menu is very hearty, but it's not plain steaks, roast beef, and potatoes—everything is richly sauced ($15.99–$27.99). Seafood—Asian Shrimp Cocktail ($9.99) and salmon with maple butter ($20.99)—get royal treatment, and the vegetarian entree ($15.99) is very tempting. Moderately priced lunches include excellent salads ($6.99–$15.99), sandwiches ($11.49–$14.99), and steaks, of course ($19.99–$21.99). The luscious cheddar cheese soup ($4.99) is a big favorite at any time. You may also find duck, venison, and a very popular buffalo ribeye (seasonal). Leave room for dessert—chocolate "moose" anyone?*

*Le Cellier is Le Cozier*

Table | Canadian | Medium noise | Reservations strongly recommended | Call 180 days | Long waits | Noon–3:00 pm, 4:00 pm–closing

| | | Jennifer's Rating | Dave's Rating | Readers' Rating |
|---|---|---|---|---|
| **Liberty Inn** [C-1] L $13, D $13, S | DD PQ | 4 | 4 | 5 |

*Hot dogs, hamburgers, and chicken strips ($5.79–$7.39) weren't as American as apple cobbler ($3.49) back in Colonial days, but they are now. A toppings bar adds relish to the basic fare, while a chicken Caesar salad ($6.99) provides an alternative. Kosher items available. Seating indoors and out.*

Counter | American | Short waits | ~11 am–closing

*Eatery descriptions and ratings are explained on page 206.*

# Epcot Eateries
(continued)

Jennifer's Rating | Dave's Rating | Readers' Rating

## Lotus Blossom Café [B-3] L $14, D $14, S — DDPQ — 3 4 5

Counter | Chinese | Med. noise | Med. waits | ~11 am–closing

*Chinese food at Epcot leaves a bit to be desired, but the menu here has become more enticing, as has its dining room after a recent facelift (see photo to left). Try Beijing barbecue, orange chicken, beef noodle soup bowl, veggie stir fry, or shrimp fried rice (each $7.29), pot stickers ($4.99), egg rolls ($3.99), and sesame chicken salad ($6.59). Desserts run $2.99–$3.99. Kids' meal (barbecue drumstick) is $5.95. Indoor and covered outdoor seating.*

*Enjoying a meal at Lotus Blossom Cafe*

## Restaurant Marrakesh [F-1] L $44, D $50 — DDPT — 9 7 8

Table | Middle Eastern | Noisy | Reservations not always needed | Call 180 days | Short waits | 11:30 am–3:45 pm, 4 pm–closing

*Enjoy exotic food in an authentic Moroccan setting as modest belly dancers and live musicians lend even more atmosphere. Lamb and chicken are the backbone of the cuisine, either grilled, roasted, or stewed ($22.95–$31.95). The flaky pastry-based appetizers ($5.95–$6.95) are a must, especially the chicken bastilla ($5.95). If you've always wanted to try couscous, the Moroccan national dish of stewed meat and/or vegetables over steamed semolina, you'll find it is quite good here ($19.95–$26.95). Order a la carte, or choose from a variety of family-style feasts ($35.95–$39.95) at dinnertime. Plan to sample a variety of appetizers and desserts ($4.95–$6.95). Check for bargain-priced specials at lunch. The kids' menu is a bit exotic, offering Moroccan pasta, chicken tenders, kefta (bun-less burgers) with fries, and veggie couscous ($6.95). Tables and chairs.*

## Nine Dragons [B-3] L $36, D $40, S — DDPT — 7 8 6

Table | Chinese | Med. noise | Reservations suggested | Call 180 days | Medium waits | 12:00 pm–4:30 pm, 4:45 pm–park closing

*Nine Dragons, decorated in traditional Chinese style with red lacquered woods and accents of gold and black has greatly improved, but the prices are still nothing like Chinatown. Many regions of China are represented by familiar menu items, including pot stickers ($5.99), hot and sour soup ($3.29), Canton pepper beef ($18.79), scallops with black bean sauce ($17.99), steamed scallops and tofu ($17.99), kung bao chicken ($16.75), and a Peking Duck dinner for two ($38.99). Lunch now offers traditional Dim Sum service—pick plates of dumplings and other items from a cart, at $3.50–$14.95 per plate. A sampler meal for two is $29.95 at lunch and $43.98 at dinner. Kids' meals are $4.75–$8.50. Note: This eatery will close in early 2008 for renovations, which will include an exhibition kitchen. Check our web site for details and a reopening date.*

*Lunching at Nine Dragons*

*Looking for Restaurant Marrakesh? See page 213.*

# Epcot Eateries
(continued)

Ratings: Jennifer's Rating / Dave's Rating / Readers' Rating

## Rose & Crown Pub and Dining Room [E-3] L $37, D $42 DDPT — 7 6 8

*They say "heck" is a place where the cooks are English, but the food in this boisterous, crowded pub is quite nice. It's so cozy inside you'd swear you just walked in out of a London fog. Traditional specialties include fish & chips ($15.99), bangers and mash ($15.99), and tea time chicken with creamed leeks ($14.99). Start your meal (or simply snack) on a fruit and cheese plate ($8.99). Pub-style entertainers put in a regular appearance. A quieter meal with a view of IllumiNations may be had out on the terrace—request a 7:30 pm (or earlier) reservation, check in early, request an outside table (no guarantee you'll get one, but ask anyway), and have a leisurely dinner. Don't forget a pint of ale, porter, or stout, a side of English "chips" ($2.99). And how about the sticky toffee pudding for dessert ($4.99)?*

Table · English · Very noisy · Reservations strongly recommended · Call 180 days · Long waits · ~11:30 am–4:00 pm, 4:30–closing

## San Angel Inn [B-4] L $39, D $48 DDPT — 7 7 7

*Where but Disney can you dine at noon in a romantic, twilit Mexican plaza, while a cool evening breeze caresses your skin, a volcano steams ominously on the horizon and boats float by on Gran Fiesta Tour (see page 147)? Despite the fine, authentic Mexican food, it's the atmosphere that makes San Angel Inn (pronounced "San Anhel") a favorite. For appetizers, we suggest the Queso Fundido ($9.25/two) or ceviche (marinated seafood, $8.50). For your entree, try their wonderful Mole Poblano (chicken in unsweetened cocoa sauce, $19.99), mahi-mahi Veracruzana ($21.50), or the basic Plato Mexicano ($20.99). Check the Chef's Selections for tempting items that go beyond simple "Mex." Vegetarians should make special requests before ordering. The kids can choose from quesadillas, chicken strips, and cheeseburgers ($5.99).*

Table · Mexican · Noisy · Reservations strongly recommended · Call 180 days · Med. waits · 11:30 am–4:00 pm 4:30–closing

## Sommerfest [B-1] L $13, D $13, S DDPQ — 5 6 7

*Hearty, German fare for light eaters. Sommerfest serves bratwurst ($6.39), frankfurters (with sauerkraut, of course—$6.09), soft pretzels ($3.29), Black Forest cake ($3.59), and apple strudel ($3.59). Wash it down with German wine ($6.00–$6.75), schnapps ($6.95–$7.50), or beer in a souvenir stein ($11.50). Covered seating is outdoors, within earshot of the oompah bands. Seasonal.*

Counter · German · Noisy · Med. waits · ~11 am–closing

## Sunshine Seasons [F-6] B $14, L $14, D DDPT — 6 7 8

*Designed to look like an airport food court (to go along with Soarin' nearby), this counter-service eatery features an open kitchen and food stations themed to the seasons. The Soup and Salad station (spring) offers a roasted beet and goat cheese salad ($7.09) and seared tuna on mixed greens ($8.39). The Asian Noodles station (summer) has a veggie and tofu noodle bowl ($5.59) and grilled vegetable and beef plate ($7.59). The Grill station (fall) has a rotisserie chicken flatbread ($9.09) and grilled salmon ($9.09). And the Sandwich station (winter) offers a Black Forest ham and salami grinder ($7.59) and a smoked turkey sandwich ($6.99). There's also a Bakery station with various desserts, pastries, cakes, pies, espresso, cappucino, and ice cream. Kids' meals ($3.99) include a mini sub, chicken stir-fry, and a chicken leg. Seating is inside at tables and chairs.*

Counter · Cuisine varies · Noisy · Long waits · ~9:00 am–closing

*A new tequila bar is being built inside the Mexico pavilion as we go to press. The bar will seat about 50 people and offerings will emphasize the cultural and historical aspects of the Mexican beverage. The bar will replace one of the retail shops inside the pavilion.*

# Epcot Eateries

(continued)

Jennifer's Rating / Dave's Rating / Readers' Rating

## Tangierine Cafe [E-1] — L $17, D $17, S — DD PQ — 7 7 7

*Tangierine Café offers traditional Middle Eastern sandwiches and combo platters served in a delightfully decorated, open-air café. Choose from shawarma (sliced chicken or lamb), roast chicken or vegetarian platters, and sandwiches and wraps ($7.95–$9.95). Desserts are a deal—for $2.50 you can add baklava to your meal. A coffee and pastry counter is tucked in the back, making this cafe an excellent choice for mid-afternoon espresso and honey-drenched desserts. Kids' meals are $6.95. Indoor and outdoor seating.*

**Counter** | Middle Eastern | Med. noise | Med. waits | Noon-closing

## Teppan Edo [E-1] — L $44, D $48 — DD PT — ? ? ?

*Formerly the Teppanyaki Dining Room, this eatery got a makeover and new menu in fall 2007, after we went to press. The fun "teppan" concept remains, however—guests sit around teppan grilling tables, upon which meat and veggies are cooked by a flamboyant chef. Expect to be able to choose from steak, chicken, and seafood in a variety of combinations, and watch as everything is cooked the same way and served with the same vegetables and rice. It's tasty, fun, and a good "adventure" for timid eaters. Teppan tables seat eight guests and are often shared by two or more parties. For a full review of this revamped eatery after it opens, visit http://www.passporter.com.*

**Table** | Japanese | Noisy | Reservations recommended | Call 180 days | Long waits | 12–3:45 pm, 4:30–closing

## Tokyo Dining [E-1] — L $33, D $40, S — DD PT — ? ? ?

*Like Teppan Edo, this restaurant was renovated from a previous incarnation (the former Tempura Kiku and Matsu No Ma eateries). All we know at press time is that Tokyo Dining is expected to showcase the traditional cuisine of Japan, with an emphasis on sushi. The good news is that Tokyo Dining should be roomier than the previous occupants. For a full review of this revamped eatery after it opens, visit http://www.passporter.com.*

**Table** | Japanese | Med. noisy | Medium waits | ~11 am-closing

## Yakitori House [D-1] — L $14, D $14, S — DD PQ — 6 5 8

*Of the Japan pavilion's three eateries, we visit here most often for tasty, filling, and economical fare (but quality is slipping recently). This classic Japanese quick-meal spot serves skewers of grilled teriyaki chicken and beef as a snack, platter, or in a combo with shrimp tempura ($1.79–$7.49), satisfying beef curry over rice ($6.49), and big, filling bowls of Udon noodle soup ($6.49). Wash it down with hot sake or cold Kirin beer. Dine at tables indoors or out, and take a few minutes to stroll through the nearby bonsai display. Kids' meal is $3.99.*

**Counter** | Japanese | Medium noise | Medium waits | ~11 am-closing

## Yorkshire County Fish Shop [E-3] — L $13, D $13, S — DD PQ — 7 8 7

*Crowds have been queuing up and strolling away with Harry Ramsden's legendary Fish & Chips ($7.99), and for good reason—it's the real thing! (Dave can't resist it!) An extra side of chips is $2.69. Wash it down with a Bass ale, Guinness, or try a refreshing, hard cider (sweet or dry). Seating at patio tables is often available to the right, or visit the United Kingdom gardens to eat.*

**Counter** | English | Med. noise | Med. waits | ~11 am-closing

*Eatery descriptions and ratings are explained on page 206.*

# Epcot Eateries

(continued)

Snacking at Epcot is every bit as diverse and rewarding as feasting in its fine restaurants. The snack carts and shops seem to appear and change regularly, however, so a definitive snack list isn't practical. Instead, we've listed our favorite treats at Epcot and where you can find them—this will give you an idea of the variety of snacks available. If you can't locate one of our favorite munchies, chances are very good you'll find a new tidbit that we haven't yet discovered!

### Our Favorite Snacks at Epcot

| Treat | Found At |
|---|---|
| Churros (fried dough rolled in cinnamon sugar) DD PS | Mexico (Cantina de San Angel) |
| Pretzels, Lefse, and School Bread DD PS | Norway (Kringla Bakeri og Kafé) |
| Italian pastries and cappuccino | Italy (along promenade) |
| Funnel cakes (deep-fried batter with powdered sugar) | The American Adventure |
| Kaki Gori (shaved ice with sweet flavoring) | Japan (along promenade) |
| Baklava (flaky pastry with honey, rosewater, and nuts) | Morocco (along promenade) |
| Wine by the glass | France (along promenade) |

*Note: Some shops and carts may be seasonal.*

### International Food and Wine Festival

Eager to sample more international cuisine and exotic tastes? Visit the "World" in autumn, when Epcot hosts the International Food and Wine Festival. Just stroll around the World Showcase Promenade and sample food and drink at more than 25 booths. The generously sized appetizer treats range in price from $1.50 to $4.50, while small plastic glasses of wine, beer, champagne, cognac, and port begin at $2 and go up from there. Guests on the Disney Dining Plan may be able to use their snack credits for many of the food items under $4. You can easily make a meal out of the offerings, stopping at booths whenever you discover another appetizing snack. Eating while strolling around isn't always the most relaxing, but there are plenty of benches and quiet nooks at which to munch away. In addition to the treats, you can watch cooking demonstrations by top chefs, participate in beer and wine seminars and tastings, and attend the Eat to the Beat concert series at the America Gardens Theater (no extra charge). With advance reservations, you can join special wine tasting events ($95–$150), a Party for the Senses (a $135 wine-sipping and food-sampling extravaganza), wine schools (day-long education programs for $150), and one-hour Food and Wine Pairings ($45). The ultimate VIP experience may be the $210–$350 reserve dinners (Exquisite Evenings), held in a VIP dining room and featuring a VIP viewing of IllumiNations. We expect the 13th annual festival to run from September 28 to November 11, 2008. For more information, call 407-WDW-INFO.

# Disney's Hollywood Studios Eateries

(park map on page 154)

| | | Jennifer's Rating | Dave's Rating | Readers' Rating |
|---|---|---|---|---|
| **ABC Commissary** [C-3] | B $8, L $13, D $13, S | 5 | 6 | 5 |
| **Backlot Express** [C-5] | L $14, D $14, S | 5 | 5 | 7 |
| **Catalina Eddie's** [G-3] | L $14, D $14, S | 4 | 5 | 6 |
| **'50s Prime Time Cafe** [E-5] | L $35, D $37 | 8 | 6 | 8 |
| **Hollywood & Vine** [E-5] | B $29, L $31, D $30 | 7 | 7 | 7 |

**ABC Commissary** [C-3] — B $8, L $13, D $13, S — Ratings: 5 / 6 / 5

*Carpeted floors, potted palms, and sleek decorating make you feel like a special employee. The International menu features fish & chips, vegetable noodle stir fry, chicken curry, tabbouleh wrap, Cuban sandwiches, and burgers ($5.49–$6.89). Kids can get chicken or fish nuggets, and stir fry ($3.99). One of the park's only breakfast spots. Kosher items available. Shady outdoor seating, too.*

Counter | American | Med. noise | Med. waits | Open all day

**Backlot Express** [C-5] — L $14, D $14, S — Ratings: 5 / 5 / 7

*Rarely crowded and often overlooked, this backstage-themed cafeteria serves up burgers, hot dogs, chicken strips, grilled turkey & cheese, and sesame chicken salad ($5.79–$6.99). The children's meal is $3.99 (includes drink). Pleasant indoor and outdoor seating. Perfect spot for watching the parade—stake out a table about a half-hour beforehand. Not always open.*

Counter | American | Noisy | Short waits | 11 am–closing

**Catalina Eddie's** [G-3] — L $14, D $14, S — Ratings: 4 / 5 / 6

*Part of the outdoor Sunset Ranch Market mini food court on Sunset Blvd. Cheese and pepperoni pizza ($5.59–$5.89), a side salad ($2.19), apple pie ($3.59), and chocolate cake ($3.59) make up the menu. Outdoor, shaded (and not-so-shaded) seating. Nearby food stands serve McDonald's fries, fresh fruit, smoked turkey legs, burgers, and ice cream.*

Counter | American | Med. noise | Short waits | 11 am–closing

**'50s Prime Time Cafe** [E-5] — L $35, D $37 — Ratings: 8 / 6 / 8

*Clean your plate in an old kitchenette, while "Mom" serves gussied-up versions of home-cooked meals like meatloaf, pot roast, grilled and fried chicken, salmon, grilled pork tenderloin, pasta ($12.49–$19.99), and scrumptious malts, milkshakes, and sundaes ($4.29–$7.49). The lunch menu adds pot pie, sandwiches, and salads ($11.99–$15.79). Vintage TV clips of "I Love Lucy" and "The Honeymooners" play while you eat, and your "brother" and "sister" (your servers) boss you around when your "Mom" isn't watching. This is a unique dining experience if you're willing to play along—not recommended for the overly shy. Veggie burgers on request. The dining areas and adjoining bar/waiting area are a wonderland of '50s-vintage Formica, television sets, and knickknacks. Table and booth seating.*

Table | American | Noisy | Reservations strongly recommended | Call 180 days | Long waits | 11 am–4 pm, 4 pm–closing

**Hollywood & Vine** [E-5] — B $29, L $31, D $30 — Ratings: 7 / 7 / 7

*This 1940s-inspired "Cafeteria of the Stars" once again has star power with a character breakfast and lunch buffet ("Play 'n Dine") with friends from Playhouse Disney, including JoJo's Circus and Little Einsteins characters. It's a tasty and economical choice for a pre-Fantasmic! dinner. Stainless steel serving areas, comfy half-booths, metal-edged Formica tables, checkerboard floor tiles, and a mural of Hollywood in its heyday set the scene. The menu changes regularly—buffet choices may include pot roast, salmon, baked chicken, and a fish specialty. The kids have their own buffet, and everyone can make sundaes. Breakfast is $22.99/$12.99, lunch is $24.99/$13.99, and dinner (no characters) is $24.99/$11.99. Available with the Fantasmic! dinner package at the same price (see page 219).*

Buffet | American | Noisy | Reservations suggested | Call 180 days | 8:00–11:20 am, 11:40–2:25 pm, 4:00 pm–closing

**Tip:** The Disney's Hollywood Studios' table-service restaurants may open 30 minutes earlier on days with Extra Magic Hour—check at 407-WDW-DINE.

# Disney's Hollywood Studios Eateries

(continued)

Jennifer's Rating | Dave's Rating | Readers' Rating

## The Hollywood Brown Derby [E-3] L $46, D $55 — 8 8 8

*The famous Brown Derby, complete with "stars," serves enticing starters like lump crab cake ($9.00), Lobster and fennel bisque ($7.00), and the yummy and original Cobb Salad ($14.00/two). Entrees include excellent pan-seared grouper with a citrus sauce, and first-rate roasts and chops ($18.00–$28.00). Desserts like the famous grapefruit cake ($6.00–$8.00) are quite good, and this is the place for a celebratory bottle of bubbly. The Brown Derby is the Studios' most elegant establishment. Off-white walls covered with caricatures of the stars, dark wood trim, crisp, white table linens, and attentive, formal service set the tone. Hollywood "personalities" may jazz up the show. This restaurant offers some special meals—for information on the Fantasmic! Meal Package, see page 219; for the Dine with an Imagineer experience, see page 239.*

Table | American | Med. noise | Reservations strongly recommended | Call 180 days | Long waits | 11:30 am–3 pm | 3:30 pm–closing

## Mama Melrose's Ristorante Italiano [A-4] L $36, D $40 — 6 5 7

*Mama's is a brick wall and booth sort of place. A variety of individual wood-fired pizzas ($11.99–$12.99), light pasta specialties, and simple meats grace the menu at Mama's, which changes regularly. Charred butcher tender steak ($20.99), chicken parmesan ($16.49), or wood-grilled salmon ($18.49) may catch your eye. The seafood pasta Fra Diavolo ($19.99) wasn't devilishly spicy or briny, but there was plenty of shellfish. Sangria, a Bellini cocktail, and desserts like hazelnut and ricotta cheesecake ($5.99) may catch your attention. Ask about the Fantasmic! Dinner Package, which offers a three-course dinner plus seating at Fantasmic! (see pages 152 and 219). Your little "bambini" can get pasta, pizza, or chicken strips for $7.49.*

© MediaMarx, Inc.

*Jennifer and Dave enjoy Mama Melrose's sangria*

Table | Italian | Med. noise | Reservations suggested | Call 180 days | Short waits | Noon–3 pm, 3:30 pm–closing

## Rosie's All-American Cafe [G-3] L $13, D $13, S — 4 4 6

*Part of the outdoor Sunset Ranch Market mini food court on Sunset Blvd., Rosie's is really a hamburger stand offering burgers ($5.89–$6.89), veggie burgers ($5.89), chicken strips ($6.69), soup ($2.59), salad ($2.19), and desserts ($3.59). Seating is outdoors at covered picnic benches. Other stands nearby offer pizza, smoked turkey legs, ice cream, McDonald's fries, and fresh fruit.*

Counter | American | Med. noise | Med. waits | 11 am–closing

## Sci-Fi Dine-In Theater Restaurant [C-4] L $35, D $37 — 7 7 6

*Build a drive-in theater in a movie soundstage, seat folks in replica vintage cars, serve souped-up drive-in fare, and show old sci-fi movie trailers. Would anyone buy that script? You and the kids will at this fanciful eatery. The menu is fun and portions are huge. Definitely get a shake ($4.29)—you can get "adult" (alcoholic) shakes, too. The kids' menu is classic "drive-in," but the adult menu has upscale choices like pan-seared tuna with veggies and rice ($13.99) and shrimp penne pasta ($17.99). At lunch, try the Angus chuck burger ($11.99) or smoked turkey sandwich ($10.99). The desserts are out of this world ($4.99–$5.99). Everyone faces the screen, so chatting is hard. Not all seats are "parked cars"—request one if you want it. Kids' menu is $7.49.*

Table | American | Noisy | Reservations strongly recommended | Call 180 days | Med. waits | 11 am–4 pm | 4 pm–closing

*Eatery descriptions and ratings are explained on page 206.*

# Disney's Hollywood Studios Eateries

(continued)

Jennifer's Rating | Dave's Rating | Readers' Rating

### Flatbread Grill (Studio Catering) [B-3] L $13, D $13, S DDPQ — 7 6 6

*This recently renovated eatery offers a melting pot of flavors. Offerings include barbeque pulled pork sub ($6.49), grilled chicken with rice and beans ($6.49), Greek salad ($5.99), Chicken Caesar Wrap ($6.49), and marble cheesecake ($3.59). Kids can have the choice of chicken wraps or a chicken drumstick ($3.99). Sangria is also offered ($5.25). Tables are outside but sheltered.*

**Counter** | Mediterranean | Med. noise | Med. waits | 11 am-closing

### Toluca Legs Turkey Co. [G-3] L $8, D $8, S DDPQ — 4 4 5

*Part of the outdoor Sunset Ranch Market mini food court on Sunset Blvd. As you may have guessed, you can get a turkey leg ($5.49) to munch on. You can also get hot dogs with chili and/or cheese ($5.19). Seating is outdoors at covered picnic benches. Other stands nearby offer burgers, chicken strips, soup, ice cream, McDonald's fries, and fresh fruit.*

**Counter** | American | Noisy | Med. waits | 11 am-closing

### Toy Story Pizza Planet [B-5] L $12, D $12 DDPQ — 3 4 6

*The name is familiar, but this pizzeria/arcade doesn't look all that much like the pizza palace in Toy Story. Choose from individual pizzas ($5.59-$6.29) or "meal deals" that combine pizza, a side salad, and drink ($7.59-$8.19). There's also a Greek Salad ($4.99) and cookies ($1.89). It's an OK place to eat and rest while your little "Andy" or "Jessie" hits the arcade. Seating upstairs and outside.*

**Counter** | American | Very noisy | Long waits | 11 am-closing

## Fantasmic! Dinner Package DDP2

If you're thinking about a table service dinner at Disney's Hollywood Studios, consider the Fantasmic! Dinner Package. You get a meal at Hollywood Brown Derby, Mama Melrose, or Hollywood and Vine *plus* seats in the reserved section at the Fantasmic! nighttime show, at the price of the meal alone. To qualify, everyone in your party must order the fixed-price meal–$21.99–$46.99 (kids are $9.99–$11.99). Credit card deposit required. Call 407-WDW-DINE to make reservations up to 180 days in advance, or ask about it at Lobby Concierge at your Disney hotel or at Guest Relations in the park (see map on page 154 for location). Availability is very limited. Note: Restaurants and details may change, lunch may be available seasonally (ask) and Fantasmic! may be canceled in bad weather. Note that no rain checks are issued for your Fantasmic! seating if it is canceled.

## Disney's Hollywood Studios Snack Shops and Carts

| Name | Location | Specialties |
|---|---|---|
| Dinosaur Gertie's Ice Cream DDPS | Echo Lake | Soft-serve ice cream |
| Min & Bill's Dockside Diner DDPS | Echo Lake | Shakes & malts, stuffed pretzels |
| Peevy's Polar Pipeline DDPS | Echo Lake | Frozen slushes, bottled drinks |
| Herbie's Drive-In DDPS | Streets of America | Steamed meat and veggie buns |
| Anaheim Produce DDPS | Sunset Boulevard | Fresh fruit, drinks |
| Hollywood Scoops DDPS | Sunset Boulevard | Hand-dipped ice cream |
| Starring Rolls Cafe DDPS | Sunset Boulevard | Baked goods, coffee, sandwiches |
| Fairfax Fries DDPS | Sunset Boulevard | McDonald's fries, beverages |

*Note: Some shops and carts may be seasonal.*

# Disney's Animal Kingdom Eateries

(park map on page 164)

Ratings columns: Jennifer's Rating | Dave's Rating | Readers' Rating

## Flame Tree Barbecue [E-4] L $7, D $7, S — 6 6 6

*Although we're not sure how barbecue fits in with the Animal Kingdom motif, at least one of us can't knock it, because it's good stuff. Pork, chicken, turkey, and beef is smoked right on premises and is available sliced on sandwiches ($7.29) and arrayed on platters ($7.99–$8.99). The condiment stations offer traditional and mustard-based barbecue sauces. A green salad with BBQ chicken in a garlic bread shell ($6.99) is the light alternative. Chicken wings and hot dogs for the kids ($3.99). Shaded outdoor seating in a lovely Asian garden or on decks overlooking the lake and Expedition Everest.*

© MediaMarx, Inc.
Outdoor seating at Flame Tree Barbecue

Counter | American/Barbecue | Quiet | No reservations | Med. waits | 10 am–5 pm

## Pizzafari [B-4] L $9, D $9, S — 4 4 7

*This popular pizzeria serves individual cheese and pepperoni pizzas ($5.59–$5.89), chicken Caesar salad ($6.99), and a hot Italian sandwich ($6.79). You can also get a basket of breadsticks ($3.99). There's lots of indoor, air-conditioned seating in brightly decorated, uniquely themed dining areas. Not surprisingly, the menu makes this a popular family dining spot. Many folks love Pizzafari, but we find the noise levels and crowds to be a bit much. Look for quieter seating toward the back of the restaurant or outside on the patio. Kosher items available here.*

Counter | Italian | Very noisy | Long waits | 10:00 am–5:00 pm

## Rainforest Cafe [B-7] B $15, L $49, D $38 — 5 6 7

*Environmentally conscious dining in an artificial rainforest hidden behind a two-story waterfall? It even rains indoors! The Rainforest Cafe puts on quite a show and piles your plate with tasty, inventive foods representing many different cuisines. Hearty breakfasts ($8.99–$13.99), enormous sandwiches ($10.99–$13.99), personal pizzas ($12.99–$13.99), pastas ($16.49–$19.99), steaks ($23.99–$39.99), comfort foods ($13.99–$19.99), and mountainous salads ($14.99) overflow the menu. Smoothies and specialty alcoholic drinks are popular. Located just outside the gates (no park admission required). This was the first table-service restaurant at Disney's Animal Kingdom. There's a special entrance for folks exiting and re-entering the park. For discounts, see page 205.*

Table | American | Very noisy | Call 407-938-9100 for reservations | Long waits | 8:30 am–1.5 hours after closing

## Restaurantosaurus [E-6] L $12, D $12, S — 5 5 8

*Disney and McDonald's teamed up to bring you DinoLand's only sit-down meal. Choices include "Dino-Size" ½-lb. burgers with McDonald's fries ($6.89), hot dogs with fries ($5.79), grilled chicken salads ($6.99), veggie plates (on request), and Chicken McNuggets ($5.49). McNuggets Happy Meals are $3.99. The food is not thrilling, but the indoor, air-conditioned dining areas are fun—it's a weathered, dig site bunker with broken equipment, humorous signs, and educational displays. Note: Donald's "Breakfastosaurus" character meal is no longer offered as of November 5, 2007—Donald's moving over to Tusker House for a safari breakfast buffet (see details on next page).*

Counter | American | Very noisy | No reservations | Long waits | 10:30 am–park closing

*Eatery descriptions and ratings are explained on page 206.*

# Disney's Animal Kingdom Eateries
(continued)

Jennifer's Rating | Dave's Rating | Readers' Rating

## Tusker House Restaurant [B-2] B $14, L $14, D $14, S DDPQ ? ? ?

*At press time, this eatery was closed but was expected to reopen on November 18, 2007, as a buffet restaurant. Mornings will see "Donald's Safari Breakfast Buffet" with friends like Mickey, Minnie, Goofy, Daisy, and Donald (of course). Lunch and dinner buffets will also be offered, but without the characters. Menu offerings at this time are not known, but please visit http://www.passporter.com after opening for a full review.*

Table
American
Noisy
Call 180 days
8:00-10:30 am
11 am-varies

## Yak & Yeti [E-3] L, D ? ? ?

*Finally ... a new table-service restaurant opened in Asia in fall 2007! The new Asian-themed eatery offers both table-service and counter-service meals, as well as a shop selling Asian-inspired items. If the restaurant/shop idea reminds you of Rainforest Cafe, you're on the money—the new restaurant is operated by Landry's Restaurants, which also runs Rainforest Cafe. The theme is evocative of the Western Himalayan foothills in India and Nepal, the dining rooms full of Asian antiques. Cuisine is reported to be "Asian-fusion." Table-service area has 250 tables indoors, while the counter-service component has 350 tables outdoors. Reservations are likely to be taken, but at press time it is not known whether you call 407-WDW DINE or another number. By the time you read this, we should have a full review at our web site.*

Table
Asian-American
Other details unknown at press time

## Disney Animal Kingdom's Snack Shops and Carts

| Name | Land | Specialties |
|---|---|---|
| Chip 'n' Dale's Cookie Cabin DDPS | Camp Minnie-Mickey | Hot dogs, chips (but NO cookies!) |
| Dawa Bar | Africa | Beer, cocktails |
| Harambe Fruit Market DDPS | Africa | Fresh fruit, juices, beverages |
| Kusafiri Coffee Shop & Bakery DDPS | Africa | Pastries, cappuccino & espresso |
| Tamu Tamu Refreshments DDPS | Africa | Ice cream, sundaes, floats |
| Anandapur Ice Cream DDPS | Asia | Ice cream and floats |
| Dino Bite Snacks DDPS | DinoLand U.S.A. | Ice cream, sundaes, nachos |
| Dino Diner DDPS | DinoLand U.S.A. | Ice cream, drinks |
| Petrifries DDPS | DinoLand U.S.A. | McDonald's French fries |

*Note: Some shops and carts may be seasonal.*

**Tip**: Want to enjoy the flavors of Walt Disney World at home? Pick up "Cooking with Mickey" (Hyperion Books) or download recipes at http://familyfun.go.com/recipes/disney.

# Downtown Disney Marketplace Eateries

(map on page 180)

Jennifer's Rating / Dave's Rating / Readers' Rating

**Cap'n Jack's Restaurant** L $38, D $46 — 7 | 4 | 6

*This casual, nautically themed restaurant hovers over the Lake Buena Vista Lagoon. Tables and chairs line the outer rim of the six-sided main dining room, giving each table glittering views through floor-to-ceiling picture windows. The lights of Downtown perform an enchanting dance on the waters, providing a romantic setting that the lackluster kitchen can't quite match. The menu includes crab cake ($9.49) and shrimp cocktail ($10.99) appetizers, chowder ($5.49), sandwiches at lunch ($8.99–$12.99), and entrees that include seafood pasta in a lobster sauce ($18.99), steak ($19.99), smoked pork ribs ($21.99), seared salmon with caper vin blanc ($23.99), and twin lobster tails ($31.99). Consider Ghirardelli for dessert and Fulton's for better seafood.*

Table | Seafood | Med. noise | Reservations at 407-WDW-DINE | Short waits | 11:30 am–10:30 pm

**Earl of Sandwich** B $10, L $10, D $10, S — 6 | 6 | 7

*Yes, the current Earl of Sandwich is involved in this attractive establishment. Perfect for a lunch or a light supper in cozy British decor, the menu offers a dozen appetizing hot sandwiches on specialty bread (roast beef & cheddar, ham & brie, and a turkey, bacon, & swiss club—all $5.75 each), Cobb and Chinese chicken salads ($5.95), and refrigerated grab 'n go items—sandwiches ($3.95), tuna, fruit, or chicken salads ($5.75), and yummy tomato soup ($1.95). Hot breakfast sandwiches ($4.95) in the morning, and a kids' menu ($3.95).*

Counter | Eclectic | Noisy | Medium waits | 8:00 am–11:00 pm

**Ghirardelli Soda Fountain & Chocolate Shop** S $9 — 6 | 6 | 8

*Who can resist the pleasures of San Francisco's famed chocolatier? Sundaes, sundaes, and more sundaes ($6.95–$7.25) tempt dessert fans, or share an eight-scoop Earthquake ($24.95). If that's too much, cones, shakes, malts, and frozen mochas beckon ($4.25–$4.95). Their whipped cream-topped hot chocolate ($3.20) is perfect on cool winter evenings. Sugar- and fat-free ice cream, too.*

Counter | American | Med. waits | 9:30 am–12:00 am

**Rainforest Cafe** L $52, D $52 — 5 | 6 | 7

*Another Rainforest Cafe? Yes, and it's very similar to the one at Disney's Animal Kingdom (see page 220 for menu items and descriptions). Differences include a smoking volcano atop the restaurant (rather than a waterfall) and lunch and dinner only (no breakfast). This is a very popular stop for families. Show up, sign up, and be prepared to wait. And wait. And wait. Occasional live animal demonstrations help pass the time. If the wait is too long, you can sit at the Juice Bar and order from the regular menu, or browse the Rainforest gift shop or the nearby Art of Disney shop. Near the Downtown Disney Marketplace bus stop. Open until midnight on Fridays and Saturdays. Reservations accepted at 407-827-8500. For discounts, see page 205.*

Table | American | Very noisy | Call 407-827-8500 for reservations | Very long waits | 11:30 am–11:00 pm

**Ronald's Fun House (McDonald's)** B $6, L $6, D $6, S — 2 | 2 | 5

*This is a classic "Mickey D's" with Big Macs ($2.69), McNuggets ($2.69–$6.29), and fries ($2.09–$2.79) at familiar prices. What sets it apart from the typical Golden Arches is the imaginative, Disneyfied architecture. The eatery is a huge McDonaldland-styled clockworks, filled with oversized gears and springs connected to a clock tower outside. It's next door to Lego and World of Disney, so it's a happy stop for young families. Open 'til 2 am on Fridays and Saturdays.*

Counter | American | Very noisy | Med. waits | 8:00 am–1:00 am

*Eatery descriptions and ratings are explained on page 206.*

# Downtown Disney Marketplace & Pleasure Island Eateries

(maps on pages 180 and 190)

Jennifer's Rating | Dave's Rating | Readers' Rating

## Marketplace Eateries *(continued)*

| Wolfgang Puck Express | B $11, L $11, D $11, S DDPQ | 6 6 7 |
|---|---|---|
| *Fast food for the trendy, upscale set. Puck's famous wood-fired pizzas ($8.25–$9.25), rotissered rosemary garlic chicken ($7.95) and pastas ($5.25–$9.95) are served hot. Salads ($4.95–$8.25), and appetizing sandwiches ($6.25) are available in the refrigerator cabinet. Desserts are $1.50–$4.25, and children's items are $4.50–$5.50. Drink homemade lemonade, frozen cafe mocha, wines by the bottle and glass, and beer on tap. Dine outside, or take out. See page 225 for Wolfgang Puck Grand Cafe over at the West Side.* | | **Counter**<br>American<br>Med. noise<br>Med. waits<br>8:30 am–11:30 am, 11:30 am–10 pm |

## Pleasure Island Eateries

| Cookes of Dublin | L $13, D $13, S DDPQ | 6 6 7 |
|---|---|---|
| *This small "chippie" beside Raglan Road offers hand-battered fish & chips ($8.95), smoked haddock ($9.95), battered chicken on a skewer ($6.95), and fried candy bars ($2.95). Seating is mostly outside and uncovered.* | | **Counter**<br>Irish<br>3 pm–11 pm |

| Fulton's Crab House | L $41, D $70 | 6 7 8 |
|---|---|---|
| *A boatload of seafood, served in a replica of a riverboat (sans paddlewheel) just outside Pleasure Island. The fish is flown in fresh every day, and the prices suggest it flew First Class. If you're looking for a fish feast, this is the right place. Preparations are straightforward–grilled, steamed, fried, or raw, with appropriate sauces. Crab lovers can choose from nearly a dozen entrees featuring crab ($28.95–$49.95). Twin Maine lobsters ($49.95), and the finest seasonal fish, shrimp, oysters, and clams ($27.95–$29.95) also appear in many forms. Steaks make a strong showing, too ($35.95). Prices aren't too bad if you avoid crab and lobster. Try the créme brulée. Kids' menu $4.95–$12.95.* | | **Table**<br>Seafood<br>Very noisy<br>Reservations accepted<br>Med. waits<br>11:30 am–3:30 pm, 5 pm–11 pm |

| Portobello Yacht Club | L $42, D $54 | 5 6 8 |
|---|---|---|
| *This is a nice way to start your night at Pleasure Island. Contemporary Italian specialties are served in a bustling setting. Meals are robust and flavorful, and sometimes memorable–we've been disappointed by mediocre meals and excess noise, but we enjoyed our most recent dinner and loved our first. Specialties focus on grilled meats and fish, including sausage ravioli ($17.95), salmon bruschetta ($22.95), and eggplant rollatini ($19.95). Pastas are from $17.95 to $31.95. There's a fine, if expensive, wine list. Desserts include sinful chocolates, fresh fruits, and sorbet ($3.95–$6.95). Call 407-WDW-DINE for reservations.* | | **Table**<br>Italian<br>Very noisy<br>Reservations accepted<br>Call 180 days<br>Med. waits<br>11:30 am–11 pm |

| Raglan Road | L $40, D $48 DDPT | 6 7 7 |
|---|---|---|
| *This large and comfortable Irish pub has a great atmosphere, four bars, live entertainment after 9:00 pm, and a new approach to old Irish comfort foods that make this a worthy stop. Starters of scallops ($9.95) and chicken kebabs ($7.50) are satisfying choices, as are main courses like "Heavenly Ham" ($20.00), a modernized Shepherd's Pie ($17.00), and a hearty chicken and mushroom pie ($17.00). Desserts ($7.00–$9.00) missed the mark. Kids' menu $6.00–$9.00.* | | **Table**<br>Irish<br>Call 180 days<br>Med. waits<br>11 am–2:45 pm, 3–11 pm |

**New Restaurant**: In 2008 or 2009, the new theme eatery, "T-Rex: A Prehistoric Family Adventure," will open with a 25,000 sq. ft., 600-seat, two-storied dining room. That's big!

# Downtown Disney West Side Eateries

(map on page 180)

| Eatery | Price | Description | Jennifer's Rating | Dave's Rating | Readers' Rating | Details |
|---|---|---|---|---|---|---|
| **Bongos Cuban Cafe** | L $36, D $37 | *The lively Latin sounds and flavors of Miami's South Beach make Gloria Estefan's Bongos a popular choice for Downtown Disney dining. This is robust, savory fare, with not a chili pepper in sight. Black bean soup ($4.95), seafood stew ($28.95), garlic shrimp ($22.95), skirt steak ($19.95), ropa vieja ($15.95), fried plantains ($3.75), and flan ($5.75) are some of the authentic Cuban choices. The lunch menu offers mainly sandwiches ($8.00–$8.50). Tastes may be too exotic for some diners, and our most recent meal was disappointing. The bar serves classic rum drinks, including the Mojito, a refreshing mix of white rum, mint, and sugar. An outdoor counter serves sandwiches and snacks (avg. meal cost=$16.00) from 9:30 am–midnight. Lunch served on Friday and Saturday only.* | 4 | 6 | 7 | **Table**; Cuban; Noisy; No reservations; Long waits (allow 20 to 60 min.); 11:00 am–2:00 am |
| **FoodQuest** | L $12, D $12, S | *FoodQuest serves a wide, appealing variety of salads ($4.95–$6.95), hot wraps ($7.50), sandwiches ($6.50–$6.95), hot dogs ($3.95), and burgers ($5.50) to guests at DisneyQuest (you must have DisneyQuest admission to dine here). Kids' hot dog available for $2.95. FoodQuest is operated by the Cheesecake Factory, which means there's also a good selection of desserts and beverages.* | 5 | 6 | 6 | **Counter**; American; Noisy; 11:30 am–10:30 pm |
| **House of Blues** | L $46, D $46 | *The funky House of Blues' menu is "Nawlins" Blues, with enough Cajun and Creole dishes to chase the blues away. The fried catfish starter ($9.95), gumbo ($5.75), and jambalaya ($18.95) are two beats ahead of any place similar in the "World," and you can get fine burgers ($9.95), Cajun meatloaf ($16.50), steaks ($24.95), ribs ($14.95), salads ($5.00–$14.00), and sandwiches ($10.95), too. Located near Cirque du Soleil and DisneyQuest, "HOB" looks like a weather-beaten wharfside dive. Inside is an equally aged interior with comfy booths. Live blues bands keep the joint cookin' (and make conversation difficult). Headliners play at the concert hall next door. A Gospel Brunch is held every Sunday (see page 238 for details). Open to 2:00 am on Thu.–Sat.* | 8 | 7 | 8 | **Table**; American; Very noisy; Reservations at 407-WDW-DINE; Call 180 days; Long waits; 11:00 am–11:00 pm |
| **Wetzel's Pretzels** | S $14 | *Former Disneyland Jungle Cruise cast member Rick Wetzel has become king of the gourmet soft pretzel. This shop in the former Forty Thirst Street Cafe offers a variety of fresh, hand-rolled soft pretzels, "pretzel dogs" (pretzel dough-wrapped weiners), fresh-squeezed lemonade, fruit drinks, and Häagen-Dazs ice cream. A second kiosk can be found at Downtown Disney Marketplace.* | 6 | 5 | 5 | **Counter**; American; Med. noise; 11:00 am–11:00 pm |

*Eatery descriptions and ratings are explained on page 206.*

**Tip**: We enjoy eating at Downtown Disney West Side before or after a night out, but we find the long lines frustrating. To offset the waits, try visiting at times least likely to be crowded (late afternoon and late night). If you can't avoid the peak times but need a good meal, try the bar seating at Wolfgang Puck Grand Cafe—seats open up frequently and you usually don't need a host to be seated. You can order any item off the regular menu at the bar, too.

# Downtown Disney West Side Eateries

(continued)

Jennifer's Rating | Dave's Rating | Readers' Rating

## Planet Hollywood — L $43, D $43 — DDPT — 5 | 5 | 6

*Everyone will be entertained and well-fed inside Planet Hollywood's big, blue globe full of movie and TV memorabilia. Every visitor gets the Hollywood treatment—you have to pass by the bouncers at the bottom of the stairs and walk under a long awning to reach the front door. There's seating on several levels, with views of projection video screens showing TV clips and movie trailers. You don't really come for the food, or do you? The menu can please almost anyone, with entree salads ($11.95–$13.95), sandwiches and burgers ($10.95–$13.95), pastas ($12.95–$18.95), fajitas ($16.95), and grilled and roasted meats ($16.95–$22.95). Kids' meals run about $7.95. Portions are huge, quality is average, and service can be slow. You won't get bored, though.*

Table | American | Very noisy | Reservations at 407-WDW-DINE | Call 180 days | Med. waits | 11 am–1 am

## Wolfgang Puck Grand Cafe — L $52, D $52 — DDPT — 7 | 6 | 7

*Puck is famous for nearly single-handedly popularizing California cuisine and for putting wood-fired, individual pizzas on the map. Menu favorites include Chinois Chicken Salad ($12.95), four cheese pizza ($11.95), Pumpkin Ravioli ($14.95), Pork and Veal Meatloaf ($17.95), seafood ($17.95) and rotisserie chicken ($17.95). Oops! Let's not forget his fabulous sushi and California Rolls ($12.95–$14.95)! The decor is trendy, the tables for two are too small, service is spotty, and dinnertime seating requires long waits. If you're in a rush, dine at the bar or outdoors. Conditions are much nicer at lunch. Note: "Grand Cafe" refers to the three restaurants under one roof. Reservations can be made up to 60 days in advance for dining times between 11:30 am–6:00 pm and 9:30 pm–closing.*

Table | American | Very noisy | Reservations at 407-WDW-DINE | Very long waits | 11:30 am–11:00 pm

## Wolfgang Puck Dining Room — D $66 — 8 | 8 | 8

*Climb the broad staircase inside Wolfgang Puck Grand Cafe and you'll reach the upscale Dining Room. This is a popular site for private parties, but when it's open to the public, it offers refined respite from the crowds below. Seafood items include shrimp Garganelli, Atlantic salmon, pan-seared rare tuna "Nicoise," and sushi ($10.00–$27.00). Main courses include rack of lamb ($36.00), beef short ribs ($28.00), braised duck Pappardelle ($22.00), and Wienerschnitzel Kartoffelsalat ($29.00). Call 24 hours in advance for the five-course Chef's Table menu ($74.95). Call 407-WDW-DINE for reservations and parties.*

Table | American | Noisy | Reservations recommended | Call 180 days | Long waits | 6–10:00 pm

## Wolfgang Puck Express — L $12, D $12 — DDPQ — 5 | 6 | 8

*Fast food for the trendy, upscale set. Puck's famous wood-fired pizzas, rotisseried rosemary garlic chicken, real macaroni and cheese, soups, and pastas are served hot. Enjoy a wide choice of salads and appetizing sandwiches, soft drinks, and alcoholic beverages. Part of Wolfgang Puck Grand Cafe. Dine outside, or take out. See page 223 for Wolfgang Puck Express at Marketplace.*

Counter | American | Med. noise | Med. waits | 11 am–11 pm

## Wonderland Cafe — S $8 — 7 | 7 | 7

*This is truly a coffee and dessert wonderland! It's the place to go for virtually every possible kind of hot and cold coffee drink plus to-die-for desserts, such as cheesecakes ($4.95–$5.95), mud pie blackout cake ($5.50), and hot fudge brownie sundae ($5.95). Comfy seating. The Cheesecake Factory runs the joint. Located inside DisneyQuest—admission required.*

Counter | American | Med. noise | 10:30 am–11:45 pm

# Resort Restaurants

## (Disney's Animal Kingdom Lodge and BoardWalk Resorts)

Jennifer's Rating | Dave's Rating | Readers' Rating

## Disney's Animal Kingdom Lodge Resort Restaurants

### Boma–Flavors of Africa — B $21, D $32 — DDP — 7 8 9

*Savor the many flavors of Africa at a fabulous buffet (breakfast is $16.99/adults and $9.99/kids; dinner is $25.99/adults and $11.99/kids). At dinner, a dazzling array of unusual soups, stews, salads, veggies, and wood-grilled meats tempt both timid and adventuresome diners (including kids and vegetarians). The wood-burning grill and exhibit kitchen add extra flavor to the marketplace décor. And the dessert station is fabulous—be sure to try the Zebra Domes. Breakfast is equally wonderful but more down-to-earth. This has become one of Disney's most talked-about restaurants. Diners are consistently amazed by the wide variety of pleasing new tastes, and even plain meat-and-potatoes lovers are delighted. Book ahead and arrive early. Even the line to check in can be long. Enjoy the Animal Kingdom Lodge's lobby and animal overlooks while you wait to be seated.*

**Buffet** | African | Very noisy | Reservations strongly suggested | Call 180 days | Long waits | 7:30 am–11:00 am, 5:00–10:00 pm

### Jiko–The Cooking Place — D $59 — DDP2 — 9 9 9

*African flavorings meet Californian and Asian influences with grace and style at Jiko. Savory appetizers like maize and sweet potato tamales and beef bastela come from wood-burning ovens ($8-$9). Entrees include pan-roasted jumbo scallops ($29), Durban shrimp curry ($28), grains, peas, and veggies with tandoori tofu ($24), and simmered berkshire pork shoulder ($26). Jiko boasts a AAA Four Diamond rating, among other honors. Fish and vegetarian items take the limelight, and you'll also find a strong Afro-Mediterranean influence. For dessert, try the Jiko dream pyramid ($8). Phenomenal South African wines. Kids have their own menu with appetizers ($3) and entrees ($6–$11). Dress code is "business casual" (see page 204).*

**Table** | African | Noisy | Reservations strongly suggested | Call 180 days | Short waits | 5:30 pm–10:00 pm

## BoardWalk Resort Restaurants

*See page 233 for Beach Club eateries.*

### Big River Grille & Brewing Works — L $36, D $40 — 3 4 4

*No, you won't see Brewmaster Mickey, but this brewpub chain is a popular family dining spot at the BoardWalk (ESPN Club seems to siphon off the rowdier drinking crowd). Choices range from chicken quesadilla ($8.99) to a grilled chicken cashew salad ($11.99), barbecue pork sandwich ($8.50, lunch only), burgers ($8.99), or meatloaf ($11.99 or $13.99). Steaks and ribs are also plentiful ($13.99–$24.99). The decor and seating are simple—we suggest you dine outdoors on the boardwalk in good weather. Our most recent visit was disappointing, with lackluster service, mediocre food, and a dirty floor. They do take reservations 24 hours in advance as well as reservations on the same day at 407-560-0253.*

**Table** | American | Noisy | Reservations accepted within 24 hrs. | Med. waits | 11:30 am–11:00 pm

### ESPN Club — L $33, D $33 — DDP — 4 4 7

*100 TVs pipe the big games into every nook and cranny of this very popular (and loud) sports bar. You can even go on camera for a live sports trivia quiz. The lineup is familiar—hot wings ($8.99), chili ($5.49), burgers and sandwiches ($8.99–$12.99), or try a ESPN sundae ($4.99), plus beer and mixed drinks. Sit at booths or on stools. Open until 2:00 am on weekends. This eatery is very busy during any sport playoff as well as Sunday afternoons. No reservations.*

**Table** | American | Very noisy | Med. waits | 11:30 am–1:00 am

*Eatery descriptions and ratings are explained on page 206.*

# Resort Restaurants

**(BoardWalk, Caribbean Beach, and Contemporary Resorts)**

Jennifer's Rating | Dave's Rating | Readers' Rating

## BoardWalk Resort Restaurants *(continued)*

**Flying Fish Cafe** — D $70 — DDP2 — 8 8 8

*This is a Disney dining hot spot and one of our favorites, serving uniquely prepared, fresh seafood in a trendy-but-fun atmosphere. The menu changes to suit the season and the catch. Appetizers are special. Dave was blown away by plump steamed mussels in a pastis-flavored cream. The "Chef's Thunder" portion of the menu offers daily specialties, such as coriander-crusted Yellowfin Tuna ($32), while the main menu may offer a remarkable red snapper in a crispy, sliced-potato wrapper ($34) or herb-crusted alaskan halibut ($34). There's strip steak, chicken, and pasta for the fish-shy ($38–$39) and not-to-be-missed desserts. The crowds here are loud—ask for a quieter table in the back. Open to 10:30 on Fri. and Sat. Dress code is "business casual" (see page 204).*

Table | Seafood | Very noisy | Reservations strongly recommended | Call 180 days | Med. waits | 5:30 pm–10 pm

**Spoodles** — B $14, D $48 — DDPT — 6 7 6

*Fresh seafood, grilled meats, oak-fired flatbreads, pastas, and other Italian, Greek, and Spanish specialties grace the menu. A satisfying breakfast offers popular items plus Italian frittata and breakfast flatbread ($8.99–$9.99) and an all-you-can-eat breakfast platter ($11.99). At dinner, start with flatbread ($9.99) or grilled lamb kebubs with chickpea salad ($7.99), or make a meal of these Spanish-style appetizers. Entrees include a rigatoni ($17.99); Tuscan-pressed cornish game hen ($19.49); and lemon-garlic shrimp linguine ($18.99). Desserts ($4.49–$11.99) include gelato, creme brulee, and chocolate apricot pistachio cake. A take-out pizza window is available, too.*

Table | Mediterranean | Noisy | Reservations recommended | Call 180 days | Short waits | 7:30–11 am, 5–10 pm

## Caribbean Beach Resort Restaurant

**Shutters** — D $41 — DDPT — 6 6 6

*Serving American cuisine inspired by the flavors of the Caribbean, this 120-seat, casual family restaurant has a breezy, island atmosphere. In all ways, a big improvement over the old Captain's Tavern. Menu items include a delicious baked onion soup ($5.49), penne pasta with shrimp ($13.49–$16.99), and herb-roasted chicken ($15.99). Their signature smoked prime rib ($20.99) is just average. For dessert, go with the key lime tart ($5.49).*

Table | Caribbean/American | Reservations suggested | 5:30–10 pm

## Contemporary Resort Restaurants

**California Grill** — D $66 — DDP2 — 8 8 8

*High atop the Contemporary, overlooking the Magic Kingdom, the California Grill pours fine wines, serves yummy California cuisine, and keeps getting better! The noise can be deafening, but the fireworks bursting over Cinderella Castle are spectacular. The menu changes weekly, but count on inventive sushi ($16–$24), flatbreads ($10–$14), grilled or roasted seafood and meats ($23–$35), and sinful desserts. Perennial picks include grilled pork tenderloin ($24) and oak-fired beef filet ($35). Vegetarians do well. Warm Valrhona chocolate cake ($10) is a sinful dessert. When available, the peaceful Wine Room has the same menu, and you may see Epcot's IllumiNations. Sushi bar seating, too. Kids' menu is $7–$11. Dress code is "business casual" (see page 204). Note: Diners check in on the second floor of the Contemporary and are escorted up to the 15th floor when their table is ready. $20/person cancellation fee.*

Table | American | Very noisy | Reservations strongly recommended | Call 180 days | Long waits | 5:30 pm–10:00 pm

# Resort Restaurants
## (Contemporary, Coronado Springs, and Fort Wilderness Resorts)

Jennifer's Rating | Dave's Rating | Readers' Rating

## Contemporary Resort Restaurants *(continued)*

### Chef Mickey's — B $24, D $35 — DDPT — 6 | 6 | 8

*Chef Mickey's fills the Contemporary's cavernous lobby with all sorts of Goofy antics (not to mention Mickey, Minnie, and friends). Mickey's offers separate adult and kid's dinner buffets ($27.99/$12.99 kids 3-9) and a sundae bar. Breakfast buffet ($18.99/$10.99) includes omelettes and pancakes cooked to order. Dinner items change, but on our last visit, we had flavorful roast beef, tasty pork loin, and cod with a curry crust, all of a quality and presentation befitting a deluxe resort.* *See pages 234–235 for character meal details.*

**Buffet** | American | Very noisy | Reservations suggested | 7-11:30 am, 5:00-9:30 pm

### Concourse Steakhouse — B $18, L $37, D $43 — DDPT — 6 | 7 | 8

*Appealing touches on the appetizers and entrees lift the Concourse a cut above your typical steakhouse. Situated in the towering lobby of the Contemporary, it's a sane alternative when the California Grill is busy. Concourse's morning menu ($6.99-$14.99) includes eggs Benedict ($9.99). Lunch brings sandwiches ($9.99-$13.99) and penne pasta ($13.99). Dinner includes lobster bisque ($6.99), roasted half chicken ($15.99), steaks and prime rib ($19.99-$26.99), and a salmon BLT ($13.99). This eatery is expected to close in spring 2008—the space will be converted into a counter-service spot that will open in mid-August 2008.*

**Table** | Steakhouse | Reservations suggested | Call 180 days | 7:30-11 am, Noon-2:00 pm, 5:30-10:00 pm

The Contemporary's ground floor will host a new restaurant in late 2008 or 2009. Tentatively named "**The Wave**", this eatery is rumored to offer inventive sushi and Pan-Asian cuisine. Watch our web site for updates.

## Coronado Springs Resort Restaurant

### Maya Grill — B $21, D $51 — DDPT — 5 | 6 | 5

*Alas, this formerly inventive spot has become a nearly ordinary steakhouse with appealing Mexican/Southwestern items among the appetizers, catering to the resort's conventioneers. If you're hankering for Mexican food, try the resort's food court instead. The restaurant is almost too elegant for a moderate resort, with grand, soaring architecture evoking a Mayan temple in warm yellows and accents of deep blue, shimmering gold, and rich woods. The breakfast buffet offers the standards with a Southwestern flair ($16.95/$9.95). The dinner menu includes steaks and mixed grill ($19.99-$29.99), BBQ ribs ($19.99), marinated rack of lamb ($23.99), and salmon filet ($22.99). Kids' menu available ($8.25-$8.95).*

**Table** | American | Med. noise | Reservations suggested | Call 180 days | Short waits | 7-11 am, 5-10 pm

## Fort Wilderness Resort Restaurant

### Trail's End Restaurant — B $15, L $18, D $28 — DDPT — 7 | 6 | 6

*One of the best dining deals on Disney property. While the vittles at Trail's End won't win awards for elegance, the food is plentiful, fresh, and tasty. Breakfasts ($11.99/$7.99 kids 3-9) are hearty and heavy on home-style classics—eggs, French toast, Mickey waffles, hash, donuts, biscuits and gravy, cereals, yogurt, and fruit. Lunch ($12.99/$8.99) brings rib-stickin' fare like fried chicken, mac and cheese, BBQ, pizza, turkey wraps, and a passable salad bar. Dinner is gentle on the wallet at $17.99 ($9.99 ages 3-9) and you still get a tasty soup, salad bar, peel-and-eat shrimp, chicken, ribs, carved meat, fish, good veggies, pizza, a daily regional specialty like venison stew, and fruit cobbler for dessert. Soup & Salad bar is $11.50.*

**Buffet** | American | Med. noise | Reservations accepted | Short waits | 7:30-11 am, Noon-2:30 pm, 4:30-9:30 pm

*Eatery descriptions and ratings are explained on page 206.*

# Resort Restaurants

**(Grand Floridian Resort)**

## Grand Floridian Resort Restaurants

Jennifer's Rating | Dave's Rating | Readers' Rating

### Cítricos — D $61 — DDP2 — 9 | 8 | 9

*A grand restaurant at the Grand Floridian, Cítricos blends the fresh flavors of Florida and the Mediterranean with simplicity and elegance. Warm colors, tall windows, and well-spaced tables make this a very comfortable place. The menu changes frequently, but the sauteed shrimp ($12.00) and mushroom ravioli ($9.00) are appealing appetizers. A wonderful braised veal shank is available as an entree ($33.00), along with sauteed wild king salmon ($34.00), and seared tofu ($23.00). The wine pairings ($29.50) are a fine idea, and the desserts ($8.00) are gorgeous! Closed Mondays and Tuesdays. Kids' menu ($5.49–$12.00) available. Dress code is "business casual" (see page 204).*

**Table** | Floridian | Med. noise | Reservations suggested | Call 180 days | Short waits | 5:30–9:30 pm

### Garden View Lounge — S $25 — 8 | 7 | 5

*If you've ever yearned for afternoon tea, this is the place for it. The quiet, genteel Victorian setting is perfect for tea sandwiches, scones, and pastries ($2.75–$12.75), or do it right with an all-inclusive tea "offering" ($10.50–$25.50). A good variety of teas is served. Site of "My Disney Girl's Tea Party" (see page 246).*

**Lounge** | English | Call 180 days | 2–6 pm

### Grand Floridian Cafe — B $30, L $33, D $41 — DDPT — 5 | 6 | 6

*This "informal" cafe features an American menu with all the extra flourishes found in finer restaurants. Hearty breakfasts include corned beef hash or eggs Benedict ($8.99–$16.99). Lunch brings entree salads ($12.99–$15.99), shrimp and pasta ($17.99), and sandwiches including a Reuben and Philly cheese steak ($9.99–$12.99). Dinner offers a short menu with steak, prime rib, grilled fish, and pasta ($16.99–$25.99), plus burgers ($11.99).*

**Table** | American | Very noisy | 7–11 am, 11:45 am–2 pm, 5–9 pm

### Narcoossee's — D $73 — DDP2 — 8 | 8 | 8

*Narcoossee's open kitchen serves an ever-changing menu of grilled seafoods with savory accompaniments. Perched on the edge of Seven Seas Lagoon, the restaurant has a sedate and casual dockside atmosphere, with lots of bare wood and windows affording views of the Magic Kingdom fireworks and the Electrical Water Pageant. The huge appetizer of steamed mussels was heavenly ($15.00), as was the grilled salmon ($31.00). Sesame-crusted Ahi tuna ($32.00), and steamed Maine lobster ($59.00) are also tempting choices, and meat lovers can order filet mignon ($35.00) or Tanglewood chicken breast ($26.00). Desserts ($7.00–$12.00) include assorted berry pyramid and Key Lime créme brulée. Kids' menu ($6.00–$13.00) available. Dress code is "business casual" (see page 204).*

**Table** | Seafood | Noisy | Reservations recommended | Call 180 days | Short waits | 6–10 pm (lounge open 5–10 pm)

### 1900 Park Fare — B $24, D $36 — DDPT — 7 | 7 | 7

*Daily character meals in a jolly Victorian setting renovated in fall 2007, complete with an orchestrion ("player" organ). The upscale buffet breakfast ($18.99/$10.99 kids 3–9) features Mary Poppins, Alice in Wonderland, and their friends. Waits can be long, but characters may be on hand to keep you occupied. At dinner time ($28.99/$13.99), Cinderella and friends take their turn hosting. You don't really come for the food, but this is one of Disney's finer buffets (keep your eyes open for the strawberry soup—it's scrumptious). The Wonderland Tea Party is held here for kids on Mondays–Fridays. See pages 234–235 and 246 for details.*

**Buffet** | American | Very noisy | Reservations recommended | Call 180 days | 8:00–11:30 am 4:30–8:30 pm

# Resort Restaurants

**(Grand Floridian, Old Key West, and Polynesian Resorts)**

Jennifer's Rating | Dave's Rating | Readers' Rating

## Grand Floridian Resort Restaurants *(continued)*

| Victoria & Albert's | D $158 | 10 | 10 | 9 |
|---|---|---|---|---|

*You have to dress up for Walt Disney World's five-star dining experience—jackets are required and a tux or gown isn't entirely out of place. The continental, five-course, prix fixe menu ($125) is redesigned daily, a harpist fills the air with music, and ladies receive roses at meal's end. For an extra-special evening, reserve the "Chef's Table," an alcove in the kitchen where you observe and interact with the chef and staff ($125, reserve six months in advance). Consider a wine pairing ($60) to perfectly match your meal. Is it all worth it? Without a doubt! Your dinner is elegantly prepared, and each course brings new delights. We held our wedding dinner here. Need we say more? State special dietary needs in advance. Call 407-824-1089 to confirm 24 hours in advance.*

Table | French | Quiet | Reservations required—call 407-824-1089 | Call 180 days | Short waits | 5:45 pm & 9:00 pm

## Old Key West Resort Restaurant

| Olivia's Cafe | B $20, L $35, D $42 | 6 | 6 | 5 |
|---|---|---|---|---|

*Olivia's Cafe serves an enticing array of Southern- and Caribbean-tinged specialties in a homey, small-island atmosphere. Breakfast includes the classics and a lineup of healthy items ($7.99–$9.99). Lunchtime brings conch chowder ($4.69), salads ($5.49–$13.99), Reuben and roast beef sandwiches ($9.99). At dinner, the crab cake ($10.49), prime rib ($20.99), barbecue grouper ($19.99), and park chop glazed with dark rum ($18.99) will make you smile, and don't pass up the Key Lime tart ($5.49) or individual apple pies ($5.49). Reservations are not always necessary here.*

Table | Floridian | Med. noise | Short waits | Call 180 days | 7:30–10:30 am, 11:30 am–5 pm, 5–10 pm

## Polynesian Resort Restaurants

*See page 237 for the Polynesian Luau*

| Kona Cafe | B $18, L $36, D $45 | 8 | 7 | 8 |
|---|---|---|---|---|

*A stylish spot for coffee and full meals. Its Asian/eclectic menu brings welcome sophistication to the Polynesian Resort. Breakfasts include banana-stuffed "Tonga Toast" ($8.99) and tropical fruit punch ($3.99). Lunch offers a huge teriyaki beef salad ($11.99), a satisfying Asian noodle bowl ($13.99), and a tasty BBQ pork sandwich ($9.99). The appetizers are attractive, and dinners offer steaks, chicken, and seafood with an Asian flair ($14.49–$25.49), including Macadamia-crusted Mahi Mahi ($19.99). Fabulous coffee bar (mornings only) and desserts, too! (The specialty is "Ko Ko Puffs.")*

Table | International | Noisy | Reservations recommended | Call 180 days | 7:30–11:30 am, Noon–3:00 pm, 5–10 pm

| 'Ohana | B $19, D $31 | 8 | 7 | 7 |
|---|---|---|---|---|

*Aloha, cousins! The Polynesian Resort welcomes you warmly to 'Ohana, a great, fun spot for families and groups. This is an all-you-care-to-eat feast ($25.99/$11.99 kids 3–9). Appetizers (salad, wonton, and wings) and veggies are served family-style, then the cast members circulate with long skewers of grilled steak, turkey, sausage, and pork. Kids can do coconut races and hula hoop contests, and entertainers sing Hawaiian melodies. If you work things right, you may even see the Magic Kingdom fireworks! Soft drinks and bread pudding dessert included. The tropical drinks in unusual containers are extra. 'Ohana also hosts a character breakfast ($18.99/$10.99 ages 3–9) with Lilo and Stitch: "'Ohana means family-style dining, which means no one gets leftovers!" See pages 234–235.*

Table | Polynesian | Very noisy | Reservations strongly recommended | Call 180 days | Long waits | 7:30–11 am, 5–10 pm

*Eatery descriptions and ratings are explained on page 206.*

# Resort Restaurants

**(Port Orleans, Saratoga Springs, and Swan and Dolphin Resorts)**

Jennifer's Rating | Dave's Rating | Readers' Rating

## Port Orleans Riverside Resort Restaurant

**Boatwright's Dining Hall** — B $18, D $42 — DDP — 7 | 5 | 7

*Cajun cooking from down the bayou fits the bill perfectly. In keeping with the restaurant's theme, a wooden boat hangs overhead and boat-builders' tools hang on the rustic walls. This is a place for hearty, Southern-style breakfasts such as big omelettes ($8.99) and sweet potato pancakes ($7.29). Dinner offers crab cakes ($9.49), jambalaya ($17.49), penne pasta ($16.99), herb-roasted chicken ($15.99), and sirloin steak ($19.99). Kids' meals are $4.29 at breakfast and $7.49 at dinner.*

Table | American | Call 180 days | Short waits | 7:30–11:30 am, 5–10 pm

## Saratoga Springs Resort Restaurant

**Turf Club Bar and Grill** — L $39, D $41 — DDP — 6 | 6 | 6

*Recently expanded from its former incarnation as a lounge, this table-service eatery offers wholesome American fare. Menu items include crab cakes ($10.49) and fried calamari ($9.49) for starters. Entrees include spiced salmon salad ($16.99), Angus chuck cheeseburger ($11.49), barbecued spare ribs ($17.99), and penne pasta with shrimp ($18.99). Desserts are $5.49–$5.99. Kids' meals are $7.49 (pita pizza, grilled chicken, fruit, mac & cheese, or hamburger).*

Table | American | Call 180 days | Short waits | 12:00–5:00 pm, 5:00–9:00 pm

## Swan and Dolphin Resort Restaurants

**bluezoo** [Dolphin] — D $70 — 6 | 7 | 7

*Star chef Todd English presents upscale, inventively prepared seafood at this visually striking establishment. The scallop appetizer with braised short rib ($12) was a savory adventure, the "Dancing Fish" ($27) disappointing, filo baked salmon a winner, and other choices ($20–$52) were satisfying. Separate, lighter menu at the crowded cafe/bar. Not kid-friendly. Dave prefers nearby Flying Fish Cafe.*

Table | Seafood | Noisy | Call 180 days | 5 pm–11 pm

**Fresh Mediterranean Market** [Dolphin] — B $19, L $29 — 8 | 7 | 8

*This cheery and appealing variation on a buffet offers a wide variety of cooked-to-order items at breakfast ($17.95/$10.95) and lunch ($18.95/$11.95). The very attentive chefs ply you with all sorts of temptations, both Mediterranean-style and American, all prepared with a light, "fresh" hand. Grilled and rotisseried meats, pastas, cold salads, veggies, and lots of desserts, too!*

Buffet | Mediterranean | Med. noise | Call 180 days | 6 am–2 pm

**Gulliver's Grill at Garden Grove** [Swan] — B $19, L $35, D $50 — 5 | 6 | 8

*By day, this is the Garden Grove Cafe, offering breakfast and lunch. There's a satisfying breakfast buffet ($16.99/$10.99 kids 3–9), a Japanese breakfast ($17.95), a la carte selections, and a character breakfast on weekends from 8:00 to 11:00 am ($18.99/$11.99). Lunch offers salads, sandwiches, and light entrees ($6.50–$14.95). Each night of the week, this eatery is transformed into Gulliver's, a character dining experience (see pages 234–235). Dinner offers a buffet ($28.99–$31.99/$12.99 kids 3–9) with a rotating theme. A la carte also available. Reserve at 407-934-1609.*

Table | American | Noisy | Call 180 days | 6:30–11:30 am, 11:30 am–2 pm, 5:30–10 pm

**Kimonos** [Swan] — D $46, S — 6 | 7 | 6

*In search of excellent late-night sushi, drinks, and karaoke? Try the Swan! Dinner is possible ($19.50–$23.50), or snack on sushi by the piece ($4.00–$12.95) and hot appetizers ($3.25–$13.95) while you get up the nerve to sing (if you want). Very noisy. Reservations accepted for parties of 6+ (call 407-934-1609).*

Table | Japanese | Noisy | 5:30 pm–12 am

# Resort Restaurants
## (Swan and Dolphin and Wilderness Lodge Resorts)

Jennifer's Rating | Dave's Rating | Readers' Rating

## Swan and Dolphin Resorts Restaurants *(continued)*

### Il Mulino New York Trattoria (formerly Palio) [Swan] D $65 — 8 8 7

*This traditional Italian eatery replaced Palio in early 2007. The extensive (if pricey) menu features dishes from the Abruzzi region of Italy, including arancini rice balls ($8), a raw bar platter ($36 for two), carpaccio ($14), pizzas ($16), risotto con funghi ($26), gnocchi bolognese ($24), bistecca ribeye steak ($36), saltimbocca ($33), and seared red snapper ($29). Desserts are heavenly, especially the torta di cioccolati (flourless chocolate cake–$8). At meal's end, adults are served complimentary glasses of limoncello, a sweet digestif.*

*Il Mulino's Dining Room*

Table | Italian | Very noisy | Reservations suggested–407-WDW-DINE | 5 pm–11 pm

### Shula's Steak House [Dolphin] D $79 — 8 8 9

*This is the most upscale steakhouse on Disney property. Beautifully grilled, flavorful beef is the focus (if you finish the 48-oz. porterhouse, they'll engrave your name on a plaque!) but perfectly succulent fish ($25.95–$26.95) gets the utmost respect. Grilled meats cost from $22.95 to $75.00. If you need to ask the "market price" of the 4-lb. lobster, you can't afford it! With dark wood paneling, Sinatra on the speakers, gilt-framed football photos, and formal, attentive service, you may prefer to wear a jacket or dress. Veggies are $6.95–$7.95 (split an order, and get the potato pancake, too) but the "garnish" of peppers, watercress, and mushrooms on every plate may be enough. The wine list is expansive and expensive. And order the chocolate soufflé for two ($13.00)!*

Table | Steakhouse | Med. noise | Reservations suggested; call 407-WDW-DINE | Call 180 days | Short waits | 5 pm–11 pm

## Wilderness Lodge Resort Restaurants

### Artist Point D $62 DDP2 — 10 9 8

*This visually stunning restaurant serves flavorful contemporary fare from the Pacific Northwest and is among our favorites. The dining room is a soaring, log-beamed space graced by large murals of Western landscapes and furnished with comfortable, Mission-style tables and chairs. The menu changes seasonally. For starters, try venison spring rolls ($8), braised mussels ($12), or smoky portobello soup ($7). The old-standby cedar plank salmon ($32) is always rewarding, or try Berkshire pork chop ($28), potato chive pot stickers ($21), or seafood and vegetarian entrees ($21–$27). For dessert, the hot berry cobbler is a must ($8). The wine list is excellent–try a wine pairing. Dress code is "business casual" (see page 204). This restaurant offers the Dine with an Imagineer experience–see page 239.*

Table | American | Med. noise | Reservations suggested | Call 180 days | Short waits | 5:30 pm–10:00 pm

### Whispering Canyon Cafe B $29, L $35, D $43 DDPT — 8 6 8

*If you hanker for really fine barbecue in a rustic Wild West setting, sashay over to the Wilderness Lodge. There are a la carte choices ($13.99–$20.99 at dinner), but most get the family-style, all-you-can-eat "skillets." The breakfast skillet is $10.99/$6.29 kids 3–9. Lunch ($14.99/$9.49) and dinner ($22.49/$9.49) bring oven-roasted chicken, ribs, pork, shrimp, and all the fixin's. This is "dry" barbecue–marinated and smoked, with four sauces on the side. Just don't ask for ketchup. Trust us! There are activities for the kids, and the servers make sure all have fun. Hours: 7:30–11:00 am, Noon–3:00 pm, and 5:00–10:00 pm.*

Table | Barbecue | Very noisy | Reservations a must | Call 180 days | Long waits | 7:30 am–10 pm

*Eatery descriptions and ratings are explained on page 206.*

# Resort Restaurants

## (Yacht and Beach Club Resorts and Wide World of Sports)

Jennifer's Rating | Dave's Rating | Readers' Rating

## Yacht and Beach Club Resorts Restaurants

| Cape May Cafe [Beach Club] B $24, D $33 DDPT | 7 7 8 |
|---|---|
| *Seafood lovers line up for this dinner buffet ($25.99/$11.99 kids 3-9), which is within walking distance of Epcot and five resort hotels. An endless supply of chowder, steamed hard shell clams, mussels, baked fish, prime rib, corn on the cob, and all the trimmings will make any seafood lover happy as a clam. There's plenty for the fish-shy, a kids' buffet (mac & cheese, mini hot dogs, fish nuggets, and chicken strips), a dessert bar, and they bring taffy with the check. The character breakfast buffet ($18.99/$10.99) is prized for its relaxed atmosphere (see pages 234-235). Chairs and booths.* | **Buffet**<br>Seafood<br>Noisy<br>Reservations recommended<br>Call 180 days<br>7:30-11 am, 5:30-9:30 pm |

| Yacht Club Galley [Yacht Club] B $24, L $33, D $41 DDPT | 4 5 8 |
|---|---|
| *This casual-yet-typical hotel café offers pleasant surroundings at breakfast, lunch, and dinner. Traditional favorites and a healthy helping of meat and seafood dishes are the specialty here. Breakfast offers a buffet ($15.99/$8.99 kids 3-9) and a la carte selections ($4.99-$13.99). Lunch brings salads ($5.49-$13.99), cheeseburgers ($10.99), and a crab cake sandwich ($13.99). Dinner resembles lunch: sandwiches, dinner salads, and a few entrees ($9.99-$16.99).* | **Table**<br>American<br>Short waits<br>7:00-11 am, 11:30 am-2 pm, 6:00-10:00 pm |

| Yachtsman Steakhouse [Yacht Club] D $76 DDP2 | 7 7 9 |
|---|---|
| *Until Shula's opened, Yachtsman Steakhouse was the best steakhouse at Disney and it still comes close. Hardwood-grilled steaks are the main attraction at dinner, but vegetarians haven't been neglected (try the squash ravioli, $21). Appetizers include lobster bisque ($9), Maine diver scallops ($13), and salads ($8-$11). Plain and sauced meats ($28-$80) including a popular peppercorn-glazed strip steak ($36), porterhouse ($42), filet mignon ($34), rib eye ($42), and prime rib ($32) fill the menu, plus chateaubriand for two ($80). Excellent wine and beer list. Kids entrees are $6-$12. Dress code is "business casual" (see page 204).* | **Table**<br>Steakhouse<br>Med. noise<br>Reservations strongly suggested<br>Call 180 days<br>5:30-9:45 pm |

| Beaches and Cream L $27, D $27, S DDPT | 8 6 8 |
|---|---|
| *This small, seaside-style ice cream parlor is always jammed. Sure, you can get classic luncheonette items like burgers ($7.89-$9.89), roast beef sandwiches ($8.99), veggie burgers ($7.49), and hot dogs ($6.49), plus shakes and malts ($4.99), but you know everyone is here for the ice cream. Why not cut to the chase and go for an ice cream soda, float, ice cream, frozen yogurt, or sundae ($2.69-$7.99). Or get the Kitchen Sink ($21.99), a huge sundae with every topping. Sit at tables, booths, or at the counter. The average meal costs above are for a "light" meal (no appetizers are available). No reservations. Take-out for ice cream is also available.* | **Table**<br>American<br>Very noisy<br>No reservations<br>Long waits<br>11:00 am-11:00 pm |

## Wide World of Sports

| All-Star Cafe | ? ? ? |
|---|---|
| *The All-Star Cafe is slated to close in fall 2007 and reopen by November 20 as a new counter-service eatery. Details are not known at this time, but we think it's likely the eatery's star-powered decor, 55 TVs for watching the game, a video arcade, and sports memorabilia may remain, along with American fare. Expect it to be closed when no events are held.* | **Counter?**<br>American<br>Reservations not accepted<br>Hours unknown |

# Character Meals

Disney offers many opportunities to dine with characters, both those in full guise (like Mickey Mouse) and "face characters" in costume (like Cinderella). While they don't actually sit with you throughout your meal, they do roam around the restaurant and visit your table for interludes. Character meals are generally more expensive than regular meals (ranging from $19 to $45 for adults and $12 to $28 for kids ages 3–9), but the chance to meet the characters in an unhurried atmosphere makes it worthwhile. Even if characters aren't at the top of your menu, character dinners are a good deal—the cost of these buffets and family style meals is usually less than comparable full-service meals when you factor all costs. Character meals are *extremely* popular—make reservations as far in advance as possible at 407-WDW-DINE. Bring your camera and an autograph book!

Be aware that there's a mad rush for reservations for breakfast and lunch at Cinderella's Royal Table in the Magic Kingdom. Folks start phoning at 7:00 am Eastern time, exactly 180 days prior to their desired date, and tables are often gone in a matter of minutes. If you get a table at Cinderella's, expect to pay for the meal in full by credit card at the time of reservation—this payment is refunded if you cancel 48 hours in advance. If you miss out, don't despair. Try again once you get to Disney. Cancellations are possible, so it never hurts to ask for a table, even as you're walking through Cinderella Castle. If you are set on dining with a princess, try the character meals at Akershus Royal Banquet Hall or the character dinner at 1900 Park Fare.

- ✔ Some character breakfasts start prior to park opening. All Disney resorts offer special Disney bus transportation to the early character breakfasts.
- ✔ For the best character experience, dine off-hours. While Mickey may only give you a quick hello during busy mealtimes, you might end up with a close, personal relationship when tables are empty.
- ✔ Don't be shy, grown-ups! Even if you aren't dining with kids, the characters visit your table. If you'd rather sit things out, they will simply give you a nod or handshake.
- ✔ The "head" characters don't speak, but that doesn't mean you have to keep quiet around them. Talk to them and they'll pantomime and play along!

*Alexander holds hands with a furry friend at the Crystal Palace character meal. (His friend asked to remain anonymous because he's so bashful.)*

- ✔ Most character meals take just one table-service credit on the Disney Dining Plan.

# Character Dining Location Chart

The chart below shows all the character meals at the time of writing. The location of each meal is given in parentheses, along with the meal served (B=breakfast or brunch, L=lunch, D=dinner, All=all three meals), the type (buffet=buffet-style, family=family-style, plate=buffet items brought to you on a plate, menu=from the menu), and the prominent characters (note that a specific character's appearance is not guaranteed).

| Restaurant | Meal | Type | Characters |
|---|---|---|---|
| Akershus Royal Banquet Hall DDPT | All | Family | Snow White, Belle, Jasmine |
| *Dine in a castle with princesses (but don't expect Cinderella). (Page 210)* | | | |
| Cape May Cafe (Beach Club) DDPT | B | Buffet | Goofy, Chip, Dale, Pluto |
| *Casual, beach party atmosphere and good, standard breakfast foods. (Page 233)* | | | |
| Chef Mickey's (Contemporary) DDPT | B/D | Buffet | Mickey, Minnie Goofy, Pluto |
| *Bustling, popular destination. Superior food. Try to dine at off-hours. (Page 228)* | | | |
| Cinderella's Royal Table (MK) DDP2 | B/L | Plate | Cinderella, Belle, Aurora |
| *Gorgeous setting, hottest reservation at WDW. Original "princess" meal. (Page 207)* | | | |
| Crystal Palace (MK) DDPT | All | Buffet | Pooh, Tigger, Eeyore, Piglet |
| *A favorite spot for satisfying meals in bright and airy surroundings. (Page 207)* | | | |
| Donald's Breakfastosaurus (AK) DDPT | B | Buffet | Donald, Mickey, Goofy |
| *Ends November 5, 2007. Crowded and noisy, but lots of fun. (Page 220)* | | | |
| Donald's Safari Breakfast (AK) DDPT | B | Buffet | Donald, Mickey, Goofy |
| *Begins November 18, 2007. Details not known at press time. (Page 221)* | | | |
| The Garden Grill (Epcot) DDPT | L/D | Plate | Mickey, Chip, Dale, Pluto |
| *Tasty dining in an unusual setting. Good spur-of-the-moment choice. (Page 212)* | | | |
| Gulliver's/Garden Grove (Swan) | B/D[1] | Buffet/Menu | Timon or Goofy |
| *A la carte menu makes this an expensive character dinner. (Page 231)* | | | |
| Hollywood & Vine (Studios) DDPT | B/D | Buffet | JoJo, Goliath, Little Einsteins |
| *Play 'n Dine character meal appeals to the Playhouse Disney set. (Page 217)* | | | |
| Liberty Tree Tavern (MK) DDPT | D | Family | Goofy, Pluto, Minnie |
| *Thanksgiving-style feast with Colonial-garbed characters. (Page 208)* | | | |
| My Disney Girl's Tea Party (GF) | Tea[2] | Snack | Princess Aurora |
| *A special tea and brunch, plus a My Disney Girl doll. (Pages 229 and 246)* | | | |
| 1900 Park Fare (Grand Floridian) DDPT | B/D | Buffet | Mary Poppins (B) Cinderella (D) |
| *First-rate food, comfy Victorian surroundings, and lots of character. (Page 229)* | | | |
| 'Ohana (Polynesian) DDPT | B | Family | Lilo, Stitch, Mickey, Pluto |
| *Aloha, Cousins! A relaxed atmosphere (no more Minnie, alas!). (Page 230)* | | | |
| Wonderland Tea Party (GF) | Tea[3] | Snack | Alice in Wonderland |
| *"Tea," stories, and cupcakes with Alice at 1900 Park Fare. (Page 229)* | | | |

1 *Character breakfasts are weekends at 8:00–11:00 am; dinners are held 6:00–10:00 pm every night (Timon and Rafiki on Mon. and Fri., and Goofy and Pluto on all other nights).*

2 *My Disney Girl's Princess Tea Party has limited availability—see page 246 for details.*

3 *Wonderland Tea Parties are held Monday through Friday, 1:30–2:30 pm.*

# Dinner Shows

## Hoop-Dee-Doo Musical Revue DD P2

The Hoop-Dee-Doo Musical Revue is a **hilarious hoedown** in an Old West-style dance hall at the Fort Wilderness Resort. The song-and-dance vaudeville act relies heavily on slapstick humor, hokey gags, corny puns, and lots of audience participation. The Wild West performers interact with the audience, and guests celebrating birthdays and anniversaries may be singled out for special attention.

*We've been lucky to get this stage-side table at the Hoop-Dee-Doo twice!*

The **all-you-care-to-eat meal** includes salad, barbecue ribs, fried chicken, corn, baked beans, and bread, with strawberry shortcake for dessert (kids can request mac and cheese and hot dogs instead). Complimentary beverages include soda, beer, and sangria—cocktails can be ordered, but they are not included in the price.

**Prices vary by seat category**—cheapest seats are in category 3 (left or right side of the balcony) at $50.99/adults and $25.99/kids 3–9 (prices include taxes and gratuities). Category 2 seats are $54.99/adults and $26.99/kids 3–9 and are located in the back of the main floor or in the center of the balcony. Category 1 premium seats are $58.99/adults and $29.99/kids 3–9, located front and/or center on the main floor. Guests who need wheelchair access may only be seated in category 1. Disney Dining Plan credits are accepted here (two credits per person) for categories 2 and 3 only. Shows are at 5:00 pm, 7:15 pm, and 9:30 pm nightly (the 9:30 pm show is the easiest to get in). A photo is taken before the show, and you can purchase photo packages from a cast member who circulates during dinner.

This show is **very popular**—reserve up to 180 days in advance at 407-WDW-DINE. The earlier you reserve, the better your table (within your category, of course). Full payment is required with reservation, refundable up to 48 hours in advance. Hoop-Dee-Doo Musical Revue is located in Pioneer Hall at the Fort Wilderness Resort. See travel directions below.

### Mickey's Backyard Barbecue DD P2

This old-fashioned, open-air barbecue features good ol' Disney characters (Minnie, Mickey, Goofy, Chip, and Dale), live country music, carnival games, and line dancing. Vittles include chicken, hot dogs, ribs, salads, corn, cole slaw, beans, vegetables, rolls, and (of course!) watermelon—all served buffet-style at picnic tables under a huge pavilion. Includes all-you-can-drink soft drinks and beer. Typically held on Thursdays and Sundays at 6:30 (ends at 9:30 pm) from March through December. Cost: $44.99/adults and $26.99/kids 3–9 (prices include all taxes and gratuities). Call 407-WDW-DINE to inquire about availability and reservations. Full payment is now required with your reservations, refundable up to 48 hours in advance.

### Getting to the Fort Wilderness Dinner Shows

To get to either Hoop-Dee-Doo or Backyard Barbecue, take the boat to Fort Wilderness from the Magic Kingdom, Contemporary, or Wilderness Lodge. Special buses run to and from some resorts, or take any Fort Wilderness-bound theme park bus. Driving (parking is free) is an option, too. The Hoop-Dee-Doo is in Pioneer Hall; Backyard Barbecue is next door to Pioneer Hall (around back). Allow 60 to 90 minutes for travel.

# Spirit of Aloha Dinner (Polynesian Luau) DD PP2

Aloha! The Spirit of Aloha Dinner is an **exotic, South Pacific-style celebration** of color, style, history, music, and dance. Everything you expect from a luau is here—women in "grass" skirts, men in face paint, fire dancers, plus traditional music and a little bit of Elvis—showcasing the cultures and traditions of Polynesia and connecting them all to the modern Hawaii seen in Lilo and Stitch. The show is held together by Auntie Wini, the heart of a group of young islanders who have learned to love traditional values including 'ohana (family). The show is held nightly in Luau Cove, an outdoor stage surrounded by a torch-lit garden. Upon arrival, guests are presented with a complimentary lei and entertained in the garden before dinner. While you wait for the show, you can buy drinks and souvenirs and have a family photo taken. Guests are seated at long, wooden tables that fan out from the stage, all under shelter in the event of rain.

The **all-you-care-to-eat meal**, served family-style for your party, includes salad, fresh pineapple, roasted chicken, BBQ ribs, rice, and sautéed vegetables, with a special "volcano dessert" (shown in photo below—the name is the most exciting part). Included with your meal is your choice of unlimited soda, coffee, iced tea, milk, beer, and wine. Specialty drinks are extra. The show begins after dinner with Hawaiian music and plenty of South Seas dancing by both men and women. Kids are quite welcome at the Luau—young ones will be invited on stage for a special dance number. Photos taken before the show are circulated during dinner by a cast member.

**Prices vary by seat category**—cheapest seats are in category 3 (extreme far left or right of the stage on the lower level, or on the upper level) at $50.99/adults and $25.99/kids 3-9 (prices include taxes and gratuities). Category 2 seats are $54.99/adults and $26.99/kids 3-9 and are located on the left or right side of the stage, or on the upper level tables in the center. Category 1 premium seats are $58.99/adults and $29.99/kids 3-9, located front and/or center on the lower level. Disney Dining Plan credits are accepted here (two credits per person) for categories 2 and 3 only. Shows are held at 5:15 pm and 8:00 pm, Tuesdays through Saturdays. We prefer the later seating as the darkness adds to the mystique and romance of the show. Ask about discounts for the late show. In the cooler months, the late show may be canceled.

*The Spirit of "Alooooha!"*

**Make your reservations as early as possible** (up to 180 days in advance)—they book up early. Full payment is required with your reservation, refundable up to 48 hours prior to the show.

### Getting to the Polynesian Dinner Show

To get to the Polynesian dinner show, either drive directly to the Polynesian Resort or take the monorail from the Magic Kingdom or Epcot. From other parks and resorts, bus to the Magic Kingdom and take the monorail (daytime) or bus to Downtown Disney and transfer to a Polynesian bus. Once inside the resort, follow signs to Luau Cove. Allow plenty of time for travel, especially if coming from another resort.

# Special Shows

### Holidays

Holidays are always special at the Walt Disney World Resort. The parks and resorts overflow with special entertainment and decorations that vary from season to season and year to year (see pages 258–259 for details). The Christmas and New Year's season is especially magical, with all kinds of celebrations throughout the property. One big Christmas favorite is the Candlelight Processional at World Showcase in Epcot, which is available free to Epcot guests (show only) or as an Epcot lunch or dinner package PP offering special seating for the show (call 407-WDW-DINE).

### House of Blues

House of Blues has a concert hall separate from its restaurant (page 224) that features performances by top musicians. On Sundays at 10:30 am and 1:00 pm, they serve an all-you-care-to-eat Gospel Brunch with soul food and glorious gospel music—price is $33.50/adults and $17.25/kids 3–9. Reservations can be made up to a month in advance at the House of Blues box office (or call 407-934-2583). Tickets for evening performances are available through the box office or Ticketmaster, and range from $13 to $60. The House of Blues is located at Downtown Disney West Side.

### MurderWatch Mystery Dinner Show

The Grosvenor Resort, a Hotel Plaza Resort on Disney property (see page 104), stages a popular murder mystery dinner show at 6:00 pm on Saturday nights in Baskervilles restaurant. The show includes an all-you-care-to-eat roast beef buffet and a healthy serving of (optional) audience participation. Tickets may be reserved in advance ($39.95/adult and $10.95/kids 9 and under) at 407-827-6534. Ask about discounts, too! Visit http://www.murderwatch.com for more information.

### Restaurants With Entertainment

Several Disney restaurants offer performances or entertainment during meals. At the Magic Kingdom, a piano player may tickle the ivories at Casey's Corner. At Epcot, Biergarten has traditional German music and dancing, Restaurant Marrakesh features belly dancing and Moroccan musicians, and Rose & Crown plays host to pub performers. At Disney's Hollywood Studios, '50s Prime Time Cafe has TVs and cast members who act like "sisters" and "brothers," and the Sci-Fi Dine-In Theater Restaurant shows old movie trailers. Both 'Ohana (Polynesian Resort) and Whispering Canyon Cafe (Wilderness Lodge Resort) offer fun activities for the kids (big and little). And Raglan Road at Downtown Disney promises Irish music, dancing, and storytelling.

# Special Dining Opportunities

On Mother's Day during Epcot's International Flower & Garden Festival (March 19–June 1, 2008), you can experience the **Food Among the Flowers Brunch**. This is an elaborate meal offering dozens of inventive and tantalizing choices—some may even include edible flower blossoms. Then, during the Epcot's International Food & Wine Festival (anticipated dates are September 28–November 11, 2008), there are special **wine tasting dinners** and other special meals (see page 216 for more about the Festival). Finally, during the **Christmas season**, when all the familiar eateries are overflowing, there is often a **holiday buffet** at a special location. For all these meals, call 407-WDW-DINE for information and reservations, but walk-up diners are often welcome at the holiday buffet.

**Holiday dinners at the resorts** and selected theme park restaurants usually go unheralded. Disney has no need to promote attendance during its busiest seasons, but you can be fairly certain that many resorts will have something happening on Easter Sunday, Mother's Day, Thanksgiving Day, Christmas week, and New Year's Eve. Start by phoning your Disney resort to see whether the restaurants there are serving a special holiday dinner. If you strike out at your resort, call around to the various deluxe resorts (holiday meals aren't always listed with 407-WDW-DINE). Magic Kingdom and Epcot full-service restaurants are also good candidates. Call 407-WDW-DINE to see if special meals are being offered at the theme parks during your visit.

**Dine with a Disney Imagineer** is a special part of the Disney's Hollywood Studios dining lineup and offers a close-up peek at the people who create Disney's entertainment, attractions, parks, and resorts. These special meals are typically available three times a week and feature intimate conversations with an Imagineer. Held in a private room at the Hollywood Brown Derby (see page 218), guests are served a special four-course meal while they learn about "their" Imagineer's work. Each guest receives a souvenir that may be autographed. Available for groups of 2–10 guests, and groups may be combined. Lunch is \$60.99/adults (\$34.99/kids 3–9), though it's not really a kids' event (and Disney suggests that it would be most appreciated by those 14 and older). Lunches are held on Mondays, Wednesdays, and Fridays. A similar meal is also offered at 5:30 pm on Thursdays at the Artist Point (Wilderness Lodge Resort)—price is \$89/adult and \$40/child (ages 3–9). Reserve these dining experiences up to 60 days in advance at 407-WDW-DINE—note that prepayment is required and you must cancel at least 48 hours in advance to get your money back.

Planning | Getting There | Staying in Style | Touring | Feasting | Making Magic | Index | Notes & More

Electronic, interactive worksheet available—see page 287

# Meal Worksheet

The first step in planning your meals is determining your needs. Start by checkmarking the meals you'll need in the worksheet below. Next, write down where you would like to eat your meals—be specific ("cereal in room" or "Brown Derby at Studios"). If you're using the Dining Plan (see pages 202-203), indicate the number of snacks S, quick-service Q, and table-service T credits to be used per meal. Circle the meals that require reservations, then use the worksheet on the next page to make the arrangements.

| Meal | Location | S | Q | T | Meal | Location | S | Q | T |
|---|---|---|---|---|---|---|---|---|---|
| **Day One—Date:** | | | | | **Day Six—Date:** | | | | |
| ❑ Breakfast | | | | | ❑ Breakfast | | | | |
| ❑ Lunch | | | | | ❑ Lunch | | | | |
| ❑ Dinner | | | | | ❑ Dinner | | | | |
| ❑ Other | | | | | ❑ Other | | | | |
| **Day Two—Date:** | | | | | **Day Seven—Date:** | | | | |
| ❑ Breakfast | | | | | ❑ Breakfast | | | | |
| ❑ Lunch | | | | | ❑ Lunch | | | | |
| ❑ Dinner | | | | | ❑ Dinner | | | | |
| ❑ Other | | | | | ❑ Other | | | | |
| **Day Three—Date:** | | | | | **Day Eight—Date:** | | | | |
| ❑ Breakfast | | | | | ❑ Breakfast | | | | |
| ❑ Lunch | | | | | ❑ Lunch | | | | |
| ❑ Dinner | | | | | ❑ Dinner | | | | |
| ❑ Other | | | | | ❑ Other | | | | |
| **Day Four—Date:** | | | | | **Day Nine—Date:** | | | | |
| ❑ Breakfast | | | | | ❑ Breakfast | | | | |
| ❑ Lunch | | | | | ❑ Lunch | | | | |
| ❑ Dinner | | | | | ❑ Dinner | | | | |
| ❑ Other | | | | | ❑ Other | | | | |
| **Day Five—Date:** | | | | | **Day Ten—Date:** | | | | |
| ❑ Breakfast | | | | | ❑ Breakfast | | | | |
| ❑ Lunch | | | | | ❑ Lunch | | | | |
| ❑ Dinner | | | | | ❑ Dinner | | | | |
| ❑ Other | | | | | ❑ Other | | | | |

(S, Q, T columns: Dining Plan Credits)

# Advance Reservations Worksheet

Electronic, interactive worksheet available– see page 287

Once you've determined what meals you plan to eat in table-service restaurants, note them in the chart below, along with your preferred dining time. Next, call 407-WDW-DINE to make advance reservations (have a credit card handy for certain reservations). Note the actual meal time and confirmation number below. When dining arrangements are finalized, transfer the information to your PassPockets.

**Our Resort:**
**Our Arrival Date:**

*Before calling, fill in everything to the left of this line.*

| Date | Restaurant Name | Preferred Time | Actual Time | Confirmation Number |
|---|---|---|---|---|
| | | | | |

# A Recipe for Fun

Make the most of your dining experience at Walt Disney World with these tips and tricks we've collected over the years:

"On our recent trip to Walt Disney World, we **ordered groceries** from http://www.GardenGrocer.com to have extra food and snacks in the room. When we checked in, our items were waiting at the front desk. We had ordered bottled water, yogurt, juice, snacks, and fresh fruit. The prices were comparable to home, and now that most of the Disney resorts have refrigerators in the room at no extra charge, this was a great money-saving and time-saving route! The fruit was fresh and nice, and we could pack extra snacks and beverages in our daily backpack before heading out. This is something we will definitely do again!" – *Contributed by Laura B., a winner in our 2007 Dining Tip Contest*

"In Liberty Square is **Columbia Harbour House**, a snug counter-service place to lunch. Go to the second floor and dine in the little room that extends over the passage between Liberty Square and Fantasyland. Enjoy watching the crowds passing between the park sections. Even on crowded days, this room tends to be empty."
– *Contributed by Chris Oakleaf, a winner in our 2007 Dining Tip Contest*

If you are celebrating a **special occasion**, be sure to mention it at the podium before you are seated. You may be pleasantly surprised.

If you want to **linger over your meal**, don't place your entire order all at once. This keeps your food from arriving too fast. Do let your server know you intend to order a full meal, however, or they might assume you're just snacking on appetizers and leave you alone.

## Magical Memory

*"Every evening at the end of a hot, harrowing day enjoying the wonders of Walt Disney World, my husband and I chose a wonderful Disney resort for our family dinner with the help of our PassPorter, which we carried everywhere. One night at Artist Point at Wilderness Lodge (a definite don't miss), the next night at the Grand Floridian (a beautiful place with beautiful views of the park), and the next night at Disney's Animal Kingdom Lodge resort (where you can view the animals from different points in the hotel). What a wonderful reward for a busy, adventure-filled day."*

*...as told by Disney vacationer Sandra Johnson*

PEEK behind the magic with tours and classes

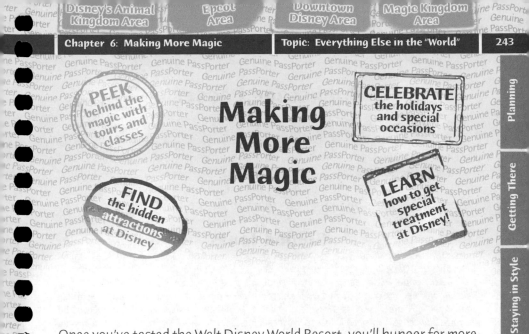

# Making More Magic

FIND the hidden attractions at Disney

Once you've tasted the Walt Disney World Resort, you'll hunger for more. Most visits can only *nibble* at the many wonders the "World" holds. There is much, much more that can be done to make your vacation magical. We've been to Disney more than most and yet there are *still* things we haven't done, and we add new discoveries to the wish list after every trip. It can all be a bit overwhelming, not to mention habit-forming. If you tried to keep up with each new activity on the Disney horizon, you'd have a full-time job on your hands.

To help you undertake your own magical explorations of the Walt Disney World Resort, we present a collection of useful information about some of its lesser-known aspects and attractions. This is our "everything else" chapter. To begin, we give you a backstage pass to the guided tours, special classes, and educational programs Disney offers—from peeks behind the scenes to dives under the seas. From there, we lead you on a treasure hunt for fun tucked away inside the parks—both real "treasure hunts" and hunts for items you'll treasure. We've even added a mini worksheet for those of you who love to shop! Next we share our special tricks for feeling and looking like a VIP on your trip—a little extra-special attention can go a long way! Then we give you the lowdown on childcare programs. Your kids may find these more fun than the theme parks themselves—no kidding! Special occasions and events aren't forgotten either, with ideas, tips, and details on celebrating birthdays, engagements, honeymoons, anniversaries, holidays, and more. Before we say goodbye, we'll leave you with information for explorations beyond the Walt Disney World Resort at other Disney vacation spots—from exotic ports of call, to foreign lands, to home lands.

So get out that pixie dust and don your sorcerer's hat—we're making magic, Disney-style!

# Backstage Passes

Disney does such a good job of hiding the figurative ropes and pulleys that you'll be disappointed if you hope to catch a glimpse of what makes Disney really work. To meet the growing demands of interminably curious guests, Disney offers tours and programs that satisfy the need to "peek."

## Guided Tours

*Unless otherwise noted, advance reservations may be (and should be) made up to 90–180 days in advance at 407-939-8687, or through your resort's Lobby Concierge desk. Some discounts are available to Annual Passholders, Disney Visa cardholders, AAA, or Disney Vacation Club members. Tours are only open to guests 16 and older unless otherwise noted. Many tours require substantial walking and most are wheelchair accessible. In general, no photos of backstage areas are allowed on the tours. Cancel 48 hours in advance to avoid penalties. Tours that require regular park admission are noted with the ticket (🎟) icon. Important: Bring photo ID with you for tour check-in.*

| ☐ **Around the World at Epcot (on a Segway!)** [Epcot] 🎟 | |
|---|---|
| *This two-hour tour offers a unique opportunity to ride a Segway (a self-balancing, two-wheeled "vehicle"). Learn to ride for the first hour, then practice riding around World Showcase. Max. weight is 250 lbs.; pregnant and special needs guests may not participate. Offered daily at 7:45, 8:30, 9:00, and 9:30 am. (A one-hour tour, Simply Segway Experience, is also available on most days—see next page.)* | **$85**<br>Ages 16 & up<br>On-stage only |

| ☐ **Backstage Magic** [Magic Kingdom, Disney's Hollywood Studios, and Epcot] | |
|---|---|
| *This seven-hour tour of three major parks explores how Disney's magic is created and maintained. Go beneath the Magic Kingdom to explore the underground "utilidors," enjoy a special lunch at Disney's Hollywood Studios, and see the computer systems at Epcot. Tours depart Monday–Friday at 8:45 am. Price includes lunch. Park admission is not required. Reserve well in advance.* | **$199**<br>Ages 16 & up<br>Backstage peek at three theme parks |

| ☐ **Backstage Safari Tour** [Disney's Animal Kingdom] 🎟 | |
|---|---|
| *A three-hour, behind-the-scenes peek at Disney's Animal Kingdom park to see how they care for our four-legged friends. No photography is allowed in backstage areas. Tours depart at 8:15 am on Mondays, Wednesdays, Thursdays, and Fridays. Park admission is required (not included in price).* | **$65**<br>Ages 16 & up<br>Backstage peek |

| ☐ **Family Magic Tour** [Magic Kingdom] 🎟 | |
|---|---|
| *This fun, 2 ½-hour tour offers guests an interactive adventure through the Magic Kingdom in search of a Disney character (such as Hook or Maleficent). The popular tour is open to all and is held daily at 10:00 am. This is a popular tour and reservations are strongly recommended. Park admission required.* | **$27**<br>Ages 3 & up<br>On-stage only |

| ☐ **Keys to the Kingdom** [Magic Kingdom] 🎟 | |
|---|---|
| *This 4 ½-hour guided tour of Magic Kingdom gives an overview of the park's highlights, history, and backstage areas, plus lunch at Columbia Harbour House. The route varies, but usually visits three attractions and two backstage areas (even a peek in the "utilidors"). Offered daily at 8:30, 9:00, and 9:30 am. Guests without reservations can inquire at City Hall, but the tour is very popular and we recommend you book it well in advance. Park admission is required.* | **$60**<br>Ages 16 & up<br>Backstage peek (including the utilidors) |

Looking for Epcot Seas Aqua Tour, Dolphins in Depth, or Divequest? See page 247.

### The Magic Behind Our Steam Trains [Magic Kingdom]

| | |
|---|---|
| Railroad fans get an inside look at the Walt Disney World Railroad in the Magic Kingdom. Join the opening crew, view the roundhouse, and explore Walt's passion for steam trains. The three-hour tour is held on Mondays, Tuesdays, Thursdays, and Saturdays at 7:15 am. Park admission is required. | **$40**<br>Ages 10 & up<br>Backstage peek |

### Mickey's Magical Milestones [Magic Kingdom]

| | |
|---|---|
| Walk in Mickey's footsteps as you retrace his fabled career in this two-hour tour through the Magic Kingdom. You may even get to meet the Big Cheese himself. Tours are on Mondays, Wednesdays, and Fridays at 9:00 am. | **$25**<br>Ages 10 & up<br>On-stage only |

### Simply Segway Experience [Epcot]

| | |
|---|---|
| Want to try a Segway without committing to two hours with the Around the World tour? This is the "Segway Lite" tour where you get instruction, but only ride the two-wheeled vehicles inside. The one-hour experience is held on Sundays, Mondays, Wednesdays, and Saturdays at 11:30 am. Park admission is required. Age and weight restrictions are the same as the Around the World tour. | **$35**<br>Ages 16 & up<br>On-stage only (no backstage) |

### Undiscovered Future World [Epcot]

| | |
|---|---|
| This 4 1/2-hour walking tour of the pavilions in Future World goes backstage. Tour highlights include a visit to a VIP lounge, a walk-through of the Cast Services building, an opportunity to meet an International Ambassador, and a peek at where the IllumiNations barges are stored. Guests may receive a limited edition trading pin, discounts on lunch and purchases in the China pavilion, and/or special seating for IllumiNations that evening. Tours are offered on Mondays, Wednesdays, and Fridays at 8:45 am. Park admission is required. | **$49**<br>Ages 16 & up<br>Backstage peek (including Epcot marina) |

### VIP Tours

| | |
|---|---|
| Custom-designed six- to eight-hour tours may be booked by individuals or groups of up to ten people. Tours must include a meal. Cost is $125–$150 per hour per tour guide (six-hour minimum) and does not include park admission. VIP Tours may be booked from 24 hours to three months in advance. Blackout dates apply; call 407-560-4033 for availability and reservations. | **$125+/hour**<br>All ages<br>On-stage only (no backstage) |

### Wild By Design [Disney's Animal Kingdom]

| | |
|---|---|
| This three-hour walking tour takes you around Disney's Animal Kingdom to learn about the represented cultures, historic artifacts, and storytelling. Guests wear headphones to hear the tour guide better. Tours leave at 8:30 am on Thursdays and Fridays. Price includes a light continental breakfast. | **$58**<br>Ages 14 & up<br>On-stage only |

### Yuletide Fantasy [Theme Parks and Resort Hotels]

| | |
|---|---|
| Offered daily during the holiday season at 8:45 am, this three-hour tour gives a behind-the-scenes peek at the magical holiday transformations. The tour visits theme parks and resorts to view the decorations. Guests under 16 are not allowed. Park admission is not required. Meet at Epcot Guest Relations (outside turnstiles). | **$69**<br>Ages 16 & up<br>Backstage peek |

*Tip: In summer 2007, a new tour called "Wilderness Back Trail Adventure Segway Tour" was offered at Fort Wilderness on the Segway X2 off-road vehicles. The tour was in testing mode and it was not known if it would continue beyond the summer, but if you're interested, call 407-WDW-TOUR to inquire about it. During testing, price was $65/person and the tour was offered on Tuesdays, Fridays, and Saturdays at 8:30 am and 11:30 am.*

*Note: Gardens of the World and Hidden Treasures of World Showcase tours ended in 2007.*

# Children's Tours, Parties, and Activities

Fun stuff for kids! You can reserve fee-based activities by calling 407-WDW-DINE up to 180 days in advance; free activities take no reservations.

**Albatross Treasure Cruise** [Yacht Club Resort]

|  |  |
|---|---|
| *Follow the clues on this cruise around Crescent Lake, visit "exotic" ports of call, and listen to a reading of "The Legend of the Albatross." Cruise includes lunch (PB&J sandwich, cookie, and juice) and a split of the "buried treasure."* | **$28.17**<br>Ages 4–10<br>9:30–11:30 am |

**Disney's Pirate Adventure** [Grand Floridian Resort]

|  |  |
|---|---|
| *Ahoy, mateys! Cast off from the Grand Floridian marina on a cruise around the Seven Seas Lagoon in search of treasure. Little buccaneers get a bandana to wrap around their heads, hear a reading of "The Legend of Gasparilla," learn pirate songs, and receive a bag of "loot" (treats). Lunch is included.* | **$28.17**<br>Ages 4–10<br>9:30–11:30 am<br>M, W, Th, Sa |

**Wonderland Tea Party** [Grand Floridian Resort]

|  |  |
|---|---|
| *Take tea with Alice in Wonderland! Kids make and eat cupcakes, participate in projects, and meet Alice, the Mad Hatter, and friends. Held in the 1900 Park Fare restaurant in the Grand Floridian Resort on Monday–Friday.* | **$28.17**<br>Ages 4–10<br>1:30–2:30 pm |

**My Disney Girl's Perfectly Princess Tea Party** [Grand Floridian Resort]

|  |  |
|---|---|
| *Pure pampering for your little princess. This five-part party is held in the Grand Floridian's Garden View Tea Lounge and features a visit from Princess Aurora. Includes tea, brunch, dessert, a My Disney Girl doll, and the participation of one adult. Siblings or friends can attend for $135 each and extra adults are $65 each.* | **$200.00**<br>Ages 3–11<br>10:30–noon<br>Su, M, W, Th, F |

**Grand Adventures in Cooking** [Grand Floridian Resort]

|  |  |
|---|---|
| *Kids listen to a story, get aprons and chef's hats to decorate, then share their kitchen creations. Offered from 10:00 to 11:45 am on Tue. and Fri. in the Mouseketeer Clubhouse. Cancellations less than 24 hours before charged the full amount.* | **$28.17**<br>Ages 4–10<br>10–11:45 am |

**Bayou Pirate Adventure Cruise** [Port Orleans Riverside]

|  |  |
|---|---|
| *Cruise along the Sassagoula River and hunt for Pirate Jean Lafitte's treasure. Includes a light lunch (PB&J and juice) and a share of the "treasure." Held on Sundays, Tuesdays, and Thursdays. Formerly the Sassagoula River Adventure.* | **$28.17**<br>Ages 4–10<br>9:30–11:30 am |

**Islands of the Caribbean Pirate Adventure** [Caribbean Beach Resort]

|  |  |
|---|---|
| *Discover the story of Old Port Royale as you sail about Barefoot Bay in a boat resembling an old battle relic. Kids wear pirate bandanas, search for hidden treasure, rustle up grub (PB&J, juice), and divide the loot. Held on Tuesdays and Sundays.* | **$28.17**<br>Ages 4–10<br>9:30–11:30 am |

**Boma Kids' Activities** [Disney's Animal Kingdom Lodge]

|  |  |
|---|---|
| *Daily activities for kids—such as cookie decorating—are available in the restaurant (Boma) and lobby of Disney's Animal Kingdom Lodge. Ask for the daily schedule of events at the hotel's front desk or at Boma.* | **Free**<br>Ages 3–12<br>Times vary |

**Junior Chef Program at The Land** [Epcot]

|  |  |
|---|---|
| *Don your chef hats and help make a batch of yummy chocolate chip cookies! Just go to the bright yellow "bakery" downstairs in The Land to participate. Offered at 12:30, 1:30, 2:30, 3:30, and 4:30 pm daily. Limited to 20 participants.* | **Free**<br>Ages 3–10<br>Times vary |

# Classes and Educational Programs

**Behind the Seeds: A Special Guided Greenhouse Tour**—This one-hour walking tour delves deeper into the innovative greenhouses seen in the Living With the Land exhibit at Epcot. Cost is $14/adult and $10/child age 3–9 (no minimum age), 13 people max. per tour. Park admission to Epcot is required. Sign up at the counter outside Soarin' (in The Land) or call 407-WDW-TOUR. Tours leave every 45 minutes between 9:45 am and 4:30 pm.

**Dolphins in Depth**—This unique three-hour program highlights the dolphin research at The Seas with Nemo & Friends in Epcot. Guests play an active part in the research as they learn about dolphin behavior. Guests must be 13 or older, and 13- to 17-year-olds must be with a participating adult. Offered on Mondays–Fridays beginning at 9:30 am. Cost is $150/person and includes a photo, soda, and souvenir T-shirt. Dolphin interaction is not guaranteed. Park admission to Epcot is not required to participate in this program.

**Epcot Divequest**—Open Water SCUBA-certified divers ages 10 and older can dive the 6-million-gallon pool at The Seas with Nemo & Friends (guests 10–14 must be with a participating adult). The three-hour program includes a presentation on marine research and conservation. Divers suit up and are guided in small groups for a 40-minute dive. The cost includes use of gear, refreshments, a certificate, a dive log stamp, and a shirt. Proof of certification must be shown and divers have to sign medical and legal waivers. Dives are daily at 4:30 and 5:30 pm. Cost is $140/person. Park admission to Epcot is not required. Advance reservations are required.

**Epcot Seas Aqua Tour**—A 2½-hour SCUBA-assisted snorkel that takes place in the largest indoor aquarium in the world at The Seas with Nemo & Friends. You do not need to be SCUBA certified; equipment and instructions are provided. Actual snorkel time is 30 minutes. Offered daily at 12:30 pm for guests ages 8 and up (8- to 16-year-olds must be with an adult). Cost is $100/person and includes use of gear, a shirt, and a group photo. Park admission not required.

**Typhoon Lagoon Learn-to-Surf Program**—Surf's up! This exciting class at Typhoon Lagoon water park teaches guests surfing basics. Learn on dry land for the first half-hour, then try your new skills on the big waves in the park's huge wave pool for the remaining two hours. The 2½-hour class is offered on Mondays, Tuesdays, and Fridays at 6:45 am, though starting time may vary with park operating hours (class is held before the park opens). Class is open to resort guests ages 8 and up who are strong swimmers. Cost is $140/person, and park admission is not required. Call 407-WDW-PLAY for reservations. See pages 171–174 for details on Typhoon Lagoon. (You can book special "private surf parties" at Typhoon Lagoon—call 407-WDW-SURF for details.)

### Recreation and Water Sports

A variety of options are available at moderate and deluxe resort hotels, water parks, and the Downtown Disney marina. While not all activities are offered in all locations, you can expect to find biking (regular and surrey), fishing, canoeing, boating, sailing, parasailing, waterskiing, wakeboarding, tubing, surfing, horseback riding, and carriage rides somewhere in the World. Call 407-WDW-PLAY or your resort to get details. Sammy Duvall's Watersports Centre at the Contemporary offers personal watercraft excursions, waterskiing, parasailing, and wakeboarding (included in some packages)—call 407-939-0754 or visit http://www.sammyduvall.com. Also see page 194.

# Treasure Hunts

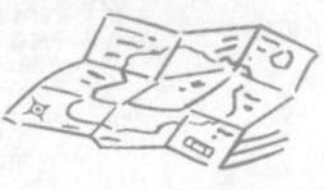

There is hidden treasure at the Walt Disney World Resort. While it may not consist of golden doubloons, it is every bit as priceless. There are countless sets of often-hidden and always-valuable Disneyesque items for you to find during your vacation. Sometimes these items are purposefully hidden; other times they are out in plain view for all to see but few to notice. Hunting for your favorite item can add a new dimension to your vacation! If you enjoy treasure hunting, check out *PassPorter's Treasure Hunts at Walt Disney World* book (see page 285). Here are our favorite things to collect:

**Disney Characters and Autographs**

Live Disney characters abound, and kids of all ages delight in spotting them. You can discover where some characters are "hiding" by checking with Guest Relations at each major park. If you want to "bag your catch," take photographs—and try to get yourself or your family in the picture! Keep in mind that characters are popular and crowds will form. If you know when your characters will appear, show up early to greet them. (Tip: Ask a Disney cast member about character appearances for the day.) You can also collect autographs from characters who are able to sign their name. Special autograph books are available at most shops, or you can bring your own. Or use the PassPorter's autograph space on pages 276–279. Try to bring a wide-barreled pen or marker so the character can hold it easily. You can also have the characters sign hats or shirts (which must be Disney or non-commercial), but shirts cannot be worn while they are being signed and you need something to slip under the fabric to provide a writing surface. We now have an entire 266-page e-book called *PassPorter's Disney Character Yearbook*, which is all about finding, meeting, photographing, and getting character autographs, and includes a full page dedicated to each character you can meet at Walt Disney World—for details, see http://www.passporter.com/disney-character-yearbook.asp.

**Pressed Pennies and Quarters**

One of the least expensive souvenirs at the Walt Disney World Resort is pressed coins. Souvenir Pressed Coin machines, found throughout the "World," press different Disney designs onto pennies or quarters. Cost is 51 cents for a pressed penny and $1.25 for a pressed quarter. Designs differ from machine to machine, making a complete collection a worthy achievement. Bring rolls of shiny pennies and quarters along with you—the hunt for a money-changing machine isn't as much fun. While there are good lists of pressed coin machine locations on the Internet (try http://www.intercot.com/infocentral/coins), finding them is half the fun! **Tip**: Buy a keepsake book at Disney's gift shops to store your coins.

*A pressed coin machine at Caribbean Beach Resort*

**Free Stuff**

Disney may seem to be a mecca to capitalism, but there are still free things for the taking, and they make great souvenirs! Some may even become collector's items one day. You can collect guidemaps, brochures, napkins, paper cups and plates, containers, bags, menus, and more.

# Hidden Mickeys

Believe it or not, Disney intentionally hides "Mickeys" all over the place! The internationally recognized Mickey Mouse head (one big circle and two smaller circles for the ears) has been discovered hidden in murals, fences, shows—you name it, you can probably find a Mickey hidden somewhere in it! Disney fans maintain lists of these Hidden Mickeys—try http://www.hiddenmickeys.org and http://www.hiddenmickeysguide.com. You will also enjoy the "Hidden Mickeys" field guide by Steven M. Barrett, available in bookstores and at our web site (http://www.passporterstore.com/store). We made a list of our favorite Hidden Mickeys for a rainy day activity—how many hiding places can you find? Write your answers below.

| # Location | Hint | Hiding Place |
|---|---|---|
| 1. General | Isn't it good to know Disney cares for the environment? | |
| 2. General | Ka-ching! Look at what you get when the cash register rings! | |
| 3. General | Bubble, bubble, toil, and trouble, look to laundry for three bubbles. | |
| 4. Magic Kingdom | Clippity clop, clippity clop! I pull a trolley past the Main St. shops. | |
| 5. Magic Kingdom | Look to your feet for the holes in the street. | |
| 6. Magic Kingdom | A Mickey up a sleeve—no joke—check the Grim Reaper's cloak. | |
| 7. Epcot | Test the Track, can you cope? Find the Mickey in the rope. | |
| 8. Epcot | As you stand in Maelstrom's line, find him in the hands of time. | |
| 9. Epcot | Now turn your glance to the gardens of France. | |
| 10. Disney's Hollywood Studios | Look for a tower and we'll bet if you say "terror" you're all wet. | |
| 11. Disney's Hollywood Studios | All around the park I run, my thin black bars protect the fun. | |
| 12. Disney's Hollywood Studios | On your tour of the backlot put the refrigerator on the spot! | |
| 13. Disney's Animal Kingdom | Amid the trees near Simba's fest hangs a house that holds a nest. | |
| 14. Disney's Animal Kingdom | Near Pangani you'll pass some fruit. Don't squish Mickey under your boot! | |
| 15. Disney's Animal Kingdom | There is a froggie near Pizzafari. Now that's the end of this safari! | |

*Hidden Mickey hiding places are found on page 261.*

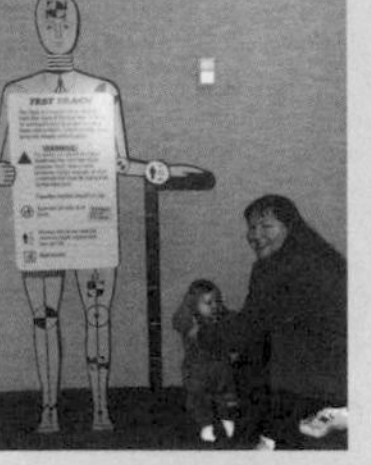

*A photo "growth chart" at Epcot's Test Track (Alexander at 0, 1, & 2)*

### Photographs and Memories

Many vacationers bring a camera or a camcorder to record their trip. Most seem content to simply take pictures as the mood strikes them, but you can also "collect" pictures as well! Here are some ideas for fun photograph collections: Disney puns and visual gags that often go unnoticed (try "holding up" Spaceship Earth in your photos); your favorite spot at different times of the day; all of the "Kodak Picture Spot" signs; and pictures through the eyes of your children (give them their own camera). How about a photo of each family member next to their favorite attraction? If you take these same photos on return trips, you can make a "growth chart" over time. Another idea is to hold a family photo scavenger hunt for fun things and places around Walt Disney World. And don't forget about Disney's PhotoPass—see the details on page 150.

### Souvenirs

If you enjoy taking home souvenirs but you're tired of the usual T-shirts or postcards, consider beginning a new collection. Chances are that if you can collect it, Disney has it somewhere on its property. Here are favorite collectibles: enamel pins (see page 253 for details), patches (you can sew them onto your packs), mugs, figurines, hats, clothing, stuffed animals, mini bean bags, and Pal Mickey (see below). Love shopping? Here's a mini worksheet to help you organize the items you want to purchase for yourself and others at Walt Disney World!

| Who | What | Size/Color | $$ | ✓ |
|---|---|---|---|---|
| | | | | |

### Pal Mickey – "The Talk of the Parks"

Who's 10 inches tall and is destined to become the most popular tour guide at Walt Disney World? Pal Mickey! Pal Mickey is Disney Imagineering's plush innovation, a soft, loveable toy that plays games wherever he goes, and becomes an instant tour guide whenever he enters a Disney theme park. While Pal Mickey is no substitute for a real tour guide (be that a person or a guidebook) and he mainly appeals to kids, he's still an amusing diversion. You can purchase Pal Mickey for $70—rentals are no longer available. Be sure to keep his black nose pointed outward and uncovered, as he is literally guided by his nose. Pal Mickey is available in English or Spanish.

# In Search Of...

Quite often we're on the lookout for specific items, whether they be souvenirs or necessities. To help hunt down your treasures, here is a partial list of places to find some of the more commonly sought items:

**Alcohol**—You can buy a mixed drink or beer at any of the resorts or parks with the notable exception of the Magic Kingdom. You can also purchase alcohol at most resort general stores and at Downtown Disney.

**Baby Needs**—The baby care centers in the four major parks sell common baby items, such as diapers, wipes, and formula. Your resort's gift shop stocks these items as well.

**Groceries**—Snacks are available at most of the resort stores, and a small selection of groceries is available at resorts with in-room cooking facilities. For more serious marketing, visit the Winn-Dixie half a mile north of the Crossroads Shopping Center. You may also want to try GardenGrocer.com (http://www.gardengrocer.com) for deliveries!

**Gum**—Gum is not sold on Disney property nor at the airport to avoid messes. If you need it, bring it with you or buy it off-property.

**Lost Items**—Lost and Found centers are located everywhere you go—generally near the front of the park or complex. Jennifer dropped a favorite scarf at Downtown Disney and within 15 minutes she had recovered it at Lost and Found (much to her relief). You can also call Lost and Found at 407-824-4245. Lost and found items are generally kept at each park only until closing. After that, they are usually transferred to Central Lost and Found at the Transportation and Ticket Center (inside the Kennel). Remember to label everything!

**Medicine**—Order prescription and over-the-counter drugs through Turner Drugs at 407-828-8125 from 8:00 am to 8:00 pm. Deliveries (for a fee) are available between 9:00 am and 9:00 pm. (Insurance paperwork is available so you may file claims upon your return.) Tip: Check with your insurance company to see which pharmacies will accept your insurance. Over-the-counter medicine and bandages are kept under the counter at many Disney shops—ask a cast member. Aspirin and bandages are also available at no charge at the first-aid stations staffed by licensed medical personnel in each park and resort front desks.

**Missing or Lost Persons**—Should you become separated, immediately alert a cast member or go to Guest Relations. Teach kids how to recognize cast members by their white nametags. A message system is available at Guest Relations to help coordinate things, even if you aren't lost (yet). It's a good idea to choose a meeting place each day in the event you are separated from your family or friends. You may also find it helpful to give each member of your party a two-way radio or cell phone to stay in touch with one another. We also suggest you take a digital photo of kids each morning—this will help you if a child is lost. Consider using "Who's Shoes ID" tags (http://www.whosshoesid.com), too!

**Money**—ATMs (cash machines) are located in all the parks and resorts. See our park maps or Disney's guidemaps for locations. The Walt Disney World Resort accepts American Express, MasterCard, Visa, Discover, JCB, Diner's Club, traveler's checks, cash, Disney Dollars and Gift Cards, and the Disney Dream Reward Dollars card (see page 10 for details on the Disney Rewards Visa card). Personal checks are not accepted on property, however.

**Rain Gear**—If you didn't bring an umbrella or poncho along, Disney will sell you one at virtually any shop. You may need to ask, but chances are they'll have something. Tip: If your poncho rips, bring it back to any shop and they'll replace it. Disney sells clear ponchos to make it easier to spot your companions in the rain.

# VIP Tips

**Wake-Up Call**

If you're staying at a Disney resort, start your day with a call from Mickey. Just use the phone system to arrange a wake-up call, and when the phone rings, Mickey, Stitch, or one of their friends welcomes you to the new day! When the phone rings with your wake-up call, press the speakerphone button so everyone in the room can hear it! Tip: Make your wake-up call for an off-time, such as 7:03, to help ensure you get Mickey.

**Box Seats**

**Monorail**—If you're at one of the monorail resorts, ask the cast member on the platform about riding in the front cab. The view is fabulous! Keep in mind that you may need to wait for a specific monorail to arrive. Monorail cab rides are available on the Express and Epcot lines when traffic and crowds permit, too. Seating is limited to four guests, and you may be seated with others (as Allie was in the photo above). The front cab is often not available when boarding a resort monorail from the Magic Kingdom or Transportation and Ticket Center (TTC). Note that wheelchairs cannot ride in the front cab; ask for a "pilot's license" in lieu of riding up front!

© MediaMarx, Inc.

*Look at the view you get from the monorail cab!*

**Contemporary Resort**—Enjoy a meal in the California Grill during the Magic Kingdom fireworks (the music that normally accompanies the fireworks is broadcast in the restaurant). While the California Grill observation deck is open only to diners, there's another viewing area on the north end of the Grand Concourse (4th floor).

**Fireworks Cruises**—Do you have something to celebrate? Rent a pontoon boat, the Breathless II speedboat, or the new Grand 1 Yacht to view the fireworks at Epcot or the Magic Kingdom. Cruises are booked per boat rather than per passenger, and all include a pilot. Call 407-WDW-PLAY for rates and reservations. You can book up to 90 days in advance, and we recommend you call at 7:00 am Eastern Time exactly 90 days in advance, as these cruises are extremely popular. Note: These are sometimes called "specialty" cruises by Disney, as they can't promise that the fireworks won't be cancelled.

Note: Disney no longer sells photos for the Leave a Legacy monument in front of Epcot's Spaceship Earth.

### Trading Pins

Colorful, enameled commemorative pins are a favorite Disney collectible, available at nearly every shop for $6.95 and up. Disney designs thousands of these colorful, cloisonné pins, which commemorate the theme parks, resorts, attractions, characters, and events. Over the years, Disney stepped up pin trading activity by introducing Pin Trading Stations at the parks and the Disney's Pin Traders shop at Downtown Disney, where you can buy and swap pins. Bring (or buy) your own Disney pins, and trade pins with other guests and with cast members wearing special pin-trading lanyards around their neck or boards at their waist. Look for "Scoop Sanderson," a special Main Street, U.S.A. cast member who offers pin trading classes and tips. Note that cast members wearing green lanyards trade only with children. Pin trading is a fun way to meet fellow vacationers and learn more about the world of Disney. Buy a Disney pin lanyard, or display your pins in a scrapbook, or on a vest or hat.

*Dave trades a pin on his hat with a cast member at Disney's Animal Kingdom*

### Name Badges and Pins

Show everyone how special you are with an oval Disney name badge, personalized with your first name. The badges make great conversation starters—you may even get more personal attention from cast members while wearing one. You can purchase badges in the parks and at Downtown Disney for $6. Have an unusual name? Visit the engraving shop at Disney's Hollywood Studios or at Disney's Days of Christmas at Downtown Disney. Another option is our own PassPorter Badge, which our readers requested to help them spot fellow fans in the parks. PassPorter Badges are $4 and also come with free personalization. You can order PassPorter Badges at our web site. We also issue our own collectible, cloisonné PassPorter Pins each year for $6 each—see page 283).

### Park Passports

Disney has passports, too! The Epcot Passport is a great way to tour the World Showcase. Once you have a passport, you can get it "stamped" at each pavilion or land by a cast member. The passports—which kids love—can be purchased at shops and carts for about $10 and include an "I'm a World Showcase Traveler" pin and a set of stickers. A similar passport is available at Disney's Animal Kingdom.

# Childcare Programs

"We're going to Walt Disney World. Why in the 'World' would we need childcare?" The Walt Disney World Resort is an adult playground, too! The "World" offers an exciting nightlife and leaves lots of room for romance. All you need is a sitter. Not surprisingly, Disney delivers with a variety of childcare options and a few programs that may seem like childcare to you (but don't tell the kids). The two main options are childcare programs at the resorts and private, in-room baby-sitting.

Many of Disney's deluxe resorts offer childcare programs. These childcare programs are a good bit like daycare, but unlike daycare, their "day" usually starts at around 4:00 pm and runs until midnight. They offer a variety of structured activities and entertainment and usually include a full meal. All programs accept children from 4 to 12 years of age, and all children must be potty-trained. Rates are $11/hour, and some programs have minimum stays. Programs usually also have an overtime rate—the kids won't be evicted if your coach turns into a pumpkin on the way back from Cinderella Castle. Parents are given pagers, too. Some programs are available only to Disney resort guests, and some only for guests staying or dining in the particular resort. Make your status clear when you phone so there are no disappointments. No matter which program you contact, we recommend you call well in advance and ask plenty of questions. Reservations can be made with the club itself or at 407-WDW-DINE. Each resort offers different services and rules, and all are subject to change. Cancel at least 24 hours in advance to avoid a $15/kid fee. **Allie's KidTip:** "It's cool to stay at the kids' clubs so you can do what you like to do and grown-ups can do what they want to do." Read on for more of Allie's KidTips on the clubs she's visited.

## Childcare Near Epcot and Disney's Hollywood Studios

| **Sandcastle Club** [Beach Club] | 407-934-3750 |
|---|---|
| *Large club with plenty of Legos, games, computers, and video games (free) to play with. Meals are served at 6:00, 7:00, or 8:00 pm. This club is available only to Disney resort guests.* **Allie's KidTip:** *"There are fun games to play."* | **$11/hour**<br>4:30 pm–Midnight |

| **Harbor Club** [Boardwalk Inn & Villas] (currently closed) | 407-939-6301 |
|---|---|
| *Smaller club with kid-friendly activities. Price includes a meal and a snack—meals are served at 6:00, 7:00, or 8:00 pm. Note that this club was closed at the time of writing, and it is not known if it will reopen.* | **$11/hour**<br>4:00 pm–Midnight |

| **Camp Dolphin** [Swan and Dolphin] | 407-934-4000 ext. 4241 |
|---|---|
| *Kids have fun with arts and crafts, video games, and movies. Price includes a meal at 7:00 pm—kids are usually taken to the Picabu eatery in the resort. Note that participation is not limited to Swan and Dolphin guests.* | **$11/hour**<br>5:30 pm–Midnight |

## Childcare Near Disney's Animal Kingdom

| **Simba's Cubhouse** [Disney's Animal Kingdom Lodge] | 407-938-4785 |
|---|---|
| *The club with a view of the savanna and animals. Plenty of movies and games. Price includes a meal (serving time varies).* Allie's Kid Tip: *"This is my first choice! I liked the people and the decorations. And I loved watching the animals."* | **$11/hour** 4:30 pm–Midnight |

## Childcare Near the Magic Kingdom

| **Mouseketeer Club** [Grand Floridian] | 407-824-2985 |
|---|---|
| *A medium-sized club with movies, games, and crafts. Price includes a meal if child is checked in by 6:30 pm (meal is at 7:30 pm). Two-hour minimum stay. This club is available only to Grand Floridian resort and restaurant guests.* | **$11/hour** 4:30 pm–Midnight |

| **Cub's Den** [Wilderness Lodge] | 407-824-1083 |
|---|---|
| *A smallish club with structured activities, movies, arts and crafts, and games. Price includes a meal (choice of hot dog, hamburger, cheeseburger, chicken strips, mac & cheese, or PB&J, plus ice cream) served between 6:30–8:00 pm.* | **$11/hour** 4:30 pm–Midnight |

| **Never Land Club** [Polynesian] | 407-824-2000 |
|---|---|
| *This is the largest, most creatively themed club! Price includes a meal (buffet of kid-friendly items) served 6:00–8:00 pm. Open house daily from noon to 4:00 pm for Polynesian resort guests.* Allie's Kid Tip: *"I like the people here, and the toy stairs are fun to sit on and watch movies. The TV here is big!"* | **$11/hour** 4:00 pm–Midnight |

Note: The Mouseketeer Clubhouse at the Contemporary closed on October 1, 2004.

# Other Childcare Options

**Kids Nite Out** offers Disney-sanctioned, private in-room babysitting, 24 hours a day. Two other independent childcare agencies, **Fairy Godmothers** and **All About Kids**, offer similar services. The professional sitters will take kids to the theme parks if you make arrangements in advance (ask at time of reservation) and watch infants and children with some special needs. The sitters show up equipped to keep the kids occupied with games and activities. They are well-trained, bonded, and insured. Rates vary, depending on the age and number of kids under care. For reservations, call Kids Nite Out at 800-696-8105 or 407-828-0920, the Fairy Godmothers at 407-275-7326, or All About Kids at 407-812-9300.

# Special Occasions

It seems natural to celebrate a special occasion at Disney. It's designed for fun and comes predecorated! So whether you plan a trip around a special day or want to celebrate one that falls during your vacation, you can do it at Disney! Here are our tips and tricks for a magical celebration:

**Birthdays**—What better place to celebrate a birthday than at Disney? If you're at a Disney resort, press "0" on your room phone and ask for the special "birthday message." Be sure to request a free "It's My Birthday!" pin at the Guest Relations desk at the theme parks. If you want to celebrate in style, all sorts of birthday parties and cruises can be arranged in advance—you can even "invite" Disney characters (though they're very expensive). For kids ages 4–12, you can arrange a birthday party at the BoardWalk or the Yacht & Beach Club—call 407-WDW-PLAY. For parties in other restaurants, call 407-WDW-DINE. Birthday cruises (407-WDW-PLAY) are also available—we surprised Dave's father with one and he loved it! And in March 2003, Jennifer surprised her mom Carolyn with a special birthday event, planned in part by Gifts of a Lifetime (see sidebar below). Families that celebrate **Quinceañera**, a celebration of a daughter's 15th birthday, can choose from a variety of special events—visit http://www.disneyworld.com/quinceanera or call 321-939-4555.

**Engagements**—Disney is a magical place to propose to a loved one. Alas, you'll have to devise your own scheme as Disney no longer offers official assistance.

**Weddings**—Of course you can get married at Disney—in fact, we tied the knot at a delightful "Intimate Wedding" with our immediate family at the Polynesian in May 2004! From intimate to traditional to themed, Disney's Fairy Tale Weddings have something for virtually every budget. Visit http://www.disneyweddings.com or call 407-828-3400. Vow renewals are also available. You can also get free "Just Married" buttons to wear—ask about them at Guest Relations in any of the four major parks and resort front desks. You may wish to purchase and wear the bridal Mickey ears (white veil and black top hat) for $10 each—see our photo on the next page!

*Jennifer and Dave walk up the "aisle" at the Polynesian Resort*

### Special Services for Special Occasions

It's a challenge to organize a special occasion long-distance. An innovative company, **Presentations: Gifts of a Lifetime**, helps you shop for that perfect gift, arrange a magical event, and even put on the whole show! To learn more, visit their web site at http://www.giftsofalifetime.com or call 407-909-0593.

You can also have the **Walt Disney World Florist** (407-827-3505) prepare a fruit or snack basket and deliver it to a guest room.

Need a little help remembering that special occasion? Another unique service, **MouseMemories**, can create custom memory albums from your own photos. If you prefer to create your own memory albums, they offer scrapbooking supplies. To learn more, visit http://www.mousememories.com.

**Honeymoons**—Walt Disney World is the #1 honeymoon destination in the world, believe it or not. Not only are romantic spots found around virtually every corner, but Disney goes out of its way to make newlyweds welcome. Special honeymoon packages, romantic rooms, candlelit dinners, and adult-oriented entertainment abound. Even if you do nothing more than mention that it is your honeymoon to cast members, you may be in for a special treat. For details, call Disney at 407-934-7639.

*Jennifer and Dave share a Mickey Rice Krispie Bar on their honeymoon*

**Anniversaries**—Like birthdays, anniversaries are always in style at the Walt Disney World Resort. You can get free "Happy Anniversary" buttons to wear—ask about them at Guest Relations in any of the four major parks. You can plan a special night out at a romantic restaurant or shape an entire vacation around your special day. Be sure to mention your anniversary when making advance dining reservations (especially at Cinderella's Royal Table)—you may be pleasantly surprised. If you're staying at a resort, mention your anniversary at check-in, too.

**Group Events**—With all the conventions it hosts each year, Disney is a pro at group parties and functions. We've planned several ourselves and found plenty of options and many helpful cast members. And with the introduction of "Magical Gatherings" (see sidebar below), group events are even easier to plan! You can have a private party virtually anywhere in the "World," for small or large groups. For parties in any of the resorts, call 407-828-3074. If you're interested in having a private party at one of the parks, including Pleasure Island (can we come?), call Group Sales at 407-828-3200. We can't say it'll be cheap, but you can plan one within a reasonable budget if you're careful. Of course, you can go all-out, too—companies rent entire theme parks. Planet Hollywood at Downtown Disney hosts private functions, too. In fact, your authors host special gatherings for readers who want to meet us and other like-minded folks who just can't get enough of Disney. If you'd like to learn about our next reader and Disney fan gathering, please visit http://www.mousefest.org and see page 282.

### Magical Gatherings DDP2 *(selected experiences)*

Disney's Magical Gatherings program is designed to help bring friends and family together at Walt Disney World. If you've got eight or more people staying at a Walt Disney World resort, you can book special experiences (**Grand Gatherings**) only available to groups. These events include the International Storybook Dinner (with storytelling and a VIP viewing of IllumiNations at Epcot), Good Morning Gathering (a Magic Kingdom character breakfast with Mickey Mouse), Safari Celebration Dinner (an end-of-day safari followed by a dinner reception at Tusker House with characters, live entertainment, and animal experiences), and the Magical Fireworks Voyage (an evening cruise to view the Wishes fireworks show over the Magic Kingdom). Disney also provides helpful services to plan your gathering, such as web-based tools to help your group stay in touch and build consensus. And Disney has increased the number of restaurants that accommodate larger parties. To plan a Magical Gathering, call 407-WDW-MAGIC or 800-327-2989, or visit http://www.disneyworld.com/magicalgatherings.

# Special Events and Holidays

Disney really knows how to celebrate. Nearly every holiday seems to have at least one event, and Easter, Halloween, Christmas, and New Year's Eve spark extended festivities. Disney also is a master at battling periods of slow attendance with specially themed events throughout the year. Call Disney's main information line at 407-824-4321 or visit their web site at http://www.disneyworld.com for more information.

**Sports**

January brings the sell-out **Walt Disney World Marathon Weekend** (Jan. 10–13, 2008), which includes Family Fun Run (Jan. 11) and the Health and Fitness Expo (Jan. 10–12)—call 407-939-7810. The **Atlanta Braves** baseball spring training is in February and March, and the **Tampa Bay Buccaneers** football team has their training camp again in July and August. The **Walt Disney World Inline Marathon** is May 4, 2008. Many more sport opportunities are available at Disney's Wide World of Sports Complex—for more details, visit http://www.disneyworldsports.com.

**Celebrations at Pleasure Island**

Pleasure Island throws special parties throughout the year. **Mardi Gras** is February 5, 2008, and the island celebrates for several days with "Party Gras." Pleasure Island typically celebrates Valentine's Day, St. Patrick's Day, Cinco de Mayo (May 5), and New Year's Eve, too.

**Festivals and Fun**

The popular **Pirates & Princesses Party** at the Magic Kingdom (advance ticket price: $41.49/$35.10 ages 3–9) with treats, swashbuckling, dancing, a special parade, character meets, and popular attractions have historically been held in the late winter/early spring and summer. The **Epcot International Flower & Garden Festival** (March 19–June 1, 2008) fills the park with exhibits, seminars, tours, demonstrations, the Food Among the Flowers Brunch (see page 239), and special entertainment at the America Gardens Theatre. On selected dates in May and June, Disney's Hollywood Studios has **Star Wars Weekends** with celebrity appearances and special events. **Grad Nights** party down at the Magic Kingdom (April 18, 19, 25, and 26, 2008) from 10:00 pm to 4:00 am—for details, visit http://www.disneyyouthgroups.com. **Disney's 8th Grade Jam** is May 2, 2008. The Friday and Saturday after Labor Day bring the popular **Nights of Joy** to Magic Kingdom to celebrate contemporary Christian music ($45/person in advance; see http://www.nightofjoy.com). The 11th Annual **Epcot International Food & Wine Festival**, which we anticipate will be held September 28–November 11, 2008, turns the World Showcase into an even greater gourmet delight (see page 216). November is also heaven for soap opera fans—**ABC Super Soap Weekend** brings many favorite soap stars to Disney's Hollywood Studios.

**Easter** *(March 23, 2008)*

Spring crowds reach a peak during Easter week. Easter egg hunts and candy scrambles may be held at some of the resorts for their guests (in 2007, nearly every Disney resort hotel held Easter events for their hotel guests). Check with your resort for details. Some restaurants offer Easter breakfasts or dinners, such as Chef Mickey's (see page 228), 'Ohana (see page 230), Whispering Canyon Cafe (see page 232), and Mickey's Backyard BBQ (see page 236). Note that the Magic Kingdom no longer has an Easter parade.

**Independence Day** *(July 4, 2008)*
The Magic Kingdom traditionally puts on a spectacular fireworks show, as does Disney's Hollywood Studios. Pleasure Island adds patriotic entertainment as well. Epcot's IllumiNations is enhanced with Fourth of July fun, too!

**Halloween** *(October 31, 2008)*
Mickey's Not So Scary Halloween Party brings kid-friendly spookiness to the Magic Kingdom for about 20 nights (7:00 pm–midnight) in September and October (usually Tuesdays, Fridays, and Sundays, plus Halloween night). Enjoy Mickey's Boo to You Halloween Parade, a kids' costume parade, trick-or-treating around the park, Halloween-themed fireworks, storytellers, fortune tellers, and access to most rides. We recommend you make time for the Liberty Belle Riverboat, which offers Halloween cruises with storytellers and live entertainment—it was the highlight of our night! Advance tickets are $41.49/adult, $35.10/child (price includes tax). Call 407-934-7639 well in advance as tickets sell out, especially for Halloween night—tickets usually go on sale on May 1.

**Thanksgiving** *(November 27, 2008)*
Crowds take a bump up for this All-American holiday. Disney's holiday decorations are on their way up, and a number of the full-service restaurants at the parks and almost all of the Disney resorts host special holiday dinners, with and without Disney characters.

**Christmas** *(December 25, 2008)*
Christmas is a very special time, with delightful decorations, holiday entertainment, and countless ways to enjoy the season. Decorations go up around Thanksgiving, so there's more than a month of merriment. Try to come during the first two weeks of December when the crowds are thinner, rates are lower, the party is in full swing, and the "World" is decked with holiday cheer. **Mickey's Very Merry Christmas Party** is a big favorite. Packed full of special shows and special fun, the Magic Kingdom is open for five extra hours for about 20 nights in November and December. Snow falls on Main Street, fireworks and music fill the air, and the big rides are open. And let's not forget the Main Street tree lighting ceremony, holiday-themed shows in the Galaxy Palace Theatre (in Tomorrowland), strolling carolers, and complimentary cookies and hot cocoa. Advance tickets are $43.62/adults, $36.16/kids, prices include tax (add $7 if you buy at the gate)—tickets usually go on sale May 1. At Epcot, the **Candlelight Processional** runs two to three times nightly. A celebrity narrator, chorus, and orchestra present the Christmas tale. No extra admission required, but a special dinner package offers reserved seating (call 407-WDW-DINE). Be sure to **view the resort decorations** (try the Yuletide Tour—see page 245) and enjoy merriment at **Downtown Disney**. The **Osborne Family Spectacle of Lights** sparkles throughout the Streets of America Set at Disney's Hollywood Studios—see page 158.

**New Year's Eve** *(December 31, 2008)*
The Magic Kingdom, Epcot, Disney's Hollywood Studios, Pleasure Island, and Atlantic Dance at the BoardWalk all host big New Year's celebrations. The theme parks overflow during the Christmas–New Year's week, and reservations at resorts are extremely hard to get. Disney charges regular admission to the parks on New Year's Eve, but Pleasure Island hosts a popular $89/person event featuring headliners, food, and a holiday toast.

**Other Parties, Holidays, and Observances**
All parks participate in February's **Black Heritage Celebration**. June 3–9, 2008 are the **Unofficial Gay Days events** (visit both http://www.gayday.com and http://www.gaydays.com). The **Tom Joyner Family Reunion** (see http://www.tomjoyner.com) is held around Labor Day. And our very own **MouseFest** Disney Fan Gathering is December 2–10, 2007, December 7–15, 2008, and December 6–14, 2009—see page 282 for all the details.

# Beyond Walt Disney World

We're pretty infatuated with Disney, but there is life beyond Walt Disney World. At least that's what we hear. We don't venture far beyond the gates, preferring to spend more time immersed in Disney's magic rather than battle traffic to get to another park. We do know that families hope to visit other theme parks during their visit to central Florida, so here is a list of Florida parks and attractions, along with their numbers and web sites. You may also be interested in "The Other Orlando" guidebook by Kelly Monaghan, available at our web site and at your local bookstore.

| Name | Number | Web Site |
|---|---|---|
| Busch Gardens | 813-987-5082 | http://www.buschgardens.com |
| Cypress Gardens | 863-324-2111 | http://www.cypressgardens.com |
| Gatorland | 800-393-JAWS | http://www.gatorland.com |
| Green Meadows Farm | 407-846-0770 | http://greenmeadowsfarm.com |
| Kennedy Space Center | 321-452-2121 | http://kennedyspacecenter.com |
| Medieval Times | 407-396-1518 | http://medievaltimes.com |
| Sea World | 407-363-2613 | http://seaworld.com |
| Universal Studios/Islands of Adv. | 407-363-8000 | http://www.usf.com |
| Wet 'n' Wild | 407-351-1800 | http://www.wetnwild.com |

Note: *Cypress Gardens reopened in December 2004 after hurricane damage was repaired.*

## Beyond Orlando

Like any other forward-thinking organization, The Walt Disney Company has expanded into other locales. Here are a few of them:

**Disney Cruise Line**—"Take the magic of Disney and just add water!" The Disney Cruise Line set sail in 1998 with the same enthusiasm and energy you find at the Walt Disney World Resort. See pages 100–101, and pick up a copy of our popular guidebook, *PassPorter's Disney Cruise Line and Its Ports of Call* (available in bookstores or order at http://www.passporter.com/dcl—more details on page 285).

© MediaMarx, Inc.

**Disney's Vero Beach Resort**—Vero Beach, Florida, is Disney's first oceanside resort, a two-hour drive from Disney World. Relaxing and definitely laid-back compared to the theme parks, Vero Beach Resort offers the chance to get some real rest. But there's also plenty to do nearby—nightclubs, theatre, movies, restaurants, cultural events, recreation, and, of course, walking on the beach (very important). Call 561-234-2000 for more information, or visit http://www.disneyvacationclub.com and click Resorts.

**Disney's Hilton Head Island Resort**—For southern grace and charm, experience the Carolina Low Country lifestyle at Disney's Hilton Head Island Resort. Hilton Head is a golfer's nirvana, boasting 12 nearby golf courses. The tennis and beaches are also big draws. It's an ideal spot for small group retreats. For more information, call 843-341-4100.

© MediaMarx, Inc.

**Disneyland Resort (California)**—The original "Magic Kingdom," near Los Angeles. Disneyland was the model for the Magic Kingdom in Florida and still keeps a step or two ahead of its offspring, since Disney's Imagineers live close by. The official Disneyland hotels are right next door if you want to make a week out of it. An entirely different park, Disney's California Adventure, opened in 2001, with beautiful vistas and many great attractions. We cover the entire Disneyland Resort and other area attractions, such as Universal Studios, Knott's Berry Farm, LEGOLAND, Hollywood, San Diego Zoo, and SeaWorld in our award-winning guidebook: *PassPorter's Disneyland Resort and Southern California Attractions*. For more details and to order a copy, visit http://www.passporter.com/dl (see page 285).

© MediaMarx, Inc.

**Disneyland Paris Resort (France)**—The first (and only) Disney resort in Europe, the park has a similar layout to Disneyland, with the major change being a substitution of Discoveryland for Tomorrowland. It is said by many to be the most beautiful of all the Disney parks, and we tend to agree. In April 2002, the Walt Disney Studios theme park opened, featuring several popular attractions from Disney's Hollywood Studios in Florida—and one of its original attractions (Lights, Motors, Action!) made its way to Florida, too. Visit http://www.disneylandparis.com. We visited in late February 2005 and found it snowing (real snow!) on Main Street. We stayed at the Disneyland Hotel—immediately adjacent to the park—and adored it.

**Tokyo Disney Resort (Japan)**—Disney, Japan-style! Tokyo Disney Resort is located in Urayasu, just outside Tokyo. It is similar to Disneyland in California, incorporating the quintessential "American" things. When Jennifer visited, she found it squeaky clean and definitely Disney, with just a touch of Japanese peeking through. In 2001, the Tokyo DisneySea theme park opened immediately adjacent to Tokyo Disneyland. The aquatically themed park has seven lands and a resort, Hotel MiraCosta. Visit http://www.tokyodisneyresort.co.jp and click English.

**Hong Kong Disneyland**—Opened in September 2005, this theme park overlooks the water of Penny's Bay, Lantau. For details, visit http://www.hongkongdisneyland.com.

**DisneyQuest**—Plans originally called for DisneyQuests around the country, but only one outside of Orlando was built in Chicago (which is now closed). For details on DisneyQuest, visit http://www.disneyquest.com.

**Hidden Mickey Hiding Places (from list on page 249)**

*1) In the Disney Recycles logo on bags, napkins, etc.; 2) On cash register receipts; 3) The "Soap Stop" vending machines in the resort laundry rooms; 4) Main Street Vehicle horse harnesses; 5) In the center of manhole covers; 6) In the sleeve of a cloak on a Grim Reaper ghost in the Haunted Mansion; 7) In coiled ropes on Test Track (visible in the ride photo); 8) Drilling platform worker's watch; 9) Hedges trimmed into circles; 10) Earffel water tower; 11) The ironwork fence around Disney's Hollywood Studios; 12) The yellow refrigerator on the Backlot Tour; 13) Birdhouse near Festival of the Lion King; 14) On the sidewalk near the Harambe Fruit Market; and 15) On the frog statue outside of the women's restroom near Pizzafari.*

# Your Own Walt Disney World

Make Walt Disney World your personal playground with these tips:

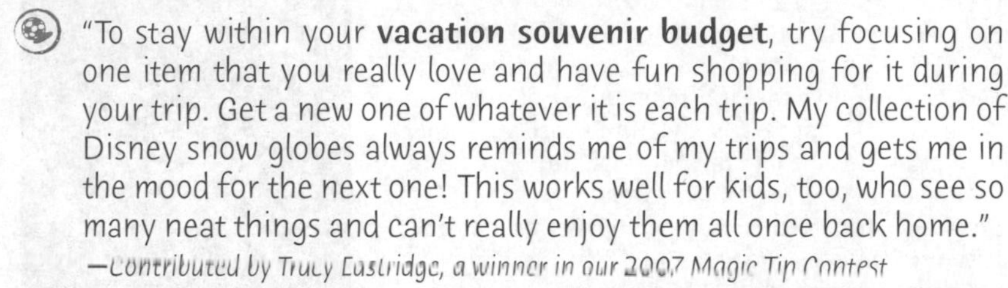

"To stay within your **vacation souvenir budget**, try focusing on one item that you really love and have fun shopping for it during your trip. Get a new one of whatever it is each trip. My collection of Disney snow globes always reminds me of my trips and gets me in the mood for the next one! This works well for kids, too, who see so many neat things and can't really enjoy them all once back home."
*—Contributed by Tracy Eastridge, a winner in our 2007 Magic Tip Contest*

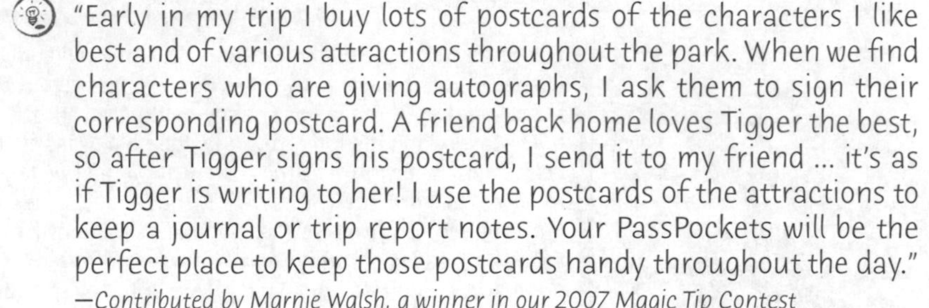

"Early in my trip I buy lots of postcards of the characters I like best and of various attractions throughout the park. When we find characters who are giving autographs, I ask them to sign their corresponding postcard. A friend back home loves Tigger the best, so after Tigger signs his postcard, I send it to my friend ... it's as if Tigger is writing to her! I use the postcards of the attractions to keep a journal or trip report notes. Your PassPockets will be the perfect place to keep those postcards handy throughout the day."
*—Contributed by Marnie Walsh, a winner in our 2007 Magic Tip Contest*

Write to us and **share your experiences, memories, and tips**. If we use them, we'll credit you in PassPorter and send you a copy! Visit http://www.passporter.com/customs/tipsandstories.asp.

## Magical Memory

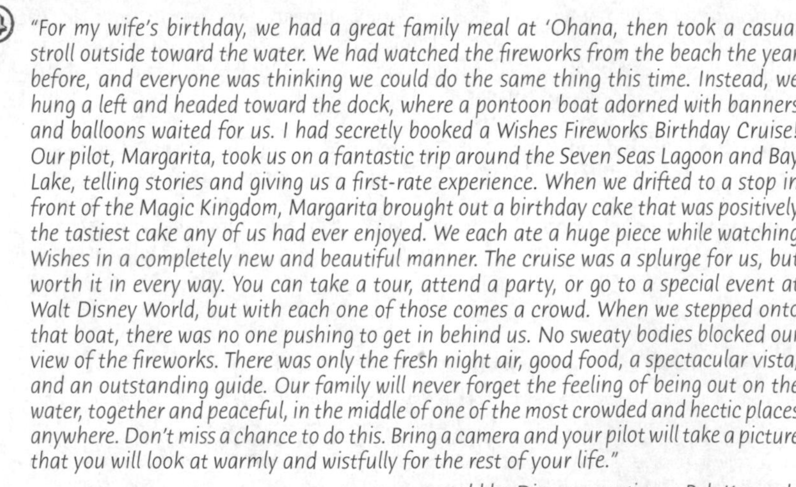

*"For my wife's birthday, we had a great family meal at 'Ohana, then took a casual stroll outside toward the water. We had watched the fireworks from the beach the year before, and everyone was thinking we could do the same thing this time. Instead, we hung a left and headed toward the dock, where a pontoon boat adorned with banners and balloons waited for us. I had secretly booked a Wishes Fireworks Birthday Cruise! Our pilot, Margarita, took us on a fantastic trip around the Seven Seas Lagoon and Bay Lake, telling stories and giving us a first-rate experience. When we drifted to a stop in front of the Magic Kingdom, Margarita brought out a birthday cake that was positively the tastiest cake any of us had ever enjoyed. We each ate a huge piece while watching Wishes in a completely new and beautiful manner. The cruise was a splurge for us, but worth it in every way. You can take a tour, attend a party, or go to a special event at Walt Disney World, but with each one of those comes a crowd. When we stepped onto that boat, there was no one pushing to get in behind us. No sweaty bodies blocked our view of the fireworks. There was only the fresh night air, good food, a spectacular vista, and an outstanding guide. Our family will never forget the feeling of being out on the water, together and peaceful, in the middle of one of the most crowded and hectic places anywhere. Don't miss a chance to do this. Bring a camera and your pilot will take a picture that you will look at warmly and wistfully for the rest of your life."*

*...as told by Disney vacationer Bob Kennedy*

# Index

We feel that a comprehensive index is very important to a successful travel guide. Too many times we've tried to look something up in other books only to find there was no entry at all, forcing us to flip through pages and waste valuable time. When you're on the phone with a reservation agent and looking for that little detail, time is of the essence.

You'll find the PassPorter index is complete and detailed. Whenever we reference more than one page for a given topic, the major topic is in **bold** and map references are in *italics* to help you home in on exactly what you need. For those times you want to find everything there is to be had, we include all the minor references. We have plenty of cross-references, too, just in case you don't look it up under the name we use.

P.S. This isn't the end of the book. More nifty features begin on page 276!

## Symbols

Planning Getting There Staying in Style Touring Feasting Making Magic Index Notes & More

# Web Site Index

| Site Name | Page | Address (URL) |
|---|---|---|
| AAA | 11 | http://www.aaa.com |
| AllEars.net | 6 | http://www.allears.net |
| All Star Vacation Homes | 109 | http://www.allstarvacationhomes.com |
| Along Interstate 75 | 15 | http://www.i75online.com |
| AmeriSuites Lake Buena Vista | 108 | http://www.amerisuites.com |
| Amtrak | 18 | http://www.amtrak.com |
| AutoPilot | 15 | http://www.freetrip.com |
| Buena Vista Scooter/ECV Rental | 34 | http://www.buenavistascooters.com |
| Busch Gardens | 260 | http://www.buschgardens.com |
| Care Medical Equipment | 34 | http://www.caremedicalequipment.com |
| Disney's Magical Gatherings | 257 | http://www.disneyworld.com/magicalgatherings |
| Disney Cruise Line | 100-101 | http://www.disneycruise.com |
| DisneyEcho | 7 | http://disneyecho.emuck.com |
| Disneyland (California) | 260 | http://www.disneyland.com |
| Disneyland Paris | 261 | http://www.disneylandparis.com |
| DisneyQuest | 186 | http://www.disneyquest.com |
| Disney Vacation Club | 102-103 | http://www.disneyvacationclub.com |
| Disney Rewards Visa | 10 | http://chase.com/disney |
| DoomBuggies.com (Haunted Mansion) | 131 | http://www.doombuggies.com |
| DoubleTree Club Hotel | 108 | http://www.doubletreeclublbv.com |
| Drive I-95 | 15 | http://www.drivei95.com |
| DVC By Resale | 103 | http://www.dvcbyresale.com |
| EarPlanes | 23 | http://www.earplanes.com |
| E Pass | 15 | http://www.epass.com |
| Entertainment Book | 11 | http://www.entertainment.com |
| Expedia | 16 | http://www.expedia.com |
| Florida Residents Information | 10 | http://www.disneyworld.com/flresidents |
| Florida's Turnpike | 15 | http://www.floridasturnpike.com |
| Florida Orlando Tickets | 117 | http://www.floridaorlandotickets.net |
| Florida Spirit Vacation Homes | 109 | http://www.floridaspiritvacationhome.com |
| Friends of Bill W. in Orlando | 112 | http://aaorlandointergroup.org |
| Gatorland | 260 | http://gatorland.com |
| Gay Days | 259 | http://www.gayday.com |
| Gaylord Palms | 108 | http://www.gaylordpalms.com |
| Gifts of a Lifetime | 256 | http://www.giftsofalifetime.com |
| Green Meadows Farm | 260 | http://greenmeadowsfarm.com |
| Greyhound | 18 | http://www.greyhound.com |
| Grosvenor Resort | 104 | http://www.grosvenorresort.com |
| Happy Limo | 20 | http://www.happylimo.com |
| Hard Rock Hotel | 107 | http://www.hardrockhotelorlando.com |
| Hidden Mickeys of Disney | vii, 249 | http://www.hiddenmickeys.org |
| Hidden Mickeys Guide | 249 | http://www.hiddenmickeysguide.com |
| The Hilton | 104 | http://www.downtowndisneyhotels.com/Hilton.html |
| Holiday Inn (Hotel Plaza) | 104 | http://www.downtowndisneyhotels.com/HolidayInn.html |
| Hotel Royal Plaza | 105 | http://www.royalplaza.com |
| Iago & Zazu's Attraction of the Week | vi | http://aotw.figzu.com |
| Intercot | vii, 7 | http://www.intercot.com |
| Interstate 95 Exit Information Guide | 15 | http://www.usastar.com/i95/homepage.htm |
| Kennedy Space Center | 260 | http://kennedyspacecenter.com |
| LaughingPlace.com | vii | http://www.laughingplace.com |

| Site Name | Page | Address (URL) |
|---|---|---|
| Lynx (local buses) | 20 | http://www.golynx.com |
| Magical Disney Cruise Guide | 101 | http://allearsnet.com/cruise/cruise.shtml |
| MapQuest | 24 | http://www.mapquest.com |
| Marc Schwartz's Unofficial Disney Golf | 192 | http://www.wdwgolf.com |
| Medieval Times | 260 | http://medievaltimes.com |
| The Mouse For Less | 7, 11 | http://www.themouseforless.com |
| MouseFest Fan Gathering | 284 | http://www.mousefest.org |
| MouseMemories | 256 | http://www.mousememories.com |
| Mouse Pads Vacation Rentals | 109 | http://www.mousepadsorlando.com |
| MousePlanet Trip Reports | 12 | http://www.mouseplanet.com/dtp/trip.rpt |
| MousePlanet Disney Vacation Club | 103 | http://www.mouseplanet.com/dtp/dvc |
| MousePlanet Trip Planner | vii | http://www.mouseplanet.com/dtp/wdwguide |
| MouseSavers.com | vii, 11 | http://www.mousesavers.com |
| MurderWatch Mystery Dinner Show | 238 | http://www.murderwatch.com |
| Nature Conservancy | 193 | http://www.nature.org |
| Nickelodeon Family Suites | 106 | http://www.nickhotel.com |
| Orbitz | 16 | http://www.orbitz.com |
| Orlando Houses of Worship | 112 | http://orlando.areaconnect.com/churches.htm |
| Orlando International Airport | 17 | http://www.orlandoairports.net |
| Orlando Magicard | 11 | http://www.orlandoinfo.com/magicard |
| PassPorter Online | 281 | http://www.passporter.com *(see more on page 281)* |
| PassPorter Book Updates | 4, 280 | http://www.passporter.com/customs/bookupdates.htm |
| PhotoPass | 115, 150 | http://www.disneyphotopass.com |
| PhotoPass Unofficial Guide | 150 | http://www.stitchkingdom.com/photopass |
| Portofino Bay Hotel | 107 | http://www.portofinobay.com |
| Pressed Coin Collector Page | 248 | http://www.liss.olm.net/ec |
| Priceline | 16 | http://www.priceline.com |
| Planning Strategy Calculator | vii, 203 | http://pscalculator.net |
| Quicksilver Tours & Transportation | 20 | http://www.quicksilver-tours.com |
| Radisson Resort Orlando-Celebration | 106 | http://www.radissonparkway.com |
| Rainforest Cafe | 206 | http://www.rainforestcafe.com |
| Rodeway Inn International | 109 | http://www.rodewayinnorlando.com |
| Royal Pacific Resort | 107 | http://www.loewshotels.com/hotels/orlando_royal_pacific |
| Sea World | 260 | http://seaworld.com |
| Shades of Green | 98 | http://www.shadesofgreen.org |
| Sheraton Safari | 106 | http://www.sheratonsafari.com |
| Sheraton's Vistana Resort | 108 | http://www.sheraton.com |
| Southwest Airlines | 16 | http://www.southwest.com |
| Spencer Family's Disney Page | vi, 62 | http://home.hiwaay.net/~jlspence |
| Steve Soares' Disney Entertainment | 122 | http://pages.prodigy.net/stevesoares |
| Swan and Dolphin Resorts | 99 | http://www.swandolphin.com |
| Tagrel | 7 | http://www.tagrel.com |
| TicketMania | 117 | http://www.ticketmania.com |
| Transportation Security Administration | 16 | http://www.tsa.gov |
| Travelocity | 16, 28 | http://www.travelocity.com |
| Universal Studios Florida | 260 | http://www.usf.com |
| Unofficial Disney Information Station | vii, 7 | http://www.wdwinfo.com |
| Unofficial Walt Disney World Info Guide | vii, 7, 205 | http://www.allearsnet.com |
| Walker Mobility | 34 | http://www.walkermobility.com |
| Walt Disney Travel Co. | 8 | http://www.disneytravel.com |
| Walt Disney World Resort | 7, 120 | http://www.disneyworld.com |
| Walt Disney World Spas | 193 | http://www.relaxedyet.com |
| Walt Disney World Sports & Rec. | 194 | http://www.disneyworldsports.com |
| Wet 'n' Wild | 260 | http://www.wetnwild.com |
| Wyndham Palace Resort & Spa | 105 | http://www.wyndham.com |

# Notes & Autographs

Whether you run out of space somewhere else or want to get your favorite character's autograph, these pages stand ready!

# Scribbles & Doodles

Whether you scribble and doodle or just scoodle and dribble, this page is specially treated to accept ink and resist moisture!

*(Okay, so all paper does this... but hey, we just can't resist mentioning hidden features!)*

# Autographs

Kids and kids-at-heart love to get autographs from Disney characters! These two pages beg to be filled with signatures, paw prints, and doodles from your favorite characters. We've even provided places to write the actual name of the character (they can be hard to read—they are autographs, after all), plus the location where you discovered the character and the date of your find. Even if you bring or purchase an autograph book, use these pages when you fill it up or just plain forget it. (Been there, done that!) Be sure to see page 248 for tips and tricks on how to get character autographs, too!

*Character:* *Location:* *Date:*

*Character:* *Location:* *Date:*

*Character:* *Location:* *Date:*

# Autographs Anonymous

We know. We understand. Bouncing tigers and giant mice can be intimidating. After several months of research and development, we came up with the following system that can help both the interminably shy and the overstimulated. Just write your name in the blank below, take a deep breath, and hold out your book. Now, wasn't that easy?

**Hi, my name is ___________. May I have your autograph?**

(write your name here)

*Character:*
*Location:* *Date:*

*Character:*
*Location:* *Date:*

*Character:* *Location:* *Date:*

*Character:* *Location:* *Date:*

# Register Your PassPorter

We are very interested to learn how your vacation went and what you think of the PassPorter, how it worked (or didn't work) for you, and your opinion on how we could improve it! We encourage you to register your copy of PassPorter with us—in return for your feedback, we'll send you **two valuable coupons** good for discounts on PassPorters and PassHolder pouches when purchased directly from us. You can register your copy of PassPorter at http://www.passporter.com/register.asp, or you can send us a postcard or letter to P.O. Box 3880, Ann Arbor, Michigan 48106.

## Report a Correction or Change

Keeping up with the changes at Walt Disney World is virtually impossible without your help. When you notice something is different than what is printed in PassPorter, or you just come across something you'd like to see us cover, please let us know! You can report your news, updates, changes, and corrections at http://www.passporter.com/wdw/report.htm.

## Contribute to the Next Edition of PassPorter

You can become an important part of the 2009 edition of PassPorter Walt Disney World! The easiest way is to rate the resorts, rides, and/or restaurants at http://www.passporter.com/wdw/rate.htm. Your ratings and comments become part of our reader ratings throughout the book and help future readers make travel decisions. Want to get more involved? Send us a vacation tip or magical memory—if we use it in a future edition of PassPorter, we'll credit you by name in the guidebook and send you a free copy of the edition!

## Get Your Questions Answered

We love to hear from you! Alas, due to the thousands of e-mails and hundreds of phone calls we receive each week, we cannot offer personalized advice to all our readers. But there's a great way to get your questions answered: Ask your fellow readers! Visit our message boards at http://www.passporterboards.com, join for free, and post your question. In most cases, fellow readers and Disney fans will offer their ideas and experiences! Our message boards also function as an ultimate list of frequently asked questions. Just browsing through to see the answers to other readers' questions will reap untold benefit! This is also a great way to make friends and have fun while planning your vacation. But be careful—our message boards can be addictive!

# PassPorter Online

A wonderful way to get the most from your PassPorter is to visit our active web site at http://www.passporter.com. We serve up valuable PassPorter updates, plus useful Walt Disney World information and advice we couldn't jam into our book. You can swap tales (that's t-a-l-e-s, Mickey!) with fellow Disney fans, play contests and games, find links to other sites, get plenty of details, and ask us questions. You can also order PassPorters and shop for PassPorter accessories and travel gear! The latest information on new PassPorters to other destinations is available on our web site as well. To go directly to our latest list of page-by-page PassPorter updates, visit http://www.passporter.com/customs/bookupdates.htm.

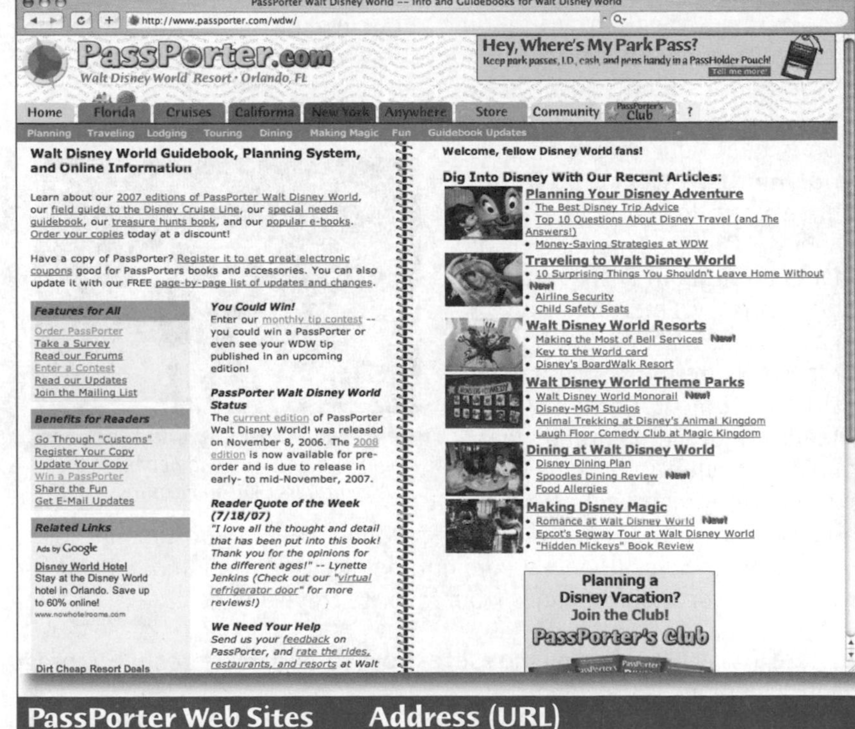

| PassPorter Web Sites | Address (URL) |
|---|---|
| Main Page: PassPorter Online | http://www.passporter.com |
| Walt Disney World Forum | http://www.passporter.com/wdw |
| PassPorter Posts Message Boards | http://www.passporterboards.com |
| PassPorter: Best of Times Links Page | http://www.passporter.com/wdw/bestoftimes.htm |
| Book Updates | http://www.passporter.com/customs/bookupdates.htm |
| Luggage Log and Tag Maker | http://www.passporter.com/wdw/luggagelog.asp |
| Rate the Rides, Resorts, Restaurants | http://www.passporter.com/wdw/rate.htm |
| Register Your PassPorter | http://www.passporter.com/register.asp |
| PassPorter Deluxe Edition Information | http://www.passporter.com/wdw/deluxe.htm |

Planning
Getting There
Staying in Style
Touring
Feasting
Making Magic
Index
Notes & More

# Vacation With Fellow Fans

Join PassPorter authors Jennifer and Dave Marx, AllEarsNet's Deb Wills, and a host of webmasters, guidebook authors, and online communities for a grand gathering at Walt Disney World and on the Disney Cruise Line! Each year in early December, we **gather and share our love for Disney** in a little event we call "MouseFest." 2007 dates are December 2-6 (Disney cruise) and December 6-10 (Walt Disney World). Our 2008–2010 dates are posted on the MouseFest web site at http://www.mousefest.org.

**What better time to visit** Walt Disney World? Disney's holiday festivities are in full swing, lodging can be had at value season pricing, and crowds are a whole lot smaller than they'll be later in December. Spice up your regular family vacation by attending a couple of events, or build an entire vacation around MouseFest activities. It's a whole new way to enjoy Walt Disney World and the Disney cruise.

Come meet your online friends and **make new friends** who share your love of all things Disney. • Choose from dozens of meets throughout Disney's parks and resorts. • Find new ways to experience familiar attractions. • Enjoy treasure hunts and guided tours. • Come together at the MegaMouseMeet, a grand meet-and-greet where you can meet friends from many communities and hobnob with dozens of authors, webmasters, and other notables. • Ask if your favorite online communities will be attending. • Look for MouseFest vacation packages from favorite travel agencies.

*Old fashioned fun and ribbing at the Adventurers Club on Pleasure Island*

Be sure to visit **http://www.mousefest.org** to learn more about this great event! Everyone is welcome!

*Preparing to board Kilimanjaro Safaris at Disney's Animal Kingdom*

# PassPorter Goodies

PassPorter was born out of the necessity for more planning, organization, and a way to preserve the memories of a great vacation! Along the way we've found other things that either help us use the PassPorter better, appreciate our vacation more, or just make our journey a little more comfortable. Others have asked us about them, so we thought we'd share them with you. Order online at http://www.passporterstore.com, call us toll-free at 877-929-3273, or use the order form below.

**PassPorter® PassHolder** is a small, lightweight nylon pouch that holds passes, ID cards, passports, money, and pens. Wear it around your neck for hands-free touring, and for easy access at the airport. The front features a clear compartment, a zippered pocket, and a velcro pocket; the back has a small pocket (perfect size for FASTPASS) and two pen slots. Adjustable cord. Royal blue. 4 7/8" x 6 1/2"

**Quantity**: ____ x $7.95

**PassPorter® Badge** personalized with your name! Go around the "World" in style with our lemon yellow oval pin. Price includes personalization with your name, shipping, and handling. Please indicate badge name(s) with your order.

**Quantity**: ___ x $4.00

Name(s): ________

**PassPorter® Pin** is our collectible, cloissone pin. Our current version depicts our colorful PassPorter logo, the pages of a book, and the words, "The World is an Open Book." The pin measures nearly 1 1/2" in diameter. Watch for new pins to be introduced in the future, too!

**Quantity**: ___ x $6.00

**Please ship my PassPorter Goodies to:**

Name ..........

Address ..........

City, State, Zip ..........

Daytime Phone ..........

Payment: ❑ check (to "MediaMarx") ❑ charge card

❑ MasterCard ❑ Visa ❑ American Express ❑ Discover

Card number .......... Exp. Date. ..........

Signature ..........

Sub-Total:

Tax*:

Shipping**:

**Total**:

* Please include sales tax if you live in Michigan.
**Shipping costs are:
$5 for totals up to $9
$6 for totals up to $19
$7 for totals up to $29
$8 for totals up to $39
Delivery takes 1-2 weeks.

*Send your order form to P.O. Box 3880, Ann Arbor, MI 48106, call us toll-free at 877-WAYFARER (877-929-3273), or order online http://www.passporterstore.com/store.*

# More PassPorters

You've asked for more PassPorters—we've listened! We have five PassPorter books and seven e-books (and growing), all designed to make your Disney vacation the best it can be. And if you've wished for a PassPorter with all the flexibility and features of a daily planner, check out our Deluxe Editions (described below). To learn more about the new PassPorters and get release dates, please visit us at http://www.passporter.com.

## PassPorter Walt Disney World Deluxe Edition

Design first-class vacations with this loose-leaf ring binder edition. The Deluxe Edition features the same great content as the PassPorter Walt Disney World spiral guide. Special features of the Deluxe Edition include ten interior storage slots in the binder to hold guidemaps, ID cards, and a pen (we even include a pen). The Deluxe binder makes it really easy to add, remove, and rearrange pages ... you can even download, print, and add in updates and supplemental pages from our web site, and refills are available for purchase. Learn more at http://www.passporter.com/wdw/deluxe.htm. The Deluxe Edition is available through bookstores by special order—just give your favorite bookstore the ISBN is 978-1-58771-050-6 (2008 Deluxe Edition) and 978-1-58771-061-2 (2009 Deluxe Edition).

## PassPorter's Open Mouse for Walt Disney World and the Disney Cruise Line—Second Edition

It's hardly a one-size-fits-all world at Disney's Orlando resort, yet everyone seems to fit. Consider the typical multi-generational family planning a vacation: pregnant and nursing moms, parents with infants, cousins "keeping Kosher," grandparents with declining mobility, a child with food allergies, an uncle struggling with obesity, a teenaged daughter recently "converted" to vegetarianism ... everyday people coping with everyday needs. And Walt Disney World does more to accommodate their many challenges than just about anyone. You'll see more wheelchairs and electric scooters in Disney parks than you're likely to see anywhere else. If you know to ask, Disney has devices to help a hearing- or vision-impaired guest enjoy a show, park maps and translation devices in six languages, "Special Assistance" passes for children with autism or ADD, a sheltered spot to breastfeed an infant, chefs and waiters schooled to serve a wide spectrum of special dietary needs, rides sized to fit guests of various abilities and dimensions ... you could fill a book, and indeed, that's what authors Deb Wills and Debra Martin Koma have done in this updated edition (formerly *PassPorter's Walt Disney World for Your Special Needs*)! *Open Mouse* has more than 440 pages of in-depth information for Walt Disney World vacationers of all abilities, delivering in-depth coverage of every ride, attraction, and resort on Walt Disney World property from a distinctive "special challenges" perspective. Learn more and order your copy at http://www.passporter.com/wdw/openmouse/guidebook.asp or get a copy at your favorite bookstore (ISBN: 978-1-58771-048-3).

➢

# Even More PassPorters

## PassPorter's Disney Cruise Line and its Ports of Call

***Updated annually!*** Get your cruise plans in shipshape with our updated field guide ... includes details on the West Coast/Mexican Riviera cruises! Authors Jennifer and Dave Marx cover the Disney Cruise Line in incredible detail, including deck plans, stateroom floor plans, original photos, menus, entertainment guides, port/shore excursion details, and plenty of worksheets to help you budget, plan, and record your cruise information. Now in its sixth edition, this is the original and most comprehensive guidebook devoted to the Disney Cruise Line! Learn more and order your copy at http://www.passporter.com/dcl or get a copy at your favorite bookstore (paperback, no PassPockets: ISBN: 978-1-58771-055-1). Also available in a Deluxe Edition with organizer PassPockets (ISBN: 978-1-58771-056-8).

*(January 2008)*

## PassPorter Disneyland Resort and Southern California Attractions–Second Edition

PassPorter tours the park that started it all in this updated book! California's Disneyland, Disney's California Adventure, and Downtown Disney get PassPorter's expert treatment, and we throw in Hollywood and Downtown Los Angeles, San Diego, SeaWorld, the San Diego Zoo and Wild Animal Park, LEGOLAND, and Six Flags Magic Mountain. All this, and PassPorter's famous PassPockets and planning features.Whether you're making the pilgrimage to Disneyland for a big celebration or planning a classic Southern California family vacation, you can't miss. Learn more at http://www.passporter.com/dl, or pick it up at your favorite bookstore (ISBN: 978-1-58771-042-1). Also available as a Deluxe Edition in a padded, six-ring binder (ISBN: 978-1-58771-043-8).

## PassPorter's Treasure Hunts at Walt Disney World

Have even more fun at Walt Disney World! Jennifer and Dave's treasure hunts have long been a favorite part of PassPorter reader gatherings at Walt Disney World, and now you can join in the fun. Gain a whole new appreciation of Disney's fabulous attention to detail as you search through the parks and resorts for the little (and big) things that you may never have noticed before. Great for individuals, families, and groups, with hunts for people of all ages and levels of Disney knowledge. Special, "secure" answer pages make sure nobody can cheat. Learn more and order at http://www.passporter.com/hunts or get a copy at your favorite bookstore (ISBN: 978-1-58771-026-1).

## PassPorter E-Books

We have many e-books that cover narrower topics in delightful depth! See all the details on the next page!

To order our guides or e-books, visit http://www.passporterstore.com or call toll-free 877-929-3273. PassPorter guidebooks are also available at your local bookstore. If you don't see it on the shelf, just ask!

# PassPorter E-Books

Looking for more in-depth coverage on specific topics? Look no further than PassPorter E-Books! Our e-books are inexpensive (most just $4.95) and available immediately as a download on your computer (Adobe PDF format). If you prefer your books printed, we have options for that, too! And unlike most e-books, ours are fully formatted just like a regular PassPorter print book. A PassPorter e-book will even fit into a Deluxe PassPorter Binder, if you have one. We offer seven e-books at press time, and have plans for many, many more!

**PassPorter's Cruise Clues**: ***First-Class Tips for Disney Cruise Trips***
Get the best tips for the Disney Cruise Line—all categorized and coded—as well as cruise line comparisons, a teen perspective, and ultimate packing lists! This e-book is packed with 250 cruiser-tested tips—all edited by award-winning author Jennifer Marx.

**PassPorter's Disney 500**: ***Fast Tips for Walt Disney World Trips***
Our most popular e-book has more than 500 time-tested Walt Disney World tips—all categorized and coded! We chose the best of our reader-submitted tips over a six-year period for this e-book and each has been edited by author Jennifer Marx.

**PassPorter's Disney Character Yearbook**
***Who, What, and Where at Walt Disney World, Disneyland, and the Disney Cruise Line***
A 268-page compendium of all the live Disney characters you can find at Walt Disney World, Disneyland, and on the Disney Cruise Line. Also includes tips on finding, meeting, photographing, and getting autographs, plus a customizable autograph book to print!

**PassPorter's Disney Speed Planner**: ***The Easy Ten-Step Program***
A fast, easy method for planning practically perfect vacations—great for busy people or those who don't have lots of time to plan. Follow this simple, ten-step plan to help you get your vacation planned in short order so you can get on with your life. It's like a having an experienced friend show you the ropes step by step—and have fun doing it!

**PassPorter's Free-Book**
***A Guide to Free and Low-Cost Activities at Walt Disney World***
It's hard to believe anything is free at Walt Disney World, but there are actually a number of things you can get or do for little to no cost. This e-book documents more than 150 free or cheap things to do before you go and after you arrive. It's the most comprehensive collection!

**PassPorter's Sidekick for the Walt Disney World Guidebook**
***An interactive collection of worksheets, journal pages, and charts***
This is a customizable companion to our general Walt Disney World guidebook—you can personalize worksheets, journals, luggage tags, and charts, plus click links to all the URLs in the guidebook and get transportation pages for all points within Walt Disney World!

**PassPorter's Walt Disney World for Brit Holidaymakers**
Brits, you can get super in-depth information for your Walt Disney World vacation from fellow Brit and PassPorter feature columnist Cheryl Pendry. More than 300 pages long!

Learn more about these and other titles and order e-books at:
http://www.passporterstore.com/store/ebooks.aspx

Do you want more help planning your Walt Disney World vacation? Join the PassPorter's Club and get all these benefits:

- ✔ "All-you-can-read" access to EVERY e-book we publish (see current list on the previous page). PassPorter's Club passholders also get early access to these e-books before the general public. New e-books are added on a regular basis, too.
- ✔ Interactive, customizable "e-worksheets" to help make your trip planning easier, faster, and smoother. These are the electronic, interactive worksheets we've been mentioning throughout this book. The worksheets are in PDF format and can be printed for a truly personalized approach! We have more than 35 worksheets, with more on the way. You can see a sample e-worksheet to the right.

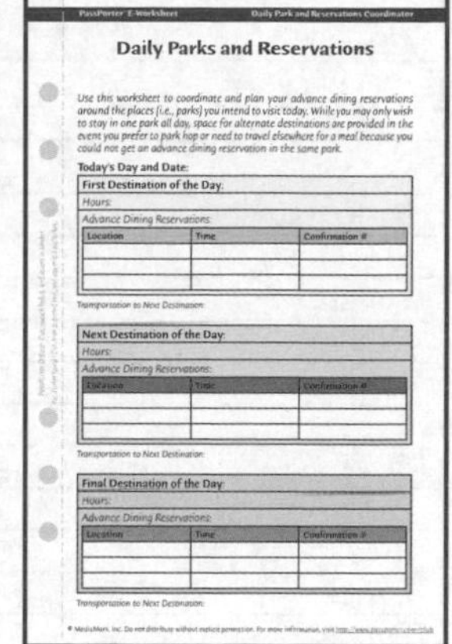

PassPorter E-Worksheet — Daily Park and Reservations Coordinator

**Daily Parks and Reservations**

*Use this worksheet to coordinate and plan your advance dining reservations around the places (i.e., parks) you intend to visit today. While you may only wish to stay in one park all day, space for alternate destinations are provided in the event you prefer to park hop or need to travel elsewhere for a meal because you could not get an advance dining reservation in the same park.*

**Today's Day and Date:**

**First Destination of the Day:**
*Hours:*
*Advance Dining Reservations:*

| Location | Time | Confirmation # |
|---|---|---|
| | | |
| | | |
| | | |

*Transportation to Next Destination:*

**Next Destination of the Day:**
*Hours:*
*Advance Dining Reservations:*

| Location | Time | Confirmation # |
|---|---|---|
| | | |
| | | |
| | | |

*Transportation to Next Destination:*

**Final Destination of the Day:**
*Hours:*
*Advance Dining Reservations:*

| Location | Time | Confirmation # |
|---|---|---|
| | | |
| | | |
| | | |

*Transportation to Next Destination:*

- ✔ Access to super-sized "e-photos" in the PassPorter Photo Archives—photos can be zoomed in up to 25 times larger than standard web photos. You can use these e-photos to see detail as if you're actually standing there—or use them for desktop wallpaper, scrapbooking, whatever!
- ✔ Our best discount on print guidebooks ... 35% off!

There's more features, too! For a full list of features and current e-books, e-worksheets, and e-photos, visit http://www.passporter.com/club. You can also take a peek inside the Club's Gallery at http://www.passporterboards.com/forums/passporters-club-gallery. The Gallery is open to everyone—it contains two FREE interactive e-worksheets to try out!

**Price**: A PassPorter's Club pass is currently $4.95/month, or the cost of just one e-book!

## How to Get Your Pass to the PassPorter's Club

**Step 1. Get a free community account**. Register simply and quickly at http://www.passporterboards.com/forums/register.php.

**Step 2. Log in** at http://www.passporterboards.com/forums/login.php using the Member Name and password you created in step 1.

**Step 3. Get your pass.** Select the type of pass you'd like and follow the directions to activate it immediately. We currently offer monthly and annual passes. (Annual passes save 25% and get extra perks!)

Questions? Assistance? We're here to help! Please send e-mail to club@passporter.com.

You may also find many of your questions answered in our FAQ (Frequently Asked Questions) in the Gallery forum (see link above).

Electronic, interactive worksheet available–see page 287

# Vacation At-A-Glance

Create an overview of your itinerary in the chart below for easy reference. You can then make copies of it and give one to everyone in your traveling party, as well as to friends and family members who stay behind. Get a FREE electronic version of this worksheet at http://www.passporter.com/club.

| Name(s): | | |
|---|---|---|
| Departing on: | Time: | #: |
| Arriving at: | | |
| Staying at: | | Phone: |

| | |
|---|---|
| Date: | Date: |
| Park/Activity: | Park/Activity: |
| Breakfast: | Breakfast: |
| Lunch: | Lunch: |
| Dinner: | Dinner: |
| Other: | Other: |
| Date: | Date: |
| Park/Activity: | Park/Activity: |
| Breakfast: | Breakfast: |
| Lunch: | Lunch: |
| Dinner: | Dinner: |
| Other: | Other: |
| Date: | Date: |
| Park/Activity: | Park/Activity: |
| Breakfast: | Breakfast: |
| Lunch: | Lunch: |
| Dinner: | Dinner: |
| Other: | Other: |
| Date: | Date: |
| Park/Activity: | Park/Activity: |
| Breakfast: | Breakfast: |
| Lunch: | Lunch: |
| Dinner: | Dinner: |
| Other: | Other: |
| Date: | Date: |
| Park/Activity: | Park/Activity: |
| Breakfast: | Breakfast: |
| Lunch: | Lunch: |
| Dinner: | Dinner: |
| Other: | Other: |

| Departing on: | Time: | #: |
|---|---|---|
| Returning at: | | |

# Customize Your PassPorter

Use these labels to personalize your PassPockets for your trip. The color rectangles at the right can be folded over the edge of pages to create your own tabs or flags!

Our Cruise

Our Honeymoon

Our Wedding

Our Anniversary

Our Reunion

Our Gathering

My Birthday

Our Special Day

Our Journey

Our Eleventh Day

Our Twelvth Day

Our Thirteenth Day

Our Fourteenth Day

Our Return

PLANS PLANS

TRAVELS TRAVELS

ROOMS ROOMS

PLAY PLAY

FOOD FOOD

PLACES PLACES

MAGIC MAGIC

*Create Your Own Labels & ← Tabs →*

*Keep everything you need for your journey together here in one place, such as maps, tickets, coupons, reservation numbers... even passports!*

# Our Journey

Departing at ____________ Arriving at ____________

Airline/Train/Bus Company ____________

Flight/Route Number(s) ____________

Flight Reservation Number(s) ____________ Seat(s) ____________

Cruise Reservation Number ____________ Stateroom ____________

Auto/Trip Insurance ____________

Rental Car/Shuttle/Limo Company ____________

Type ____________ Reservation Number ____________

Details ____________

Returning at ____________ Arriving home at ____________

Flight/Route Number(s) ____________ Seat(s) ____________

Note(s) ____________

*Store small items in here like baggage claim tickets and receipts*

## Things to Do

- [ ] ____________
- [ ] ____________
- [ ] ____________
- [ ] ____________
- [ ] ____________
- [ ] ____________
- [ ] ____________
- [ ] ____________

## Notes

# Memories of Our Journey

The weather was... ____________ ... when we left

and... ____________ ... when we arrived

The best thing about our journey was... ____________

The worst thing about our journey was... ____________

The funniest thing about our journey was... ____________

During our journey we tried... ____________

and the result was... ____________

The most magical moment during our journey was... ____________

## Photos and Snapshots

☐ Photos taken today (card/roll # ____)

| Shot # | Description |
|---|---|
| | |
| | |
| | |
| | |
| | |
| | |

## Meals and Snacks

Breakfast: ____________ $

Lunch: ____________ $

Dinner: ____________ $

Snacks: ____________ $

## Budget and Expenses

Target travel budget: $

Fares: $
$

Fuel: $

Tips: $

Meals: $
$

Other: $
$

**Total:** $

## Notes for Next Time

*Use your notes here to remind yourself to inquire about special requests at check-in, such as room preferences, discounts, and amenities.*

# Our Room(s)

Hotel/Motel/Ship: ______________ Phone: ______________

Arriving: ______________ Departing: ______________

Room Type: ______________ Location: ______________

Special Requests: ______________

Reservation Number: ______________

Room Number: ______________ Floor/Building: ______________

Additional Stay: ______________ Phone: ______________

Arriving: ______________ Departing: ______________

Room Type: ______________ Location: ______________

Special Requests: ______________

Reservation Number: ______________

Room Number: ______________ Floor/Building: ______________

↓ *Store small items in here like card keys, receipts, and luggage tags* ↓

## Things to Do

- ☐ ______________
- ☐ ______________
- ☐ ______________
- ☐ ______________
- ☐ ______________
- ☐ ______________
- ☐ ______________
- ☐ ______________

## Notes

# Memories of Our First Day

The weather today was... ________

The best thing today was... ________

The worst thing today was... ________

The funniest thing today was... ________

Today we tried... ________

and the result was... ________

The most magical moment today was... ________

## Photos and Snapshots

❑ Photos taken today (card/roll # ___)

| Shot # | Description |
|---|---|
| | |
| | |
| | |
| | |
| | |
| | |

## Budget and Expenses

First day budget: $

Admission: $

Meals: $

$

$

Shopping: $

$

Other: $

$

**Total:** $

## Meals and Snacks

Breakfast: ________ $

Lunch: ________ $

Dinner: ________ $

Snacks: ________ $

## Notes for Next Time

*Remember to drink plenty of fluids,
eat substantial meals, use sunblock, wear a hat,
and take frequent breaks as necessary during your day.*

# Our Second Day

**Confirmation Numbers**

: Wake up:

: Early Morning:

: Breakfast:

: Morning:

:

: Lunch:

: Afternoon:

:

: Dinner:

: Evening:

:

: Before bed:

Special plans for today:

*Store small items in here like ticket stubs and receipts for meals and purchases*

## Things to Do, Places to Go, Attractions to Visit

- [ ]
- [ ]
- [ ]
- [ ]
- [ ]
- [ ]
- [ ]
- [ ]

## Notes

**Day:** **Date:**

# Memories of Our Second Day

The weather today was... ______

The best thing today was... ______

The worst thing today was... ______

The funniest thing today was... ______

Today we tried... ______
and the result was... ______

The most magical moment today was... ______

## Photos and Snapshots

☐ Photos taken today (card/roll # ___)

Shot # Description

## Budget and Expenses

Second day budget: $

Admission: $
Meals: $
$
$
Shopping: $
$
Other: $
$
**Total:** $

## Meals and Snacks

Breakfast: $
Lunch: $
Dinner: $
Snacks: $

## Notes for Next Time

*When you skip activities for lack of time or energy, flip ahead in your PassPorter and jot them down for another day so you don't forget to return!*

# Our Third Day

**Confirmation Numbers**

___:___ Wake up: ______

___:___ Early Morning: ______

___:___ Breakfast: ______

___:___ Morning: ______

___:___ ______

___:___ Lunch: ______

___:___ Afternoon: ______

___:___ ______

___:___ Dinner: ______

___:___ Evening: ______

___:___ ______

___:___ Before bed: ______

Special plans for today: ______

______

↓ *Store small items in here like ticket stubs and receipts for meals and purchases* ↓

## Things to Do, Places to Go, Attractions to Visit

- ❑ ______
- ❑ ______
- ❑ ______
- ❑ ______
- ❑ ______
- ❑ ______
- ❑ ______
- ❑ ______

## Notes

______

______

______

______

**Day:** **Date:**

# Memories of Our Fourth Day

The weather today was... ______

The best thing today was... ______

The worst thing today was... ______

The funniest thing today was... ______

Today we tried... ______

and the result was... ______

The most magical moment today was... ______

## Photos and Snapshots

☐ Photos taken today (card/roll # ___)

| Shot # | Description |
|---|---|
| | |
| | |
| | |
| | |
| | |
| | |

## Meals and Snacks

Breakfast: ______ $

Lunch: ______ $

Dinner: ______ $

Snacks: ______ $

## Budget and Expenses

Fourth day budget: $

Admission: $

Meals: $

$

$

Shopping: $

$

Other: $

$

**Total:** $

## Notes for Next Time

*Take stock of what you wanted to do and what you've actually done while you still have time, then make the time to fulfill your dreams!*

# Our Fifth Day

**Confirmation Numbers**

: Wake up:

: Early Morning:

: Breakfast:

: Morning:

:

: Lunch:

: Afternoon:

:

: Dinner:

: Evening:

:

: Before bed:

Special plans for today:

*Store small items in here like ticket stubs and receipts for meals and purchases*

## Things to Do, Places to Go, Attractions to Visit

- ❑
- ❑
- ❑
- ❑
- ❑
- ❑
- ❑
- ❑

## Notes

**Day:** **Date:**

# Memories of Our Fifth Day

The weather today was...

The best thing today was...

The worst thing today was...

The funniest thing today was...

Today we tried...

and the result was...

The most magical moment today was...

## Photos and Snapshots

☐ Photos taken today (card/roll # ___)

Shot # Description

## Meals and Snacks

Breakfast: $

Lunch: $

Dinner: $

Snacks: $

## Budget and Expenses

Fifth day budget: $

Admission: $

Meals: $

$

$

Shopping: $

$

Other: $

$

**Total:** $

## Notes for Next Time

*Break out of the typical tourist mold and customize your vacation with one of the tips in your PassPorter. Don't forget the sunglasses!*

# Our Sixth Day

**Confirmation Numbers**

___:___ Wake up: ______

___:___ Early Morning: ______

___:___ Breakfast: ______

___:___ Morning: ______

___:___ ______

___:___ Lunch: ______

___:___ Afternoon: ______

___:___ ______

___:___ Dinner: ______

___:___ Evening: ______

___:___ ______

___:___ Before bed: ______

Special plans for today: ______

↓ *Store small items in here like ticket stubs and receipts for meals and purchases* ↓

## Things to Do, Places to Go, Attractions to Visit

- ❑ ______
- ❑ ______
- ❑ ______
- ❑ ______
- ❑ ______
- ❑ ______
- ❑ ______
- ❑ ______

## Notes

**Day:** **Date:**

# Memories of Our Sixth Day

The weather today was... ______

The best thing today was... ______

The worst thing today was... ______

The funniest thing today was... ______

Today we tried... ______

and the result was... ______

The most magical moment today was... ______

## Photos and Snapshots

☐ Photos taken today (card/roll # ____)

| Shot # | Description |
|---|---|
| | |
| | |
| | |
| | |
| | |
| | |

## Meals and Snacks

Breakfast: ______ $

Lunch: ______ $

Dinner: ______ $

Snacks: ______ $

## Budget and Expenses

Sixth day budget: $ ______

Admission: $ ______

Meals: $ ______

$ ______

$ ______

Shopping: $ ______

$ ______

Other: $ ______

$ ______

**Total:** $ ______

## Notes for Next Time

*Address your postcards and store them in your PassPorter for safe keeping until you can mail them. This also helps you remember to send them!*

# Our Seventh Day

**Confirmation Numbers**

|  |  |
|---|---|
| : | Wake up: |
| : | Early Morning: |
| : | Breakfast: |
| : | Morning: |
| : | |
| : | Lunch: |
| : | Afternoon: |
| : | |
| : | Dinner: |
| : | Evening: |
| : | |
| : | Before bed: |

Special plans for today:

↓ *Store small items in here like ticket stubs and receipts for meals and purchases* ↓

## Things to Do, Places to Go, Attractions to Visit

- ❑
- ❑
- ❑
- ❑
- ❑
- ❑
- ❑
- ❑

## Notes



**Day:** **Date:**

# Memories of Our Seventh Day

The weather today was... ______

The best thing today was... ______

The worst thing today was... ______

The funniest thing today was... ______

Today we tried... ______

and the result was... ______

The most magical moment today was... ______

## Photos and Snapshots

☐ Photos taken today (card/roll # ____)

| Shot # | Description |
| --- | --- |
| | |
| | |
| | |
| | |
| | |
| | |

## Meals and Snacks

Breakfast: ______ $

Lunch: ______ $

Dinner: ______ $

Snacks: ______ $

## Budget and Expenses

Seventh day budget: $

Admission: $

Meals: $

$

$

Shopping: $

$

Other: $

$

**Total:** $

## Notes for Next Time

*Running out of steam? Try taking a day to relax away from the excitement. Take a dip in the pool, or just hang out in your room.*

# Our Eighth Day

**Confirmation Numbers**

: Wake up:

: Early Morning:

: Breakfast:

: Morning:

:

: Lunch:

: Afternoon:

:

: Dinner:

: Evening:

:

: Before bed:

Special plans for today:

*Store small items in here like ticket stubs and receipts for meals and purchases*

## Things to Do, Places to Go, Attractions to Visit

- [ ]
- [ ]
- [ ]
- [ ]
- [ ]
- [ ]
- [ ]
- [ ]

## Notes

**Day:** **Date:**

# Memories of Our Eighth Day

The weather today was... ______

The best thing today was... ______

The worst thing today was... ______

The funniest thing today was... ______

Today we tried... ______

and the result was... ______

The most magical moment today was... ______

## Photos and Snapshots

☐ Photos taken today (card/roll # ____)

| Shot # | Description |
|---|---|
| | |
| | |
| | |
| | |
| | |
| | |

## Meals and Snacks

Breakfast: ______ $

Lunch: ______ $

Dinner: ______ $

Snacks: ______ $

## Budget and Expenses

Eighth day budget: $ ______

Admission: $ ______

Meals: $ ______

$ ______

$ ______

Shopping: $ ______

$ ______

Other: $ ______

$ ______

**Total:** $ ______

## Notes for Next Time

*On the next to last day of your trip, confirm your return travel arrangements and pack whatever you can for a less stressful departure.*

# Our Ninth Day

**Confirmation Numbers**

: Wake up:

: Early Morning:

: Breakfast:

: Morning:

:

: Lunch:

: Afternoon:

:

: Dinner:

: Evening:

:

: Before bed:

Special plans for today:

↓ *Store small items in here like ticket stubs and receipts for meals and purchases* ↓

## Things to Do, Places to Go, Attractions to Visit

- ❑
- ❑
- ❑
- ❑
- ❑
- ❑
- ❑
- ❑

## Notes

OUR NINTH DAY: Memories, Photos, Expenses, Meals, and Notes

# Memories of Our Ninth Day

The weather today was... ______

The best thing today was... ______

______

The worst thing today was... ______

______

The funniest thing today was... ______

______

Today we tried... ______

and the result was... ______

______

The most magical moment today was... ______

______

## Photos and Snapshots

☐ Photos taken today (card/roll # ____)

| Shot # | Description |
|---|---|
| | |
| | |
| | |
| | |
| | |
| | |

## Meals and Snacks

Breakfast: ______ $

Lunch: ______ $

Dinner: ______ $

Snacks: ______ $

## Budget and Expenses

Ninth day budget: $ ______

Admission: $ ______

Meals: $ ______

$ ______

$ ______

Shopping: $ ______

$ ______

Other: $ ______

$ ______

**Total:** $ ______

## Notes for Next Time

______

*Your visit may be ending soon, but the memories you've made can last a lifetime. Record them in your PassPorter now before you forget.*

# Our Tenth Day

**Confirmation Numbers**

: Wake up:

: Early Morning:

: Breakfast:

: Morning:

:

: Lunch:

: Afternoon:

:

: Dinner:

: Evening:

:

: Before bed:

Special plans for today:

↓ *Store small items in here like ticket stubs and receipts for meals and purchases* ↓

## Things to Do, Places to Go, Attractions to Visit

❑ ❑

❑ ❑

❑ ❑

❑ ❑

## Notes

**Day:** **Date:**

# Memories of Our Tenth Day

The weather today was... ____________________

The best thing today was... ____________________

The worst thing today was... ____________________

The funniest thing today was... ____________________

Today we tried... ____________________

and the result was... ____________________

The most magical moment today was... ____________________

## Photos and Snapshots

☐ Photos taken today (card/roll # ____)

| Shot # | Description |
|---|---|
| | |
| | |
| | |
| | |
| | |
| | |

## Meals and Snacks

Breakfast: ____________________ $

Lunch: ____________________ $

Dinner: ____________________ $

Snacks: ____________________ $

## Budget and Expenses

Tenth day budget: $

Admission: $

Meals: $

$

$

Shopping: $

$

Other: $

$

**Total**: $

## Notes for Next Time

Design your own PassPocket!
Use it for extra days, special events, projects, or
remove it and bring it along on days you don't carry your book.

**Confirmation Numbers**

*Write your day, event, or subject above.*

Store small items in here like ticket stubs and receipts for meals and purchases

## Notes

**Day:** **Date:**

OUR SPECIAL DAY: Itinerary, Information, Tickets, Guides, Maps

Write your subject above.

*Your memories will last longer if you record them while they are fresh in your mind. What made you laugh? Smile? Cry? Write it down here!*

# Our Magic Memories

Our most memorable day was... __________

because... __________

Our most memorable place was... __________

because... __________

Our most memorable attraction was... __________

because... __________

Our most memorable activity was... __________

because... __________

↓ *Store small items in here that you want to save as souvenirs and mementos* ↓

Our most memorable meal was... __________

because... __________

Our most magic moment of all was... __________

because... __________

Special memories of our vacation: __________

# Our Trip Report

Use this page to write about your vacation for your family and friends, or even for the benefit of others at school, work, or on the Internet. A trip report is also a good activity for school-age children, especially if they missed school during their adventure. If you run out of room on this page, just continue it on paper and tuck the sheets in this PassPocket for safekeeping.

When did you go? ______________________________

Who did you go with? What are their ages? ______________________________

______________________________

Was this your first trip? _____ If not, how many trips have you had? _____

Where did you sleep? ______________________________

______________________________

What attractions did you visit? ______________________________

______________________________

______________________________

______________________________

What special things did you do? ______________________________

______________________________

______________________________

______________________________

What would you do again? Why? ______________________________

______________________________

______________________________

What would you never do again? Why not? ______________________________

______________________________

______________________________

What tips do you have for your fellow vacationers? ______________________________

______________________________

______________________________

______________________________

______________________________

______________________________

______________________________

______________________________

Would you like to share your trip report with other PassPorter readers? Visit us on the web at http://www.passporter.com. You can also make a copy of this page and mail it to us—our address is P.O. Box 3880, Ann Arbor, MI, 48106. Please include your full name, address, and phone number so we may contact you if necessary.